129992

Limited Classical Reprint Library

THE PSALMS

BY

ALEXANDER MACLAREN, D.D.

VOLUME III.

PSALMS XC.—CI.

Foreword by
Dr. Cyril J. Barber

Klock & Klock Christian Publishers, Inc.
2527 GIRARD AVE. N.
MINNEAPOLIS, MINNESOTA 55411

Originally published by
Hodder & Stroughton
New York
n.d.

ISBN: 0-86524-038-8

Printed by Klock & Klock in the U.S.A.
1981 Reprint

CONTENTS

BOOK IV.

PSALMS XC.—CVI.

PSALM XC.

1 Lord, a dwelling-place hast Thou been for us
  In generation after generation.
2 Before the mountains were born,
  Or Thou gavest birth to the earth and the world,
  Even from everlasting, Thou art God.
3 Thou turnest frail man back to dust,
  And sayest, "Return, ye sons of man."
4 For a thousand years in Thine eyes are as yesterday when
      it was passing,
  And a watch in the night.
5 Thou dost flood them away, a sleep do they become,
  In the morning they are like grass [which] springs afresh.
6 In the morning it blooms and springs afresh,
  By evening it is cut down and withers.

7 For we are wasted away in Thine anger,
  And by Thy wrath have we been panic-struck.
8 Thou hast set our iniquities before Thee,
  Our secret [sins] in the radiance of Thy face.
9 For all our days have vanished in Thy wrath,
  We have spent our years as a murmur.
10 The days of our years—in them are seventy years,
  Or if [we are] in strength, eighty years,
  And their pride is [but] trouble and vanity,
  For it is passed swiftly, and we fly away.
11 Who knows the power of Thine anger,
  And of Thy wrath according to the [due] fear of Thee?
12 To number our days—thus teach us,
  That we may win ourselves a heart of wisdom.

13 Return, Jehovah; how long?
  And have compassion upon Thy servants.
14 Satisfy us in the morning [with] Thy loving-kindness,
  And we shall ring out joyful cries and be glad all our days

3

15 Gladden us according to the days [when] Thou hast afflicted us,
　　The years [when] we have seen adversity.
16 To Thy servants let Thy working be manifested,
　　And Thy majesty upon their children.
17 And let the graciousness of the Lord our God be upon us,
　　And the work of our hands establish upon us,
　　Yea, the work of our hands establish it.

THE sad and stately music of this great psalm befits the dirge of a world. How artificial and poor, beside its restrained emotion and majestic simplicity, do even the most deeply felt strains of other poets on the same themes sound ! It preaches man's mortality in immortal words. In its awestruck yet trustful gaze on God's eternal being, in its lofty sadness, in its archaic directness, in its grand images so clearly cut and so briefly expressed, in its emphatic recognition of sin as the occasion of death, and in its clinging to the eternal God who can fill fleeting days with ringing gladness, the psalm utters once for all the deepest thoughts of devout men. Like the God whom it hymns, it has been " for generation after generation " an asylum.

The question of its authorship has a literary interest, but little more. The arguments against the Mosaic authorship, apart from those derived from the as yet unsettled questions in regard to the Pentateuch, are weak. The favourite one, adduced by Cheyne after Hupfeld and others, is that the duration of human life was greater, according to the history, in Moses' time than seventy years ; but the prolonged lives of certain conspicuous persons in that period do not warrant a conclusion as to the average length of life ; and the generation that fell in the wilderness can clearly not have lived beyond the psalmist's limit. The characteristic Mosaic tone in regarding death as the wages of sin, the massive simplicity and the entire absence

of dependence on other parts of the Psalter, which
separate this psalm from almost all the others of the
Fourth Book, are strongly favourable to the correctness
of the superscription.   Further, the section vv. 7–12 is
distinctly historical, and is best understood as referring
not to mankind in general, but to Israel ; and no period
is so likely to have suggested such a strain of thought
as that when the penalty of sin was laid upon the people,
and they were condemned to find graves in the wilderness.   But however the question of authorship may be
settled, the psalm is " not of an age, but for all time."

It falls into three parts, of which the two former
contain six verses each, while the last has but five.   In
the first section (vv. 1–6), the transitoriness of men
is set over against the eternity of God ; in the second,
(vv. 7–12) that transitoriness is traced to its reason,
namely sin ; and in the third, prayer that God would
visit His servants is built upon both His eternity and
their fleeting days.   The short ver. 1 blends both the
thoughts which are expanded in the following verses,
while in it the singer breathes awed contemplation
of the eternal God as the dwelling-place or asylum of
generations that follow each other, swift and unremem-
bered, as the waves that break on some lonely shore.
God is invoked as " Lord," the sovereign ruler, the
name which connotes His elevation and authority.
But, though lofty, He is not inaccessible.   As some
ancestral home shelters generation after generation of
a family, and in its solid strength stands unmoved,
while one after another of its somewhile tenants is
borne forth to his grave, and the descendants sit in the
halls where centuries before their ancestors sat, God is
the home of all who find any real home amidst the
fluctuating nothings of this shadowy world.   The con-

trast of His eternity and our transiency is not bitter,
though it may hush us into wisdom, if we begin with
the trust that He is the abiding abode of short-lived man.
For this use of *dwelling-place* compare Deut. xxxiii. 27.

What God has been to successive generations results
from what He is in Himself before all generations.
So ver. 2 soars to the contemplation of His absolute
eternity, stretching boundless on either side of " this
bank and shoal of time "—" From everlasting to everlasting Thou art God "; and in that name is proclaimed
His self-derived strength, which, being eternal, is
neither derived from nor diminished by time, that first
gives to, and then withdraws from, all creatures their
feeble power.   The remarkable expressions for the
coming forth of the material world from the abyss of
Deity regard creation as a birth.   The Hebrew text
reads in ver. 2 *b* as above, " Thou gavest birth to"; but a
very small change in a single vowel gives the possibly
preferable reading which preserves the parallelism of a
passive verb in both clauses, " Or the earth and the
world were brought forth."

The poet turns now to the other member of his
antithesis.   Over against God's eternal Being is set the
succession of man's generations, which has been already
referred to in ver. 1.   This thought of successiveness
is lost unless ver. 3 *b* is understood as the creative
fiat which replaces by a new generation those who
have been turned back to dust.   Death and life, decay
and ever-springing growth, are in continual alternation.
The leaves, which are men, drop; the buds swell and
open.   The ever-knitted web is being ever run down
and woven together again.   It is a dreary sight, unless
one can say with our psalm, " *Thou* turnest . . . *Thou*
sayest, Return."   Then one understands that it is not

aimless or futile. If a living Person is behind the
transiencies of human life, these are still pathetic and
awe-kindling, but not bewildering. In ver. 3 *a* there
is clear allusion to Gen. iii. 19. The word rendered
"dust" may be an adjective taken as neuter = *thai
which is crushed, i.e.* dust; or, as others suppose, a
substantive = *crushing*; but is probably best understood
in the former sense. The psalm significantly uses the
word for *man* which connotes frailty, and in *b* the
expression "sons of man" which suggests birth.

The psalmist rises still higher in ver. 4. It is much
to say that God's Being is endless, but it is more to
say that He is raised above Time, and that none of
the terms in which men describe duration have any
meaning for Him. A thousand years, which to a man
seem so long, are to Him dwindled to nothing, in
comparison with the eternity of His Being. As Peter
has said, the converse must also be true, and "one
day be with the Lord as a thousand years." He
can crowd a fulness of action into narrow limits
Moments can do the work of centuries. The longest
and shortest measures of time are absolutely equivalent, for both are entirely inapplicable, to His timeless
Being. But what has this great thought to do here,
and how is the "For" justified? It may be that
the psalmist is supporting the representation of ver. 2,
God's eternity, rather than that of ver. 3, man's transiency; but, seeing that this verse is followed by one
which strikes the same note as ver. 3, it is more
probable that here, too, the dominant thought is the
brevity of human life. It never seems so short, as
when measured against God's timeless existence. So,
the underlying thought of ver. 3, namely, the brevity
of man's time, which is there illustrated by the picture

of the endless flux of generations, is here confirmed
by the thought that all measures of time dwindle to
equal insignificance with Him.

The psalmist next takes his stand on the border-
moment between to-day and yesterday. How short
looks the day that is gliding away into the past! "A
watch in the night" is still shorter to our consciousness,
for it passes over us unnoted.

The passing of mortal life has hitherto been contemplated in immediate connection with God's permanence, and the psalmist's tone has been a wonderful
blending of melancholy and trust. But in ver. 5 the
sadder side of his contemplations becomes predominant.
Frail man, frail because sinful, is his theme. The
figures which set forth man's mortality are grand in
their unelaborated brevity. They are like some of
Michael Angelo's solemn statues. "Thou floodest
them away"—a bold metaphor, suggesting the rush
of a mighty stream, bearing on its tawny bosom
crops, household goods, and corpses, and hurrying
with its spoils to the sea. "They become a sleep."
Some would take this to mean falling into the sleep
of death ; others would regard life as compared to
a sleep—"for before we are rightly conscious of being
alive, we cease to live" (Luther, quoted by Cheyne);
while others find the point of comparison in the disappearance, without leaving a trace behind, of the
noisy generations, sunk at once into silence, and
"occupying no more space on the scroll of Time than
a night's sleep" (so Kay). It is tempting to attach
"in the morning" to "a sleep," but the recurrence
of the expression in ver. 7 points to the retention of
the present division of clauses, according to which the
springing grass greets the eye at dawn, as if created

by· a night's rain. The word rendered "springs afresh" is taken in two opposite meanings, being by some rendered *passes away*, and by others as above. Both meanings come from the same radical notion of change, but the latter is evidently the more natural and picturesque here, as preserving, untroubled by any intrusion of an opposite thought, the cheerful picture of the pastures rejoicing in the morning sunshine, and so making more impressive the sudden, sad change wrought by evening, when all the fresh green blades and bright flowers lie turned already into brown hay by the mower's scythe and the fierce sunbeams.

> "So passeth, in the passing of an hour,
> Of mortal life, the leaf, the bud, the flower."

The central portion of the psalm (vv. 7–12) narrows the circle of the poet's vision to Israel, and brings out the connection between death and sin. The transition from truths of universal application is marked by the use of *we* and *us*, while the past tenses indicate that the psalm is recounting history. That transitoriness assumes a still more tragic aspect, when regarded as the result of the collision of God's "wrath" with frail man. How can such stubble but be wasted into ashes by such fire? And yet this is the same psalmist who has just discerned that the unchanging Lord is the dwelling-place of all generations. The change from the previous thought of the eternal God as the dwelling-place of frail men is very marked in this section, in which the destructive anger of God is in view. But the singer felt no contradiction between the two thoughts, and there is none. We do not understand the full blessedness of believing that God is our asylum, till we understand that He is our asylum

from all that is destructive in Himself; nor do we
know the significance of the universal experience of
decay and death, till we learn that it is not the result
of our finite being, but of sin.

That one note sounds on in solemn persistence
through these verses, therein echoing the characteristic
Mosaic lesson, and corresponding with the history of
the people in the desert. In ver. 7 the cause of their
wasting away is declared to be God's wrath, which
has scattered them as in panic (Psalm xlviii. 5). The
occasion of that lightning flash of anger is confessed
in ver. 8 to be the sins which, however hidden, stand
revealed before God. The expression for "the light
of Thy face" is slightly different from the usual one, a
word being employed which means a luminary, and is
used in Gen. i. for the heavenly bodies. The ordinary
phrase is always used as expressing favour and blessing;
but there is an illumination, as from an all-revealing
light, which flashes into all dark corners of human
experience, and "there is nothing hid from the heat
thereof." Sin smitten by that light must die. Therefore, in ver. 9, the consequence of its falling on Israel's
transgressions is set forth. Their days vanish as mists
before the sun, or as darkness glides out of the sky in
the morning. Their noisy years are but as a murmur,
scarce breaking the deep silence, and forgotten as soon
as faintly heard. The psalmist sums up his sad contemplations in ver. 10, in which life is regarded as not
only rigidly circumscribed within a poor seventy or, at
most, eighty years, but as being, by reason of its transitoriness, unsatisfying and burdensome. The "pride"
which is but trouble and vanity is that which John
calls "the pride of life," the objects which, apart
from God, men desire to win, and glory in possess-

ing. The self-gratulation would be less ridiculous or
tragic, if the things which evoke it lasted longer, or we
lasted longer to possess them. But seeing that they
swiftly pass and we fly too, surely it is but "trouble"
to fight for what is "vanity" when won, and what
melts away so surely and soon.

Plainly, then, things being so, man's wisdom is to
seek to know two things—the power of God's anger,
and the measure of his own days. But alas for human
levity and bondage to sense, how few look beyond the
external, or lay to heart the solemn truth that God's
wrath is inevitably operative against sin, and how few
have any such just conception of it as to lead to reverential awe, proportioned to the Divine character which
should evoke it! Ignorance and inoperative knowledge
divide mankind between them, and but a small remnant
have let the truth plough deep into their inmost being
and plant there holy fear of God. Therefore, the
psalmist prays for himself and his people, as knowing
the temptations to inconsiderate disregard and to inadequate feeling of God's opposition to sin, that His
power would take untaught hearts in hand and teach
them this—to count their days. Then we shall bring
home, as from a ripened harvest field, the best fruit
which life can yield, "a heart of wisdom," which, having
learned the power of God's anger, and the number of
our days, turns itself to the eternal dwelling-place, and no
more is sad, when it sees life ebbing away, or the generations moving in unbroken succession into the darkness.

The third part (vv. 13–17) gathers all the previous
meditations into a prayer, which is peculiarly appropriate to Israel in the wilderness, but has deep meaning
for all God's servants. We note the invocation of God
by the covenant name "Jehovah," as contrasted with

the " Lord " of ver. 1.   The psalmist draws nearer to
God, and feels the closer bond of which that name is the
pledge.   His prayer is the more urgent, by reason of
the brevity of life.   So short is his time that he cannot
afford to let God delay in coming to him and to his
fellows.   " How long ? " comes pathetically from lips
which have been declaring that their time of speech is
so short.   This is not impatience, but wistful yearning,
which, even while it yearns, leaves God to settle His
own time, and, while it submits, still longs.   Night has
wrapped Israel, but the psalmist's faith " awakes the
morning," and he prays that its beams may soon dawn
and Israel be satisfied with the longed-for loving-
kindness (compare Psalm xxx. 5); for life at its longest
is but brief, and he would fain have what remains of it be
lit with sunshine from God's face.   The only thing that
will secure life-long gladness is a heart satisfied with
the experience of God's love.   That will make morning
in mirk midnight ; that will take all the sorrow out of
the transiency of life.   The days which are filled with
God are long enough to satisfy us ; and they who have
Him for their own will be " full of days," whatever the
number of these may be.

The psalmist believes that God's justice has in store
for His servants joys and blessings proportioned to
the duration of their trials.   He is not thinking of any
future beyond the grave ; but his prayer is a prophecy,
which is often fulfilled even in this life and always
hereafter.   Sorrows rightly borne here are factors
determining the glory that shall follow.   There is a
proportion between the years of affliction and the
millenniums of glory.   But the final prayer, based
upon all these thoughts of God's eternity and man's
transitoriness, is not for blessedness, but for vision and

Divine favour on work done for Him. The deepest
longing of the devout heart should be for the manifestation to itself and others of God's work. The
psalmist is not only asking that God would put forth
His acts in interposition for himself and his fellow-
servants, but also that the full glory of these far-reaching
deeds may be disclosed to their understandings as well
as experienced in their lives. And since he knows
that " through the ages an increasing purpose runs,"
he prays that coming generations may see even more
glorious displays of Divine power than his contemporaries have done. How the sadness of the thought
of fleeting generations succeeded by new ones vanishes
when we think of them all as, in turn, spectators and
possessors of God's " work " ! But in that great work
we are not to be mere spectators. Fleeting as our
days are, they are ennobled by our being permitted to
be God's tools ; and if " the work of our hands " is the
reflex or carrying on of His working, we can confidently ask that, though we the workers have to pass,
it may be " established." " In our embers " may be
" something that doth live," and that life will not all
die which has done the will of God, but it and its
doer will " endure for ever." Only there must be the
descent upon us of " the graciousness " of God, before
there can flow from us " deeds which breed not
shame," but outlast the perishable earth and follow
their doers into the eternal dwelling-place. The
psalmist's closing prayer reaches further than he knew.
Lives on which the favour of God has come down like
a dove, and in which His will has been done, are not
flooded away, nor do they die into silence like a whisper,
but carry in themselves the seeds of immortality, and
are akin to the eternity of God.

PSALM XCI.

1 He that sits in the secret place of the Most High,
In the shadow of the Almighty shall he lodge.

2 I will say to Jehovah, "My refuge and my fortress,
My God, in whom I will trust."

3 For He, He shall deliver thee from the snare of the fowler
From the pestilence that destroys.

4 With His pinions shall He cover thee,
And under His wings shalt thou take refuge,
A shield and target is His Troth.

5 Thou shalt not be afraid of the terror of the night,
Of the arrow [that] flies by day,

6 Of the pestilence [that] stalks in darkness,
Of the sickness [that] devastates at noonday.

7 A thousand may fall at thy side,
And a myriad at thy right hand,
To thee it shall not reach.

8 Only with thine eyes shalt thou look on,
And see the recompense of the wicked.

9a "For Thou, Jehovah, art my refuge."

9b The Most High thou hast made thy dwelling-place,
10 No evil shall befall thee,
And no scourge shall come near thy tent.

11 For His angels will He command concerning thee,
To keep thee in all thy ways.

12 Upon [their] hands shall they bear thee,
Lest thou strike thy foot against a stone.

13 Upon lion and adder shalt thou tread,
Thou shalt trample upon young lion and dragon.

14 "Because to Me he clings, therefore will I deliver him
I will lift him high because he knows My name.

14

15 He shall call on Me, and I will answer him;
With him will I, even I, be in trouble,
I will rescue him and bring him to honour.
16 [With] length of days will I satisfy him,
And give him to gaze on My salvation."

THE solemn sadness of Psalm xc. is set in strong relief by the sunny brightness of this song of happy perfect trust in the Divine protection. The juxtaposition is, however, probably due to the verbal coincidence of the same expression being used in both psalms in reference to God. In Psalm xc. 1, and in xci. 9, the somewhat unusual designation "dwelling-place" is applied to Him, and the thought conveyed in it runs through the whole of this psalm.

An outstanding characteristic of it is its sudden changes of persons; "He," "I," and "thou" alternate in a bewildering fashion, which has led to many attempts at explanation. One point is clear—that, in vv. 14–16, God speaks, and that He speaks of, not to, the person who loves and clings to Him. At ver. 14, then, we must suppose a change of speaker, which is unmarked by any introductory formula. Looking back over the remainder of the psalm, we find that the bulk of it is addressed directly *to* a person who must be the same as is spoken *of* in the Divine promises. The "him" of the latter is the "thee" of the mass of the psalm. But this mass is broken at two points by clauses alike in meaning, and containing expressions of trust (vv. 2, 9 *a*). Obviously the unity of the psalm requires that the "I" of these two verses should be the "thou" of the great portion of the psalm, and the "he" of the last part. Each profession of trust will then be followed by assurances of safety thence resulting, ver. 2 having for pendant vv. 3–8, and ver. 9 *a* being followed by vv. 9 *b*–13. The two utterances of personal faith are substantially identical, and the assurances which succeed them are also in effect the same. It is by some supposed that this alternation of persons is due simply to the poet expressing partly " his own feelings as from himself, and partly as if they were uttered by another " (Perowne after Ewald). But that is not an explanation of the structure; it is only a statement of the structure which requires to be explained. No doubt the poet is expressing his own feelings or convictions all through the psalm : but why does he express them in this singular fashion ?

The explanation which is given by Delitzsch, Stier, Cheyne and many others takes the psalm to be antiphonal, and distributes the parts among the voices of a choir, with some variations in the allocation.

But ver. 1 still remains a difficulty. As it stands it sounds flat and tautological, and hence attempts have been made to amend it, which will presently be referred to. But it will fall into the general antiphonal scheme, if it is regarded as a prelude, sung by the same voice which twice answers the single singer with choral assurances that reward his trust. We, then, have this distribution of parts : ver. 1, the broad statement of the blessedness of dwelling with God ; ver. 2, a solo, the voice of a heart encouraged thereby to exercise personal trust ; vv. 3–8, answers, setting forth the security of such a refuge ; ver. 9 *a*, solo, reiterating with sweet monotony the word of trust ; vv. 9 *b*–13, the first voice or chorus repeating with some variation the assurances of vv. 3–8 ; and vv. 14–16, God's acceptance of the trust and confirmation of the assurances.

There is, no doubt, difficulty in ver. 1 ; for, if it is taken as an independent sentence, it sounds tautological, since there is no well-marked difference between "sitting" and "lodging," nor much between "secret place" and "shadow." But possibly the idea of safety is more strongly conveyed by "shadow" than by "secret place," and the meaning of the apparently identical assertion may be, that he who quietly enters into communion with God thereby passes into His protection ; or, as Kay puts it, "Loving faith on man's part shall be met by faithful love on God's part." The LXX. changes the person of "will say" in ver. 2, and connects it with ver. 1 as its subject ("He that sits . . . that lodges . . . shall say"). Ewald, followed by Baethgen and others, regards ver. 1 as referring to the "I" of ver. 2, and translates "Sitting . . . I say." Hupfeld, whom Cheyne follows, cuts the knot by assuming that "Blessed is " has dropped out at the beginning of ver. 1, and so gets a smooth run of construction and thought ("Happy is he who sits . . . who lodges . . . who says"). It is suspiciously smooth, obliterates the characteristic change of persons, of which the psalm has other instances, and has no support except the thought that the psalmist would have saved us a great deal of trouble, if he had only been wise enough to have written so. The existing text is capable of a meaning in accordance with his general drift. A wide declaration like that of ver. 1 fittingly preludes the body of the song, and naturally evokes the pathetic profession of faith which follows.

According to the accents, ver. 2 is to be read "I will say, ' To Jehovah [belongs] my refuge,'" etc. But it is better to divide as above. Jehovah *is* the refuge. The psalmist speaks *to* Him, with the exclamation of yearning trust. He can only call Him by precious names, to use which, in however broken a fashion, is

an appeal that goes straight to His heart, as it comes
straight from the suppliant's. The singer lovingly
accumulates the Divine names in these two first verses.
He calls God " Most High," " Almighty," when he
utters the general truth of the safety of souls that enter
His secret place ; but, when he speaks his own trust,
he addresses Jehovah, and adds to the wide designation "God" the little word " my," which claims personal possession of His fulness of Deity. The solo
voice does not say much, but it says enough. There
has been much underground work before that clear jet
of personal "appropriating faith" could spring into
light.

We might have looked for a Selah here, if this psalm
had stood in the earlier books, but we can feel the brief
pause before the choral answer comes in vv. 3–8. It
sets forth in lofty poetry the blessings that such a trust
secures. Its central idea is that of safety. That safety
is guaranteed in regard to two classes of dangers—those
from enemies, and those from diseases. Both are conceived of as divided into secret and open perils. Ver. 3
proclaims the trustful soul's immunity, and ver. 4 beautifully describes the Divine protection which secures it.
Vv. 5, 6, expand the general notion of safety, into
defence against secret and open foes and secret and
open pestilences ; while vv. 7, 8, sum up the whole, in
a vivid contrast between the multitude of victims and
the man sheltered in God, and looking out from his
refuge on the wide-rolling flood of destruction. As in
Psalm xviii. 5, Death is represented as a " fowler " into
whose snares men heedlessly flutter, unless held back
by God's delivering hand. The mention of pestilence
in ver. 3 somewhat anticipates the proper order, as the
same idea recurs in its appropriate place in ver. 6.

Hence the rendering "word," which requires no consonantal change, is adopted from the LXX. by several moderns. But that is feeble, and the slight irregularity of a double mention of one form of peril, which is naturally suggested by the previous reference to Death, is not of much moment. The beautiful description of God sheltering the trustful man beneath His pinions recalls Deut. xxxii. 11 and Psalms xvii. 8, lxiii. 7. The mother eagle, spreading her dread wing over her eaglets, is a wonderful symbol of the union of power and gentleness. It would be a bold hand which would drag the fledglings from that warm hiding-place and dare the terrors of that beak and claws. But this pregnant verse (4) not only tells of the strong defence which God is, but also, in a word, sets in clear light man's way of reaching that asylum. "Thou shalt take refuge." It is the word which is often vaguely rendered "trust," but which, if we retain its original signification, becomes illuminative as to what that trust is. The flight of the soul, conscious of nakedness and peril, to the safe shelter of God's breast is a description of faith which, in practical value, surpasses much learned dissertation. And this verse adds yet another point to its comprehensive statements, when, changing the figure, it calls God's *Troth*, or faithful adherence to His promises and obligations, our "shield and target." We have not to fly to a dumb God for shelter, or to risk anything upon a Peradventure. He has spoken, and His word is inviolable. Therefore, trust is possible. And between ourselves and all evil we may lift the shield of His Troth. His faithfulness is our sure defence, and Faith is our shield only in a secondary sense, its office being but to grasp our true defence, and to keep us well behind that.

The assaults of enemies and the devastations of pestilence are taken in vv. 5, 6, as types of all perils. These evils speak of a less artificial stage of society than that in which our experience moves, but they serve us as symbols of more complex dangers besetting outward and inward life. "The terror of the night" seems best understood as parallel with the "arrow that flies by day," in so far as both refer to actual attacks by enemies. Nocturnal surprises were favourite methods of assault in early warfare. Such an explanation is worthier than the supposition that the psalmist means demons that haunt the night. In ver. 6 Pestilence is personified as stalking, shrouded in darkness, the more terrible because it strikes unseen. Ver. 6 *b* has been understood, as by the Targum and LXX., to refer to demons who exercise their power in noonday. But this explanation rests upon a misreading of the word rendered "devastates." The other translated "sickness" is only found, besides this place, in Deut. xxxii. 24 ("destruction") and Isa. xxviii. 2 ("a destroying storm," lit. a storm of destruction), and in somewhat different form in Hosea xiii. 14. It comes from a root meaning *to cut*, and seems here to be a synonym for pestilence. Baethgen sees in "the arrow by day" the fierce sunbeams, and in "the *heat* (as he renders) which rages at noonday" the poisonous simoom. The trustful man, sheltered in God, looks on while thousands fall round him, as Israel looked from their homes on the Passover night, and sees that there is a God that judges and recompenses evil-doers by evil suffered.

Heartened by these great assurances, the single voice once more declares its trust. Ver. 9 *a* is best separated from *b*, though Hupfeld here again assumes that "thou hast said" has fallen out between "For" and "Thou."

This second utterance of trust is almost identical with
the first.　Faith has no need to vary its expression.
"Thou, Jehovah, art my refuge" is enough for it.
God's mighty name and its personal possession of all
which that name means, as its own hiding-place, are
its treasures, which it does not weary of recounting.
Love loves to repeat itself.　The deepest emotions, like
song-birds, have but two or three notes, which they
sing over and over again all the long day through.
He that can use this singer's words of trust has a
vocabulary rich enough.

The responsive assurances (vv. 9 *b*–13) are, in like
manner, substantially identical with the preceding
ones, but differences may be discerned by which these
are heightened in comparison with the former.　The
promise of immunity is more general.　Instead of two
typical forms of danger, the widest possible exemption
from all forms of it is declared in ver. 10.　*No* evil
shall come near, *no* scourge approach, the "tent" of
the man whose real and permanent "dwelling-place"
is Jehovah.　There are much beauty and significance
in that contrast of the two homes in which a godly
man lives, housing, as far as his outward life is concerned, in a transitory abode, which to-morrow may
be rolled up and moved to another camping-place in
the desert, but abiding, in so far as his true being is
concerned, in God, the permanent dwelling-place through
all generations.　The transitory outward life has reflected
on it some light of peaceful security from that true
home.　It is further noteworthy that the second group
of assurances is concerned with active life, while the
first only represented a passive condition of safety
beneath God's wing.　In vv. 11, 12, His angels take
the place of protectors, and the sphere in which they

protect is " in all thy *ways* "—*i.e.*, in the activities of ordinary life. The dangers *there* are of stumbling, whether that be construed as referring to outward difficulties or to temptations to sin.

The perils, further specified in ver. 13, correspond to those of the previous part in being open and secret . the lion with its roar and leap, the adder with its stealthy glide among the herbage and its unlooked-for bite. So, the two sets of assurances, taken together, cover the whole ground of life, both in its moments of hidden communion in the secret place of the Most High, and in its times of diligent discharge of duty on life's common way. Perils of communion and perils of work are equally real, and equally may we be sheltered from them. God Himself spreads His wing over the trustful man, and sends His messengers to keep him, in all the paths appointed for him by God. The angels have no charge to take stones out of the way. Hinderances are good for us. Smooth paths weary and make persumptuous. Rough ones bring out our best and drive us to look to God. But His messengers have for their task to lift us on their palms over difficulties, not so that we shall not feel them to be difficult, but so that we shall not strike our foot against them. Many a man remembers the elevation and buoyancy of spirit which strangely came to him when most pressed by work or trouble. God's angels were bearing him up. Active life is full of open and secret foes as well as of difficulties. He that keeps near to God will pass unharmed through them all, and, with a foot made strong and firm by God's own power infused into it, will be able to crush the life out of the most formidable and the most sly assailants. " The God of peace shall bruise Satan under your feet shortly."

Finally, God Himself speaks, and confirms and deepens the previous assurances. That He is represented as speaking *of*, not *to*, His servant increases the majesty of the utterance, by seeming to call the universe to hear, and converts promises to an individual into promises to every one who will fulfil the requisite conditions. These are threefold.

God desires that men should cling to Him, know His name, and call on Him. The word rendered "cling" includes more than "setting love upon" one. It means to bind or knit oneself to anything, and so embraces the cleaving of a fixed heart, of a "recollected" mind, and of an obedient will. Such clinging demands effort; for every hand relaxes its grasp, unless ever and again tightened. He who thus clings will come to "know" God's "name," with the knowledge which is born of experience, and is loving familiarity, not mere intellectual apprehension. Such clinging and knowledge will find utterance in continual converse with God, not only when needing deliverance, but in perpetual aspiration after Him.

The promises to such an one go very deep and stretch very far. "I will deliver him." So the previous assurance that no evil shall come nigh him is explained and brought into correspondence with the facts of life. Evil may be experienced. Sorrows will come. But they will not touch the central core of the true life, and from them God will deliver, not only by causing them to cease, but by fitting us to bear. Clinging to Him, a man will be "drawn out of many waters," like Peter on the stormy lake. " I will set him on high " is more than a parallel promise to that of deliverance. It includes that ; for a man lifted to a height is safe from the flood that sweeps through the valley, or from the enemies that ravage the plain. But that elevation, which comes from knowing God's name, brings more than safety, even a life lived in a higher region than that of things seen. "I will answer him." How can He fail to hear when they who trust Him cry? Promises, especially for the troubled, follow, which do not conflict with the earlier assurances, rightly understood. "I will be with him in trouble." God's presence is the answer to His servant's call. God comes nearer to devout and tried souls, as a mother presses herself caressingly closer to a weeping child. So, no man need add solitude to sadness, but may have God sitting with him, like Job's friends, waiting to comfort him with true comfort. And His presence delivers from, and glorifies after, trouble borne as becomes God's friend. The bit of dull steel might complain, if it could feel, of the pain of being polished, but the result is to make it a mirror fit to flash back the sunlight.

"With length of days will I satisfy him" is, no doubt, a promise belonging more especially to Old Testament times ; but if we put emphasis on " satisfy," rather than on the extended duration, it may fairly suggest that, to the trustful soul, life is long enough, whatever its duration, and that the guest, who has sat at God's table here, is not unwilling to rise from it, when his time comes, being "satisfied with favour, and full of the goodness of the Lord." The vision of God's salvation, which is set last, seems from its position in the series to point, however dimly, to a vision which comes after earth's troubles and length of days. The psalmist's language implies not a mere casual beholding, but a fixed gaze. Delitzsch renders " revel in My salvation " (English translation). Cheyne has " feast his eyes with." Such seeing is possession. The crown of God's promises to the man who makes God his dwelling-place is a full, rapturous experience of a full salvation, which follows on the troubles and deliverances of earth, and brings a more dazzling honour and a more perfect satisfaction.

PSALM XCII.

1 Good is it to give thanks to Jehovah,
And to harp to Thy name, Most High ;
2 To declare in the morning Thy loving-kindness,
And thy faithfulness in the night seasons,
3 Upon a ten-stringed [instrument], even upon the psaltery,
With skilful music on the lyre.

4 For Thou hast gladdened me, Jehovah, with Thy working,
In the works of Thy hands will I shout aloud my joy.
5 How great are Thy works, Jehovah,
Exceeding deep are Thy purposes !
6 A brutish man knows not,
And a fool understands not this.

7 When the wicked sprang like herbage,
And all the workers of iniquity blossomed,
[It was only] for their being destroyed for ever.
8 But Thou art [enthroned] on high for evermore Jehovah !
9 For behold Thy enemies, Jehovah,
For behold Thy enemies—shall perish,
All the workers of iniquity shall be scattered.

10 But Thou hast exalted my horn like a wild ox,
I am anointed with fresh oil (?).
11 My eye also gazed on my adversaries,
Of them that rose against me as evil-doers my ear heard
12 The righteous shall spring like the palm,
Like a cedar in Lebanon shall he grow.

13 Planted in the house of Jehovah,
They shall spring in the courts of our God.
14 Still shall they bear fruit in old age,
Full of sap and verdant shall they be.
15 To declare that Jehovah is upright,
My Rock, and there is no unrighteousness in Him.

AUTHORITIES differ in their arrangement of this psalm. Clearly, the first three verses are a prelude ; and if these are left out of account, the remainder of the psalm consists of twelve verses, which fall into two groups of six each, the former of which mainly deals with the brief prosperity and final overthrow of the wicked, while the latter paints the converse truth of the security and blessedness of the righteous. Both illustrate the depth of God's works and purposes, which is the psalmist's theme. A further division of each of these six verses into groups of three is adopted by Delitzsch, and may be accepted. There will then be five strophes of three verses each, of which the first is introductory ; the second and third, a pair setting forth the aspect of Providence towards the wicked ; and the fourth and fifth, another pair, magnifying its dealings with the righteous. Perowne takes the eighth verse, which is distinguished by containing only one clause, as the kernel of the psalm, which is preceded by seven verses, constituting the first division, and followed by seven, making the second. But this arrangement, though tempting, wrenches ver. 9 from its kindred ver. 7.

Vv. 1–3 are in any case introductory. In form they are addressed to Jehovah, in thankful acknowledgment of the privilege and joy of praise. In reality they are a summons to men to taste its gladness, and to fill each day and brighten every night by music of thanksgiving. The devout heart feels that worship is "good," not only as being acceptable to God and conformable to man's highest duty, but as being the source of delight to the worshipper. Nothing is more characteristic of the Psalter than the joy which often dances and sings through its strains. Nothing affords a surer test of the reality of worship than the worshipper's joy in it. With much significance and beauty, " Thy loving-kindness " is to be the theme of each morning, as we rise to a new day and find His mercy, radiant as the fresh sunshine, waiting to bless our eyes, and " Thy faithfulness " is to be sung in the night seasons, as we part from another day which has witnessed to His fulfilment of all His promises.

The second strophe contains the reason for praise— namely, the greatness and depth of the Divine works and purposes. The works meant are, as is obvious from the whole strain of the psalm, those of God's government of the world. The theme which exercised earlier psalmists reappears here, but the struggles of faith with unbelief, which are so profoundly and pathetically recorded in Psalm lxxiii., are ended for this singer. He bows in trustful adoration before the greatness of the works and the unsearchable depth of the purpose of God which directs the works. The sequence of vv. 4–6 is noteworthy. The central place is occupied by ver. 5—a wondering and reverent exclamation, evoked by the very mysteries of Providence. On either side of it stand verses describing the con- trasted impression made by these on devout and on gross minds. The psalmist and his fellows are " gladdened," though he cannot see to the utmost verge or deepest abyss of Works or Plans. What he does see is good; and if sight does not go down to the depths, it is because eyes are weak, not because these are less pellucid than the sunlit shallows. What gladdens the trustful soul, which is in sympathy with God, only bewilders the " brutish man "—*i.e.*, the man who, by immersing his faculties in sense, has descended to the animal level; and it is too grave and weighty for the "fool," the man of incurable levity and self-conceit, to trouble himself to ponder. The eye sees what it is capable of seeing. A man's judgment of God's dealings depends on his relation to God and on the dispositions of his soul.

The sterner aspect of Providence is dealt with in the next strophe (vv. 7–9). Some recent signal destruction of evil-doers seems to be referred to. It exemplifies once more the old truth which another psalmist had sung (Psalm xxxvii. 2), that the prosperity of evil-doers is short-lived, like the blossoming herbage, and not only short-lived, but itself the occasion of their destruction. The apparent success of the wicked is as a pleasant slope that leads downwards. The quicker the blossoming, the sooner the petals fall. "The prosperity of fools shall destroy them." As in the previous strophe the middle verse was central in idea as well as in place, so in this one. Ver. 8 states the great fact from which the overthrow of the wicked, which is declared in the verses before and after, results. God's eternal elevation above the Transitory and the Evil is not merely contrasted with these, but is assigned as the reason why what is evil is transitory. We might render "Thou, Jehovah, art high (lit. a height) for evermore," as, in effect, the LXX. and other old versions do; but the application of such an epithet to God is unexampled, and the rendering above is preferable. God's eternal exaltation "is the great pillar of the universe and of our faith" (Perowne). From it must one day result that all God's enemies shall perish, as the psalmist reiterates, with triumphant reduplication of the designation of the foes, as if he would make plain that the very name "God's enemies" contained a prophecy of their destruction. However closely

banded, they "shall be scattered." Evil may make
conspiracies for a time, for common hatred of good
brings discordant elements into strange fellowship, but
in its real nature it is divisive, and, sooner or later,
allies in wickedness become foes, and no two of them
are left together. The only lasting human association
is that which binds men to one another, because all
are bound to God.

From the scattered fugitives the psalmist turns first
to joyful contemplation of his own blessedness, and
then to wider thoughts of the general well-being of all
God's friends. The more personal references are com-
prised in the fourth strophe (vv. 10–12). The metaphor
of the exalted horn expresses, as in Psalms lxxv. 10,
lxxxix. 17, triumph or the vindication of the psalmist
by his deliverance. Ver. 10 *b* is very doubtful. The
word usually rendered " I am anointed " is peculiar.
Another view of the word takes it for an infinitive used
as a noun, with the meaning " growing old," or, as
Cheyne renders, " wasting strength." This translation
(" my wasting strength with rich oil ") is that of the
LXX. and other ancient versions, and of Cheyne and
Baethgen among moderns. If adopted, the verb must
be understood as repeated from the preceding clause,
and the slight incongruity thence arising can be lessened
by giving a somewhat wider meaning to " exalted,"
such as " strengthen " or the like. The psalmist would
then represent his deliverance as being like refreshing
a failing old age, by anointing with fresh oil.

Thus triumphant and quickened, he expects to gaze
on the downfall of his foes. He uses the same expression as is found in Psalm xci. 8, with a similar con-
notation of calm security, and possibly of satisfaction.
There is no need for heightening his feelings into

" desire," as in the Authorised and Revised Versions.
The next clause (ver. 11 *b*) "seems to have been
expressly framed to correspond with the other ; it
occurs nowhere else in this sense " (Perowne). A less
personal verse (ver. 12) forms the transition to the last
strophe, which is concerned with the community of the
righteous. Here the singular number is retained. By
" the righteous" the psalmist does not exactly mean
himself, but he blends his own individuality with that
of the ideal character, so that he is both speaking of his
own future and declaring a general truth. The wicked
" spring like herbage" (ver. 7), but the righteous "spring
like the palm." The point of comparison is apparently
the gracefulness of the tree, which lifts its slender but
upright stem, and is ever verdant and fruitful. The
cedar in its massive strength, its undecaying vigour,
and the broad shelves of its foliage, green among the
snows of Lebanon, stands in strong contrast to the
palm. Gracefulness is wedded to strength, and both
are perennial in lives devoted to God and Right. Evil
blooms quickly, and quickly dies. What is good lasts.
One cedar outlives a hundred generations of the grass
and flowers that encircle its steadfast feet.

The last part extends the thoughts of ver. 12 to
all the righteous. It does not name them, for it is
needless to do so. Imagery and reality are fused
together in this strophe. It is questionable whether
there were trees planted in the courts of the Temple ;
but the psalmist's thought is that the righteous will
surely be found there, and that it is their native soil, in
which rooted, they are permanent. The facts underlying the somewhat violent metaphor are that true
righteousness is found only in the dwellers with God,
that they who anchor themselves in Him, as a tree in

the earth, are both stayed on, and fed from, Him.
The law of physical decay does not enfeeble all the
powers of devout men, even while they are subject to
it.   As aged palm trees bear the heaviest clusters, so
lives which are planted in and nourished from God
know no term of their fruitfulness, and are full of sap
and verdant, when lives that have shut themselves off
from Him are like an old stump, gaunt and dry, fit
only for firewood.   Such lives are prolonged and made
fruitful, as standing proofs that Jehovah is upright,
rewarding all cleaving to Him and doing of His will,
with conservation of strength, and ever-growing power
to do His will.

Ver. 15 is a reminiscence of Deut. xxxii. 4.   The
last clause is probably to be taken in connection
with the preceding, as by Cheyne (" And that in my
Rock there is no unrighteousness ").   But it may also
be regarded as a final avowal of the psalmist's faith,
the last result of his contemplations of the mysteries of
Providence.   These but drive him to cling close to
Jehovah, as his sole refuge and his sure shelter, and to
ring out *this* as the end which shall one day be manifest as the net result of Providence—that there is no
least trace of unrighteousness in Him.

PSALM XCIII.

1 Jehovah is King, with majesty has He clothed Himself,
  Jehovah has clothed Himself, has girded Himself with strength,
  Yea, the world is set fast [that] it cannot be moved.
2 Fast is set Thy throne from of yore,
  From eternity art Thou.

3 The streams, Jehovah, have lifted up,
  The streams have lifted up their voice,
  The streams lift up their tumult.
4 Above the voices of many waters,
  Mighty [waters], ocean breakers,
  Mightier is Jehovah on high.

5 Thy testimonies are utterly to be trusted:
  Holiness fits Thy house,
  Jehovah, for length of days.

THIS is the first of a group of psalms celebrating Jehovah as King. It is followed by one which somewhat interrupts the unity of subject in the group, but may be brought into connection with them by being regarded as hymning Jehovah's kingly and judicial providence, as manifested in the subjugation of rebels against His throne. The remaining members of the group (Psalms xcv.–c.) rise to a height of lyric exultation in meditating on the reign of Jehovah. Psalms xciii. and xciv. are followed by two (xcv: vi.) beginning with ringing calls for new songs to hail the new manifestation of Himself, by which Jehovah has, as it were, inaugurated a new stage in His visible reign on earth. Psalm xcvii again breaks out into the joyful proclama-

tion "Jehovah is King," which is followed, as if by a
chorus, with a repeated summons for a new song (Psalm
xcviii.).   Once more the proclamation "Jehovah is King"
is sounded out in Psalm xcix., and then the group is
closed by Psalm c., with its call to all lands to crowd
round Jehovah's throne with "tumult of acclaim."
Probably the historical fact underlying this new conviction of, and triumph in, the Kingdom of Jehovah is
the return from exile.   But the tone of prophetic anticipation in these exuberant hymns of confident joy can
scarcely fail of recognition.   The psalmists sang of an
ideal state to which their most glorious experiences but
remotely approximated.   They saw "not yet all things
put under Him," but they were sure that He is King,
and they were as sure, though with the certitude of
faith fixed on His word and not with that of sight, that
His universal dominion would one day be universally
recognised and rejoiced in.

This short psalm but strikes the keynote for the
group.   It is overture to the oratorio, prelude of the
symphony.   Jehovah's reign, the stability of His
throne, the consequent fixity of the natural order, His
supremacy over all noisy rage of opposition and law-
lessness, either in Nature or among men, are set forth
with magnificent energy and brevity.   But the King of
the world is not a mere Nature-compelling Jove.   He
has spoken to men, and the stability of the natural
order but faintly shadows the firmness of His "testimonies," which are worthy of absolute reliance, and
which make the souls that do rely on them stable as
the firm earth, and steadfast with a steadfastness
derived from Jehovah's throne.   He not only reigns
over, but dwells among, men, and His power keeps His
dwelling-place inviolate, and lasting as His reign.

Ver. 1 describes an act rather than a state. " Jehovah has become King " by some specific manifestation of His sovereignty. Not as though He had not been King before, as ver. 2 immediately goes on to point out, but that He has shown the world, by a recent deed, the eternal truth that He reigns. His coronation has been by His own hands. No others have arrayed Him in His royal robes. The psalmist dwells with emphatic reiteration on the thought that Jehovah has clothed *Himself* with majesty and girded *Himself* with strength. All the stability of Nature is a consequence of His self-created and self-manifested power. That Strength holds a reeling world steady. The psalmist knew nothing about the fixity of natural law, but his thought goes down below that fixity, and finds its reason in the constant forth-putting of Divine power. Ver. 2 goes far back as well as deep down or high up, when it travels into the dim, unbounded past, and sees there, amidst its mists, one shining, solid substance, Jehovah's throne, which stood firm before every " then." The word rendered *from of yore* is literally " from then," as if to express the priority of that throne to every period of defined time. And even that grand thought can be capped by a grander climax : " From eternity art Thou." Therefore the world stands firm.

But there are things in the firm world that are not firm. There are " streams " or perhaps " floods," which seem to own no control, in their hoarse dash and devastating rush. The sea is ever the symbol of rebellious opposition and of ungoverned force. Here both the natural and symbolic meanings are present. And the picture is superbly painted. The sound of the blows of the breakers against the rocks, or as they clash with each other, is vividly repeated in the word rendered "tumult," which means rather a blow or collision, and here seems to express the thud of the waves against an obstacle.

Ver. 4 is difficult to construe. The word rendered "mighty" is, according to the accentuation, attached to "breakers," but stands in an unusual position if it is to be so taken. It seems better to disregard the accents, and to take "mighty" as a second adjective belonging to "waters." These will then be described as both multitudinous and proud in their strength, while "ocean breakers" will stand in apposition to *waters*. Jehovah's might is compared with these. It would be but a poor measure of it to say that it was more than they ; but the comparison means that He subdues the floods, and proves His power by taming and calming them. Evidently we are to see shining through the nature-picture Jehovah's triumphant subjugation of rebellious men, which is one manifestation of His kingly power. That dominion is not such as to make opposition impossible. Antagonism of the wildest sort neither casts doubt on its reality nor impinges a hair's-breadth on its sovereignty. All such futile rebellion will be subdued. The shriek of the storm, the dash of the breakers, will be hushed when He says "Peace," and the highest toss of their spray does not wet, much less shake, His stable throne. Such was the psalmist's faith as he looked out over a revolted world. Such may well be ours, who "hear a deeper voice across the storm."

That sweet closing verse comes by its very abruptness with singular impressiveness. We pass from wild commotion into calm. Jehovah speaks, and His words are witnesses both of what He is and of what men should and may be. Power is not an object for trust to fasten on, unless it is gracious, and gives men account of its motives and ends. Words are not objects for trust to fasten on, unless they have power for fulfilment behind them. But if the King, who sets fast earth and bridles seas, speaks to us, we may utterly confide in His word, and, if we do, we shall share in His stable being, in so far as man is capable of resemblance to the changeless God. Trust in firm promises is the secret of firmness. Jehovah has not only given Israel His word, but His house, and His kingly power preserves His dwelling-place from wrong.

"Holiness" in ver. 5 expresses an attribute of Jehovah's house, not a quality of the worshippers therein. It cannot but be preserved from assault, since He dwells there. A king who cannot keep his own palace safe from invaders can have little power. If this psalm is, as it evidently is, post-exilic, how could the singer, remembering the destruction of the Temple, speak thus? Because he had learned the lesson of that destruction, that the earthly house in which Jehovah dwelt among men had ceased to be His, by reason of the sins of its frequenters. Therefore, it was " burned with fire." The profaned house is no longer Jehovah's, but, as Jesus said with strong emphasis on the first word, " *Your* house is left unto you desolate." The Kingship of Jehovah is proclaimed eloquently and tragically by the desolated shrine.

PSALM XCIV.

1 God of vengeances, Jehovah,
  God of vengeances, shine forth.
2 Lift up Thyself, Judge of the earth,
  Return recompense to the proud.

3 For how long, Jehovah, shall the wicked,
  For how long shall the wicked exult?
4 They well out, they speak—arrogance,
  They give themselves airs like princes—all these workers
      of iniquity.
5 Thy people, Jehovah, they crush in pieces,
  And Thine inheritance they afflict.
6 Widow and stranger they kill,
  And orphans they murder.

7 And they say, "Jah sees [it] not,
  And the God of Jacob considers it not."
8 Consider, ye brutish among the people,
  And ye fools, when will ye be wise?
9 The Planter of the ear, shall He not hear?
  Or the Former of the eye, shall He not see?
10 The Instructor of the nations, shall He not punish,—
  The Teacher of knowledge to man?
11 Jehovah knows the thoughts of men,
  For they are [but] a breath.

12 Happy the man whom Thou instructest, Jehovah,
  And teachest from Thy law,
13 To give him rest from the days of evil,
  Till there be digged for the wicked a pit.
14 For Jehovah will not spurn away His people,
  And His inheritance He will not forsake.
15 For to righteousness shall judgment return,
  And after it shall all the upright in heart [follow].

38

16 Who will rise up for me against the evil-doers ?
  Who will set himself for me against the workers of
      iniquity ?
17 Unless Jehovah had been a help for me,
  My soul had soon dwelt in silence.
18 When I say, "My foot slips,"
  Thy loving-kindness, Jehovah, stays me.
19 In the multitude of my divided thoughts within me,
  Thy comforts delight my soul.

20 Can the throne of destruction be confederate with Thee,
  Which frameth mischief by statute ?
21 They come in troops against the soul of the righteous,
  And innocent blood they condemn.
22 But Jehovah is to me a high tower,
  And my God the rock of my refuge.
23 And He brings back upon them their iniquities,
  And by their own evil will He root them out,
  Jehovah our God will root them out.

THE theme of God the Judge is closely allied to
that of God the King, as other psalms of this
group show, in which His coming to judge the world
is the subject of rapturous praise. This psalm hymns
Jehovah's retributive sway, for which it passionately
cries, and in which it confidently trusts. Israel is
oppressed by insolent rulers, who have poisoned the
fountains of justice, condemning the innocent, enacting
unrighteous laws, and making a prey of all the helpless.
These "judges of Sodom" are not foreign oppressors,
for they are "among the people"; and even while they
scoff at Jehovah's judgments they call Him by His
covenant names of "Jah" and "God of Jacob." There
is no need, therefore, to look beyond Israel for the
originals of the dark picture, nor does it supply data
for fixing the period of the psalm.

The structure and course of thought are transparent.
First comes an invocation to God as the Judge of the
earth (vv. 1, 2); then follow groups of four verses

each, subdivided into pairs,—the first of these (vv. 3–6) pictures the doings of the oppressors; the second (vv. 7–11) quotes their delusion that their crimes are unseen by Jehovah, and refutes their dream of impunity, and it is closed by a verse in excess of the normal number, emphatically asserting the truth which the mockers denied. The third group declares the blessedness of the men whom God teaches, and the certainty of His retribution to vindicate the cause of the righteous (vv. 12–15). Then follow the singer's own cry for help in his own need, as one of the oppressed community, and a sweet reminiscence of former aid, which calms his present anxieties. The concluding group goes back to description of the lawless law-makers and their doings, and ends with trust that the retribution prayed for in the first verses will verily be dealt out to them, and that thereby both the singer, as a member of the nation, and the community will find Jehovah, who is both " my God " and " our God," a high tower.

The reiterations in the first two verses are not oratorical embellishments, but reveal intense feeling and pressing need. It is a cold prayer which contents itself with one utterance. A man in straits continues to cry for help till it comes, or till he sees it coming. To this singer, the one aspect of Jehovah's reign which was forced on him by Israel's dismal circumstances was the judicial. There are times when no thought of God is so full of strength as that He is " the God of recompenses," as Jeremiah calls Him (li. 56), and when the longing of good men is that He would flash forth, and slay evil by the brightness of His coming. They who have no profound loathing of sin, or who have never felt the crushing weight of legalised wickedness, may shrink from such aspirations as the psalmist's, and brand them as ferocious; but hearts longing for the triumph of righteousness will not take offence at them.

The first group (vv. 3–6) lifts the cry of suffering Faith, which has almost become impatience, but turns to, not from, God, and so checks complaints of His delay, and converts them into prayer. " How long, O Lord ? " is the burden of many a tried heart ; and the Seer heard it from the souls beneath the altar. This psalm passes quickly to dilate on the crimes of the rulers which forced out that prayer. The portrait has many points of likeness to that drawn in Psalm lxxiii. Here, as there, boastful speech and haughty carriage are made prominent, being put before even cruelty and oppression. " They well out, they speak—arrogance " : both verbs have the same object. Insolent self-exalta-tion pours from the fountain of their pride in copious jets. " They give themselves airs like princes." The verb in this clause may mean *to say among themselves* or *to boast*, but is now usually regarded as meaning *to behave like a prince*—*i.e.*, to carry oneself insolently. Vain-glorious arrogance manifest in boasting speech and masterful demeanour characterises Eastern rulers, especially those who have risen from low origin. Every little village tyrant gave himself airs, as if he were a king ; and the lower his rank, the greater his insolence. These oppressors were grinding the nation to powder, and what made their crime the darker was that it was Jehovah's people and inheritance which they thus harassed. Helplessness should be a passport to a ruler's care, but it had become a mark for murderous attack. Widow, stranger, and orphan are named as types of defencelessness.

Nothing in this strophe indicates that these oppres-sors are foreigners. Nor does the delusion that

Jehovah neither saw nor cared for their doings, which
the next strophe (vv. 7–11) states and confutes, imply
that they were so.   Cheyne, indeed, adduces the name
"God of Jacob," which is put into their mouths, as
evidence that they are pictured as knowing Jehovah
only as one among many tribal or national deities; but
the name is too familiar upon the lips of Israelites, and
its use by others is too conjectural, to allow of such a
conclusion.   Rather, the language derives its darkest
shade from being used by Hebrews, who are thereby
declaring themselves apostates from God as well as
oppressors of His people.   Their mad, practical atheism
makes the psalmist blaze up in indignant rebuke and
impetuous argumentation.   He turns to them, and
addresses them in rough, plain words, strangely contrasted with their arrogant utterances regarding themselves.   They are "brutish" (cf. Psalm lxxiii. 22) and
"fools."   The psalmist, in his height of moral indignation, towers above these petty tyrants, and tells them
home truths very profitable for such people, however
dangerous to their utterer.   There is no obligation to
speak smooth words to rulers whose rule is injustice
and their religion impiety.   Ahab had his Elijah, and
Herod his John Baptist.   The succession has been
continued through the ages.

Delitzsch and others, who take the oppressors to be
foreigners, are obliged to suppose that the psalmist
turns in ver. 8 to those Israelites who had been led
to doubt God by the prosperity of the wicked ; but
there is nothing, except the exigencies of that mistaken
supposition, to show that any others than the deniers
of God's providence who have just been quoted are
addressed as "among the people."   Their denial was
the more inexcusable, because they belonged to the

people whose history was one long proof that Jehovah did see and recompense evil. Two considerations are urged by the psalmist, who becomes for the moment a philosophical theologian, in confutation of the error in question. First, he argues that nothing can be in the effect which is not in the cause, that the Maker of men's eyes cannot be blind, nor the Planter of their ears deaf. The thought has wide applications. It hits the centre, in regard to many modern denials as well as in regard to these blunt, ancient ones. Can a universe plainly full of purpose have come from a purposeless source? Can finite persons have emerged from an impersonal Infinity? Have we not a right to argue upwards from man's make to God his maker, and to find in Him the archetype of all human capacity. We may mark that, as has been long ago observed, the psalm avoids gross anthropomorphism, and infers, not that the Creator of the ear has ears, but that He hears. As Jerome (quoted by Delitzsch) says, "Membra sustulit, efficientias dedit."

In ver. 10 a second argument is employed, which turns on the thought that God is the educator of mankind. That office of instructor cannot be carried out unless He is also their chastiser, when correction is needed. The psalmist looks beyonds the bounds of Israel, the recipient of special revelation (cf. ver. 12), and recognises, what seldom appears in the Old Testament, but is unquestionably there, the great thought that He is teaching all mankind by manifold ways, and especially by the law written in their hearts. Jewish particularism, the exaggeration into a lie of the truth of God's special revelation to Israel, came to forget or deny God's education of mankind. Alas that the same mistake was inherited by so many epochs of the Church!

The teaching of the strophe is gathered up in ver. 11, which exceeds the normal number of four verses in each group, and asserts strongly the conclusion for which the psalmist has been arguing. The rendering of *b* is, " For (not That) they (*i.e.* men) are but a breath." " The ground of the Omniscience which sees the thoughts of men through and through is profoundly laid in the vanity, *i.e.* the finiteness, of men, as the correlative of the Infiniteness of God " (Hupfeld).

In the strophe vv. 12–15, the psalmist turns from the oppressors to their victims, the meek of the earth, and changes his tone from fiery remonstrance to gracious consolation. The true point of view from which to regard the oppressors' wrong is to see in it part of God's educational processes. Jehovah, who "instructs" all men by conscience, "instructs" Israel, and by the Law "teaches" the right interpretation of such afflictive providences. Happy he who accepts that higher education! A further consolation lies in considering the purpose of the special revelation to Israel, which will be realised in patient hearts that are made wise thereby—namely, calm repose of submission and trust, which are not disturbed by any stormy weather. There is possible for the harassed man "peace subsisting at the heart of endless agitation."

If we recognise that life is mainly educational, we shall neither be astonished nor disturbed by sorrows. It is not to be wondered at that the schoolmaster has a rod, and uses it sometimes. There is rest from evil even while in evil, if we understand the purpose of evil. Yet another consolation lies in the steadfast anticipation of its transiency and of the retribution measured to its doers. That is no unworthy source of comfort. And the ground on which it rests is the impossibility of God's forsaking His people, His inheritance. These designations of Israel look back to ver. 5, where the crushed and afflicted are designated by the same words. Israel's relation to Jehovah made the calamities more startling; but it also makes their cessation, and retribution for them on their inflicters, more certain. It is the trial and triumph of Faith to be sure, while tyrants grind and crush, that Jehovah has not deserted their victims. He cannot change His purpose; therefore, sorrows and prosperity are but divergent methods, concurring in carrying out His unalterable design. The individual sufferer may take comfort from his belonging to the community to which the presence of Jehovah is guaranteed for ever. The singer puts his convictions as to what is to be the upshot of all the perplexed riddles of human affairs into epigrammatic form, in the obscure, gnome-like saying, "To righteousness shall judgment return," by which he seems to mean that the administration of justice, which at present was being trampled under foot, "shall come back to the eternal principle of all judicial action, namely, righteousness,"—in shorter words, there shall be no schism between the judgments of earthly tribunals and justice. The psalmist's hope is that of all good men and sufferers from unjust rulers. All the upright in heart long for such a state of things and follow after it, either in the sense of delight in it ("Dem Recht müssen alle frommen Herzen zufallen"—Luther), or of seeking to bring it about. The psalmist's hope is realised in the King of Men, whose own judgments are truth, and who infuses righteousness and the love of it into all who trust in Him.

The singer comes closer to his own experience in the next strophe (vv. 16-19), in which he claims his share in these general sources of rest and patience, and thankfully thinks of past times, when he found that they yielded him streams in the desert. He looks out upon the multitude of "evil-doers," and, for a moment, asks the question which faithless sense is ever suggesting and pronouncing unanswerable: "Where shall I find a champion?" As long as our eyes range along the level of earth, they see none such. But the empty earth should turn our gaze to the occupied throne. There sits the Answer to our almost despairing question. Rather, there He stands, as the proto-martyr saw Him, risen to His feet in swift readiness to help His servant. Experience confirms the hope of Jehovah's aid; for unless in the past He had been the singer's help, he could not have lived till this hour, but must have gone down into the silent land. No man who still draws breath is without tokens of God's sufficient care and ever-present help. The mystery of continued life is a witness for God. And not only does the past thus proclaim where a man's help is, but devout reflection on it will bring to light many times when doubts and tremors were disappointed. Conscious weakness appeals to confirming strength. If we feel our foot giving, and fling up our hands towards Him, He will grasp them and steady us in the most slippery places. Therefore, when divided thoughts (for so the picturesque word employed in ver. 19 means) hesitate between hope and fear, God's consolations steal into agitated minds, and there is a great calm.

The last strophe (vv. 20–23) weaves together in the finale, as a musician does in the last bars of his composition, the main themes of the psalm—the evil deeds of unjust rulers, the trust of the psalmist, his confidence in the final annihilation of the oppressor's

and the consequent manifestation of God as the God
of Israel.   The height of crime is reached when rulers
use the forms of justice as masks for injustice, and
give legal sanction to "mischief."   The ancient world
groaned under such travesties of the sanctity of Law ;
and the modern world is not free from them.   The
question often tortures faithful hearts, " Can such
doings be sanctioned by God, or in any way be allied
to Him ? "   To the psalmist the worst part of these
rulers' wickedness was that, in his doubting moments,
it raised the terrible suspicion that God was perhaps
on the side of the oppressors.   But when such thoughts
came surging on him, he fell back, as we all have to
do, on personal experience and on an act of renewed
trust.   He remembered what God had been to him
in past moments of peril, and he claimed Him for the
same now, his own refuge and fortress.   Strong in
that individual experience and conviction, he won the
confidence that all which Jehovah had to do with the
throne of destruction was, not to connive at its evil,
but to overthrow it and root out the evil-doers, whose
own sin will be their ruin.   Then Jehovah will be
known, not only for the God who belongs to, and
works for, the single soul, but who is " our God, ' tne
refuge of the community, who will not forsake His
inheritance.

PSALM XCV.

1 Come, let us raise shrill cries of joy to Jehovah,
   Let us shout aloud to the Rock of our Salvat on.
2 Let us go to meet His face with thanksgiving,
   With songs let us shout aloud to Him.
3 For Jehovah is a great God,
   And a great King above all gods.
4 In whose hand are the deep places of the earth,
   And the peaks of the mountains are His.
5 Whose is the sea, and He made it,
   And the dry land His hands formed.

6 Come, let us worship and bow down,
   Let us kneel before Jehovah our Maker,
7 For He is our God,
   And we are the people of His pasture and the sheep of
      His hand.

   To-day, if ye would listen to His voice,
8 Harden not your hearts, as [at] Meribah,
   As [in] the day of Massah in the wilderness,
9 Where your fathers tempted Me,
   Proved Me and saw My work.
10 Forty years loathed I [that] generation,
   And said, "A peopl going astray in heart are they,
   And they know not My ways."
11 So that I sware in My wrath,
   "Surely they shall not come into My rest."

THIS psalm is obviously divided into two parts,
but there is no reason for seeing in these two
originally unconnected fragments. Rather does each
part derive force from the other ; and nothing is more
natural than that, after the congregation has spoken its
joyful summons to itself to worship, Jehovah should

48

speak warning words as to the requisite heart-preparation, without which worship is vain. The supposed fragments are fragmentary indeed, if considered apart. Surely a singer has the liberty of being abrupt and of suddenly changing his tone. Surely he may as well be credited with discerning the harmony of the change of key as some later compiler. There could be no more impressive way of teaching the conditions of acceptable worship than to set side by side a glad call to praise and a solemn warning against repeating the rebellions of the wilderness. These would be still more appropriate if this were a post-exilic hymn ; for the second return from captivity would be felt to be the analogue of the first, and the dark story of former hard-heartedness would fit very close to present circumstances.

The invocation to praise in vv. 1, 2, gives a striking picture of the joyful tumult of the Temple worship. Shrill cries of gladness, loud shouts of praise, songs with musical accompaniments, rang simultaneously through the courts, and to Western ears would have sounded as din rather than as music, and as more exuberant than reverent. The spirit expressed is, alas ! almost as strange to many moderns as the manner of its expression. That swelling joy which throbs in the summons, that consciousness that jubilation is a conspicuous element in worship, that effort to rise to a height of joyful emotion, are very foreign to much of our worship. And their absence, or presence only in minute amount, flattens much devotion, and robs the Church of one of its chief treasures. No doubt, there must often be sad strains blended with praise. But it is a part of Christian duty, and certainly of Christian wisdom, to try to catch that tone of joy in worship which rings in this psalm.

The three following verses (3–5) give Jehovah's
creative and sustaining power, and His consequent
ownership of this fair world, as the reasons for worship. He is King by right of creation. Surely it is
forcing unnatural meanings on words to maintain that
the psalmist believed in the real existence of the
"gods" whom he disparagingly contrasts with Jehovah.
The fact that these were worshipped sufficiently warrants the comparison. To treat it as in any degree
inconsistent with Monotheism is unnecessary, and
would scarcely have occurred to a reader but for the
exigencies of a theory. The repeated reference to the
"hand" of Jehovah is striking. In it are held the
deeps; it is a plastic hand, "forming" the land, as
a potter fashioning his clay; it is a shepherd's hand,
protecting and feeding his flock (ver. 7). The same
power created and sustains the physical universe, and
guides and guards Israel. The psalmist has no time
for details; he can only single out extremes, and leave
us to infer that what is true of these is true of all
that is enclosed between them. The depths and the
heights are Jehovah's. The word rendered "peaks" is
doubtful. Etymologically it should mean "fatigue," but
it is not found in that sense in any of the places where
it occurs. The parallelism requires the meaning of
heights to contrast with *depths*, and this rendering is
found in the LXX., and is adopted by most moderns.
The word is then taken to come from a root meaning
"to be high." Some of those who adopt the translation
summits attempt to get that meaning out of the root
meaning *fatigue*, by supposing that the labour of getting
to the top of the mountain is alluded to in the name.
Thus Kay renders "the mountains' toilsome heights,"
and so also Hengstenberg. But it is simpler to trace

the word to the other root, *to be high.* The ownerless
sea is owned by Him; He made both its watery waste
and the solid earth.

But that all-creating Hand has put forth more wondrous energies than those of which heights and depths,
sea and land, witness. Therefore, the summons is
again addressed to Israel to bow before " Jehovah our
Maker." The creation of a people to serve Him is the
work of His grace, and is a nobler effect of His power
than material things. It is remarkable that the call to
glad praise should be associated with thoughts of His
greatness as shown in creation, while lowly reverence
is enforced by remembrance of His special relation to
Israel. We should have expected the converse. The
revelation of God's love, in His work of creating a
people for Himself, is most fittingly adored by spirits
prostrate before Him. Another instance of apparent
transposition of thoughts occurs in ver. 7 *b*, where we
might have expected " people of His hand and sheep of
His pasture." Hupfeld proposes to correct accordingly,
and Cheyne follows him. But the correction buys
prosaic accuracy at the cost of losing the forcible
incorrectness which blends figure and fact, and by
keeping sight of both enhances each. " The sheep of
His hand " suggests not merely the creative but the
sustaining and protecting power of God. It is hallowed
for ever by our Lord's words, which may be an echo of
it : " No man is able to snatch them out of the Father's
hand."

The sudden turn from jubilant praise and recognition of Israel's prerogative as its occasion to grave
warning is made more impressive by its occurring in
the middle of a verse. God's voice breaks in upon the
joyful acclamations with solemn effect. The shouts of

the adoring multitude die on the poet's trembling ear, as that deeper Voice is heard.   We cannot persuade ourselves that this magnificent transition, so weighty with instruction, so fine in poetic effect, is due to the after-thought of a compiler.   Such an one would surely have stitched his fragments more neatly together than to make the seam run through the centre of a verse—an irregularity which would seem small to a singer in the heat of his inspiration.   Ver. 7 c may be either a wish or the protasis to the apodosis in ver. 8.   " If ye would but listen to His voice ! " is an exclamation, made more forcible by the omission of what would happen then.   But it is not necessary to regard the clause as optative.   The conditional meaning, which connects it with what follows, is probably preferable, and is not set aside by the expression " His voice " instead of " My voice " ; for " similar change of persons is very common in utterances of Jehovah, especially in the Prophets " (Hupfeld).   " To-day " stands first with strong emphasis, to enforce the critical character of the present moment.   It may be the last opportunity. At all events, it is an opportunity, and therefore to be grasped and used.   A doleful history of unthankfulness lay behind ; but still the Divine voice sounds, and still the fleeting moments offer space for softening of heart and docile hearkening.   The madness of delay when time is hurrying on, and the longsuffering patience of God, are wonderfully proclaimed in that one word, which the Epistle to the Hebrews lays hold of, with so deep insight, as all-important.

The warning points Israel back to ancestral sins, the tempting of God in the second year of the Exodus, by the demand for water (Exod. xvii. 1–7).   The scene of that murmuring received both names, Massah (temptation) and Meribah (strife). It is difficult to decide the exact force of ver. 9 *b*. "Saw My work" is most naturally taken as referring to the Divine acts of deliverance and protection seen by Israel in the desert, which aggravated the guilt of their faithlessness. But the word rendered "and" will, in that case, have to be taken as meaning "although"—a sense which cannot be established. It seems better, therefore, to take "work" in the unusual meaning of acts of judgment—His "strange work." Israel's tempting of God was the more indicative of hardheartedness that it was persisted in, in spite of chastisements. Possibly both thoughts are to be combined, and the whole varied stream of blessings and punishments is referred to in the wide expression. Both forms of God's work should have touched these hard hearts. It mattered not whether He blessed or punished. They were impervious to both. The awful issue of this obstinate rebellion is set forth in terrible words. The sensation of physical loathing followed by sickness is daringly ascribed to God. We cannot but remember what John heard in Patmos from the lips into which grace was poured: "I will spue thee out of My mouth."

But before He cast Israel out, He pled with them, as ver. 10 *b* goes on to tell: "He said, 'A people going astray in heart are they.'" He said so, by many a prophet and many a judgment, in order that they might come back to the true path. The desert-wanderings were but a symbol, as they were a consequence, of their wanderings in heart. They did not know His ways; therefore they chose their own. They strayed in heart; therefore they had an ever-increasing ignorance of the right road. For the averted heart and the blind understanding produce each other.

The issue of the long-protracted departure from the path which God had marked was, as it ever is, condemnation to continue in the pathless wilderness, and exclusion from the land of rest which God had promised them, and in which He Himself had said that He would make His resting-place in their midst. But what befell Israel in outward fact was symbolical of universal spiritual truth. The hearts that love devious ways can never be restful. The path which leads to calm is traced by God, and only those who tread it with softened hearts, earnestly listening to His voice, will find repose even on the road, and come at last to the land of peace. For others, they have chosen the desert, and in it they will wander wearily, " for ever roaming with a hungry heart."

The author of the Epistle to the Hebrews is laying hold of the very kernel of the psalm, when he adduces the fact that, so many centuries after Moses, the warning was still addressed to Israel, and the possibility of entering the Rest of God, and the danger of missing it, still urged, as showing that the Rest of God remained to be won by later generations, and proclaiming the eternal truth that " we which have believed do enter into rest."

PSALM XCVI.

1 Sing to Jehovah a new song,
  Sing to Jehovah, all the earth.
2 Sing to Jehovah, bless His name,
  Publish the glad tidings of His salvation from day to day.
3 Recount among the nations His glory,
  Among all peoples His wonders.

4 For great is Jehovah, and to be praised exceedingly,
  Dread is He above all gods.
5 For all the gods of the people are Nothings,
  And Jehovah made the heavens.
6 Honour and majesty are before Him,
  Strength and beauty are in His sanctuary.

7 Give to Jehovah, ye families of the peoples,
  Give to Jehovah glory and strength.
8 Give to Jehovah the glory of His name,
  Take an offering and come into His courts.
9 Worship Jehovah in holy attire,
  Tremble before Him, all the earth.

10 Say among the nations, "Jehovah is King,"
   Yea, the world is set fast [that] it cannot be moved,
   He shall deal judgment to the peoples in equity.
11 Let the heavens rejoice and let the earth exult,
   Let the sea thunder and its fulness,
12 Let the plain rejoice and all that is in it,
   Then shall all the trees of the forest ring out joyful cries,
13 Before Jehovah, for He comes,
   He comes to judge the earth,
   He will judge the world in righteousness,
   And peoples in His faithfulness.

THE praise of Jehovah as King has, in the preceding psalms, chiefly celebrated His reign over Israel. But this grand coronation anthem takes a wider sweep, and hymns that kingdom as extending to all nations,

55

and as reaching beyond men, for the joy and blessing of a renovated earth. It falls into four strophes, of which the first three contain three verses each, while the last extends to four. These strophes are like concentric circles, drawn round that eternal throne. The first summons Israel to its high vocation of Jehovah's evangelist, the herald who proclaims the enthronement of the King. The second sets Him above all the "Nothings" which usurp the name of gods, and thus prepares the way for His sole monarchy. The third summons outlying nations to bring their homage, and flings open the Temple gates to all men, inviting them to put on priestly robes, and do priestly acts there. The fourth calls on Nature in its heights and depths, heaven and earth, sea, plain and forest, to add their acclaim to the shouts which hail the establishment of Jehovah's visible dominion.

The song is to be new, because a new manifestation of Jehovah's Kinghood has wakened once more the long-silent harps, which had been hung on the willows of Babylon. The psalm is probably a lyric echo of the Restoration, in which the prophet-singer sees the beginning of Jehovah's world-wide display of His dominion. He knew not how many weary years were to pass in a weary and God-defying world, before his raptures became facts. But though His vision tarries, His song is no over-heated imagining, which has been chilled down for succeeding generations into a baseless hope. The perspective of the world's chronology hid from him the deep valley between His standpoint and the fulfilment of his glowing words. Mankind still marches burdened, down among the mists, but it marches towards the sunlit heights. The call to sing a new song is quoted from Isa. xlii. 10. The word

in ver. 2 *b* rendered "publish glad tidings" is also a
favourite word with Isaiah II. (xl. 9, lii. 7, etc.). Ver. 3 *a*
closely resembles Isa. lxvi. 19.

The second strophe is full of allusions to earlier
psalms and prophets. The new manifestation of
Jehovah's power has vindicated His supremacy above
the vanities which the peoples call gods, and has thereby
given new force to old triumphant words which magnified His exalted name. Long ago a psalmist had
sung, after a signal defeat of assailants of Jerusalem,
that God was "great and greatly to be praised" (Psalm
xlviii. 1), and this psalmist makes the old words new.
"Dread" reminds us of Psalm xlvii. 2. The contemptuous name of the nations' gods as "Nothings" is
frequent in Isaiah. The heavens, which roof over all
the earth, declare to every land Jehovah's creative
power, and His supremacy above all gods. But the
singer's eye pierces their abysses, and sees some
gleams of that higher sanctuary of which they are
but the floor. There stand Honour and Majesty,
Strength and Beauty. The psalmist does not speak of
"attributes." His vivid imagination conceives of these
as servants, attending on Jehovah's royal state. Whatsoever things are lovely, and whatsoever are august,
are at home in that sanctuary. Strength and beauty
are often separated in a disordered world, and each
is maimed thereby, but, in their perfection, they are
indissolubly blended. Men call many things strong
and fair which have no affinity with holiness ; but the
archetypes of both excellences are in the Holy Place,
and any strength which has not its roots there is
weakness, and any beauty which is not a reflection
from "the beauty of the Lord our God" is but a mask
concealing ugliness.

The third strophe builds on this supremacy of Jehovah, whose dwelling-place is the seat of all things worthy to be admired, the summons to all nations to render praise to Him. It is mainly a variation of Psalm xxix. 1, 2, where the summons is addressed to angels. Here "the families of the peoples" are called on to ascribe to Jehovah "glory and strength," or "the glory of His name (*i.e.*, of His character as revealed). The call presupposes a new manifestation of His Kingship, as conspicuous and earth-shaking as the thunder-storm of the original psalm. As in it the "sons of God" were called to worship in priestly garb, so here, still more emphatically, Gentile nations are invited to assume the priestly office, to "take an offering and come into His courts." The issue of Jehovah's manifestation of kingly sway will be that Israel's prerogative of priestly access to Him will be extended to all men, and that the lowly worship of earth will have characteristics which assimilate it to that of the elder brethren who ever stand before Him, and also characteristics which distinguish it from that, and are necessary while the worshippers are housed in flesh. Material offerings and places consecrated to worship belong to earth. The "sons of God" above have them not, for they need them not.

The last strophe has four verses, instead of the normal three. The psalmist's chief purpose in it is to extend his summons for praise to the whole creation ; but he cannot refrain from once more ringing out the glad tidings for which praise is to be rendered. He falls back in ver. 10 on Psalm xciii. 1, and Psalm ix. 8. In his quotation from the former psalm, he brings more closely together the thoughts of Jehovah's reign and the fixity of the world, whether that is taken with a material reference, or as predicting the calm perpetuity of the moral order established by His merciful rule and equitable judgment. The thought that inanimate nature will share in the joy of renovated humanity inspires many glowing prophetic utterances, eminently those of Isaiah—as, *e.g.*, Isa. **xxxv.** The converse thought, that it shared in the consequences of man's sin, is deeply stamped on the Genesis narrative. The same note is struck with unhesitating force in Rom. viii., and elsewhere in the New Testament. A poet invests Nature with the hues of his own emotions, but this summons of the psalmist is more than poetry. How the transformation is to be effected is not revealed, but the consuming fires will refine, and at last man will have a dwelling-place where environment will correspond to character, where the external will image the inward state, where a new form of the material will be the perpetual ally of the spiritual, and perfected manhood will walk in a "new heaven and new earth, where dwelleth righteousness."

In the last verse of the psalm, the singer appears to extend his prophetic gaze from the immediate redeeming act by which Jehovah assumes royal majesty, to a still future "coming," in which He will judge the earth. "The accession is a single act; the judging is a continual process. Note that 'judging' has no terrible sound to a Hebrew" (Cheyne, *in loc.*). Ver. 13 *c* is again a verbatim quotation from Psalm ix. 8.

PSALM XCVII.

1 Jehovah is King, let the earth exult,
   Let many lands be glad.
2 Cloud and deep darkness are round Him,
   Righteousness and judgment are the foundation of His
      throne.
3 Fire goes before Him,
   And devours His enemies round about.
4 His lightnings lighted up the world,
   The earth saw and trembled.
5 Mountains melted like wax, from before the face of Jehovah,
   From before the face of the Lord of the whole earth.
6 The heavens declared His righteousness,
   And all the peoples saw His glory.

7 Shamed are all they who serve graven images,
   Who boast themselves of the Nothings,
   Worship Him, all ye gods!
8 Zion heard and was glad,
   And the daughters of Judah exulted,
   Because of Thy judgments, Jehovah.
9 For Thou, Jehovah, art most high above all the earth,
   Thou art exceedingly exalted above all gods.

10 Ye who love Jehovah, hate evil;
   He keeps the souls of His favoured ones,
   From the hand of the wicked He delivers them.
11 Light is sown for the righteous man,
   And for the upright-hearted, gladness.
12 Be glad, ye righteous, in Jehovah,
   And give thanks to His holy memorial.

THE summons to praise the King with a new song
(Psalm xcvi.) is followed by this psalm, which
repeats the dominant idea of the group, "Jehovah is

King," but from a fresh point of view. It represents His rule under the form of a theophany, which may possibly be regarded as the fuller description of that coming of Jehovah to judgment with which Psalm xcvi. closes. The structure of both psalms is the same, each being divided into four strophes, normally consisting of three verses each, though the last strophe of Psalm xcvi. runs over into four verses. In this psalm, the first group of verses celebrates the royal state of the King (vv. 1–3) ; the second describes His coming as a past fact (vv. 4–6) ; the third portrays the twofold effects of Jehovah's appearance on the heathen and on Zion (vv. 7–9) ; and the last applies the lessons of the whole to the righteous, in exhortation and encouragement (vv. 10–12). The same dependence on earlier psalms and prophets which marks others of this group is obvious here. The psalmist's mind is saturated with old sayings, which he finds flashed up into new meaning by recent experiences. He is not " original," and does not try to be so ; but he has drunk in the spirit of his predecessors, and words which to others were antiquated and cold blaze with light for him, and seem made for his lips. He who reads aright the solemn significance of to-day will find it no less sacred than any past, and may transfer to it all which seers and singers have said and sung of Jehovah's presence of old.

The first strophe is mosaic-work. Ver. 1 (*lands=isles*) may be compared with Isa. xlii. 10, li. 5. Ver. 2 *a* is from Exod. xix. 9, 16, etc., and Psalm xviii. 9. Ver. 2 *b* is quoted from Psalm lxxxix. 14. Ver. 3 *a* recalls Psalms l. 3 and xviii. 8. The appearance of God on Sinai is the type of all later theophanies, and the reproduction of its principal features witnesses to the conviction that that transient manifestation was the unveiling of permanent reality. The veil had dropped again, but what had been once seen continued always, though unseen ; and the veil could and would be drawn aside, and the long-hidden splendour blaze forth again. The combination of the pieces of mosaic in a new pattern here is striking. Three thoughts fill the singer's mind. God is King, and His reign gladdens the world, even away out to the dimly seen lands that are washed by the western ocean. " The islands" drew Isaiah's gaze. Prophecy began in him to look seawards and westwards, little knowing how the course of empire was to take its way thither, but feeling that whatever lands might lie towards the setting sun were ruled, and would be gladdened, by Jehovah.

Gladness passes into awe in ver. 2 a, as the seer beholds the cloud and gloom which encircle the throne. The transcending infinitude of the Divine nature, the mystery of much of the Divine acts, are symbolised by these ; but the curtain is the picture. To know that God cannot be known is a large part of the knowledge of Him. Faith, built on experience, enters into the cloud, and is not afraid, but confidently tells what it knows to be within the darkness. " Righteousness and judgment "—the eternal principle and the activity thereof in the several acts of the King—are the bases of His throne, more solid than the covering cloud. Earth can rejoice in His reign, even though darkness may make parts of it painful riddles, if the assurance is held fast that absolute righteousness is at the centre, and that the solid core of all is judgment. Destructive power, symbolised in ver. 3 by fire which devours His adversaries, the fire which flashed first on Sinai, is part of the reason for the gladness of earth in His reign. For His foes are the world's foes too ; and a God who could not smite into nothingness that which lifted itself against His dominion would be no God for whom the isles could wait. These three cha- racteristics, mystery, righteousness, power to consume, attach to Jehovah's royalty, and should make every heart rejoice.

In the second strophe, the tenses suddenly change into pure narative. The change may be simply due, as Cheyne suggests, to the influence of the earlier passages descriptive of theophanies, and in which the same tense occurs ; but more probably it points to some event fresh in the experience of Israel, such as the return from Babylon. In this strophe again, we have mosaic. Ver. 4 *a* is quoted from Psalm lxxvii. 18. With ver. 4 *b* may be compared Psalm lxxvii. 16. Ver. 5 *a* is like Micah i. 4, and, in a less degree, Psalm lxviii. 2. " The Lord of the whole earth " is an unusual designa- tion, first found in a significant connection in Josh. iii. 11, 13, as emphasising His triumph over heathen gods, in leading the people into Canaan, and afterwards found in Zech. iv. 14, vi. 5, and Micah iv. 13. Ver. 6 *a* comes from the theophany in Psalm l. 6 ; and ver. 6 *b* has parallels in both parts of Isaiah—*e.g.,* Isa. xxxv. 2, xl. 5, lii. 10—passages which refer to the restoration from Babylon. The picture is grand as a piece of word-paint- ing. The world lies wrapped in thunder-gloom, and is suddenly illumined by the fierce blaze of lightning. The awestruck silence of Nature is wonderfully given by ver. 4 *b* : " The earth saw and trembled." But the picture is symbol, and the lightning-flash is meant to set forth the sudden, swift forth-darting of God's delivering power, which awes a gazing world, while the hills melting like wax from before His face solemnly proclaim how terrible its radiance is, and how easily the mere showing of Himself annihilates all high things that oppose themselves. Solid-seeming and august powers, which tower above His people's ability to overcome them, vanish when He looks out from the deep darkness. The end of His appearance and of the consequent removal of obstacles is the manifestation of His righteousness and glory. The heavens are the scene of the Divine appearance, though earth is the theatre of its working. They "declare His righteousness," not because, as in Psalm xix. they are said to tell forth His glory by their myriad lights, but because in them He has shone forth, in His great act of deliverance of His oppressed people. Israel receives the primary blessing, but is blessed, not for itself alone, but that all peoples may see in it Jehovah's glory. Thus once more the psalm recognises the world-wide destination of national mercies, and Israel's place in the Divine economy as being of universal significance.

The third strophe (vv. 7–9) sets forth the results of the theophany on foes and friends. The worshippers of "the Nothings" (xcvi. 5) are put to confusion by the demonstration by fact of Jehovah's sovereignty over their helpless deities. Ver. 7 a, b, recall Isa. xlii. 17, xliv. 9. As the worshippers are ashamed, so the gods themselves are summoned to fall down before this triumphant Jehovah, as Dagon did before the Ark. Surely it is a piece of most prosaic pedantry to argue, from this flash of scorn, that the psalmist believed that the gods whom he had just called "Nothings" had a real existence, and that therefore he was not a pure Monotheist.

The shame of the idolaters and the prostration of their gods heighten the gladness of Zion, which the psalm describes in old words that had once celebrated another flashing forth of Jehovah's power (Psalm xlviii. 11). Hupfeld, whom Cheyne follows, would transpose vv. 7 and 8, on the grounds that " the transposition explains what Zion heard, and brings the summons to the false gods into connection with the emphatic claim on behalf of Jehovah in ver. 9." But there is no need for the change, since there is no ambiguity as to what Zion heard, if the existing order is retained, and her gladness is quite as worthy a consequence of the exaltation of Jehovah in ver. 9 as the subjugation of the false gods would be. With ver. 9 compare Psalm lxxxiii. 18, and Psalm xlvii. 2.

The last strophe (vv. 10–12) draws exhortation and promises from the preceding. There is a marked diminution of dependence on earlier passages in this strophe, in which the psalmist points for his own generation the lessons of the great deliverance which he has been celebrating. Ver. 12 *a* is like Psalm xxxii. 11 ; ver. 12 *b* is from Psalm xxx. 4 ; but the remainder is the psalmist's own earnest exhortation and firm faith, cast into words which come warm from his own heart's depths. Love to Jehovah necessarily implies hatred of evil, which is His antagonist, and which He hates. That higher love will not be kept in energy, unless it is guarded by wholesome antipathy to everything foul. The capacity for love of the noble is maimed unless there is hearty hatred of the ignoble. Love to God is no idle affection, but withdraws a man from rival loves. The stronger the attraction, the stronger the recoil. The closer we cleave to God, the more decided our shrinking from all that would weaken our hold of Him. A specific reference in the exhortation to temptations to idolatry is possible, though not necessary. All times have their "evil," with which God's lovers are ever tempted to comply. The exhortation is never out of place, nor the encouragement which accompanies it ever illusory. In such firm adherence to Jehovah, many difficulties will rise, and foes be made ; but those who obey it will not lack protection. Mark the alternation of names for such. They are first called "lovers of God" ; they are then designated as His " favoured ones." That which is first in time is last in mention. The effect is in view before it is traced to its cause. "We love Him because He first loved us." Then follow names drawn from the moral perfecting which will ensue on recognition and reception of God's favour, and on the cherishing of the love which fulfils the law. They who love because they are loved, become righteous and upright-hearted because they love. For such the psalmist has promise as well as exhortation. Not only are they preserved in and from dangers, but " light is sown " for them. Many commentators think that the figure of light being sown, as seeds are buried in the ground to shoot up in beauty in a future spring-time, is too violent, and they propose to understand " sown " in the sense of *scattered on,* not *deposited in,* the earth, " so that he, the righteous, goes forward step by step in the light " (Delitzsch). Others would correct into " is risen " or "arises." But one is reluctant to part with the figure, the violence of which is permissible in an Eastern singer. Darkness often wraps the righteous, and it is not true to experience to say that his way is always in the sunlight. But it is consolation to know that light is sown, invisible and buried, as it were, but sure to germinate and fruit. The metaphor mingles figures and offends purists, but it fits closer to fact than the weakening of it which fits the rules of composition.

If we are God's lovers, present darkness may be quieted by hope, and we may have the " fruit of the light " in our lives now, and the expectation of a time when we shall possess in fulness and in perpetuity all that light of knowledge, purity, and gladness which Jesus the Sower went forth to sow, and which had been ripened by struggles and sorrows and hatred of evil while we were here.

Therefore, because of this magnificent theophany, and because of its blessed consequences for loving souls, the psalmist ends with the exhortation to the righteous to rejoice. He began with bidding the world be glad. He now bids each of us concentrate that universal gladness in our own hearts. Whether earth obeys Him or not, it is for us to clasp firmly the great facts which will feed the lamp of our joy. God's holy memorial is His name, or His self-revealed character. He desires to be known and remembered by His acts. If we rightly retain and ponder His utterance of Himself, not in syllables, but in deeds, we shall not be silent in His praise. The righteous man should not be harsh and crabbed, but his soul should dwell in a serene atmosphere of joy in Jehovah, and his life be one thanksgiving to that mighty, never-to-be-forgotten Name.

PSALM XCVIII.

1 Sing to Jehovah a new song,
  For wonders He has done,
  His right hand has brought Him salvation, and His holy arm
2 Jehovah has made known His salvation,
  To the eyes of the nations He has revealed His righteousness.
3 He has remembered His loving-kindness and His faithfulness
      to the house of Israel,
  All the ends of the earth have seen the salvation of our God.

4 Shout aloud to Jehovah, all the earth,
  Break forth into shrill cries of joy and make melody,
5 Make melody to Jehovah with the lyre,
  With lyre and voice of melody.
6 With trumpets and blast of horn,
  Shout aloud before Jehovah, the King.

7 Let the sea thunder and its fulness,
  The world and the dwellers therein,
8 Let streams clap hands,
  Together let mountains ring out joyful cries,
9 Before Jehovah, for He comes to judge the earth,
  He will judge the world in righteousness,
  And peoples in equity.

THE two preceding psalms correspond in number
and division of verses. The first begins with a
summons to sing to Jehovah; the second, with a proclamation that He is King. A precisely similar connection exists between this and the following psalm.
Psalm xcviii. is an echo of Psalm xcvi., and Psalm xcix.
of Psalm xcvii. The number of verses in each of the
second pair is nine, and in each there is a threefold
division. The general theme of both pairs is the same,
but with considerable modifications. The abundant

allusions to older passages continue here, and the
second part of Isaiah is especially familiar to the singer.

The first strophe (vv. 1–3), though modelled on
the first of Psalm xcvi., presents the theme in a different fashion. Instead of reiterating through three
verses the summons to Israel to praise Jehovah, and
declare His glory to the nations, this psalm passes at
once from the summons to praise, in order to set forth
the Divine deed which evokes the praise, and which,
the psalmist thinks, will shine by its own lustre to
" the ends of the earth," whether it has human voices
to celebrate it or not. This psalmist speaks more
definitely of Jehovah's wonders of deliverance. Israel
appears rather as the recipient than as the celebrator of
God's loving-kindness. The sun shines to all nations,
whether any voices say " Look," or no. Ver. 1 *a* is
from Psalm xcvi. 1 ; vv. 1 *c*–3 weave together snatches
of various passages in the second part of Isaiah, especially Isa. lii. 10, lix. 16, lxiii. 5. The remarkable expression " brought salvation to Him " (from the second
passage in Isaiah) is rendered by many " helped Him,"
and that rendering gives the sense but obliterates the
connection with " salvation," emphatically repeated in
the two following verses. The return from Babylon
is naturally suggested as best corresponding to the
psalmist's words. That was " the salvation of our
God," who seemed to have forgotten His people, as
Isa. xlix. 2 represents Israel as complaining, but now,
before "the eyes of all nations," has shown how well
He remembers and faithfully keeps His covenant obligations. Israel is, indeed, Jehovah's witness, and should
ring out her grateful joy ; but Jehovah's deed speaks
more loudly than Israel's proclamation of it can ever do.

The second strophe (vv. 4–6) corresponds to the

third of Psalm xcvi.; but whereas there the Gentiles
were summoned to bring offerings into the courts of
Jehovah, here it is rather the glad tumult of vocal
praise, mingled with the twang of harps, and the blare
of trumpets and horns, which is present to the singer's
imagination. He hears the swelling chorus echoing
through the courts, which are conceived as wide enough
to hold "all the earth." He has some inkling of the
great thought that the upshot of God's redeeming self-
manifestation will be glad music from a redeemed world.
His call to mankind throbs with emotion, and sounds
like a prelude to the melodious commingling of voice
and instrument which he at once enjoins and foretells.
His words are largely echoes of Isaiah. Compare Isa.
xliv. 23, xlix. 13, lii. 9, for "break forth into," and li. 3
for "voice of melody."

The final strophe is almost identical with that of
Psalm xcvi., but, in accordance with the variation found
in vv. 1–3, omits the summons to Israel to proclaim
God's Kinghood among the nations. It also inverts the
order of clauses in ver. 7, and in ver. 7 *b* quotes from
Psalm xxiv. 1, where also "the fulness of it" precedes,
with the result of having no verb expressed which
suits the nouns, since "the world and the dwellers
therein" cannot well be called on to "thunder." Instead of the "plain" and "trees of the forest" in the
original, ver. 8 substitutes streams and mountains.
The bold figure of the streams clapping hands, in token
of homage to the King (2 Kings xi. 12; Psalm xlvii. 1)
occurs in Isa. lv. 12. The meeting waves are conceived
of as striking against each other, with a sound resembling that of applauding palms. Ver. 9 is quoted from
Psalm xcvi., with the omission of the second "He
cometh" (which many versions of the LXX. retain),
and the substitution of "equity" for "His faithfulness."

PSALM XCIX.

1 Jehovah is King the peoples tremble ;
  Throned [on] the cherubim—the earth totters.
2 Jehovah in Zion is great,
  And exalted above all the peoples.
3 Let them praise Thy great and dread name,
  Holy is He.

4 And the strength of the King loves judgment,
  Thou, Thou hast established equity,
  Judgment and righteousness in Jacob hast Thou wrought.
5 Exalt Jehovah our God,
  And prostrate yourselves at His footstool,
  Holy is He.

6 Moses and Aaron among His priests,
  And Samuel among them that call [on] His name ;
  They called on Jehovah, and He, He answered them.
7 In a pillar of cloud He spoke to them,
  They kept His testimonies,
  And the statute [which] He gave them.
8 Jehovah our God ! Thou, Thou didst answer them,
  A forgiving God wast Thou unto them,
  And executing retribution for their deeds.
9 Exalt Jehovah our God,
  And prostrate yourselves at His holy mountain,
  For holy is Jehovah our God.

DELITZSCH has well called this psalm " an earthly echo of the seraphic Trisagion," the threefold proclamation of the Divine holiness, which Isaiah heard (Isa. vi. 3). It is, as already noted, a pendant to Psalm xcviii., but is distinguished from the other psalms of this group by its greater originality, the absence of distinct allusion to the great act of deliverance celebrated in them, and its absorption in the one thought of the Divine holiness. Their theme is the event by which Jehovah manifested to the world His sovereign rule ; this psalm passes beyond the event, and grasps the eternal central principle of that rule—namely, holiness. The same thought has been touched on in the other members of the group, but here it is the single subject of praise. Its exhibition in God's dealings with Israel is here traced in ancient examples, rather than in recent instances ; but the view-point of the other psalms is retained, in so far as the Divine dealings with Israel are regarded as the occasion for the world's praise.

The first strophe (vv. 1–3) dwells in general terms on Jehovah's holiness, by which august conception is meant, not only moral purity, but separation from, by elevation above, the finite and imperfect. Ver. 1 vividly paints in each clause the glory reigning in heaven, and its effect on an awestruck world. We might render the verbs in the second part of each clause as futures or as optatives (*shall tremble, shall totter,* or *Let peoples tremble,* etc.), but the thought is more animated if they are taken as describing the result of the theophany. The participial clause "throned on the cherubim" adds detail to the picture of Jehovah as King. It should not, strictly speaking, be rendered with a finite verb. When that vision of Him sitting in royal state is unveiled, all people are touched with reverence, and the solid earth staggers. But the glory which is made visible to all men has its earthly seat in Zion, and shines from thence into all lands. It is by His deeds in Israel that God's exaltation is made known. The psalmist does not call on men to

bow before a veiled Majesty, of which they only know
that it is free from all creatural limitations, lowliness
and imperfections ; but before a God, who has revealed
Himself in acts, and has thereby made Himself a name.
" Great and dread " is that name, but it is a sign of
His loving-kindness that it is known by men, and
thanksgiving, not dumb trembling, befits men who know
it. The refrain might be rendered " It is holy,"
referring to the name, but vv. 5 and 9 make the
rendering *Holy is He* more probable. The meaning
is unaffected whichever translation is adopted.

Jehovah is holy, not only because lifted above and
separated from creatural limitations, but because of His
righteousness. The second strophe therefore proclaims
that all His dominion is based on uprightness, and is
a continual passing of that into acts of " judgment and
righteousness." The " And " at the beginning of ver. 4,
following the refrain, is singular, and has led many
commentators to link the words with ver. 3 *a*, and,
taking the refrain as parenthetical, to render, " Let
them give thanks to Thy great and dread name, [for
it is holy], and [to] the strength of the King [who]
loveth," etc. But the presence of the refrain is an
insuperable bar to this rendering. Others, as Delitzsch
and Cheyne, regard "the strength of the king" as
dependent on "established" in ver. 4 *b*, and suppose
that the theocratic monarch of Israel is represented as
under Jehovah's protection, if he reigns righteously.
But surely one King only is spoken of in this psalm,
and it is the inmost principle and outward acts of His
rule which are stated as the psalmist's reason for
summoning men to prostrate themselves at His footstool. The " And " at the beginning of the strophe
links its whole thought with that of the preceding,

and declares eloquently how closely knit together
are Jehovah's exaltation and His righteousness.   The
singer is in haste to assert the essentially moral character of infinite power.   Delitzsch thinks that love
cannot be predicated of " strength," but only of the
possessor of strength ; but surely that is applying the
measuring line of prosaic accuracy to lyric fervour.
The intertwining of Divine power and righteousness
could not be more strongly asserted than by that very
intelligible attribution to His power of the emotion of
love, impelling it ever to seek union with uprightness.
He is no arbitrary ruler.   His reign is for the further-
ance of justice.   Its basis is " equity," and its separate
acts are "judgment and righteousness."   These have
been done in and for Jacob.   Therefore the call to
worship rings out again.   It is addressed to an un-
defined multitude, which, as the tone of all this group
of psalms leads us to suppose, includes the whole race
of man.   They are summoned to lift high the praise
of Him who in Himself is so high, and to cast themselves low in prostrate adoration at His footstool—*i.e.,*
at His sanctuary on Zion (ver. 9).   Thus again, in the
centre strophe of this psalm, as in Psalms xcvi. and
xcviii., mankind are called to praise the God who has
revealed Himself in Israel ; but while in the former of
these two psalms worship was represented as sacrificial,
and in the second as loud music of voice and instrument, here silent prostration is the fitting praise of
the holiness of the infinitely exalted Jehovah.

The third strophe turns to examples drawn from the
great ones of old, which at once encourage to worship
and teach the true nature of worship, while they also
set in clear light Jehovah's holiness in dealing with His
worshippers.   Priestly functions were exercised by

Moses, as in sprinkling the blood of the covenant (Exod. xxiv.), and in the ceremonial connected with the consecration of Aaron and his sons (Lev. viii.), as well as at the first celebration of worship in the Tabernacle (Exod. xl. 18 *sqq.*). In the wider sense of the word *priest*, he acted as mediator and intercessor, as in Exod. xvii. 12, in the fight against Amalek, and xxxii. 30–32, after the worship of the golden calf. Samuel, too, interceded for Israel after their seeking a king (1 Sam. xii. 19 *sqq.*), and offered sacrifices (1 Sam. vii. 9). Jeremiah couples them together as intercessors with God (xv. 1).

From these venerable examples the psalmist draws instruction as to the nature of the worship befitting the holiness of Jehovah. He goes deeper than all sacrifices, or than silent awe. To call on God is the best adoration. The cry of a soul, conscious of emptiness and need, and convinced of His fulness and of the love which is the soul of His power, is never in vain. "They called, and He"—even He in all the unreachable separation of His loftiness from their lowliness—"answered them." There is a commerce of desire and bestowal between the holy Jehovah and us. But these answers come on certain conditions, which are plain consequences of His holiness—namely, that His worshippers should keep His testimonies, by which He has witnessed both to His own character and to their duty. The psalmist seems to lose sight of his special examples, and to extend his view to the whole people, when he speaks of answers from the pillar of cloud, which cannot apply to Samuel's experience. The persons spoken of in ver. 8 as receiving answers may indeed be Moses, Aaron, and Samuel, all of whom were punished for evil deeds, as well as answered when they cried; but more probably they are the whole community. The great principle, firmly grasped and clearly proclaimed by the singer, is that a holy God is a forgiving God, willing to hearken to men's cry, and rich to answer with needed gifts, and that indissolubly interwoven with the pardon, which He in His holiness gives, is retribution for evil. God loves too well to grant impunity. Forgiveness is something far better than escape from penalties. It cannot be worthy of God to bestow or salutary for men to receive, unless it is accompanied with such retribution as may show the pardoned man how deadly his sin was. "Whatsoever a man soweth that shall he also reap" is a law not abrogated by forgiveness. The worst penalty of sin, indeed—namely, separation from God—is wholly turned aside by repentance and forgiveness; but for the most part the penalties which are inflicted on earth, and which are the natural results of sin, whether in character, memory, habit, or circumstances, are not removed by pardon. Their character is changed; they become loving chastisement for our profit.

Such, then, is the worship which all men are invited to render to the holy Jehovah. Prostrate awe should pass into the cry of need, desire, and aspiration. It will be heard, if it is verified as real by obedience to God's known will. The answers will be fresh witnesses of God's holiness, which declares itself equally in forgiveness and in retribution. Therefore, once more the clear summons to all mankind rings out, and once more the proclamation of His holiness is made.

There is joyful confidence of access to the Inaccessible in the reiteration in ver. 9 of *Jehovah our God*. "Holy is He," sang the psalmist at first, but all the gulf between Jehovah and us is bridged over when to the name which emphasises the eternal, self-existent being of the holy One we can add " our God." Then humble prostration is reconcilable with confident approach ; and His worshippers have not only to lie lowly at His footstool, but to draw near, with children's frankness to His heart.

PSALM C.

1 Shout aloud to Jehovah, all the earth.
2 Serve Jehovah with gladness,
  Come before His face with joyful cry.
3 Know ye that Jehovah He is God,
  He, He has made us, and His are we,
  His people and the sheep of His pasture.
4 Enter His gates with thanksgiving,
  His courts with praise,
  Give thanks to Him, bless His name.
5 For Jehovah is good, for ever endures His loving-kindness,
  And to generation after generation His faithfulness.

THE Psalms of the King end with this full-toned call to all the earth to do Him homage. It differs from the others of the group, by making no distinct mention either of Jehovah's royal title or of the great act of deliverance which was His visible exercise of sovereignty. But it resembles them in its jubilant tone, its urgent invitation to all men to walk in the light which shone on Israel, and its conviction that the mercies shown to the nation had blessing in them for all the world. The structure is simple. A call to praise Jehovah is twice given, and each is followed by reasons for His praise, which is grounded, in the first instance (ver. 3), on His dealings with Israel, and, in the second, on His character as revealed by all His works.

Ver. 1 consists of but a single clause, and, as Delitzsch says, is like the signal-blast of a trumpet. It rings out a summons to "all the earth," as in Psalm xcviii. 4, which is expanded in ver. 2. The service

there enjoined is that of worship in the Temple, as in
ver. 4. Thus, the characteristic tone of this group of
psalms echoes here, in its close, and all men are called
and welcomed to the Sanctuary. There is no more a
Court of the Gentiles. Not less striking than the universality of the psalm is its pulsating gladness. The
depths of sorrow, both of that which springs from
outward calamities and of that more heart-breaking
sort which wells up from dark fountains in the soul,
have been sounded in many a psalm. But the Psalter
would not reflect all the moods of the devout soul,
unless it had some strains of unmingled joy. The
Christian Year has perfect days of sunlit splendour,
when all the winds are still, and no cloud darkens the
unbroken blue. There is no music without passages
in minor keys ; but joy has its rights and place too, and
they know but little of the highest kind of worship who
do not sometimes feel their hearts swell with gladness
more poignant and exuberant than earth can minister.

The reason for the world's gladness is given in
ver. 3. It is Jehovah's special relation to Israel. So far
as the language of the verse is concerned, it depends
on Psalm xcv. 7. " He hath made us " does not refer
to creation, but to the constituting of Israel the people
of God. " We are His " is the reading of the Hebrew
margin, and is evidently to be preferred to that of the
text, " Not we ourselves." The difference in Hebrew
is only in one letter, and the pronunciation of both
readings would be the same. Jewish text-critics count
fifteen passages, in which a similar mistake has been
made in the text. Here, the comparison of Psalm xcv.
and the connection with the next clause of ver. 3 are
decidedly in favour of the amended reading. It is to
be observed that this is the only place in the psalm in

which "we" and "us" are used; and it is natural to
lay stress on the opposition between "ye" in ver. 3 *a*,
and "we" and "us" in *b*. The collective Israel
speaks, and calls all men to rejoice in Jehovah, because
of His grace to it. The psalm is, then, not, as
Cheyne calls it, "a national song of thanksgiving, with
which an universalistic element is not completely fused,"
but a song which starts from national blessings, and
discerns in them a message of hope and joy for all
men. Israel was meant to be a sacred hearth on which
a fire was kindled, that was to warm all the house.
God revealed Himself *in* Israel, but *to* the world.

The call to praise is repeated in ver. 4 with more
distinct reference to the open Temple gates into which
all the nations may now enter. The psalmist sees, in
prophetic hope, crowds pouring in with glad alacrity
through the portals, and then hears the joyful tumult
of their many voices rising in a melodious surge of
praise. His eager desire and large-hearted confidence
that so it will one day be are vividly expressed by the
fourfold call in ver. 4. And the reason which should
draw all men to bless God's revealed character is that
His self-revelation, whether to Israel or to others,
shows that the basis of that character is goodness—*i.e.*,
kindness or love—and that, as older singers have sung,
"His loving-kindness endures for ever," and, as a
thousand generations in Israel and throughout the
earth have proved, His faithful adherence to His word,
and discharge of all obligations under which He has
come to His creatures, give a basis for trust and a perpetual theme for joyful thanksgiving. Therefore, all the
world has an interest in Jehovah's royalty, and should,
and one day shall, compass His throne with joyful
homage, and obey His behests with willing service.

PSALM CI.

1 Of loving-kindness and judgment will I sing,
  To Thee, Jehovah, will I harp.
2 I will give heed to the way of perfectness,
  When wilt Thou come to me?
  I will walk with a perfect heart
  Within my house.
3 I will not set before my eyes any villainous thing,
  The doing of transgressions do I hate,
  It shall not cleave to me.
4 A perverse heart shall depart from me,
  Evil will I not know.

5 The secret slanderer of his neighbour,
  Him will I root out,
  The lofty-eyed and proud-hearted,
  Him will I not endure.
6 My eyes are on the faithful of the land,
  That they may dwell with me,
  He who walks in the way of perfectness,
  He shall serve me.
7 He shall not dwell in my house
  Who practises deceit,
  He that speaks lies
  Shall not be established before my eyes.
8 Every morning will I root out
  All the wicked of the land,
  To cut off from the city of Jehovah
  All workers of iniquity.

THE contents of this psalm go far towards confirming the correctness of the superscription in
ascribing it to David, as Ewald acknowledges. To call
it an ideal description of a Jewish king, dramatically

put into such a ruler's mouth, does not do justice to the ring of earnestness in it. No doubt, subjective impressions are unreliable guides, but it is difficult to resist the impression that a kingly voice is audible here, speaking no ideal description, but his own stern resolves. It is a royal "proclamation against vice and immorality," appropriate to the beginning of a reign. If we accept the superscription, and interpret the abrupt question in ver. 2 " When wilt Thou come to me ? " as the utterance of David's longing to see the Ark set in Jerusalem, we get a most fitting period for the psalm. He had but recently ascended the throne. The abuses and confusions of Saul's last troubled years had to be reformed. The new king felt that he was God's viceroy, and here declares what he will strive to make his monarchy—a copy of God's. He gives evil-doers fair warning, and bids all true men be sure of his favour. But he will take heed to himself, before he seeks to purge his court. So the psalm, though it has no strophical arrangement, falls into two main parts, in the first of which the king lays down the rule of his own conduct, and, in the second, declares war against the vermin that infest especially an Eastern court— slanderers, arrogant upstarts, traffickers in lies. His ambition is to have Jehovah's city worthy of its true King, when He shall deign to come and dwell in it. Therefore his face will be gracious to all good men, and his hand heavy on all evil-doers. The psalm is " A Mirror for Magistrates," to quote the title of an old English book.

The first words of the psalm seem at first sight incongruous with its contents, which are singularly devoid of praise. But they are not meant to refer to the psalm, but declare the singer's purpose for his whole life. If the speaker is a real character, he is a poet-king. Of whom is that singular combination of royalty and minstrelsy so true as of David? If the speaker is an ideal, is it not peculiar that the first qualification of the ideal king should be that he is a poet? The suggestion that " loving-kindness and judgment" are here the monarch's virtues, not Divine attributes, is negatived by usage and by the following clause, " To Thee, *Jehovah*, will I sing." But it is as a king that the psalmist vows to praise these twin characteristics of the Divine rule; and his song is to be accompanied by melodious deeds, which shape themselves after that pattern for rulers and all men. Earthly power is then strongest when, like God's, it is informed by loving-kindness and based on righteousness. In this connection, it is significant that this psalm, describing what a king should be, has been placed immediately after the series which tells who the true King of Israel and the world is, in whom these same attributes are ever linked together.

Vv. 2–4 outline the king's resolves for himself. With noble self-control, this ruler of men sets before himself the narrow, thorny way of perfectness, not the broad, flowery road of indulgence. He owns a law above himself and a far-off goal of moral completeness, which, he humbly feels, is yet unattained, but which he vows will never be hidden from his undazzled eyes, by the glitter of lower earthly good, or the rank mists of sensual pleasures. He had abundant facilities for reaching lower aims, but he turns from these to " give heed " to the way of perfectness. That resolve must be clearly and strongly made by every man, prince or peasant, who would attain to the dominion over self and externals, which is man's true royalty.

The suddenly interjected question of longing, " When wilt Thou come to me ? " is best explained by connecting it with David's desire that the Ark should be permanently domiciled in Jerusalem—a desire which was checked by his reflections on his own unworthiness (2 Sam. vi. 9). Now he feels that, on the one hand, his whole-hearted desire after righteousness makes him capable of receiving such a guest ; and that, on the other, his firmest resolves will be evanescent, without God's presence to confirm his wavering and to help him to make his resolves into acts. He longed for that " coming " of the symbol of God's dwelling with men, not with heathenish desire to have it as a magic-working charm against outward foes, but as helping his faith to grasp the fact that God was with him, as his ally in the nobler fight against his own baseness and his position's temptations. We dare not ask God to come to us, unless we are conscious of desire to be pure ; we cannot hope to realise that desire, unless He is with us. So, the natural sequel of determination to give heed to the way of perfectness is petition to Him, to come very near and take up His abode with us.

After this most significant interruption, the stream of resolutions runs on again. In the comparative privacy of his house, he will " walk with a perfect heart," ever seeking to translate his convictions of right into practice, and regulating his activities by conscience. The recesses of an Eastern palace were often foul with lust, and hid extravagances of caprice and self-indulgence ; but this ruler will behave there as one who has Jehovah for a guest. The language of ver. 3 is very energetic. " Any villainous thing " is literally " a thing of Belial " ; " the doing of transgressions " is literally " doing deeds that turn aside, *i.e.* from the course prescribed. He will not take the former as models for imitation or objects of desire. The latter kindle wholesome hatred ; and if ever he is tempted to dally with sin, he will shake it off, as a venomous reptile that has fastened on him. "A perfect heart" will expel "a perverse heart," but neither will the one be gained nor the other banished without vehement and persistent effort. This man does not trust the improvement of his character to chance or expect it to come of itself. He means to bend his strength to effect it. He cannot but "know evil," in the sense of being aware of it and conscious of its seductions ; but he will *not* "know" it, in the sense of letting it into his inner nature, or with the knowledge which is experience and love.

From ver. 5 onwards, the king lays down the principles of his public action, and that mainly in reference to bad men. One verse suffices to tell of his fostering care of good men. The rest describes how he means to be a terror to evil-doers. The vices against which he will implacably war are not gross crimes such as ordinarily bring down the sword of public justice. This monarch has regard to more subtle evils—slander, superciliousness, inflated vanity ("proud-hearted" in ver. 5 is literally wide in heart, *i.e.* dilated with self-sufficiency or ambition). His eyes are quick to mark "the faithful in the land." He looks for those whose faithfulness to God guarantees their fidelity to men and general reliableness. His servants shall be like himself, followers of "the way of perfectness." In that court, dignity and office will go, not to talent, or to crafty arts of servility, or to birth, but to moral and religious qualities.

In the last two verses, the psalm returns to evil-doers. The actors and speakers of lies shall be cleared out of the palace. Such base creatures crawl and sting about the purlieus of courts, but this prince will have his immediate *entourage* free from them. He longs to get rid of the stifling atmosphere of deceit, and to have honest men round him, as many a ruler before and since has longed. But not only palace, but city, has to be swept clean, and one cleansing at the beginning of a reign will not be enough. So " every morning " the work has to be done again. " Ill weeds grow apace," and the mower must not get weary of his scythe. God's city must be pure. " Without are . . . whatsoever worketh and maketh a lie."

. The psalm is a God-given vision of what a king and a kingdom might and should be. If David wrote it, his early resolves were sadly falsified. " I will set no villainous things before my eyes "—yet from his " house," where he vowed to " walk with a perfect heart," he looked on Bathsheba. " He that speaks lies shall not be established in my sight "—yet Absalom, Ahithophel, and the sons of Zeruiah stood round his throne. The shortcomings of the earthly shadows of God's rule force us to turn away to the only perfect King and Kingdom, Jesus Christ and His realm, and to the city " into which shall in nowise enter anything that defileth."

PSALM CII.

1 Jehovah, hear my prayer,
  And let my cry come to Thee.
2 Hide not Thy face from me in the day of my trouble.
  Bend to me Thine ear,
  In the day that I call answer me speedily.

3 For my days are consumed in smoke,
  And my bones are burned like a brand.
4 Smitten like herbage and dried up is my heart,
  For I have forgotten to eat my bread.
5 Because of the noise of my groaning,
  My bones stick to my flesh.
6 I am like a pelican of the desert,
  I am become like an owl of the ruins.
7 I am sleepless,
  And am become like a sparrow lonely on the roof.
8 All day long my enemies reproach me,
  They that are mad at me curse by me.
9 For ashes like bread have I eaten,
  And my drink with tears have I mingled.
10 Because of Thy indignation and Thy wrath,
  For Thou hast caught me up and flung me away
11 My days are like a long-drawn-out shadow,
  And I like herbage am dried up.

12 But Thou, Jehovah, sittest enthroned for ever,
  And Thy memorial is to generation after generation.
13 Thou, Thou shalt arise, shalt pity Zion,
  For it is time to show her favour,
  For the appointed time is come.
14 For Thy servants delight in her stones,
  And [to] her dust they show favour.
15 And the nations shall fear the name of Jehovah,
  And all the kings of the earth His glory,

16 Because Jehovah has built up Zion,
   He has been seen in His glory,
17 He has turned to the prayer of the destitute,
   And has not despised their prayer.
18 This shall be written for the generation after,
   And a people [yet] to be created shall praise Jah.
19 Because He has looked down from His holy height,
   Jehovah has gazed from heaven upon the earth,
20 To hear the sighing of the captive,
   To free the children of death,
21 That they may tell in Zion the name of Jehovah,
   And His praise in Jerusalem,
22 When the peoples are assembled together,
   And the kingdoms to serve Jehovah.

23 He has brought down my strength in the way,
   He has cut short my days.
24 I said, "My God, take me not away at the half of my days,"
   [Since] Thy years endure through all generations.
25 Of old Thou didst found the earth,
   And the heavens are the work of Thy hands.
26 They, they shall perish, but Thou, Thou shalt continue,
   And all of them like a garment shall wear out,
   Like a robe shalt Thou change them, and they shall be
     changed.
27 But Thou art He,
   And Thy years shall never end.
28 The sons of Thy servants shall dwell,
   And their seed shall be established before Thee.

VERSES 13, 14, show that the psalm was written when Zion was in ruins and the time of her restoration at hand. Sadness shot with hope, as a cloud with sunlight, is the singer's mood. The pressure of present sorrows points to the time of the Exile; the lightening of these, by the expectation that the hour for their cessation has all but struck, points to the close of that period. There is a general consensus of opinion on this, though Baethgen is hesitatingly inclined to adopt the Maccabean date, and Cheyne prefers the time of Nehemiah, mainly because the

references to the " stones " and " dust " recall to him
" Nehemiah's lonely ride round the burned walls," and
" Sanballat's mocking at the Jews for attempting to
revive the stones out of heaps of rubbish " (" Orig. of
Psalt.," p. 70). These references would equally suit any
period of desolation ; but the point of time indicated by
ver. 13 is more probably the eve of restoration than
the completion of the begun and interrupted re-esta-
blishment of Israel in its land. Like many of the later
psalms, this is largely coloured by earlier ones, as well
as by Deuteronomy, Job, and the second half of Isaiah,
while it has also reminiscences of Jeremiah. Some
commentators have, indeed, supposed it to be his work.

The turns of thought are simple. While there is no
clear strophical arrangement, there are four broadly distinguished parts : a prelude, invoking God to hearken
(vv. 1, 2) ; a plaintive bemoaning of the psalmist's
condition (vv. 3–11) ; a triumphant rising above his
sorrows, and rejoicing in the fair vision of a restored
Jerusalem, whose Temple-courts the nations tread
(vv. 12–22) ; and a momentary glance at his sorrows
and brief life, which but spurs him to lay hold the
more joyously on God's eternity, wherein he finds the
pledge of the fulfilment of his hopes and of God's
promises (vv. 23–28).

The opening invocations in vv. 1, 2, are mostly
found in other psalms. " Let my cry come unto Thee "
recalls Psalm xviii. 6. " Hide not Thy face " is like
Psalm xxvii. 9. " In the day of my straits " recurs in
Psalm lix. 16. " Bend to me Thy ear " is in Psalm
xxxi. 2. " In the day when I call " is as in Psalm
lvi. 9. " Answer me speedily " is found in Psalm lxix.
17. But the psalmist is not a cold-blooded compiler,
weaving a web from old threads, but a suffering man,

fain to give his desires voice, in words which sufferers before him had hallowed, and securing a certain solace by reiterating familiar petitions. They are none the less his own, because they have been the cry of others. Some aroma of the answers that they drew down in the past clings to them still, and makes them fragrant to him.

Sorrow and pain are sometimes dumb, but, in Eastern natures, more often eloquent; finding ease in recounting their pangs. The psalmist's first words of self-lamentation echo familiar strains, as he bases his cry for speedy answer on the swiftness with which his days are being whirled away, and melting like smoke as it escapes from a chimney. The image suggests another. The fire that makes the smoke is that in which his very bones are smouldering like a brand. The word for *bones* is in the singular, the bony framework being thought of as articulated into a whole. " Brand " is a doubtful rendering of a word which the Authorised Version, following some ancient Jewish authorities, renders *hearth*, as do Delitzsch and Cheyne. It is used in Isa. xxxiii. 14 as = " burning," but " brand " is required to make out the metaphor. The same theme of physical decay is continued in ver. 4, with a new image struck out by the ingenuity of pain. His heart is " smitten " as by sunstroke (compare Psalm cxxi. 6, Isa. xlix. 10, and for still closer parallels Hosea ix. 16, Jonah iv. 7, in both of which the same effect of fierce sunshine is described as the sufferer here bewails). His heart withers like Jonah's gourd. The " For " in ver. 4 *b* can scarcely be taken as giving the reason for this withering. It must rather be taken as giving the proof that it was so withered, as might be concluded by beholders from the fact that he refused his food (Baethgen). The psalmist apparently intends in ver. 5 to describe himself as worn to a skeleton by long-continued and passionate lamentations. But his phrase is singular. One can understand that emaciation should be described by saying that the bones adhered to the skin, the flesh having wasted away, but that they stick to the flesh can only describe it, by giving a wide meaning to "flesh," as including the whole outward part of the frame in contrast with the internal framework. Lam. iv. 8 gives the more natural expression. The psalmist has groaned himself into emaciation. Sadness and solitude go well together. We plunge into lonely places when we would give voice to our grief. The poet's imagination sees his own likeness in solitude-loving creatures. The pelican is never now seen in Palestine but on Lake Huleh. Thomson ("Land and Book," p. 260: London, 1861) speaks of having found it there only, and describes it as "the most sombre, austere bird I ever saw." "The owl of the ruins" is identified by Tristram ("Land of Israel," p. 67) with the small owl *Athene meridionalis*, the emblem of Minerva, which "is very characteristic of all the hilly and rocky portions of Syria." The *sparrow* may be here a generic term for any small song-bird, but there is no need for departing from the narrower meaning. Thomson (p. 43) says: "When one of them has lost his mate—an every-day occurrence—he will sit on the housetop alone and lament by the hour."

The division of ver. 7 is singular, as the main pause in it falls on "am become," to the disruption of the logical continuity. The difficulty is removed by Wickes ("Accentuation of the Poetical Books," p. 29), who gives several instances which seem to establish the law that, in the musical accentuation, there is "an apparent reluctance to place the main dividing accent after the first, or before the last, word of the verse." The division is not logical, and we may venture to neglect it, and arrange as above, restoring the dividing accent to its place after the first word. Others turn the flank of the difficulty by altering the text to read, "I am sleepless and must moan aloud" (so Cheyne, following Olshausen).

Yet another drop of bitterness in the psalmist's cup is the frantic hatred which pours itself out in voluble mockery all day long, making a running accompaniment to his wail. Solitary as he is, he cannot get beyond hearing of shrill insults. So miserable does he seem, that enemies take him and his distresses for a formula of imprecation, and can find no blacker curse to launch at other foes than to wish that they may be like him. So ashes, the token of mourning, are his food, instead of the bread which he had forgotten to eat, and there are more tears than wine in the cup he drinks.

But all this only tells how sad he is. A deeper depth opens when he remembers why he is sad. The bitterest thought to a sufferer is that his sufferings indicate God's displeasure; but it may be wholesome bitterness, which, leading to the recognition of the sin which evokes the wrath, may change into a solemn thankfulness for sorrows which are discerned to be chastisements, inflicted by that Love of which indignation is one form. The psalmist confesses sin in the act of bewailing sorrow, and sees behind all his pains the working of that hand whose interposition for him he ventures to implore. The tremendous metaphor of ver. 10 *b* pictures it as thrust forth from heaven to grasp the feeble sufferer, as an eagle stoops to plunge its talons into a lamb. It lifts him high, only to give

more destructive impetus to the force with which it
flings him down, to the place where he lies, a huddled
heap of broken bones and wounds. His plaint returns
to its beginning, lamenting the brief life which is being
wasted away by sore distress. Lengthening shadows
tell of approaching night. His day is nearing sunset.
It will be dark soon, and, as he has said (ver. 4), his
very self is withering and becoming like dried-up
herbage.

One can scarcely miss the tone of individual sorrow
in the preceding verses ; but national restoration, not
personal deliverance, is the theme of the triumphant
central part of the psalm. That is no reason for flatten-
ing the previous verses into the voice of the personified
Israel, but rather for hearing in them the sighing of
one exile, on whom the general burden weighed sorely.
He lifts his tear-laden eyes to heaven, and catches a
vision there which changes, as by magic, the key of his
song—Jehovah sitting in royal state (compare Psalms
ix. 7, xxix. 10) for ever. That silences complaints,
breathes courage into the feeble and hope into the
despairing. In another mood the thought of the eternal
rule of God might make man's mortality more bitter,
but Faith grasps it, as enfolding assurances which turn
groaning into ringing praise. For the vision is not
only of an everlasting Some One who works a sovereign
will, but of the age-long dominion of Him whose name
is Jehovah ; and since that name is the revelation of
His nature, it, too, endures for ever. It is the name of
Israel's covenant-making and keeping God. Therefore,
ancient promises have not gone to water, though Israel
is an exile, and all the old comfort and confidence are
still welling up from the Name. Zion cannot die while
Zion's God lives. Lam. v. 19 is probably the original

of this verse, but the psalmist has changed "throne" into "memorial," *i.e. name,* and thereby deepened the thought. The assurance that God will restore Zion rests not only on His faithfulness, but on signs which show that the sky is reddening towards the day of redemption. The singer sees the indication that the hour fixed in God's eternal counsels is at hand, because he sees how God's servants, who have a claim on Him and are in sympathy with His purposes, yearn lovingly after the sad ruins and dust of the forlorn city. Some new access of such feelings must have been stirring among the devouter part of the exiles. Many large truths are wrapped in the psalmist's words. The desolations of Zion knit true hearts to her more closely. The more the Church or any good cause is depressed, the more need for its friends to cling to it. God's servants should see that their sympathies go toward the same objects as God's do. They are proved to be His servants, because they favour what He favours. Their regards, turned to existing evils, are the precursors of Divine intervention for the remedy of these. When good men begin to lay the Church's or the world's miseries to heart, it is a sign that God is beginning to heal them. The cry of God's servants can " hasten the day of the Lord," and preludes His appearance like the keen morning air stirring the sleeping flowers before sunrise.

The psalmist anticipates that a rebuilt Zion will ensure a worshipping world. He expresses that confidence, which he shares with Isa. xl.–lxvi., in vv. 15–18. The name and glory of Jehovah will become objects of reverence to all the earth, because of the manifestation of them by the rebuilding of Zion, which is a witness to all men of His power and tender regard to His people's cry. The past tenses of vv. 16, 17, do not indicate that the psalm is later than the Restoration. It is contemplated as already accomplished, because it is the occasion of the "fear" prophesied in ver. 15, and consequently prior in time to it. "Destitute," in ver. 17, is literally *naked* or *stript*. It is used in Jer. xvii. 6 as the name of a desert plant, probably a dwarf juniper, stunted and dry, but seems to be employed here as simply designating utter destitution. Israel had been stripped of every beauty and made naked before her enemies. Despised, she had cried to God, and now is clothed again with the garments of salvation, "as a bride adorneth herself with her jewels."

A wondering world will adore her delivering God. The glowing hopes of psalmist and prophet seem to be dreams, since the restored Israel attracted no such observance and wrought no such convictions. But the singer was not wrong in believing that the coming of Jehovah in His glory for the rebuilding of Zion would sway the world to homage. His facts were right, but he did not know their perspective, nor could he understand how many weary years lay, like a deep gorge hidden from the eye of one who looks over a wide prospect, between the rebuilding of which he was thinking, and that truer establishment of the city of God, which is again parted from the period of universal recognition of Jehovah's glory by so many sad and stormy generations. But the vision is true. The coming of Jehovah in His glory will be followed by a world's recognition of its light.

That praise accruing to Jehovah shall be not only universal, but shall go on sounding, with increasing volume in its tone, through coming generations. This expectation is set forth in vv. 18–22, which substantially reiterate the thought of the preceding, with the addition that there is to be a new Israel, a people yet to be created (Psalm xxii. 31). The psalmist did not know "the deep things he spoke." He did know that Israel was immortal, and that the seed of life was in the tree that had cast its leaves and stood bare and apparently dead. But he did not know the process by which that new Israel was to be created, nor the new elements of which it was to consist. His confidence teaches us never to despair of the future of God's Church, however low its present state, but to look down the ages, in calm certainty that, however externals may change, the succession of God's children will never fail, nor the voice of their praise ever fall silent.

The course of God's intervention for Israel is described in vv. 19, 20. His looking down from heaven is equivalent to His observance, as the all-seeing Witness and Judge (compare Psalms xiv. 2, xxxiii. 13, 14, etc.), and is preparatory to His hearing the sighing of the captive Israel, doomed to death. The language of ver. 20 is apparently drawn from Psalm lxxix. 11. The thought corresponds to that of ver. 17. The purpose of His intervention is set forth in vv. 21, 22, as being the declaration of Jehovah's name and praise in Jerusalem before a gathered world. The aim of Jehovah's dealings is that all men, through all generations, may know and praise Him. That is but another way of saying that He infinitely desires, and perpetually works for, men's highest good. For our sakes, He desires so much that we should know Him, since the knowledge is life eternal. He is not greedy of adulation nor dependent on recognition, but He loves men too well not to rejoice in being understood and loved by them, since Love ever hungers for return. The psalmist

saw what shall one day be, when, far down the ages,
he beheld the world gathered in the temple-courts, and
heard the shout of their praise borne to him up the
stream of time. He penetrated to the inmost meaning
of the Divine acts, when he proclaimed that they were
all done for the manifestation of the Name, which
cannot but be praised when it is known.

If the poet was one of the exiles, on whom the burden
of the general calamity weighed as a personal sorrow,
it is very natural that his glowing anticipations of
national restoration should be, as in this psalm, enclosed
in a setting of more individual complaint and petition.
The transition from these to the purely impersonal
centre of the psalm, and the recurrence to them in
vv. 23–28, are inexplicable, if the "I" of the first and
last parts is Israel, but perfectly intelligible if it is one
Israelite. For a moment the tone of sadness is heard
in ver. 23; but the thought of his own afflicted and
brief life is but a stimulus to the psalmist to lay hold
of God's immutability and to find rest there. The
Hebrew text reads "*His* strength," and is followed
by the LXX., Vulgate, Hengstenberg, and Kay ("He
afflicted on the way with His power"); but the reading of the Hebrew margin, adopted above and by most
commentators, is preferable, as supplying an object for
the verb, which is lacking in the former reading, and
as corresponding to "*my* days" in *b*.

The psalmist has felt the exhaustion of long sorrow
and the shortness of his term. Will God do all these
glorious things of which he has been singing, and he
the singer, not be there to see? That would mingle
bitterness in his triumphant anticipations; for it would
be little to him, lying in his grave, that Zion should
be built again. The hopes with which some would

console us for the loss of the Christian assurance of immortality, that the race shall march on to new power and nobleness, are poor substitutes for continuance of our own lives and for our own participation in the glories of the future. The psalmist's prayer, which takes God's eternity as its reason for deprecating his own premature death, echoes the inextinguishable confidence of the devout heart, that somehow even its fleeting being has a claim to be assimilated in duration to its Eternal Object of trust and aspiration. The contrast between God's years and man's days may be brooded on in bitterness or in hope. They who are driven by thinking of their own mortality to clutch, with prayerful faith, God's eternity, use the one aright, and will not be deprived of the other.

The solemn grandeur of vv. 25, 26, needs little commentary, but it may be noted that a reminiscence of Isaiah II. runs through them, both in the description of the act of creation of heaven and earth (Isa. xlviii. 13, xliv. 24), and in that of their decaying like a garment (Isa. li. 6, liv. 10). That which has been created can be removed. The creatural is necessarily the transient. Possibly, too, the remarkable expression "changed," as applied to the visible creation, may imply the thought which had already been expressed in Isaiah, and was destined to receive such deepening by the Christian truth of the new heavens and new earth—a truth the contents of which are dim to us until it is fulfilled. But whatever may be the fate of creatures, He who receives no accession to His stable being by originating suffers no diminution by extinguishing them. Man's days, the earth's ages, and the æons of the heavens pass, and still " Thou art He," the same Unchanging Author of change. Measures of time fail when applied to His being, whose years have not that which all divisions of time have—an end. An unending year is a paradox, which, in relation to God, is a truth.

It is remarkable that the psalmist does not draw the conclusion that he himself shall receive an answer to his prayer, but that "the children of Thy servants shall dwell," *i.e.* in the land, and that there will always be an Israel "established before Thee." He contemplates successive generations as in turn dwelling in the promised land (and perhaps in the ancient "dwelling-place to all generations," even in God); but of his own continuance he is silent. Was he not assured of that? or was he so certain of the answer to his prayer that he had forgotten himself in the vision of the eternal God and the abiding Israel? Having regard to the late date of the psalm, it is hard to believe that silence meant ignorance, while it may well be that it means a less vivid and assured hope of immortality, and a smaller space occupied by that hope than with us. But the other explanation is not to be left out of view, and the psalmist's oblivion of self in rapt gazing on God's eternal being—the pledge of His servants' perpetuity—may teach us that we reach the summit of Faith when we lose ourselves in God.

The Epistle to the Hebrews quotes vv. 25–27 as spoken of "the Son." Such an application of the words rests on the fact that the psalm speaks of the coming of Jehovah for redemption, who is none other than Jehovah manifested fully in the Messiah. But Jehovah whose coming brings redemption and His recognition by the world is also Creator. Since, then, the Incarnation is, in truth, the coming of Jehovah, which the psalmist, like all the prophets, looked for as the consummation, He in whom the redeeming Jehovah was manifested is He in whom Jehovah the Creator " made the worlds." The writer of the Epistle is not asserting that the psalmist consciously spoke of the Messiah, but he is declaring that his words, read in the light of history, point to Jesus as the crowning manifestation of the redeeming, and therefore necessarily of the creating, God.

PSALM CIII.

1 Bless Jehovah, my soul,
  And all within me [bless] His holy name!
2 Bless Jehovah, my soul!
  And forget not all His benefits,
3 Who forgives all thy inquity,
  Who heals all thy diseases,
4 Who redeems thy life from the pit,
  Who crowns thee [with] loving-kindness and compassions,
5 Who satisfies thy mouth (?) with good,
  [So that] thy youth is renewed like the eagle.

6 Jehovah executes righteousness
  And judgments for all the oppressed.
7 He made known His ways to Moses,
  To the children of Israel His great deeds.
8 Full of compassion and gracious is Jehovah,
  Slow to anger and abundant in loving-kindness.
9 He will not continually contend,
  And will not keep His anger for ever.
10 Not according to our sins has He dealt with us,
   And not according to our iniquities has He recompensed us.
11 For as high as the heavens are above the earth,
   [So] great is His loving-kindness to them that fear Him.
12 As far as sunrise is from sunset,
   [So] far has He put our transgressions from us.
13 As a father has compassion on his children,
   Jehovah has compassion on them that fear Him.
14 For He—He knows our frame,
   Being mindful that we are dust.
15 Frail man—like grass are his days,
   Like a flower of the field, so he flowers.
16 For a wind passes over him and he is not,
   And his place knows him no more.

17 But the loving-kindness of Jehovah is from everlasting
         even to everlasting upon them that fear Him,
    And His righteousness is to children's children;
18 To those who keep His covenant,
    And to those who remember His statutes to do them

19 Jehovah has established His throne in the heavens,
    And His kingdom rules over all.
20 Bless Jehovah, ye His angels,
    Ye mighty in strength, who perform His word,
    Hearkening to the voice of His word!
21 Bless Jehovah, all His hosts,
    Ye His ministers, who perform His will!
22 Bless Jehovah, all His works,
    In all places of His dominion!
    Bless Jehovah, my soul!

THERE are no clouds in the horizon, nor notes of
sadness in the music, of this psalm. No purer
outburst of thankfulness enriches the Church. It is
well that, amid the many psalms which give voice to
mingled pain and trust, there should be one of unalloyed
gladness, as untouched by sorrow as if sung by spirits
in heaven. Because it is thus purely an outburst of
thankful joy, it is the more fit to be pondered in times
of sorrow.

The psalmist's praise flows in one unbroken stream.
There are no clear marks of division, but the river
broadens as it runs, and personal benefits and individual
praise open out into gifts which are seen to fill the
universe, and thanksgiving which is heard from every
extremity of His wide dominion of loving-kindness.

In ver. 1–5 the psalmist sings of his own experience. His *spirit*, or *ruling self*, calls on his "soul," the
weaker and more feminine part, which may be cast
down (Psalms xlii., xliii.) by sorrow, and needs stimulus
and control, to contemplate God's gifts and to praise
Him. A good man will rouse himself to such exercise,

and coerce his more sensuous and sluggish faculties to
their noblest use.   Especially must memory be directed,
for it keeps woefully short-lived records of mercies,
especially of continuous ones.   God's gifts are all
"benefits," whether they are bright or dark.   The
catalogue of blessings lavished on the singer's soul
begins with forgiveness and ends with immortal youth.
The profound consciousness of sin, which it was one
aim of the Law to evoke, underlies the psalmist's praise ;
and he who does not feel that no blessings could come
from heaven, unless forgiveness cleared the way for
them, has yet to learn the deepest music of thankfulness.
It is followed by " healing " of " all thy diseases," which
is no cure of merely bodily ailments, any more than
redeeming of life " from the pit " is simply preservation
of physical existence.   In both there is at least included,
even if we do not say that it only is in view, the
operation of the pardoning God in delivering from the
sicknesses and death of the spirit.

The soul thus forgiven and healed is crowned with
"loving-kindness and compassions," wreathed into a
garland for a festive brow, and its adornment is not
only a result of these Divine attributes, but the very
things themselves, so that an effluence from God
beautifies the soul.   Nor is even this all, for the same
gifts which are beauty are also sustenance, and God
satisfies the soul with good, especially with the only
real good, Himself.   The word rendered above " mouth "
is extremely difficult.   It is found in Psalm xxxii. 9,
where it seems best taken in the meaning of *trap-
pings* or *harness*.   That meaning is inappropriate
here, though Hupfeld tries to retain it.   The LXX.
renders " desire," which fits well, but can scarcely
be established.   Other renderings, such as " age " or

"duration"—*i.e.*, the whole extent of life—have been suggested. Hengstenberg and others regard the word as a designation of the soul, somewhat resembling the other term applied to it, "glory"; but the fact that it is the soul which is addressed negatives that explanation. Graetz and others resort to a slight textual alteration, resulting in the reading "thy misery." Delitzsch, in his latest editions, adopts this emendation doubtingly, and supposes that with the word *misery* or *affliction* there is associated the idea "of beseeching and therefore of longing," whence the LXX. rendering would originate. "Mouth" is the most natural word in such a connection, and its retention here is sanctioned by "the interpretation of the older versions in Psalm xxxii. 9 and the Arabic cognate" (Perowne). It is therefore retained above, though with some reluctance.

How should a man thus dealt with grow old? The body may, but not the soul. Rather it will drop powers that can decay, and for each thus lost will gain a stronger—moulting, and not being stripped of its wings, though it changes their feathers. There is no need to make the psalmist responsible for the fables of the eagle's renewal of its youth. The comparison with the monarch of the air does not refer to the process by which the soul's wings are made strong, but to the result in wings that never tire, but bear their possessor far up in the blue and towards the throne.

In vv. 6–18 the psalmist sweeps a greater circle, and deals with God's blessings to mankind. He has Israel specifically in view in the earlier verses, but passes beyond Israel to all "who fear Him." It is very instructive that he begins with the definite fact of God's revelation through Moses. He is not spinning a filmy idea of a God out of his own consciousness, but he has learned all that he knows of Him from His historical self-revelation. A hymn of praise which has not revelation for its basis will have many a quaver of doubt. The God of men's imaginations, consciences, or yearnings is a dim shadow. The God to whom love turns undoubting and praise rises without one note of discord is the God who has spoken His own name by deeds which have entered into the history of the world. And what has He revealed Himself to be? The psalmist answers almost in the words of the proclamation made to Moses (vv. 8, 9). The lawgiver had prayed, " I beseech Thee . . . show me now Thy ways, that I may know Thee "; and the prayer had been granted, when " the Lord passed by before him," and proclaimed His name as " full of compassion and gracious, slow to anger, and plenteous in mercy and truth." That proclamation fills the singer's heart, and his whole soul leaps up in him, as he meditates on its depth and sweetness. Now, after so many centuries of experience, Israel can repeat with full assurance the ancient self-revelation, which has been proved true by many " mighty deeds."

The psalmist's thoughts are still circling round the idea of forgiveness, with which he began his contemplations. He and his people equally need it; and all that revelation of God's character bears directly on His relation to sin. Jehovah is "long of anger"— *i.e.*, slow to allow it to flash out in punishment—and as lavish of loving-kindness as sparing of wrath. That character is disclosed by deeds. Jehovah's graciousness forces Him to " contend " against a man's sins for the man's sake. But it forbids Him to be perpetually chastising and condemning, like a harsh taskmaster. Nor does He keep His anger ever burning, though He does keep His loving-kindness aflame for a thousand generations. Lightning is transitory; sunshine, constant. Whatever His chastisements, they have been less than our sins. The heaviest is "light," and "for a moment," when compared with the "exceeding weight of" our guilt.

The glorious metaphors in vv. 11, 12, traverse heaven to the zenith, and from sunrise to sunset, to find distances distant enough to express the towering height of God's mercy and the completeness of His removal from us of our sins. That pure arch, the topstone of which nor wings nor thoughts can reach, sheds down all light and heat which make growth and cherish life. It is high above us, but it pours blessings on us, and it bends down all round the horizon to kiss the low, dark earth. The loving-kindness of Jehovah is similarly lofty, boundless, all-fructifying. In ver. 11 *b* the parallelism would be more complete if a small textual alteration were adopted, which would give "high" instead of "great"; but the slight departure which the existing text makes from precise correspondence with *a* is of little moment, and the thought is sufficiently intelligible as the words stand. Between East and West all distances lie. To the eye they bound the world. So far does God's mercy bear away our sins. Forgiveness and cleansing are inseparably united.

But the song drops—or shall we say rises?—from these magnificent measures of the immeasurable to the homely image of a father's pity. We may lose ourselves amid the amplitudes of the lofty, wide-stretching sky, but this emblem of paternal love goes straight to our hearts. A pitying God! What can be added to that? But that fatherly pity is decisively limited to "them that fear Him." It is possible, then, to put

oneself outside the range of that abundant dew, and
the universality of God's blessings does not hinder self-
exclusion from them.

In vv. 14–16 man's brief life is brought in, not as a
sorrow or as a cloud darkening the sunny joy of the
song, but as one reason for the Divine compassion.
" He, He knows our frame." The word rendered
" frame " is literally " formation " or " fashioning," and
comes from the same root as the verb employed in
Gen. ii. 7 to describe man's creation, " The Lord God
formed man of the dust of the ground." It is also used
for the potter's action in moulding earthen vessels
(Isa. xxix. 16, etc.). So, in the next clause, " dust "
carries on the allusion to Genesis, and the general idea
conveyed is that of frailty. Made from dust and fragile
as an earthen vessel, man by his weakness appeals to
Jehovah's compassion. A blow, delivered with the full
force of that almighty hand, would " break him as a
potter's vessel is broken." Therefore God handles us
tenderly, as mindful of the brittle material with which
He has to deal. The familiar figure of fading vegetation, so dear to the psalmists, recurs here ; but it is
touched with peculiar delicacy, and there is something
very sweet and uncomplaining in the singer's tone. The
image of the fading flower, burned up by the simoom,
and leaving one little spot in the desert robbed of its
beauty, veils much of the terror of death, and expresses
no shrinking, though great pathos. Ver. 16 may either
describe the withering of the flower, or the passing
away of frail man. In the former case, the pronouns
would be rendered by " it " and " its " ; in the latter, by
" he," " him," and " his." The latter seems the preferable explanation. Ver. 16 *b* is verbally the same as
Job vii. 10. The contemplation of mortality tinges the

song with a momentary sadness, which melts into the pensive, yet cheerful, assurance that mortality has an accompanying blessing, in that it makes a plea for pity from a Father's heart.

But another, more triumphant thought springs up. A devout soul, full-charged with thankfulness based on faith in God's name and ways, cannot but be led by remembering man's brief life to think of God's eternal years. So, the key changes at ver. 17 from plaintive minors to jubilant notes. The psalmist pulls out all the stops of his organ, and rolls along his music in a great *crescendo* to the close. The contrast of God's eternity with man's transitoriness is like the similar trend of thought in Psalms xc., cii. The extension of His loving-kindness to children's children, and its limitation to those who fear Him and keep His covenant in obedience, rest upon Exod. xx. 6, xxxiv. 7, Deut. vii. 9. That limitation has been laid down twice already (vv. 11–13). All men share in that loving-kindness, and receive the best gifts from it of which they are capable ; but those who cling to God in loving reverence, and who are moved by that blissful " fear " which has no torment, to yield their wills to Him in inward submission and outward obedience, do enter into the inner recesses of that loving-kindness, and are replenished with good, of which others are incapable.

If God's loving-kindness is "from everlasting to everlasting," will not His children share in it for as long ? The psalm has no articulate doctrine of a future life ; but is there not in that thought of an eternal outgoing of God's heart to its objects some (perhaps half-conscious) implication that these will continue to exist ? May not the psalmist have felt that, though the flower of earthly life " passed in the passing of an hour," the root would be somehow transplanted to the higher " house of the Lord," and " flourish in the courts of our God," as long as His everlasting mercy poured its sunshine ? We, at all events, know that His eternity is the pledge of ours. " Because I live, ye shall live also."

From ver. 19 to the end, the psalm takes a still wider sweep. It now embraces the universe. But it is noticeable that there is no more about " loving-kindness " in these verses. Man's sin and frailty make him a fit recipient of it, but we do not know that in all creation another being, capable of and needing it, is found. Amid starry distances, amid heights and depths, far beyond sunrise and sunset, God's all-including kingdom stretches and blesses all. Therefore, all creatures are called on to bless Him, since all are blessed by Him, each according to its nature and need. If they have consciousness, they owe Him praise. If they have not, they praise Him by being. The angels, "heroes of strength," as the words literally read, are " His," and they not only execute His behests, but stand attent before Him, listening to catch the first whispered indication of His will. " His hosts " are by some taken to mean the stars ; but surely it is more congruous to suppose that beings who are His " ministers " and perform His " will " are intelligent beings. Their praise consists in hearkening to and doing His word. But obedience is not all their praise ; for they, too, bring Him tribute of conscious adoration in more melodious music than ever sounded on earth. That " choir invisible " praises the King of heaven ; but later revelation has taught us that men shall teach a new song to " principalities and powers in heavenly places," because men only can praise Him whose loving-kindness to them, sinful and dying, redeemed them by His blood.

Therefore, it is no drop from these heavenly anthems, when the psalm circles round at last to its beginning, and the singer calls on his soul to add its " little human praise " to the thunderous chorus. The rest of the universe praises the mighty Ruler; he blesses the forgiving, pitying Jehovah. Nature and angels, stars and suns, seas and forests, magnify their Maker and Sustainer ; we can bless the God who pardons iniquities and heals diseases which our fellow-choristers never knew.

PSALM CIV.

1 My soul, bless Jehovah,
  Jehovah my God, Thou art exceeding great,
  Thou hast clothed Thyself with honour and majesty;
2 Covering Thyself with light as with a garment,
  Stretching out the heavens like a curtain.
3 Who lays the beams of His chambers in the waters,
  Who makes clouds His chariot,
  Who walks on the wings of the wind.
4 Making winds His messengers,
  Flaming fire His servants.

5 He sets fast the earth upon its foundations,
  [That] it should not be moved for ever and aye.
6 [With] the deep as [with] a garment Thou didst cover it,
  Above the mountains stood the waters.
7 At Thy rebuke they fled,
  At the voice of Thy thunder they were scared away.
8 —Up rose the mountains, down sank the valleys—
  To the place which Thou hadst founded for them.
9 A bound hast Thou set [that] they should not pass over,
  Nor return to cover the earth.

10 He sends forth springs into the glens,
   Between the hills they take their way.
11 They give drink to every beast of the field,
   The wild asses slake their thirst.
12 Above them dwell the birds of heaven,
   From between the branches do they give their note.
13 He waters the mountains from His chambers,
   With the fruit of Thy works the earth is satisfied.
14 He makes grass to spring for the cattle,
   And the green herb for the service of men,
   To bring forth bread from the earth,
15 And that wine may gladden the heart of feeble man;

To cause his face to shine with oil,
And that bread may sustain the heart of feeble man
16 The trees of Jehovah are satisfied,
The cedars of Lebanon which He has planted,
17 Wherein the birds nest;
The stork—the cypresses are her house.
18 The high mountains are for the wild goats,
The rocks are a refuge for the conies.

19 He has made the moon for (*i.e.*, to measure) seasons,
The sun knows its going down
20 Thou appo'ntest darkness and it is night,
Wherein all the beasts of the forest creep forth.
21 The young lions roar for their prey,
And to seek from God their meat.
22 The sun rises—they steal away,
And lay them down in their dens.
23 Forth goes man to his work
And to his labour till evening.
24 How manifold are Thy works, Jehovah!
In wisdom hast Thou made them all,
The earth is full of Thy possessions.
25 Yonder [is] the sea, great and spread on either hand,
There are creeping things without number,
Living creatures small and great.
26 There the ships go on,
[There is] that Leviathan whom Thou hast formed to sport
27 All these look to Thee,
To give their food in its season.
28 Thou givest to them—they gather;
Thou openest Thy hand—they are filled [with good.
29 Thou hidest Thy face—they are panic-struck;
Thou withdrawest their breath—they expire,
And return to their dust.
30 Thou sendest orth Thy breath—they are created,
And Thou renewest the face of the earth.

31 Let the glory of Jehovah endure for ever,
Let Jehovah rejoice in His works.
32 Who looks on the earth and it trembles,
He touches the mountains and they smoke.
33 Let me sing to Jehovah while I live,
Let me harp to my God while I have being.

34 Be my meditation sweet to Him!
　　I, I will rejoice in Jehovah.
35 Be sinners consumed from the earth,
　　And the wicked be no more!
　　Bless Jehovah, my soul!
　　　　　　　　Hallelujah!

LIKE the preceding psalm, this one begins and ends with the psalmist's call to his soul to bless Jehovah. The inference has been drawn that both psalms have the same author, but that is much too large a conclusion from such a fact. The true lesson from it is that Nature, when looked at by an eye that sees it to be full of God, yields material for devout gratitude no less than do His fatherly " mercies to them that fear Him." The key-note of the psalm is struck in ver. 24, which breaks into an exclamation concerning the manifoldness of God's works and the wisdom that has shaped them all. The psalm is a gallery of vivid Nature-pictures, touched with wonderful grace and sureness of hand. Clearness of vision and sympathy with every living thing make the swift outlines inimitably firm and lovely. The poet's mind is like a crystal mirror, in which the Cosmos is reflected. He is true to the uniform Old Testament point of view, and regards Nature neither from the scientific nor æsthetic standpoint. To him it is the garment of God, the apocalypse of a present Deity, whose sustaining energy is but the prolongation of His creative act. All creatures depend on Him ; His continuous action is their life. He rejoices in His works. The Creation narrative in Genesis underlies the psalm, and is in the main followed, though not slavishly.

Ver. 1 would be normal in structure if the initial invocation were omitted, and as ver. 35 would also be complete without it, the suggestion that it is, in both verses, a liturgical addition is plausible. The verse sums up the whole of the creative act in one grand thought. In that act the invisible God has arrayed Himself in splendour and glory, making visible these inherent attributes. That is the deepest meaning of Creation. The Universe is the garment of God.

This general idea lays the foundation for the following picture of the process of creation which is coloured by reminiscences of Genesis. Here, as there, Light is the first-born of Heaven; but the influence of the preceding thought shapes the language, and Light is regarded as God's vesture. The Uncreated Light, who is darkness to our eyes, arrays Himself in created light, which reveals while it veils Him. Everywhere diffused, all-penetrating, all-gladdening, it tells of the Presence in which all creatures live. This clause is the poetic rendering of the work of the first creative day. The next clause in like manner deals with that of the second. The mighty arch of heaven is lifted and expanded over earth, as easily as a man draws the cloth or skin sides and canopy of his circular tent over its framework. But our roof is His floor; and, according to Genesis, the firmament (lit. expanse) separates the waters above from those beneath. So the psalm pictures the Divine Architect as laying the beams of His *upper chambers* (for so the word means) in these waters, above the tent roof. The fluid is solid at His will, and the most mobile becomes fixed enough to be the foundation of His royal abode. The custom of having chambers on the roof, for privacy and freshness, suggests the image.

In these introductory verses the poet is dealing with the grander instances of creative power, especially as realised in the heavens. Not till ver. 5 does he drop to earth. His first theme is God's dominion over the elemental forces, and so he goes on to represent the clouds as His chariot, the wind as bearing Him on its swift pinions, and, as the parallelism requires, the winds as His messengers, and devouring fire as His servants. The rendering of ver. 4 adopted in Hebrews from the LXX. is less relevant to the psalmist's purpose of gathering all the forces which sweep through the wide heavens into one company of obedient servants of God, than that adopted above, and now generally recognised. It is to be observed that the verbs in vv. 2–4 are participles, which express continuous action. These creative acts were not done once for all, but are going on still and always. Preservation is continued creation.

With ver. 6 we pass to the work of the third of the Genesis days, and the verb is in the form which describes a historical fact. The earth is conceived of as formed, and already moulded into mountains and valleys, but all covered with " the deep " like a vesture —a sadly different one from the robe of Light which He wears. That weltering deep is bidden back to its future appointed bounds ; and the process is grandly described, as if the waters were sentient, and, panic-struck at God's voice, took to flight. Ver. 8 a throws in a vivid touch, to the disturbance of grammatical smoothness. The poet has the scene before his eye, and as the waters flee he sees the earth emerging, the mountains soaring, and the vales sinking, and he breaks his sentence, as if in wonder at the lovely apparition, but returns, in ver. 8 b, to tell whither the fugitive waters fled—namely, to the ocean-depths. There they are hemmed in by God's will, and, as was promised to Noah, shall not again run wasting over a drowned world.

The picture of the emerging earth, with its variations of valleys and mountains, remains before the psalmist's eye throughout vv. 10–18, which describe how it is clothed and peopled. These effects are due to the beneficent ministry of the same element, when guided and restrained by God, which swathed the world with desolation. Water runs through the vales, and rain falls on the mountains. Therefore the former bear herbs and corn, vines and olives, and the latter are clothed with trees not planted by human hand, the mighty cedars which spread their broad shelves of steadfast green high up among the clouds. " Everything lives whithersoever water cometh," as Easterns know. Therefore round the drinking-places in the vales thirsty creatures gather, birds flit and sing ; up among the cedars are peaceful nests, and inaccessible cliffs have their sure-footed inhabitants. All depend on water, and water is God's gift. The psalmist's view of Nature is characteristic in the direct ascription of all its processes to God. He makes the springs flow, and sends rain on the peaks. Equally characteristic is the absence of any expression of a sense of beauty in the sparkling streams tinkling down the gloomy wadies, or in the rain-storms darkening the hills, or in the green mantle of earth, or in the bright creatures. The psalmist is thinking of use, not of beauty. And yet it is a poet's clear and kindly eye which looks upon all, and sees the central characteristic of each,—the eager drinking of the wild ass ; the music of the birds blending with the brawling of the stream, and sweeter because the singers are hidden among the branches ; the freshly watered earth, "satisfied" with "the fruit of Thy works" (*i.e.*, the rain which God has sent from His "upper chambers"), the manifold gifts which by His wondrous alchemy are produced from the ground by help of one agency, water ; the forest trees with their foliage glistening, as if glad for the rain ; the stork on her nest ; the goats on the mountains ; the " conies " (for which we have no popular name) hurrying to their holes in the cliffs.   Man appears as depending, like the lower creatures, on the fruit of the ground ; but he has more varied supplies, bread and wine and oil, and these not only satisfy material wants, but " gladden " and " strengthen " the heart.   According to some, the word rendered " service " in ver. 14 means "tillage," a meaning which is supported by ver. 23, where the same word is rendered " labour," and which fits in well with the next clause of ver. 14, " to bring forth bread from the earth," which would describe the purpose of the tillage.   His prerogative of labour is man's special differentia in creation.   It is a token of his superiority to the happy, careless creatures who toil not nor spin.   Earth does not yield him its best products without his co-operation.   There would thus be an allusion to him as the only worker in creation, similar to that in ver. 23, and to the reference to the " ships " in ver. 26.   But probably the meaning of " service," which is suggested by the parallelism, and does not introduce the new thought of co-operation with Nature or God, is to be preferred.   The construction is somewhat difficult, but the rendering of vv. 14, 15, given above seems best.   The two clauses with infinitive verbs (*to bring forth* and *to cause to shine*) are each followed by a clause in which the construction is varied into that with a finite verb, the meaning remaining the same ; and all four clauses express the Divine purpose in causing vegetation to spring.   Then the psalmist looks up once more to the hills. "The trees of Jehovah" are so called, not so much because they are great, as because, unlike vines and olives, they have not been planted or tended by man, nor belong to him. Far above the valleys, where men and the cattle dependent on him live on earth's cultivated bounties, the unowned woods stand and drink God's gift of rain, while wild creatures lead free lives amid mountains and rocks.

With ver. 19 the psalmist passes to the fourth day, but thinks of moon and sun only in relation to the alternation of day and night as affecting creatural life on earth. The moon is named first, because the Hebrew day began with the evening. It is the *measurer*, by whose phases seasons (or, according to some, *festivals*) are reckoned. The sun is a punctual servant, knowing the hour to set and duly keeping it. "Thou appointest darkness and it is night." God wills, and His will effects material changes. He says to His servant Night, "Come," and she "comes." The psalmist had peopled the vales and mountains of his picture. Everywhere he had seen life fitted to its environment ; and night is populous too. He had outlined swift sketches of tame and wild creatures, and now he half shows us beasts of prey stealing through the gloom. He puts his finger on two characteristics— their stealthy motions, and their cries which made night hideous. Even their roar was a kind of prayer, though they knew it not ; it was God from whom they sought their food. It would not have answered the purpose to have spoken of "all the loves, Now sleeping in those quiet groves." The poet desired to show how there were creatures that found possibilities of happy life in all the variety of conditions fashioned by the creative Hand, which was thus shown to be moved by Wisdom

and Love.   The sunrise sends these nocturnal animals
back to their dens, and the world is ready for man.
" The sun looked over the mountain's rim," and the
beasts of prey slunk to their lairs, and man's day of
toil began—the mark of his pre-eminence, God's gift
for his good, by which he uses creation for its highest
end and fulfils God's purpose.   Grateful is the evening
rest when the day has been filled with strenuous toil.

The picture of earth and its inhabitants is now
complete, and the dominant thought which it leaves
on the psalmist's heart is cast into the exultant and
wondering exclamation of ver. 24.   The variety as
well as multitude of the forms in which God's creative
idea is embodied, the Wisdom which shapes all, His
ownership of all, are the impressions made by the
devout contemplation of Nature.   The scientist and
the artist are left free to pursue their respective lines
of investigation and impression ; but scientist and artist
must rise to the psalmist's point of view, if they are to
learn the deepest lesson from the ordered kingdoms of
Nature and from the beauty which floods the world.

With the exclamation in ver. 24 the psalmist has
finished his picture of the earth, which he had seen as
if emerging from the abyss, and watched as it was
gradually clothed with fertility and peopled with happy
life.   He turns, in vv. 25, 26, to the other half of his
Vision of Creation, and portrays the gathered and
curbed waters which he now calls the " sea."   As
always in Scripture, it is described as it looks to a
landsman, gazing out on it from the safe shore.   The
characteristics specified betray unfamiliarity with mari-
time pursuits.   The far-stretching roll of the waters
away out to the horizon, the mystery veiling the strange
lives swarming in its depths, the extreme contrasts in

the magnitude of its inhabitants, strike the poet.   He
sees "the stately ships go on."   The introduction
of these into the picture is unexpected.   We should
have looked for an instance of the "small" creatures,
to pair off with the "great" one, Leviathan, in the
next words.   "A modern poet," says Cheyne, *in loc.*,
"would have joined the mighty whale to the fairy
nautilus."   It has been suggested that "ship" here
is a name for the nautilus, which is common in the
Eastern Mediterranean.   The suggestion is a tempting
one, as fitting in more smoothly with the antithesis of
small and *great* in the previous clause.   But, in the
absence of any proof that the word has any other
meaning than "ship," the suggestion cannot be taken
as more than a probable conjecture.   The introduction
of "ships" into the picture is quite in harmony with
the allusions to man's works in the former parts of the
psalm, such as ver. 23, and possibly ver. 14   The
psalmist seems to intend to insert such reference to
man, the only toiler, in all his pictures.   "Leviathan"
is probably here the whale.   Ewald, Hitzig, Baethgen,
Kay, and Cheyne follow the LXX. and Vulgate in
reading "Leviathan whom Thou hast formed to sport
with him," and take the words to refer to Job xli. 5.
The thought would then be that God's power can
control the mightiest creatures' plunges ; but "the two
preceding 'there's are in favour of the usual interpretation, 'therein'" (Hupfeld), and consequently of taking
the "sporting" to be that of the unwieldy gambols of
the sea-monster.

Verses 27–30 mass all creatures of earth and sea,
including man, as alike dependent on God for sustenance and for life.   Dumbly these look expectant to
Him, though man only knows to whom all living eyes

are directed. The swift clauses in vv. 28–30, without connecting particles, vividly represent the Divine acts as immediately followed by the creatural consequences. To this psalmist the links in the chain were of little consequence. His thoughts were fixed on its two ends—the Hand that sent its power thrilling through the links, and the result realised in the creature's life. All natural phenomena are issues of God's present will. Preservation is as much His act, as inexplicable without Him, as creation. There would be nothing to "gather" unless He "gave." All sorts of supplies, which make the "good" of physical life, are in His hand, whether they be the food of the wild asses by the streams, or of the conies among the cliffs, or of the young lions in the night, or of Leviathan tumbling amidst the waves, or of toiling man. Nor is it only the nourishment of life which comes straight from God to all, but life itself depends on His continual in-breathing. His face is creation's light; breath from Him is its life. The withdrawal of it is death. Every change in creatural condition is wrought by Him. He is the only Fountain of Life, and the reservoir of all the forces that minister to life or to inanimate being. But the psalmist will not end his contemplations with the thought of the fair creation returning to nothingness. Therefore he adds another verse (30); which tells of "life re-orient out of dust." Individuals pass; the type remains. New generations spring. The yearly miracle of Spring brings greenness over the snow-covered or brown pastures and green shoots from stiffened boughs. Many of last year's birds are dead, but there are nests in the cypresses, and twitterings among the branches in the wadies. Life, not death, prevails in God's world.

So the psalmist gathers all up into a burst of praise. He desires that the glory of God, which accrues to Him from His works, may ever be rendered through devout recognition of Him as working them all by man, the only creature who can be the spokesman of creation. He further desires that, as God at first saw that all was " very good," He may ever continue thus to rejoice in His works, or, in other words, that these may fulfil His purpose. Possibly His rejoicing in His works is regarded as following upon man's giving glory to Him for them. That rejoicing, which is the manifestation both of His love and of His satisfaction, is all the more desired, because, if His works do *not* please Him, there lies in Him a dread abyss of destructive power, which could sweep them into nothingness. Superficial readers may feel that the tone of ver. 32 strikes a discord, but it is a discord which can be resolved into deeper harmony. One frown from God, and the solid earth trembles, as conscious to its depths of His displeasure. One touch of the hand that is filled with good, and the mountains smoke. Creation perishes if He is displeased. Well then may the psalmist pray that He may for ever rejoice in His works, and make them live by His smile.

Very beautifully and profoundly does the psalmist ask, in vv. 33, 34, that some echo of the Divine joy may gladden his own heart, and that his praise may be coeval with God's glory and his own life. This is the Divine purpose in creation—that God may rejoice in it and chiefly in man its crown, and that man may rejoice in Him. Such sweet commerce is possible between heaven and earth ; and they have learned the lesson of creative power and love aright who by it have been led to share in the joy of God. The psalm has been shaped in part by reminiscences of the creative days of creation. It ends with the Divine Sabbath, and with the prayer, which is also a hope, that man may enter into God's rest.

But there is one discordant note in creation's full-toned hymn, "the fair music that all creatures made." There are sinners on earth; and the last prayer of the psalmist is that that blot may be removed, and so nothing may mar the realisation of God's ideal, nor be left to lessen the completeness of His delight in His work. And so the psalm ends, as it began, with the singer's call to his own soul to bless Jehovah.

This is the first psalm which closes with Hallelujah (Praise Jehovah). It is appended to the two following psalms, which close Book IV., and is again found in Book V., in Psalms cxi.–cxiii., cxv.–cxvii., and in the final group, Psalms cxlvi.–cl. It is probably a liturgical addition.

PSALM CV.

1 **Give thanks to** Jehovah, call on His name,
   Make known among the peoples His deeds.
2 Sing to Him, harp to Him,
   Speak musingly of all His wonders.
3 Glory in His holy name,
   Glad be the heart of them that seek Jehovah!
4 Inquire after Jehovah and His strength,
   Seek His face continually.
5 Remember His wonders which He has done,
   His marvels and the judgments of His mouth.
6 O seed of Abraham His servant,
   Sons of Jacob, His chosen ones.

7 He, Jehovah, is our God,
   In all the earth are His judgments.
8 He remembers His covenant for ever,
   The word which He commanded for a thousand generations ;
9 Which He made with Abraham,
   And His oath to Isaac.
10 And He established it with Jacob for a statute,
   To Israel for an everlasting covenant,
11 Saying, " To thee will I give the land of Canaan,
   [As] your measured allotment ; "
12 Whilst they were easily counted,
   Very few, and but sojourners therein ;
13 And they went about from nation to nation,
   From [one] kingdom to another people.
14 He suffered no man to oppress them,
   And reproved kings for their sakes ;
15 [Saying], "Touch not Mine anointed ones,
   And to My prophets do no harm."

16 And He called for a famine on the land,
   Every staff of bread He broke.
17 He sent before them a man,
   For a slave was Joseph sold.

18 They afflicted his feet with the fetter,
   He was put in irons.
19 Till the time [when] his word came [to pass],
   The promise of Jehovah tested him.
20 The king sent and loosed him,
   The ruler of peoples, and let him go.
21 He made him lord over his house,
   And ruler over all his substance;
22 To bind princes at his pleasure,
   And to make his elders wise.

23 So Israel came to Egypt,
   And Jacob sojourned in the land of Ham.
24 And He made His people fruitful exceedingly,
   And made them stronger than their foes.
25 He turned their heart to hate His people,
   To deal craftily with His servants.
26 He sent Moses His servant,
   [And] Aaron whom He had chosen.
27 They set [forth] among them His signs,
   And wonders in the land of Ham.

28 He sent darkness, and made it dark,
   And they rebelled not against His words.
29 He turned their waters to blood,
   And slew their fish.
30 Their land swarmed [with] frogs,
   In the chambers of their kings.
31 He spake and the gad-fly came,
   Gnats in all their borders.
32 He gave hail [for] their rains,
   Flaming fire in their land.
33 And He smote their vine and their fig-tree,
   And broke the trees of their borders.
34 He spoke and the locust came,
   And caterpillar-locusts without number,
35 And ate up every herb in their land,
   And ate up the fruit of their ground.
36 And He smote every first-born in their land,
   The firstlings of all their strength.
37 And He brought them out with silver and gold,
   And there was not one among His tribes who stumbled.
38 Glad was Egypt at their departure,
   For the fear of them had fallen upon them.

39 He spread a cloud for a covering,
    And fire to light the night.
40 They asked and He brought quails,
    And [with] bread from heaven He satisfied them.
41 He opened the rock and forth gushed waters,
    They flowed through the deserts, a river.
42 For He remembered His holy word,
    [And] Abraham His servant;
43 And He brought out His people [with] joy,
    With glad cries His chosen [ones];
44 And He gave them the lands of the nations,
    And they took possession of the toil of the peoples,
45 To the end that they might observe His statutes,
    And keep His laws.
                    Hallelujah !

IT is a reasonable conjecture that the Hallelujah at
  the end of Psalm civ., where it is superfluous,
properly belongs to this psalm, which would then be
assimilated to Psalm cvi., which is obviously a companion psalm. Both are retrospective and didactic;
but Psalm cv. deals entirely with God's unfailing faithfulness to Israel, while Psalm cvi. sets forth the sad
contrast presented by Israel's continual faithlessness to
God. Each theme is made more impressive by being
pursued separately, and then set over against the other.
The long series of God's mercies massed together here
confronts the dark uniformity of Israel's unworthy requital of them there. Half of the sky is pure blue
and radiant sunshine; half is piled with unbroken
clouds. Nothing drives home the consciousness of
sin so surely as contemplation of God's loving acts.
Probably this psalm, like others of similar contents, is
of late date. The habit of historical retrospect for
religious purposes is likely to belong to times remote
from the events recorded. Vv. 1–15 are found in
I Chron. xvi. as part of the hymn at David's setting

up of the Ark on Zion.   But that hymn is unmistakably
a compilation from extant psalms, and cannot be taken
as deciding the Davidic authorship of the psalm.

Vv. 1–6 are a ringing summons to extol and contemplate God's great deeds for Israel.   They are full
of exultation, and, in their reiterated short clauses, are
like the joyful cries of a herald bringing good tidings
to Zion.   There is a beautiful progress of thought in
these verses.   They begin with the call to thank and
praise Jehovah and to proclaim His doings among the
people.   That recognition of Israel's office as the world's
evangelist does not require the supposition that the
nation was dispersed in captivity, but simply shows
that the singer understood the reason for the long
series of mercies heaped on it.   It is significant that
God's " deeds " are Israel's message to the world.   By
such deeds His " name " is spoken.   What God has
done is the best revelation of what God is.   His
messengers are not to speak their own thoughts about
Him, but to tell the story of His acts and let these
speak for Him.   Revelation is not a set of propositions,
but a history of Divine facts.   The foundation of audible
praise and proclamation is contemplation.   Therefore
the exhortation in ver. 2 b follows, which means not
merely " speak," but may be translated, as in margin of
the Revised Version, " meditate," and is probably best
rendered so as to combine both ideas, " musingly
speak."   Let not the words be mere words, but feel
the great deeds which you proclaim.   In like manner,
ver. 3 calls upon the heralds to " glory " for themselves
in the name of Jehovah, and to make efforts to possess
Him more fully and to rejoice in finding Him.   Aspiration after clearer and closer knowledge and experience
of God should ever underlie glad pealing forth of His

name. If it does not, eloquent tongues will fall silent, and Israel's proclamation will be cold and powerless. To seek Jehovah is to find His strength investing our feebleness. To turn our faces towards His in devout desire is to have our faces made bright by reflected light. And one chief way of seeking Jehovah is the remembrance of His merciful wonders of old, " He hath made His wonderful works to be remembered " (Psalm cxi. 4), and His design in them is that men should have solid basis for their hopes, and be thereby encouraged to seek Him, as well as be taught what He is. Thus the psalmist reaches his main theme, which is to build a memorial of these deeds for an everlasting possession. The " wonders " referred to in ver. 5 are chiefly those wrought in Egypt, as the subsequent verses show.

Ver. 6 contains, in the names given to Israel, the reason for their obeying the preceding summonses. Their hereditary relation to God gives them the material, and imposes on them the obligation and the honour, of being " secretaries of God's praise." In ver. 6 a " His servant " may be intended to designate the nation, as it often does in Isa. xl.–lxvi. " His chosen ones " in ver. 6 b would then be an exact parallel ; but the recurrence of the expression in ver. 42, with the individual reference, makes that reference more probable here.

The fundamental fact underlying all Israel's experience of God's care is His own loving will, which, self-moved, entered into covenant obligations, so that thereafter His mercies are ensured by His veracity, no less than by His kindness. Hence the psalm begins its proper theme by hymning the faithfulness of God to His oath, and painting the insignificance of the beginnings of the nation, as showing that the ground of

God's covenant relation was laid in Himself, not in them. Israel's consciousness of holding a special relation to God never obscured, in the minds of psalmists and prophets, the twin truth that all the earth waited on Him, and was the theatre of His manifestations. Baser souls might hug themselves on their prerogative. The nobler spirits ever confessed that it laid on them duties to the world, and that God had not left Himself without witness in any land. These two truths have often been rent asunder, both in Israel and in Christendom, but each needs the other for its full comprehension. " Jehovah is our God " may become the war-cry of bitter hostility to them that are without, or of contempt, which is quite as irreligious. " In all the earth are His judgments " may lead to a vague theism, incredulous of special revelation. He who is most truly penetrated with the first will be most joyfully ready to proclaim the second of these sister-thoughts, and will neither shut up all God's mercies within the circle of revelation, nor lose sight of His clearest utterances while looking on His more diffused and less perfect ones.

The obligations under which God has come to Israel are represented as a covenant, a word and an oath. In all the general idea of explicit declaration of Divine purpose, which henceforth becomes binding on God by reason of His faithfulness, is contained ; but the conception of a *covenant* implies mutual obligations, failure to discharge which on one side relieves the other contracting party from his promise, while that of a *word* simply includes the notion of articulate utterance, and that of an *oath* adds the thought of a solemn sanction and a pledge given. God swears by Himself —that is, His own character is the guarantee of His promise. These various designations are thus heaped together, in order to heighten the thought of the firmness of His promise. It stands " for ever," " to a thousand generations " ; it is an " everlasting covenant." The psalmist triumphs, as it were, in the manifold repetition of it. Each of the fathers of the nation had it confirmed to himself,—Abraham ; Isaac when, ready to flee from the land in famine, he had renewed to him (Gen. xxvi. 3) the oath which he had first heard as he stood, trembling but unharmed, by the rude altar where the ram lay in his stead (Gen. xxii. 16) ; Jacob as he lay beneath the stars at Bethel. With Jacob (Israel) the singer passes from the individuals to the nation, as is shown by the alternation of " thee " and " you " in ver. 11.

The lowly condition of the recipients of the promise not only exalts the love which chose them, but the power which preserved them and fulfilled it. And if, as may be the case, the psalm is exilic or post-exilic, its picture of ancient days is like a mirror, reflecting present depression and bidding the downcast be of good cheer. He who made a strong nation out of that little horde of wanderers must have been moved by His own heart, not by anything in them ; and what He did long ago He can do to-day. God's past is the prophecy of God's future. Literally rendered, ver. 12 a runs " Whilst they were men of number," i.e., easily numbered (Gen. xxxiv. 30, where Jacob uses the same phrase). " Very few " in b is literally " like a little," and may either apply to number or to worth. It is used in the latter sense, in reference to " the heart of the wicked," in Prov. x. 20, and may have the same meaning here. That little band of wanderers, who went about as sojourners among the kinglets of Canaan and Philistia,

with occasional visits to Egypt, seemed very vulnerable ;
but God was, as He had promised to the first of them
at a moment of extreme peril, their "shield," and in
their lives there were instances of strange protection
afforded them, which curbed kings, as in the case of
Abram in Egypt (Gen. xii.) and Gerar (Gen. xx.), and
of Isaac in the latter place (Gen. xxvi.). The patriarchs
were not, technically speaking, "anointed," but they had
that of which anointing was but a symbol. They were
Divinely set apart and endowed for their tasks, and, as
consecrated to God's service, their persons were inviolable. In a very profound sense all God's servants are
thus anointed, and are "immortal till their work is
done." "Prophets" in the narrower sense of the
word the patriarchs were not, but Abraham is called
so by God in one of the places already referred to
(Gen. xx. 7). Prior to prophetic utterance is prophetic
inspiration ; and these men received Divine communications, and were, in a special degree, possessed of the
counsels of Heaven. The designation is equivalent to
Abraham's name of the "friend of God." Thus both
titles, which guaranteed a charmed, invulnerable life to
their bearers, go deep into the permanent privileges of
God-trusting souls. All such "have an anointing from
the Holy One," and receive whispers from His lips.
They are all under the ægis of His protection, and for
their sakes kings of many a dynasty and age have been
rebuked.

In vv. 16–22 the history of Joseph is poetically and
summarily treated, as a link in the chain of providences
which brought about the fulfilment of the Covenant.
Possibly the singer is thinking about a captive Israel
in the present, while speaking about a captive Joseph
in the past. In God's dealings humiliation and afflic-

tion are often, he thinks, the precursors of glory and triumph. Calamities prepare the way for prosperity. So it was in that old time; and so it is still. In this *résumé* of the history of Joseph, the points signalised are God's direct agency in the whole—the errand on which Joseph was sent (" before them ") as a forerunner to " prepare a place for them," the severity of his sufferings, the trial of his faith by the contrast which his condition presented to what God had promised, and his final exaltation. The description of Joseph's imprisonment adds some dark touches to the account in Genesis, whether these are due to poetic idealising or to tradition. In ver. 18 *b* some would translate " Iron came over his soul." So Delitzsch, following the Vulgate (" Ferrum pertransiit animam ejus "), and the picturesque Prayer-Book Version, " The iron entered into his soul." But the original is against this, as the word for *iron* is masculine and the verb is feminine, agreeing with the feminine noun *soul*. The clause is simply a parallel to the preceding. " His soul " is best taken as a mere periphrasis for *he*, though it may be used emphatically to suggest that " his soul entered, whole and entire, in its resolve to obey God, into the cruel torture " (Kay). The meaning is conveyed by the free rendering above.

Ver. 19 is also ambiguous, from the uncertainty as to whose word is intended in *a*. It may be either God's or Joseph's. The latter is the more probable, as there appears to be an intentional contrast between " His word " in *a*, and " the promise of Jehovah " in *b*. If this explanation is adopted, a choice is still possible between Joseph's interpretation of his fellow-prisoners' dreams, the fulfilment of which led to his liberation, and his earlier word recounting his own dreams, which led to his being sold by his brethren. In any case, the thought of the verse is a great and ever true one, that God's promise, while it remains unfulfilled, and seems contradicted by present facts, serves as a test of the genuineness and firmness of a man's reliance on Him and it. That promise is by the psalmist almost personified, as putting Joseph to the test. Such testing is the deepest meaning of all afflictions. Fire will burn off a thin plating of silver from a copper coin and reveal the base metal beneath, but it will only brighten into a glow the one which is all silver.

There is a ring of triumph in the singer's voice as he tells of the honour and power heaped on the captive, and of how the king of many nations " sent," as the mightier King in heaven had done (vv. 20 and 17), and not only liberated but exalted him, giving him, whose soul had been bound in fetters, power to " bind princes according to his soul," and to instruct and command the elders of Egypt.

Vv. 23–27 carry on the story to the next step in the evolution of God's purposes. The long years of the sojourn in Egypt are summarily dealt with, as they are in the narrative in Genesis and Exodus, and the salient points of its close alone are touched—the numerical growth of the people, the consequent hostility of the Egyptians, and the mission of Moses and Aaron. The direct ascription to God of all the incidents mentioned is to be noted. The psalmist sees only one hand moving, and has no hesitation in tracing to God the turning of the Egyptians' hearts to hatred. Many commentators, both old and new, try to weaken the expression, by the explanation that the hatred was " indirectly the work of God, inasmuch as He lent increasing might to the people " (Delitzsch). But the psalmist means much more than this, just as Exodus does in attributing the hardening of Pharaoh's heart to God.

Ver. 27, according to the existing text, breaks the series of verses beginning with a singular verb of which God is the subject, which stretch with only one other interruption from ver. 24 to ver. 37. It seems most probable, therefore, that the LXX. is right in reading *He* instead of *They*. The change is but the omission of one letter, and the error supposed is a frequent one. The word literally means *set* or *planted*, and *did* is an explanation rather than a rendering. The whole expression is remarkable. Literally, we should translate " He " (or " They ") " set among them words " (or " matters ") " of His signs " ; but this would be unintelligible, and we must have recourse to reproduction of the meaning rather than of the words.

If " words of His signs " is not merely pleonastic, it may be rendered, as by Kay, " His long record of signs," or as by Cheyne, " His varied signs." But it is better to take the expression as suggesting that the *miracles* were indeed *words*, as being declarations of God's will and commands to let His people go. The phrase in ver. 5, " the judgments of His mouth," would then be roughly parallel. God's deeds are words. His signs have tongues. " He speaks and it is done " ; but also, " He does and it is spoken." The expression, however, may be like Psalm lxv. 4, where the same form of phrase is applied to sins, and where it seems to mean " deeds of iniquity." It would then mean here " His works which were signs."

The following enumeration of the " signs " does not follow the order in Exodus, but begins with the ninth plague, perhaps because of its severity, and then in the main adheres to the original sequence, though it inverts

the order of the third and forth plagues (flies and gnats
or mosquitoes, not " lice ") and omits the fifth and sixth.
The reason for this divergence is far from clear, but it
may be noted that the first two in the psalmist's order
attack the elements ; the next three (frogs, flies, gnats)
have to do with animal life ; and the next two (hail and
locusts), which embrace both these categories, are considered chiefly as affecting vegetable products. The
emphasis is laid in all on God's direct act. *He* sends
darkness, *He* turns the waters into blood, and so on.
The only other point needing notice in these verses is
the statement in ver. 28 *b*.   " They rebelled not against
His word," which obviously is true only in reference to
Moses and Aaron, who shrank not from their perilous
embassage.

The tenth plague is briefly told, for the psalm is
hurrying on to the triumphant climax of the Exodus,
when, enriched with silver and gold, the tribes went
forth, strong for their desert march, and Egypt rejoiced
to see the last of them, " for they said, We be all dead
men " (Exod. xii. 33).   There may be a veiled hope in
this exultant picture of the Exodus, that present oppression will end in like manner.   The wilderness sojourn
is so treated in ver. 39 *sqq.* as to bring into sight only
the leading instances, sung in many psalms, of God's
protection, without one disturbing reference to the sins
and failures which darkened the forty years.   These
are spread out at length, without flattery or minimising,
in the next psalm ; but here the theme is God's wonders.
Therefore, the pillar of cloud which guided, covered, and
illumined the camp, the miracles which provided food
and water, are touched on in vv. 39–41, and then the
psalmist gathers up the lessons which he would teach
in three great thoughts.   The reason for God's merciful

dealings with His people is His remembrance of His covenant, and of His servant Abraham, whose faith made a claim on God, for the fulfilment which would vindicate it. That covenant has been amply fulfilled, for Israel came forth with ringing songs, and took possession of lands which they had not tilled, and houses which they had not built. The purpose of covenant and fulfilment is that the nation, thus admitted into special relations with God, should by His mercies be drawn to keep His commandments, and in obedience find rest and closer fellowship with its God. The psalmist had learned that God gives before He demands or commands, and that " Love," springing from grateful reception of His benefits, " is the fulfilling of the Law." He anticipates the full Christian exhortation, " I beseech you, brethren, by the mercies of God, that ye present your bodies a living sacrifice."

PSALM CVI.

1   Hallelujah!
    Give thanks to Jehovah, for He is good,
    For His loving-kindness [endures] for ever.
2 Who can speak forth the mighty deeds of Jehovah?
    [Who] can cause all His praise to be heard?
3 Blessed are they who observe right,
    He who does righteousness at all times.
4 Remember me, Jehovah, with the favour which Thou bearest
       to Thy people,
    Visit me with Thy salvation;
5 That I may look on the prosperity of Thy chosen ones,
    That I may joy in the joy of Thy nation,
    That I may triumph with Thine inheritance.

6 We have sinned with our fathers,
    We have done perversely, have done wickedly.
7 Our fathers in Egypt considered not Thy wonders,
    They remembered not the multitude of Thy loving-kindnesses,
    And rebelled at the Sea, by the Red Sea.
8 And He saved them for His name's sake,
    To make known His might;
9 And He rebuked the Red Sea and it was dried up,
    And He led them in the depths as in a wilderness;
10 And He saved them from the hand of the hater,
    And redeemed them from the hand of the enemy;
11 And the waters covered their oppressors,
    Not one of them was left;
12 And they believed on His words,
    They sang His praise.

13 They hasted [and] forgot His works,
    They waited not for His counsel;
14 And they lusted a lust in the wilderness,
    And tempted God in the desert;

15 And He gave them what they asked for,
And sent wasting sickness into their soul.
16 They were jealous against Moses in the camp,
Against Aaron, the holy one of Jehovah.
17 The earth opened and swallowed Dathan,
And covered the company of Abiram;
18 And fire blazed out on their company,
Flame consumed the wicked ones.

19 They made a calf in Horeb,
And bowed down to a molten image;
20 And they changed their Glory
For the likeness of a grass-eating ox.
21 They forgot God their Saviour,
Who did great things in Egypt,
22 Wonders in the land of Ham,
Dread things by the Red Sea.
23 And He said that He would annihilate them,
Had not Moses, His chosen one, stood in the breach con-
fronting Him
To turn His anger from destroying.

24 And they despised the delightsome land,
They trusted not to His word;
25 And they murmured in their tents
They hearkened not to the voice of Jehovah;
26 And He lifted up His hand to them, [swearing]
That He would make them fall in the wilderness.
27 And that He would make their seed fall among the nations,
And scatter them in the lands.

28 And they yoked themselves to Baal-Peor,
And ate the sacrifices of dead [gods];
29 And they provoked Him by their doings,
And a plague broke in upon them;
30 And Phinehas stood up and did judgment,
And the plague was stayed;
31 And it was reckoned to him for righteousness,
To generation after generation, for ever.

32 And they moved indignation at the waters of Meribah,
And it fared ill with Moses on their account.
33 For they rebelled against [His] Spirit,
And he spoke rashly with his lips.

34 They destroyed not the peoples
[Of] whom Jehovah spoke to them;

35 And they mixed themselves with the nations
And learned their works;

36 And they served their idols
And they became to them a snare;

37 And they sacrificed their sons
And their daughters to demons;

38 And they shed innocent blood, the blood of their sons and
daughters,
Whom they sacrificed to the idols of Canaan,
And the land was profaned by bloodshed.

39 And they became unclean through their works,
And committed whoredom through their doings.

40 And the anger of Jehovah kindled on His people,
And He abhorred His inheritance;

41 And He gave them into the hand of the nations,
And their haters lorded it over them;

42 And their enemies oppressed them,
And they were bowed down under their hand.

43 Many times did He deliver them,
And they—they rebelliously followed their own counsel,
And were brought low through their iniquity;

44 And He looked on their distress
When He heard their cry;

45 And He remembered for them His covenant,
And repented according to the multitude of His loving-kindness,

46 And caused them to find compassion,
In the presence of all their captors.

47 Save us, Jehovah, our God,
And gather us from among the nations,
That we may thank Thy holy name,
That we may make our boast in Thy praise.

48 Blessed be Jehovah, the God of Israel,
From everlasting and to everlasting,
And let all the people say Amen.
Hallelujah!

THE history of God's past is a record of continuous
mercies, the history of man's, one of as continuous
sin. The memory of the former quickened the psalmist

into his sunny song of thankfulness in the previous psalm. That of the latter moves him to the confessions in this one. They are complements of each other, and are connected not only as being both retrospective, but by the identity of their beginnings and the difference of their points of view. The parts of the early history dealt with in the one are lightly touched or altogether omitted in the other. The key-note of Psalm cv. is, " Remember His mighty deeds "; that of Psalm cvi. is, " They forgot His mighty deeds."

Surely never but in Israel has patriotism chosen a nation's sins for the themes of song, or, in celebrating its victories, written but one name, the name of Jehovah, on its trophies. But in the Psalter we have several instances of such hymns of national confession ; and, in other books, there are the formulary at the presentation of the first-fruits (Deut. xxvi.), Solomon's prayer at the dedication of the Temple (I Kings viii.), Nehemiah's prayer (Neh. ix.), and Daniel's (Dan. ix.).

An exilic date is implied by the prayer of ver. 47, for the gathering of the people from among the nations. The occurrence of vv. I and 47, 48, in the compilation in I Chron. xvi. shows that this psalm, which marks the close of the Fourth Book, was in existence prior to the date of I Chronicles.

No trace of strophical arrangement is discernible. But, after an introduction in some measure like that in Psalm cv., the psalmist plunges into his theme, and draws out the long, sad story of Israel's faithlessness. He recounts seven instances during the wilderness sojourn (vv. 7–33), and then passes to those occurring in the Land (vv. 34–39), with which he connects the alternations of punishment and relenting on God's part and the obstinacy of transgression on Israel's, even

down to the moment in which he speaks (vv. 40–46).
The whole closes with a prayer for restoration to the
Land (ver. 47); to which is appended the doxology
(ver. 48), the mark of the end of Book IV., and not a
part of the psalm.

The psalmist preludes his confession and contemplation of his people's sins by a glad remembrance of
God's goodness and enduring loving-kindness and by
a prayer for himself.   Some commentators regard these
introductory verses as incongruous with the tone of the
psalm, and as mere liturgical commonplace, which has
been tacked on without much heed to fitness.   But
surely the thought of God's unspeakable goodness most
appropriately precedes the psalmist's confession, for
nothing so melts a heart in penitence as the remembrance of God's love, and nothing so heightens the evil
of sin as the consideration of the patient goodness
which it has long flouted.   The blessing pronounced in
ver. 3 on those who "do righteousness" and keep the
law is not less natural, before a psalm which sets forth
in melancholy detail the converse truth of the misery
that dogs breaking the law.

In vv. 4, 5, the psalmist interjects a prayer for himself, the abruptness of which strongly reminds us of
similar jets of personal supplication in Nehemiah.
The determination to make the "I" of the Psalter the
nation perversely insists on that personification here,
in spite of the clear distinction thrice drawn in ver. 5
between the psalmist and his people.   The "salvation"
in which he desires to share is the deliverance from
exile for which he prays in the closing verse of the
psalm.   There is something very pathetic in this
momentary thought of self.   It breathes wistful yearning, absolute confidence in the unrealised deliverance,

lowly humility which bases its claim with God on that of the nation. Such a prayer stands in the closest relation to the theme of the psalm, which draws out the dark record of national sin, in order to lead to that national repentance which, as all the history shows, is the necessary condition of " the prosperity of Thy chosen ones." Precisely because the hope of restoration is strong, the delineation of sin is unsparing.

With ver. 6 the theme of the psalm is given forth, in language which recalls Solomon's and Daniel's similar confessions (1 Kings viii. 47; Dan. ix. 5). The accumulation of synonyms for sin witnesses at once to the gravity and manifoldness of the offences, and to the earnestness and comprehensiveness of the acknowledgment. The remarkable expression " We have sinned *with* our fathers " is not to be weakened to mean merely that the present generation had sinned like their ancestors, but gives expression to the profound sense of national solidarity, which speaks in many other places of Scripture, and rests on very deep facts in the life of nations and their individual members. The enumeration of ancestral sin begins with the murmurings of the faint-hearted fugitives by the Red Sea. In Psalm cv. the wonders in Egypt were dilated on and the events at the Red Sea unmentioned. Here the signs in Egypt are barely referred to and treated as past at the point where the psalm begins, while the incidents by the Red Sea fill a large space in the song. Clearly, the two psalms supplement each other. The reason given for Israel's rebellion in Psalm cvi. is its forgetfulness of God's mighty deeds (ver. 7 *a*, *b*), while in Psalm cv. the remembrance of these is urgently enjoined. Thus, again, the connection of thought in the pair of psalms is evident. Every man has experiences enough of God's goodness stored away in the chambers of his memory to cure him of distrust, if he would only look at them. But they lie unnoticed, and so fear has sway over him. No small part of the discipline needed for vigorous hope lies in vigorous exercise of remembrance. The drying up of the Red Sea is here poetically represented, with omission of Moses' outstretched rod and the strong east wind, as the immediate consequence of God's omnipotent rebuke. Ver. 9 *b* is from Isa. lxiii. 13, and picturesquely describes the march through that terrible gorge of heaped-up waters as being easy and safe, as if it had been across some wide-stretching plain, with springy turf to tread on. The triumphant description of the completeness of the enemies' destruction in ver. 11 *b* is from Exod. xiv. 28, and " they believed on His words " is in part quoted from Exod. xiv. 31, while Miriam's song is referred to in ver. 12 *b*.

The next instance of departure is the lusting for food (vv. 13–15). Again the evil is traced to forgetfulness of God's doings, to which in ver. 13 *b* is added impatient disinclination to wait the unfolding of His counsel or plan. These evils cropped up with strange celerity. The memory of benefits was transient, as if they had been written on the blown sands of the desert. " They hasted, they forgot His works." Of how many of us that has to be said I We remember pain and sorrow longer than joy and pleasure. It is always difficult to bridle desires and be still until God discloses His purposes. We are all apt to try to force His hand open, and to impose our wishes on Him, rather than to let His will mould us. So, on forgetfulness and impatience there followed then, as there follow still, eager longings after material good and a

tempting of God. "They lusted a lust" is from Num.
xi. 4. "Tempted God" is found in reference to the
same incident in the other psalm of historical retrospect
(lxxviii. 18). He is "tempted" when unbelief demands
proofs of His power, instead of waiting patiently for
Him. In Num. xi. 33 Jehovah is said to have smitten
the people "with a very great plague." The psalm
specifies more particularly the nature of the stroke by
calling it "wasting sickness," which invaded the life
of the sinners. The words are true in a deeper sense,
though not so meant. For whoever sets his hot desires
in self-willed fashion on material good, and succeeds in
securing their gratification, gains with the satiety of his
lower sense the loss of a shrivelled spiritual nature.
Full-fed flesh makes starved souls.

The third instance is the revolt headed by Korah,
Dathan, and Abiram against the exclusive Aaronic
priesthood (vv. 16–18). It was rebellion against God,
for He had set apart Aaron as His own, and therefore
the unusual title of "the holy one of Jehovah" is here
given to the high priest. The expression recalls the
fierce protest of the mutineers, addressed to Moses and
Aaron, "Ye take too much upon you, seeing all the
congregation are holy" (Num. xvi. 3) ; and also Moses'
answer, "Jehovah will show . . . who is holy." Envy
often masquerades as the champion of the rights of the
community, when it only wishes to grasp these for
itself. These aristocratic democrats cared nothing for
the prerogatives of the nation, though they talked about
them. They wanted to pull down Aaron, not to lift
up Israel. Their end is described with stern brevity,
in language coloured by the narrative in Numbers,
from which the phrases "opened" (*i.e.*, her mouth)
and "covered" are drawn. Korah is not mentioned

here, in which the psalm follows Num. **xvi.** and Deut. xi. 6, whereas Num. xxvi. 10 includes Korah in the destruction. The difficulty does not seem to have received any satisfactory solution. But Cheyne is too peremptory when he undertakes to divine the reason for the omission of Korah here and in Deut. xi. 6, " because he was a Levite and his name was dear to temple-poets." Such clairvoyance as to motives is beyond ordinary vision. In ver. 18 the fate of the two hundred and fifty "princes of Israel" who took part in the revolt is recorded as in Num. xvi. 35.

The worship of the calf is the fourth instance (vv. 19–23) in the narrative of which the psalmist follows Exod. xxxii., but seems also to have Deut. ix. 8–12 floating in his mind, as appears from the use of the name " Horeb," which is rare in Exodus and frequent in Deuteronomy. Ver. 20 is apparently modelled on Jer. ii. 11 : " My people have changed their glory for that which doth not profit." Compare also Paul's "*changed* the *glory* of the incorruptible God for the *likeness*," etc. (Rom. i. 23). "His glory" is read instead "their glory" by Noldeke, Graetz, and Cheyne, following an old Jewish authority. The LXX., in Codd. Alex. and Sin. (second hand), has this reading, and Paul seems to follow it in the passage just quoted. It yields a worthy meaning, but the existing text is quite appropriate. It scarcely means that God was the source of Israel's glory or their boast, for the word is not found in that sense. It is much rather the name for the collective attributes of the revealed Godhead, and is here substantially equivalent to "their God," that lustrous Light which, in a special manner, belonged to the people of revelation, on whom its first and brightest beams shone. The strange perverseness which turned away from such a radiance of glory to bow down before an idol is strikingly set forth by the figure of bartering it for an image, and that of an ox that ate grass. The one true Substance given away for a shadow! The lofty Being whose light filled space surrendered: and for what? A brute that had to feed, and that on herbage! Men usually make a profit, or think they do, on their barter: but what do they gain by exchanging God for anything? Yet *we* keep making the same mistake of parting with Substance for shadows. And the reason which moved Israel is still operative. As before, the psalmist traces their mad apostasy to forgetfulness of God's deeds. The list of these is now increased by the addition of those at the Red Sea. With every step new links were added to the chain that should have bound the recipients of so many mercies to God. Therefore each new act of departure was of a darker hue of guilt, and drew on the apostates severer punishment, which also, rightly understood, was greater mercy.

"He said that He would annihilate them" is quoted from Deut. ix. 25. Moses' intercession for the people is here most vividly represented under the figure of a champion, who rushes into the breach by which the enemy is about to pour into some beleaguered town, and with his own body closes the gap and arrests the assault (cf. Ezek. xxii. 30).

The fifth instance is the refusal to go up to the land, which followed on the report of the spies (vv. 24-27). These verses are full of reminiscences of the Pentateuch and other parts of Scripture. "The delightsome land" (lit. "land of desire") is found in Jer. iii. 19 and Zech. vii. 14. "They despised" is from Num. xiv. 31. "They murmured in their tents" is from Deut. i. 27

(the only other place in which the word for murmuring occurs in this form). Lifting up the hand is used, as here, not in the usual sense of threatening to strike, but in that of swearing, in Exod. vi. 8, and the oath itself is given in Num. xiv. 28 *sqq.*, while the expression " lifted up My hand " occurs in that context, in reference to God's original oath to the patriarch. The threat of exile (ver. 27) does not occur in Numbers, but is found as the punishment of apostasy in Lev. xxvi. 33 and Deut. xxviii. 64. The verse, however, is found almost exactly in Ezek. xx. 23, with the exception that there " scatter " stands in *a* instead of *make to fall.* The difference in the Hebrew is only in the final letter of the words, and the reading in Ezekiel should probably be adopted here. So the LXX. and other ancient authorities and many of the moderns.

The sixth instance is the participation in the abominable Moabitish worship of " Baal-Peor," recorded in Num. xxv. The peculiar phrase " yoked themselves to " is taken from that chapter, and seems to refer to " the mystic, quasi-physical union supposed to exist between a god and his worshippers, and to be kept up by sacrificial meals " (Cheyne). These are called sacrifices of the dead, inasmuch as idols are dead in contrast with the living God. The judicial retribution inflicted according to Divine command by the judges of Israel slaying " every one his man " is here called a " plague," as in the foundation passage, Num. xxv. 9. The word (lit. " a stroke," *i.e.* from God) is usually applied to punitive sickness ; but God smites when He bids men smite. Both the narrative in Numbers and the psalm bring out vividly the picture of the indignant Phinehas springing to his feet from the midst of the passive crowd. He " rose up," says the former ; he " stood up," says

the latter.   And his deed is described in the psalm in
relation to its solemn judicial character, without particularising its details.   The psalmist would partially
veil both the sin and the horror of its punishment.
Phinehas' javelin was a minister of God's justice, and
the death of the two culprits satisfied that justice and
stayed the plague.   The word rendered "did judgment"
has that meaning only, and such renderings as *mediated*
or *appeased* give the effect of the deed and not the
description of it contained in the word.   "It was
reckoned to him for righteousness," as Abraham's
faith was (Gen. xv. 6).   It was indeed an act which
had its origin "in the faithfulness that had its root
in faith, and which, for the sake of this its ultimate
ground, gained him the acceptation of a righteous man,
inasmuch as it proved him to be such" (Delitzsch, Eng.
Trans.).   He showed himself a true son of Abraham
in the midst of these degenerate descendants, and it
was the same impulse of faith which drove his spear,
and which filled the patriarch's heart when he gazed
into the silent sky and saw in its numberless lights
the promise of his seed.   Phinehas' reward was the
permanence of the priesthood in his family.

The seventh instance is the rebellion at the waters
of Meribah (Strife), in the fortieth year (Num. xx.
2–13).   The chronological order is here set aside, for
the events recorded in vv. 28–31 followed those
dealt with in vv. 32, 33.   The reason is probably
that here Moses himself is hurried into sin, through
the people's faithlessness, and so a climax is reached.
The leader, long-tried, fell at last, and was shut out
from entering the land.   That was in some aspects the
master-piece and triumph of the nation's sin.   "It
fared ill with Moses on their account," as in Deut. i. 37,

iii. 26, "Jehovah was angry with me for your sakes."
"His Spirit," in ver. 33, is best taken as meaning the
Spirit of God. The people's sin is repeatedly specified
in the psalm as being rebellion against God, and the
absence of a more distinct definition of the person
referred to is like the expression in ver. 32, where
"indignation" is that of God, though His name is not
mentioned. Isa. lxiii. 10 is a parallel to this clause, as
other parts of the same chapter are to other parts of
the psalm. The question which has been often raised,
as to what was Moses' sin, is solved in ver. 33 *b*, which
makes his passionate words, wherein he lost his temper
and arrogated to himself the power of fetching water
from the rock, the head and front of his offending.
The psalmist has finished his melancholy catalogue of
sins in the wilderness with this picture of the great
leader dragged down by the prevailing tone, and he
next turns to the sins done in the land.

Two flagrant instances are given—disobedience to
the command to exterminate the inhabitants, and the
adoption of their bloody worship. The conquest of
Canaan was partial ; and, as often is the case, the
conquerors were conquered and the invaders caught
the manners of the invaded. Intermarriage poured a
large infusion of alien blood into Israel ; and the
Canaanitish strain is perceptible to-day in the fellahin
of the Holy Land. The proclivity to idolatry, which
was natural in that stage of the world's history, and
was intensified by universal example, became more
irresistible, when reinforced by kinship and neighbourhood, and the result foretold was realised—the idols
"became a snare" (Judg. ii. 1–3). The poet dwells
with special abhorrence on the hideous practice of
human sacrifices, which exercised so strong and

horrible a fascination over the inhabitants of Canaan.
The word in ver. 37 *demons* is found only here and
in Deut. xxxii. 17. The above rendering is that of the
LXX. Its literal meaning seems to be " lords." It is
thus a synonym for " Baalim." The epithet " Shaddai"
exclusively applied to Jehovah may be compared.

In vv. 40–46 the whole history of Israel is summed
up as alternating periods of sin, punishment, deliverance, recurring in constantly repeated cycles, in which
the mystery of human obstinacy is set over against
that of Divine long-suffering, and one knows not
whether to wonder most at the incurable levity which
learned nothing from experience, or the inexhaustible
long-suffering which wearied not in giving wasted
gifts. Chastisement and mercies were equally in vain.
The outcome of God's many deliverances was, " they
rebelled in their counsel "—*i.e.*, went on their own
stiff-necked way, instead of waiting for and following
God's merciful plan, which would have made them
secure and blessed. The end of such obstinacy of
disobedience can only be, " they were brought low
through their iniquity." The psalmist appears to be
quoting Lev. xxvi. 39, " they that are left of you shall
pine away in their iniquity " ; but he intentionally slightly
alters the word, substituting one of nearly the same
sound, but with the meaning of *being brought low*
instead of *fading away*. To follow one's own will
is to secure humiliation and degradation. Sin weakens
the true strength and darkens the true glory of men.

In vv. 44–46 the singer rises from these sad and
stern thoughts to recreate his spirit with the contemplation of the patient loving-kindness of God. It
persists through all man's sin and God's anger. The
multitude of its manifestations far outnumbers that of

our sins. His eye looks on Israel's distress with pity, and every sorrow on which He looks He desires to remove. Calamities melt away beneath His gaze, like damp-stains in sunlight. His merciful " look " swiftly follows the afflicted man's cry. No voice acknowledges sin and calls for help in vain. The covenant forgotten by men is none the less remembered by Him. The numberless number of His loving-kindnesses, greater than that of all men's sins, secures forgiveness after the most repeated transgressions. The law and measure of His " repenting" lie in the endless depths of His own heart. As the psalmist had sung at the beginning, that loving-kindness endures for ever ; therefore none of Israel's many sins went unchastised, and no chastisement outlasted their repentance. Solomon had prayed that God would " give them compassion before those who carried them captive " (1 Kings viii. 50) ; and thus has it been, as the psalmist joyfully sees. He may have written when the Babylonian captivity was near an end, and such instances as those of Daniel or Nehemiah may have been in his mind. In any case, it is beautifully significant that a psalm, which tells the doleful story of centuries of faithlessness, should end with God's faithfulness to His promises, His inexhaustible forgiveness, and the multitude of His loving-kindnesses. Such will be the last result of the world's history no less than of Israel's.

The psalm closes with the prayer in **ver. 47,** which shows that it was written in exile. It corresponds in part with the closing words of Psalm **cv.** Just as there the purpose of God's mercies to Israel was said to be that they might be thereby moved to keep His statutes, so here the psalmist hopes and vows that

the issue of his people's restoration will be thankfulness
to God's holy name, and triumphant pealing forth from
ransomed lips of His high praises.

Ver. 48 is the concluding doxology of the Fourth
Book.   Some commentators suppose it an integral part
of the psalm, but it is more probably an editorial
addition.

BOOK V.
PSALMS CVII—CL.

PSALM CVII.

1 **Give thanks to** Jehovah, for He is good,
   For His loving-kindness [endures] for **ever.**
2 Let the redeemed of Jehovah say [thus],
   Whom He has redeemed from the gripe of **distress,**
3 And gathered them from the lands,
   From east and west,
   From north and from [the] sea.

4 They wandered in the wilderness, in a waste of a way,
   An inhabited city they found not.
5 Hungry and thirsty,
   Their soul languished within them.
6 And they cried to Jehovah in their distress,
   From their troubles He delivered them,
7 And He led them by a straight way,
   To go to an inhabited city.
8 Let them give thanks to Jehovah [for] His loving-kindness,
   And His wonders to the sons of men.
9 For He satisfies the longing soul,
   And the hungry soul He fills with good.

10 Those who sat in darkness and in deepest gloom,
   Bound in affliction and iron,
11 Because they rebelled against the words of God,
   And the counsel of the Most High they rejected.
12 And He brought down their heart with sorrow,
   They stumbled, and helper there was none.
13 And they cried to Jehovah in their distress,
   From their troubles He saved them.
14 He brought them out from darkness and deepest gloom,
   And broke their bonds [asunder].
15 Let them give thanks to Jehovah [for] His loving-kindness,
   And His wonders to the sons of men.
16 For He broke the doors of brass,
   And the bars of iron He hewed in pieces.

17 Foolish men, because of the course of their transgression,
   And because of their iniquities, brought on themselves affliction.
18 All food their soul loathed,
   And they drew near to the gates of death.
19 And they cried to Jehovah in their distress,
   From their troubles He saved them.
20 He sent His word and healed them,
   And rescued them from their graves.
21 Let them give thanks to Jehovah [for] His loving-kindness
   And His wonders to the sons of men.
22 And let them offer sacrifices of thanksgiving,
   And tell His works with joyful joy.

23 They who go down to the sea in ships,
   Who do business on the great waters,
24 They see the works of Jehovah,
   And His wonders in the foaming deep.
25 And He spoke and raised a stormy wind,
   Which rolled high the waves thereof.
26 They went up to the sky, they went down to the depths,
   Their soul melted in trouble.
27 They went round and round and staggered like one drunk,
   And all their wisdom forsook them [was swallowed up].
28 And they cried to Jehovah in their distress,
   From their trouble He brought them out.
29 He stilled the storm into a light air,
   And hushed were their waves.
30 And they were glad because these were quieted,
   And He brought them to the haven of their desire.
31 Let them give thanks to Jehovah [for] His loving-kindness
   And His wonders to the sons of men.
32 And let them exalt Him in the assembly of the people,
   And praise Him in the session of the elders.

33 He turned rivers into a wilderness,
   And water-springs into thirsty ground,
34 A land of fruit into a salt desert,
   For the wickedness of the dwellers in it.
35 He turned a wilderness into a pool of water,
   And a dry land into water-springs.
36 And He made the hungry to dwell there,
   And they found an inhabited city.
37 And they sowed fields and planted vineyards,
   And these yielded fruits of increase.

38 And He blessed them and they multiplied exceedingly,
   And their cattle He diminished not.

39 And they were diminished and brought low,
   By the pressure of ill and sorrow.
40 "He pours contempt on princes,
   And makes them wander in a pathless waste.'
41 He lifted the needy out of affliction,
   And made families like a flock.
42 The upright see it and rejoice,
   And all perverseness stops its mouth.

43 Whoso is wise, let him observe these things,
   And let them understand the loving-kindnesses of Jehovah.

NOTWITHSTANDING the division of Books which separates Psalm cvii. from the two preceding, it is a pendant to these. The "gathering from among the heathen" prayed for in Psalm cvi. 41 has here come to pass (ver. 3). The thanksgiving which there is regarded as the purpose of that restoration is here rendered for it. Psalm cv. had for theme God's mercies to the fathers. Psalm cvi. confessed the hereditary faithlessness of Israel and its chastisement by calamity and exile. Psalm cvii. begins with summoning Israel as "the redeemed of Jehovah," to praise Him for His enduring loving-kindness in bringing them back from bondage, and then takes a wider flight, and celebrates the loving Providence which delivers, in all varieties of peril and calamity, those who cry to God. Its vivid pictures of distress and rescue begin, indeed, with one which may fairly be supposed to have been suggested by the incidents of the return from exile; and the second of these, that of the liberated prisoners, is possibly coloured by similar reminiscences; but the great restoration is only the starting-point, and the bulk of the psalm goes further afield. Its instances of Divine deliverance, though cast into narrative form, describe not specific

acts, but God's uniform way of working. Wherever
there are trouble and trust, there will be triumph and
praise.   The psalmist is propounding a partial solution of the old problem—the existence of pain and
sorrow.   They come as chastisements.   If terror or
misery drive men to God, God answers, and deliverance
is assured, from which fuller-toned praise should spring.
It is by no means a complete vindication of Providence,
and experience does not bear out the assumption of
uniform answers to prayers for deliverance from external calamities, which was more warranted before
Christ than it is now ; but the essence of the psalmist's
faith is ever true—that God hears the cry of a man
driven to cry by crushing burdens, and will give him
strength to bear and profit by them, even if He does
not take them away.

The psalm passes before us a series of pictures, all
alike in the disposition of their parts, and selected from
the sad abundance of troubles which attack humanity.
Travellers who have lost their way, captives, sick men,
storm-tossed sailors, make a strangely miscellaneous
company, the very unlikenesses of which suggest the
width of the ocean of human misery.   The artistic
regularity of structure in all the four strophes relating
to these cannot escape notice.   But it is more than
artistic.   Whatever be a man's trouble, there is but one
way out of it—to cry to God.   That way is never vain.
Always deliverance comes, and always the obligation of
praise lies on the " redeemed of Jehovah."

With ver. 33 the psalm changes its structure.   The
refrains, which came in so strikingly in the preceding
strophes, are dropped.   The complete pictures give
place to mere outline sketches.   These diversities have
suggested to some that vv. 33–43 are an excrescence ;

but they have some points of connection with the preceding, such as the peculiar phrase for "inhabited city"
(vv. 4, 5, 36), "hungry" (vv. 5, 36), and the fondness
for references to Isaiah and Job. In these latter verses
the psalmist does not describe deliverances from peril
or pain, but the sudden alternations effected by Providence on lands and men, which pass from fertility
and prosperity to barrenness and trouble, and again
from these to their opposites. Loving-kindness, which
hears and rescues, is the theme of the first part ; loving-
kindness, which "changes all things and is itself unchanged," is the theme of the second. Both converge
on the final thought (ver. 43), that the observance of
God's ways is the part of true wisdom, and will win
the clear perception of the all-embracing "loving-kindness of Jehovah."

New mercies give new meaning to old praises. Fresh
outpourings of thankfulness willingly run in well-worn
channels. The children can repeat the fathers' doxology,
and words hallowed by having borne the gratitude of
many generations are the best vehicles for to-day's
praise. Therefore, the psalm begins with venerable
words, which it bids the recipients of God's last great
mercy ring out once more. They who have yesterday
been "redeemed from captivity" have proof that "His
loving-kindness endures for ever," since it has come
down to them through centuries. The characteristic
fondness for quotations, which marks the psalm, is in
full force in the three introductory verses. Ver. 1 is,
of course, quoted from several psalms. "The redeemed
of Jehovah" is from Isa. lxii. 12. "Gathered out of the
lands" looks back to Psalm cvi. 47, and to many prophetic passages. The word rendered above "distress"
may mean *oppressor*, and is frequently rendered so here,

which rendering fits better the preceding word " hand."
But the recurrence of the same word in the subsequent
refrains (vv. 6, 13, 19, 28) makes the rendering *distress*
preferable here.   To ascribe to *distress* a " hand " is
poetical personification, or the latter word may be taken
in a somewhat wider sense as equivalent to a grasp or
grip, as above.   The return from Babylon is evidently
in the poet's thoughts, but he widens it out into a restoration from every quarter.   His enumeration of the points
from which the exiles flock is irregular, in that he says
" from north and from the *sea*," which always means the
Mediterranean, and stands for the west.   That quarter
has, however, already been mentioned, and, therefore,
it has been supposed that sea here means, abnormally,
the Red Sea, or " the southern portion of the Mediterranean."   A textual alteration has also been proposed,
which, by the addition of two letters to the word for
sea, gives that for *south*.   This reading would complete
the enumeration of cardinal points ; but possibly the
psalmist is quoting Isa. xlix. 12, where the same phrase
occurs, and the *north* is set over against the sea—*i.e.*, the
west.   The slight irregularity does not interfere with
the picture of the streams of returning exiles from
every quarter.

The first scene, that of a caravan lost in a desert, is
probably suggested by the previous reference to the
return of the "redeemed of Jehovah," but is not to be
taken as referring only to that.   It is a perfectly
general sketch of a frequent incident of travel.   It is
a remarkable trace of a state of society very unlike
modern life, that two of the four instances of " distress " are due to the perils of journeying.   By land
and by sea men took their lives in their hands, when
they left their homes.   Two points are signalised

in this description,—the first, the loss of the track; the second, the wanderers' hunger and thirst. "A waste of a way" is a singular expression, which has suggested various unnecessary textual emendations. It is like "a wild ass of a man" (Gen. xvi. 12), which several commentators quote as a parallel, and means a way which is desert (compare Acts viii. 26). The bewildered, devious march leads nowhither. Vainly the travellers look for some elevation,

> "From whence the lightened spirit sees
> That shady city of Palm Trees."

No place where men dwell appears in the wide expanse of pathless wilderness. The psalmist does not think of a particular city, but of any inhabited spot, where rest and shelter might be found. The water-skins are empty; food is finished; hopelessness follows physical exhaustion, and gloom wraps their souls; for ver. 5 *b*, literally translated, is, "Their soul covered itself"—*i.e.*, with despondency (Psalm lxxvii. 3).

The picture is not an allegory or a parable, but a transcript of a common fact. Still, one can scarcely help seeing in it a vivid representation of the inmost reality of a life apart from God. Such a life ever strays from the right road. "The labour of the foolish wearieth every one of them, because he knoweth not how to come to the city." The deepest needs of the soul are unsatisfied; and however outward good abounds, gnawing hunger and fierce thirst torment at times; and however mirth and success seem to smile, joys are superficial, and but mask a central sadness, as vineyards which clothe the outside of a volcano and lie above sulphurous fires.

The travellers are driven to God by their "distress." Happy they who, when lost in a desert, bethink themselves of the only Guide. He does not reject the cry which is forced out by the pressure of calamity; but, as the structure of vv. 6, 7, shows, His answer is simultaneous with the appeal to Him, and it is complete, as well as immediate. The track appears as suddenly as it had faded. God Himself goes at the head of the march. The path is straight as an arrow's flight, and soon they are in the city.

Ver. 6 is the first instance of the refrain, which, in each of the four pictures, is followed by a verse (or, in the last of the four, by two verses) descriptive of the act of deliverance, which again is followed by the second refrain, calling on those who have experienced such a mercy to thank Jehovah. This is followed in the first two groups by a verse reiterating the reason for praise— namely, the deliverance just granted; and, in the last two, by a verse expanding the summons. Various may be the forms of need. But the supply of them all is one, and the way to get it is one, and one is the experience of the suppliants, and one should be their praise. Life's diversities have underlying them identity of soul's wants. Waiters on God have very different outward fortunes, but the broad outlines of their inward history are identical. This is the law of His providence—they cry, He delivers. This should be the harvest from His sowing of benefits—" Let them give thanks to Jehovah." Some would translate ver. 8, " Let them thankfully confess to Jehovah His loving-kindness, and to the children of men [confess] His wonders "; but the usual rendering as above is better, as not introducing a thought which, however important, is scarcely in the psalmist's view here, and as preserving the great thought of the psalm—namely, that of God's providence to all mankind.

The second scene, that of captives, probably retains some allusion to Babylon, though an even fainter one than in the preceding strophe. It has several quotations and references to Isaiah, especially to the latter half (Isa. xl.–lxvi.). The deliverance is described in ver. 16 in words borrowed from the prophecy as to Cyrus, the instrument of Israel's restoration (Isa. xlv. 2). The gloom of the prison-house is described in language closely resembling Isa. xlii. **7**, xlix. 9. The combination of "darkness and the shade of deepest gloom" is found in Isa. ix. 2. The cause of the captivity described is rebellion against God's counsel and word. These things point to Israel's Babylonian bondage; but the picture in the psalm draws its colour rather than its subject from that event, and is quite general. The psalmist thinks that such bondage, and deliverance on repentance and prayer, are standing facts in Providence, both as regards nations and individuals. One may see, too, a certain parabolic aspect hinted at, as if the poet would have us catch a half-revealed intention to present calamity of any kind under this image of captivity. We note the slipping in of words that are not required for the picture, as when the fetters are said to be "affliction" as well as "iron." Ver. 12, too, is not specially appropriate to the condition of prisoners, persons in fetters and gloom do not *stumble*, for they do not move. There may, therefore, be a half-glance at the parabolic aspect of captivity, such as poetic imagination, and especially Oriental poetry, loves. At most it is a delicate suggestion, shyly hiding while it shows itself, and made too much of if drawn out in prosaic exposition.

We may perceive also the allegorical pertinence of

this second picture, though we do not suppose that the singer intended such a use. For is not godless life ever bondage? and is not rebellion against God the sure cause of falling under a harsher dominion? and does He not listen to the cry of a soul that feels the slavery of subjection to self and sin? and is not true enlargement found in His free service? and does He not give power to break the strongest chains of habit? The synagogue at Nazareth, where the carpenter's Son stood up to read and found the place where it was written, "The Spirit of the Lord is upon Me. . . . He hath sent Me to proclaim liberty to the captives," warrants the symbolical use of the psalmist's imagery, which is, as we have seen, largely influenced by the prophet whose words Jesus quoted. The first scene taught that devout hearts never lack guidance from God. The second adds to their blessings freedom, the true liberty which comes with submission and acceptance of His law.

Sickness, which yields the third type of suffering, is a commoner experience than the two preceding. The picture is lightly sketched, emphasis being laid on the cause of the sickness, which is sin, in accordance with the prevailing view in the Old Testament. The psalmist introduces the persons of whom he is to speak by the strongly condemnatory term "foolish ones," which refers not to intellectual feebleness, but to moral perversity. All sin is folly. Nothing is so insane as to do wrong. An ingenious correction has been suggested, and is accepted by Cheyne in the wake of Dyserinck, Graetz, and others, by which "sick men" is read for "foolish men." But it does not appear to the present writer to be so impossible as Cheyne thinks to "conceive the psalmist introducing a fresh tableau by an ethical term such as fools." The whole verse (17) lays more stress on the sin than on the sickness, and the initial designation of the sufferers as "fools" is quite in harmony with its tone. They are habitual evil-doers, as is expressed by the weighty expression "the way (or course) of their transgression." Not by one or two breaches of moral law, but by inveterate, customary sins, men ruin their physical health. So the psalmist uses a form of the verb in ver. 17 *b* which expresses that the sinner drags down his punishment with his own hands. That is, of course, eminently true in such gross forms of sin as sow to the flesh, and of the flesh reap corruption. But it is no less really true of all transgression, since all brings sickness to the soul. Ver. 18 is apparently quoted from Job xxxiii. 20-22. It paints with impressive simplicity the failing appetite and consequent ebbing strength. The grim portals, of which Death keeps the keys, have all but received the sick men; but, before they pass into their shadow, they cry to Jehovah, and, like the other men in distress, they too are heard, feeble as their sick voice may be. The manner of their deliverance is strikingly portrayed. "He sent His word and healed them." As in Psalm cv. 19, God's word is almost personified. It is the channel of the Divine power. God's uttered will has power on material things. It is the same great thought as is expressed in "He spake and it was done." The psalmist did not know the Christian teaching that the personal Word of God is the agent of all the Divine energy in the realm of nature and of history, and that a far deeper sense than that which he attached to them would one day be found in his words, when the Incarnate Word was manifested, as Himself bearing and bearing away the sicknesses of humanity, and rescuing not only the dying from going down to the grave, but bringing up the dead who had long lain there. God, who is Guide and Emancipator, is also Healer and Life-giver, and He is all these in the Word, which has become flesh, and dwelt and dwells among men.

Another travel-scene follows. The storm at sea is painted as a landsman would do it ; but a landsman who had seen, from a safe shore, what he so vividly describes. He is impressed with the strange things that the bold men who venture to sea must meet, away out there beyond the point where sea and sky touch With sure poetic instinct, he spends no time on trivial details, but dashes on his canvas the salient features of the tempest,—the sudden springing up of the gale ; the swift response of the waves rolling high, with new force in their mass and a new voice in their breaking ; the pitching craft, now on the crest, now in the trough ; the terror of the helpless crew ; the loss of steering power ; the heavy rolling of the unmanageable, clumsy ship ; and the desperation of the sailors, whose wisdom or skill was " swallowed up," or came to nothing.

Their cry to Jehovah was heard above the shriek of the storm, and the tempest fell as suddenly as it rose. The description of the deliverance is extended beyond the normal single verse, just as that of the peril had been prolonged. It comes like a benediction after the hurly-burly of the gale. How gently the words echo the softness of the light air into which it has died down, and the music which the wavelets make as they lap against the ship's sides ! With what sympathy the poet thinks of the glad hearts on board, and of their reaching the safe harbour, for which they had longed when they thought they would never see it more !

Surely it is a permissible application of these lovely
words to read into them the Christian hope of preservation amid life's tempests,—

> "Safe into the haven guide,
> O receive my soul at last."

God the guide, the emancipator, the healer, is also the
stiller of the storm, and they who cry to Him from the
unquiet sea will reach the stable shore. "And so it
came to pass, they all came safe to land."

As already observed, the tone changes with ver. 33,
from which point onwards the psalmist adduces instances of Providential working of a different kind from
those in the four vivid pictures preceding, and drops
the refrains. In vv. 33–38 he describes a double
change wrought on a land. The barrenness which
blasts fertile soil is painted in language largely borrowed from Isaiah. "Ver. 33 *a* recalls Isa. l. 2 *b*; ver.
33 *b* is like Isa. xxxv. 7 *a*" (Delitzsch). The opposite
change of desert into fertile ground is pictured as in
Isa. xli. 18. The references in ver. 36 to "the hungry"
and to "an inhabited city" connect with the previous
part of the psalm, and are against the supposition that
the latter half is not originally part of it. The incidents
described refer to no particular instance, but are as
general as those of the former part. Many a land,
which has been blasted by the vices of its inhabitants,
has been transformed into a garden by new settlers.
"Where the Turks' horse has trod, no grass will
grow."

Ver. 39 introduces the reverse, which often befalls
prosperous communities, especially in times when it is
dangerous to seem rich for fear of rapacious rulers.
"The pressure" referred to in ver 39 is the oppression
of such. If so, ver. 40, which is quoted from Job xii.

21, 24, though introduced abruptly, does not disturb the sequence of thought. It grandly paints the judgment of God on such robber-princes, who are hunted from their seats by popular execration, and have to hide themselves in the pathless waste, from which those who cry to God were delivered (vv. 41 *b* and 4 *a*). On the other hand, the oppressed are lifted, as by His strong arm, out of the depths and set on high, like a man perched safely on some crag above high-water mark. Prosperity returning is followed by large increase and happy, peaceful family life, the chief good of man on earth. The outcome of the various methods of God's unvarying purpose is that all which is good is glad, and all which is evil is struck dumb. The two clauses of ver. 42, which describe this double effect, are quoted from two passages in Job—*a* from xxii. 19, and *b* from v. 16.

The psalm began with hymning the enduring loving-kindness of Jehovah. It ends with a call to all who would be wise to give heed to the various dealings of God, as exemplified in the specimens chosen in it, that they may comprehend how in all these one purpose rules, and all are examples of the manifold loving-kindnesses of Jehovah. This closing note is an echo of the last words of Hosea's prophecy. It is the broad truth which all thoughtful observance of Providence brings home to a man, notwithstanding many mysteries and apparent contradictions. "All things work together for good to them that love God"; and the more they love Him, the more clearly will they see, and the more happily will they feel, that so it is. How can a man contemplate the painful riddle of the world, and keep his sanity, without that faith? He who has it for his faith will have it for his experience.

PSALM CVIII.

1 Steadfast is my heart, O God,
  I will sing and harp, yea, my glory [shall sing].
  Awake, harp and lute,
  I will wake the dawn.
3 I will give Thee thanks among the peoples, Jehovah,
  And I will harp to Thee among the nations.
4 For great above the heavens is Thy loving-kindness,
  And to the clouds Thy troth.
5 Exalt Thyself above the heavens, O God,
  And above all the earth Thy glory.

6 That Thy beloved ones may be delivered,
  Save with Thy right hand and answer me.
7 God has spoken in His holiness,
  I will divide Shechem and measure out the valley of Succoth.
8 Mine is Gilead, mine Manasseh,
  And Ephraim is the strength of my head,
  Judah my baton of command.
9 Moab is my wash-basin,
  Upon Edom will I throw my shoe,
  Over Philistia will I shout aloud.
10 Who will bring me into the fortified city?
  Who has guided me into Edom?
11 Hast not Thou, O God, cast us off,
  And goest not out, O God, with our hosts?
12 Give us help from trouble,
  For vain is help of man.
13 In God we shall do prowess,
  And He, He will tread down our oppressors.

TWO fragments of Davidic psalms are here tacked
together with slight variations. Vv. 1–5 are from
Psalm lvii. 7–11; and vv. 6–13 from Psalm lx. 5–12.

The return from Babylon would be an appropriate occasion for thus revivifying ancient words. We have seen in preceding psalms that Israel's past drew the thoughts of the singers of that period, and the conjecture may be hazarded that the recent deliverance suggested to some devout man, whose mind was steeped in the songs of former days, the closeness with which old strains suited new joys. If so, there is pathetic meaning in the summons to the " psaltery and harp," which had hung silent on the willows of Babylon so long, to wake their ancient minstrelsy once more, as well as exultant confidence that the God who had led David to victory still leads His people. The hopes of conquest in the second part, the consciousness that while much has been achieved by God's help, much still remains to be won before Israel can sit secure, the bar or two in the minor key in ver. 11, which heighten the exultation of the rest of the song, and the cry for help against adversaries too strong for Israel's unassisted might, are all appropriate to the early stages of the return.

The variations from the original psalms are of slight moment. In ver. 1 the reduplication of the clause " Steadfast is my heart " is omitted, and " my glory " is detached from ver. 2, where it stands in Psalm lvii., and is made a second subject, equivalent to " I." In ver. 3 *a Jehovah* is substituted for *Lord*, and the copula " and " prefixed to *b*. Ver. 4 is not improved by the change of " unto the heavens " to " above the heavens," for an anti-climax is produced by following " *above* the heavens " with " *unto* the clouds."

In the second part, the only change affecting the sense is in ver. 9, where the summons to Philistia to " shout aloud because of me," which is probably meant in sarcasm, is transformed into the plain expression of triumph, " Over Philistia will I shout aloud." The other changes are " me " for " us " in ver. 6, the omission of " and " before " mine Manasseh " in ver. 8, the substitution of a more usual synonym for " fenced " in ver. 10, and the omission of the pronoun " Thou " in ver. 11.

PSALM CIX.

1 God of my praise, be not silent,
2 For a wicked man's mouth and a mouth of deceit have they
    opened on me.
3 And with words of hate have they compassed me,
    And have fought [against] me causelessly.
4 In return for my love, they have been my adversaries,
    But I—I was [all] prayer.
5 And they have laid upon me evil in return for good,
    And hate in return for my love.

6 Set in office over him a wicked man,
    And may an adversary stand at his right hand !
7 When he is judged, let him go out guilty,
    And let his prayer be [counted] for sin !
8 Be his days few,
    His office may another take !
9 Be his children orphans,
    And his wife a widow !
10 And may his children wander up and down and beg,
    May they seek [bread] [far] from the ruins [of their house] !
11 May a creditor get into his nets all that he has,
    And may strangers plunder [the fruit of] his toil !
12 May there be no one to continue loving-kindness to him,
    And may there be no one that shows favour to his orphans !
13 May his posterity be cut off,
    In the next generation may their name be blotted out !
14 Let the iniquity of his fathers be remembered before Jehovah,
    And the sin of his mother not be blotted out !
15 May they be before Jehovah continually,
    And may He cut off their memory from the earth !

16 Because he remembered not to show loving-kindness,
    And persecuted the afflicted and poor man,
    And the heart-stricken, to do him to death.

17 And he loved cursing—and it came on him,
   And delighted not in blessing—and it remained far from him.
18 And he clothed himself [with] cursing like his garment,
   And it came like water into his inwards,
   And like oil into his bones.
19 May it be to him like a robe [with which] he covers himself,
   And for a girdle [which] he continually girds on !
20 Be this the wage of my adversaries from Jehovah,
   And of those who speak evil against my soul !

21 But Thou, Jehovah, Lord, deal with me for Thy name's sake,
   Because Thy loving-kindness is good, deliver me,
22 Because afflicted and poor am I,
   And my heart is pierced within me.
23 Like a shadow when it stretches out am I gone,
   I am shaken out, like the locust.
24 My knees give out through fasting,
   And my flesh falls away from fatness.
25 And I—I have become a reproach to them,
   They see me, they nod their head.
26 Help me, Jehovah, my God,
   Save me, according to Thy loving-kindness :
27 That they may know that this is Thy hand,
   Thou—Thou, Jehovah, hast done it.
28 They—they curse, but Thou—Thou dost bless ;
   They arose, and were put to shame,
   And Thy servant rejoices.
29 My adversaries clothe themselves [with] disgrace,
   And cover themselves like a mantle with their shame.
30 I will praise Jehovah greatly with my mouth,
   And amidst many will I praise Him.
31 For He stands at the right hand of the poor,
   To save him from those that judge his soul.

THIS is the last and the most terrible of the imprecatory psalms. Its central portion (vv. 6–20) consists of a series of wishes, addressed to God, for the heaping of all miseries on the heads of one "adversary" and of all his kith and kin. These maledictions are enclosed in prayers, which make the most striking contrast to them ; vv. 1–5 being the plaint of a loving soul, shrinkingly conscious of an atmosphere of hatred, and appealing gently to God ; while vv. 21–31 expatiate in the presentation to Him of the suppliant's feebleness and cries for deliverance, but barely touch on the wished-for requital of enemies. The combination of devout meekness and trust with the fiery imprecations in the core of the psalm is startling to Christian consciousness, and calls for an effort of " historical imagination " to deal with it fairly. The attempts to attenuate the difficulty, either by making out that the wishes are not wishes, but prophecies of the fate of evil-doers, or that vv. 6–20 are the psalmist'o quotation of his enemies' wishes about him, or that the whole is Messianic prediction of the fate of Judas or of the enemies of the Christ, are too obviously makeshifts. It is far better to recognise the discordance between the temper of the psalmist and that enjoined by Christ than to try to cover it over. Our Lord Himself has signalised the difference between His teaching and that addressed to "them of old time" on the very point of forgiveness of enemies, and we are but following His guidance when we recognise that the psalmist's mood is distinctly inferior to that which has now become the law for devout men.

Divine retribution for evil was the truth of the Old Testament, as forgiveness is that of the New. The conflict between God's kingdom and its enemies was being keenly and perpetually waged, in most literal fashion. Devout men could not but long for the triumph of that with which all good was associated, and therefore for the defeat and destruction of its opposite. For no private injuries, or for these only in so far as the suffering singer is a member of the community which represents God's cause, does he ask the descent of God's vengeance, but for the insults and hurts inflicted on righteousness. The form of these maledictions belongs to a lower stage of revelation; the substance of them, considered as passionate desires for the destruction of evil, burning zeal for the triumph of Truth, which is God's cause, and unquenchable faith that He is just, is a part of Christian perfection.

The usual variety of conjectures as to authorship exists. Delitzsch hesitatingly accepts the superscription as correct in assigning the psalm to David. Olshausen, as is his custom, says, " Maccabean "; Cheyne inclines to " the time of Nehemiah (in which case the enemy might be Sanballat), or even perhaps the close of the Persian age " (" Orig. of Psalt.," 65). He thinks that the " magnanimous David " could not have uttered " these laboured imprecations," and that the speaker is " not a brave and bold warrior, but a sensitive poet." Might he not be both ?

To address God as the " God of my praise," even at such a moment of dejection, is a triumph of faith. The name recalls to the psalmist past mercies, and expresses his confidence that he will still have cause to extol his Deliverer, while it also pleads with God what He has done as a reason for doing the like in new circumstances of need. The suppliant speaks in praise and prayer ; he asks God to speak in acts of rescuing power. A praying man cannot have a dumb God. And His mighty Voice, which hushes all others and sets His suppliants free from fears and foes, is all the more longed for and required, because of those cruel voices that yelp and snarl round the psalmist. The contrast between the three utterances—his, God's, and his enemies'—is most vivid. The foes have come at him with open mouths. " A wicked man's mouth " would read, by a slight alteration, " a mouth of wickedness" ; but the recurrence of the word "wicked man" in ver. 6 seems to look back to this verse, and to make the rendering above probable. Lies and hatred ring the psalmist round, but his conscience is clear. "They have hated me without a cause" is the experience of this ancient sufferer for righteousness' sake, as of the Prince of all such. This singer, who is charged with pouring out a flood of "unpurified passion," had, at any rate, striven to win over hatred by meekness ; and if he is bitter, it is the pain and bitterness of love flung back with contumely, and only serving to exacerbate enmity. Nor had he met with evil the first returns of evil for good, but, as he says, "I was [all] prayer" (compare Psalm cxx. 7, "I am—peace"). Repelled, his whole being turned to God, and in calm communion with Him found defence and repose. But his patient meekness availed nothing, for his foes still "laid evil" on him in return for good. The prayer is a short record of a long martyrdom. Many a foiled attempt of patient love preceded the psalm. Not till the other way had been tried long enough to show that malignity was beyond the reach of conciliation did the psalmist appeal to the God of recompenses. Let that be remembered in judging the next part of the psalm.

The terrible maledictions (vv. 6–20) need little commentary. They may be left in all their awfulness, which is neither to be extenuated nor degraded into an outburst of fierce personal vindictiveness. It is something far more noble than that. These terrible verses are prophecy, but they are prayers too ; and prayers which can only be accounted for by remembering the spirit of the old dispensation. They are the more intense, because they are launched against an individual, probably the chief among the foes. In vv. 6–15 we have imprecations pure and simple, and it is noteworthy that so large a part of these verses refers to the family of the evil-doer. In vv. 16–20 the grounds of the wished-for destruction are laid in the sinner's perverted choice, and the automatic action of sin working its own punishment is vividly set forth.

Vv. 6–8 are best taken in close connection, as representing the trial and condemnation of the object of the psalmist's imprecations, before a tribunal. He prays that the man may be haled before a wicked judge. The word rendered "set" is the root from which that rendered "office" in ver. 8 comes, and here means to set in a position of authority—*i.e.*, in a judicial one. His judge is to be "a wicked man" like himself, for such have no mercy on each other. An accuser is to stand at his right hand. The word rendered *adversary* (the verb cognate with which is used in ver. 4) is "Satan"; but the general meaning of hostile accuser is to be preferred here. With such a judge and prosecutor the issue of the cause is certain—"May he go out [from the judgment-hall] guilty." A more terrible petition follows, which is best taken in its most terrible sense. The condemned man cries for mercy, not to his earthly judge, but to God, and the psalmist can ask that the last despairing cry to Heaven may be unanswered, and even counted sin. It could only be so, if the heart that framed it was still an evil heart, despairing, indeed, but obdurate. Then comes the end: the sentence is executed. The criminal dies, and his office falls to another; his wife is a widow, and his children fatherless. This view of the connection gives unity to what is otherwise a mere heap of unconnected maledictions. It also brings out more clearly that the psalmist is seeking not merely the gratification of private animosity, but the vindication of public justice, even if ministered by an unjust judge. Peter's quotation of ver. 8 *b* in reference to Judas (Acts i. 20) does not involve the Messianic character of the psalm.

Vv. 10–15 extend the maledictions to the enemy's children and parents, in accordance with the ancient strong sense of family solidarity, which was often expressed in practice by visiting the kindred of a convicted criminal with ruin, and levelling his house with the ground. The psalmist wishes these consequences to fall in all their cruel severity, and pictures the children as vagabonds, driven from the desolation which had, in happier days, been their home, and seeking a scanty subsistence among strangers. The imprecations of ver. 11 at first sight seem to hark back to an earlier stage in the wicked man's career, contemplating him as still in life. But the wish that his wealth may be "ensnared" by creditors and stolen by strangers is quite appropriate as a consequence of his sentence and execution ; and the prayer in ver. 12. that there may be no one to "draw out loving-kindness" to him, is probably best explained by the parallel clause. A dead man lives a quasi-life in his children, and what is done to them is a prolongation of what was done to him. Thus helpless, beggars, homeless and plundered, "the seed of evil-doers" would naturally be short-lived, and the psalmist desires that they may be cut off, and the world freed from an evil race. His wishes go backwards too, and reach to the previous as well as the subsequent generation. The foe had come of a bad stock—parents, son, and son's sons are to be involved in a common doom, because partakers of a common sin. The special reason for the terrible desire that the iniquity of his father and mother may never be blotted out seems to be, the desire that the accumulated consequences of hereditary sin may fall on the heads of the third generation—a dread wish, which experience shows is often tragically fulfilled, even when the sufferers are far less guilty than their ancestors. "Father, forgive them" is the strongest conceivable contrast to these awful prayers. But the psalmist's petition implies that the sins in question were unrepented sins, and is, in fact, a cry that, as such, they should be requited in the "cutting off the memory" of such a brood of evil-doers "from the earth."

In ver. 16 a new turn of thought begins, which is pursued till ver. 20—namely, that of the self-retributive action of a perverted choice of evil. "He remembered not" to be gracious to him who needed compassion; therefore it is just that he should not be remembered on earth, and that his sin should be remembered in heaven. He deliberately chose cursing rather than blessing as his attitude and act towards others; therefore cursing comes to him and blessing remains far from him, as others' attitude and act to him. The world is a mirror which, on the whole, gives back the smile or the frown which we present to it. Though the psalmist has complained that he had loved and been hated in return, he does not doubt that, in general, the curser is cursed back again and the blesser blessed. Outwardly and inwardly, the man is wrapped in and saturated with "cursing." Like a robe or a girdle, it encompasses him; like a draught of water, it passes into his inmost nature; like anointing oil oozing into the bones, it steals into every corner of his soul. His own doings come back to poison him. The kick of the

gun which he fires is sure to hurt his own shoulder, and
it is better to be in front of the muzzle than behind the
trigger. The last word of these maledictions is not
only a wish, but a declaration of the Law of Divine
Retribution. The psalmist could not have found it in
his heart to pray such a prayer unless he had been
sure that Jehovah paid men's wages punctually in full,
and that conviction is the kernel of his awful words.
He is equally sure that his cause is God's—because he
is sure that God's cause is his, and that he suffers for
righteousness and for the righteous Jehovah.

The final part (vv. 21–31) returns to lowly, sad
petitions for deliverance, of the kind common to many
psalms. Very pathetically, and as with a tightening of
his grasp, does the singer call on his helper by the
double name " Jehovah, Lord," and plead all the pleas
with God which are hived in these names. The prayer
in ver. 21 *b* resembles that in Psalm lxix. 16, another
of the psalms of imprecation. The image of the long-
drawn-out shadow recurs in Psalm cii. 11. The word
rendered "am I gone" occurs here only, and implies
compulsory departure. The same idea of external force
hurrying one out of life is picturesquely presented in
the parallel clause. "I am shaken out," as a thing
which a man wishes to get rid of is shaken out of the
folds of a garment. The psalmist thinks of himself as
being whirled away, helpless, as a swarm of locusts
blown into the sea. The physical feebleness in ver. 24
is probably to be taken literally, as descriptive of the
havoc wrought on him by his persecutions and trouble
of soul, but may be, as often, metaphor for that trouble
itself.

The expression in ver. 24 *b* rendered above "*falls
away* from fatness" is literally " has become a liar," or

faithless, which is probably a picturesque way of saying that the psalmist's flesh had, as it were, become a rene-gade from its former well-nourished condition, and was emaciated by his sorrow.   Others would keep the literal meaning of the word rendered " fatness "—*i.e.*, oil—and translate " My flesh has shrunk up for lack of oil " (so Baethgen and Kay).

One more glance at the enemies, now again regarded as many, and one more flash of confidence that his prayer is heard, close the psalm.   Once again God is invoked by His name Jehovah, and the suppliant presses close to Him as " my God "; once again he casts himself on that loving-kindness, whose measure is wider than his thoughts and will ensure him larger answers than his desires ; once again he builds all his hope on it, and pleads no claims of his own.   He longs for personal deliverance ; but not only for personal ends, but rather that it may be an undeniable manifestation of Jehovah's power.   That is a high range of feeling which subordinates self to God even while longing for deliverance, and wishes more that He should be glorified than that self should be blessed.   There is almost a smile on the psalmist's face as he contrasts his enemies' curses with God's blessing, and thinks how ineffectual are these and how omnipotent is that.   He takes the issue of the strife between cursing men and a blessing God to be as good as already decided.   So he can look with new equanimity on the energetic preparations of his foes ; for he sees in faith their confusion and defeat, and already feels some springing in his heart of the joy of victory, and is sure of already clothing themselves with shame.   It is the prerogative of Faith to behold things that are not as though they were, and to live as in the hour of triumph even while in the thick of the fight.

The psalm began with addressing " the God of my *praise* "; it ends with the confidence and the vow that the singer will yet *praise* Him. It painted an adversary standing at the right hand of the wicked to condemn him ; it ends with the assurance that Jehovah stands at the right hand of His afflicted servant, as his advocate to protect him. The wicked man was to " go out guilty "; he whom God defends shall come forth from all that would judge his soul. " If God be for us, who can be against us ? It is God that justifieth : who is he that condemneth ? "

PSALM CX.

1 The oracle of Jehovah to my lord;
  Sit Thou [enthroned] at My right hand,
  Until I make Thine enemies the stool for Thy feet.
2 The sceptre of Thy might shall Jehovah stretch forth from Zion,
  "Rule Thou in the midst of Thine enemies."
3 Thy people are free-will offerings in the day of Thine army
  In holy attire,
  From the womb of the dawn,
  [Comes] to Thee the dew of Thy youth[s].
4 Jehovah has sworn and will not repent,
  Thou art a priest for ever,
  After the manner of Melchizedek.

5 The Lord at Thy right hand
  Has crushed kings in the day of His wrath.
6 He shall judge among the nations,
  He has filled [the land] with corpses,
  He has crushed the head over a wide land.
7 Of the brook shall He drink on the way,
  Therefore shall He lift up [His] head.

DOES our Lord's attribution of this psalm to David
foreclose the question of its authorship for those
who accept His authority? Many, who fully recognise
and reverently bow to that authority, think that it does
not, and appeal for support of their view to the unques-
tionable limitations of His earthly knowledge. It is
urged that His object in His argument with the
Pharisees, in which this psalm is quoted by Him
(Matt. xxii. 41–46 and parallels), is not to instruct them
on the authorship of the psalm, but to argue from its

contents; and though He assumes the Davidic authorship, accepted generally at the time, yet the cogency of
His argument is unimpaired, so long as it is recognised
that the psalm is a Messianic one, and that the august
language used in it of the Messiah is not compatible
with the position of One who was a mere human son of
David (Driver, "Introd.," p. 363, note).   So also Dr.
Sanday ("Inspiration," p. 420) says that "the Pharisees
were taken upon their own ground, and the fallacy of
their conclusion was shown on their own premises."
But our Lord's argument is not drawn from the
"august language" of the psalm, but from David's
relationship to the Messiah, and crumbles to pieces if
he is not the singer.   It may freely be admitted that
there are instances in our Lord's references to the Old
Testament in which He speaks from the point of view
of His hearers in regard to it; but these are cases in
which nothing turned on the question whether that
point of view was correct or not.   Here everything
turns on it; and to maintain that, in so important a
crisis, He based His arguments on an error comes
perilously near to imputing fallibility to Him as our
teacher.   Most of recent writers who advocate the
view in question would recoil from such a consequence;
but their position is divided from it by a thin line.
Whatever the limitations of our Lord's human knowledge, they did not affect His authority in regard to
what He did teach; and the present writer ventures to
believe that He did teach that *David* in this psalm
calls Messiah his Lord.

If so, the psalm stands alone, as not having primary
reference to an earthly king.   It is not, like other
Messianic psalms, typical, but directly prophetic of
Messiah, and of Him only.   We are not warranted

in denying the possibility of such direct prophecy; and the picture drawn in this psalm, so far transcending any possible original among the sons of men, has not full justice done to its majestic lines, unless it is recognised as setting forth none other than the personal Messiah. True, it is drawn with colours supplied from earthly experiences, and paints a warrior-monarch. The prophet-psalmist, no doubt, conceived of literal warfare; but a prophet did not always understand the oracles which he spoke.

The psalm falls into two parts: the Vision of the Priest-King and His army (vv. 1–4); the King's Warfare and Victory (vv. 5–7).

"The oracle of Jehovah" introduces a fresh utterance of God's, heard by the psalmist, who thus claims to be the mouthpiece of the Divine will. It is a familiar prophetic phrase, but usually found at the close—not, as here, at the beginning—of the utterance to which it refers (see, however, Isa. lvi. 8; Zech. xii. 1). The unusual position makes the Divine origin of the following words more emphatic. "My Lord" is a customary title of respect in addressing a superior, but not in speaking *of* him. Its use here evidently implies that the psalmist regards Messiah as his king, and the best comment on it is Matt. xxii. 43: "How then doth David in spirit call Him Lord?" The substance of the oracle follows. He who is exalted to sit at the right hand of a king is installed thereby as his associate in rule. He who is seated by God at His right hand is received into such mystery of participation in Divine authority and power, as cannot be imposed on frail humanity. The rigid monotheism of the Jewish singers makes this tremendous "oracle" the more remarkable. Greek gods might have their assessors from among

mortals, but who shall share Jehovah's throne?
"Solomon sat on the throne of the Lord as king"
(1 Chron. xxix. 23); but that is no parallel, nor does
it show that the oracle of this psalm simply states the
dignity of the theocratic king. Solomon's throne was
Jehovah's, as being established by Him, and since he
represented Jehovah on earth; but to sit at Jehovah's
right hand means far more than this. That session
of Messiah is represented as the prelude to the exercise
of Divine power for His triumph over His foes; and
that apparent repose, while Jehovah fights for him, is
singularly contrasted with his activity as described in
verses 6, 7. The singer speaks riddles about a union
of undisturbed tranquillity and of warlike strenuousness,
which are only solved when we see their fulfilment in
Him who sitteth at the right hand of God, and who yet
goes with His armies where they go. "He was received
up, and sat on the right hand of God, . . . the Lord
also working with them" (Mark xvi. 19, 20). The
opened heavens showed to Stephen his Master, not
sitting, but standing in the posture of readiness to help
him dying, and to receive him made more alive by death.
His foot shall be on the neck of His foes, as Joshua
bade the men of Israel put theirs on the conquered
kings'. Opposition shall not only be subdued, but shall
become subsidiary to Messiah's dominion, "a stepping-
stone to higher things."

The Divine oracle is silent, and the strain is taken
up by the psalmist himself, who speaks "in the
spirit," in the remainder of the psalm, no less than
he did when uttering Jehovah's word. Messiah's
dominion has a definite earthly centre. From Zion is
this King to rule. His mighty sceptre, the symbol and
instrument of His God-given power, is to stretch thence.

How far? No limit is named to the sweep of His
sway. But since Jehovah is to extend it, it must
be conterminous with the reach of His omnipotence.
Ver. 2 *b* may be taken as the words of Jehovah, but
more probably they are the loyal exclamation of the
psalmist, moved to his heart's depths by the vision
which makes the bliss of his solitude. The word
rendered "rule" is found also in Balaam's prophecy
of Messiah (Numb. xxiv. 19) and in the Messianic Psalm
lxxii. 8. The kingdom is to subsist in the midst of
enemies. The normal state of the Church on earth
is militant. Yet the enemies are not only a ring of
antagonists round a centre of submission, but into their
midst His power penetrates, and Messiah dominates
them too, for all their embattled hostility. A throne
round which storms of rebellion rage is an insecure
seat. But this throne is established through enmity,
because it is upheld by Jehovah.

The kingdom in relation to its subjects is the theme
of ver. 3, which accords with the warlike tone of the
whole psalm, by describing them as an army. The
period spoken of is " the day of Thy host," or array—
the time when the forces are mustered and set in order
for battle. The word rendered *free-will offerings* may
possibly mean simply "willingnesses," and the abstract
noun may be used as in "I am—prayer" (Psalm cix. 4)—
i.e., most willing ; but it is better to retain the fuller and
more picturesque meaning of glad, spontaneous sacrifices,
which corresponds with the priestly character afterwards
ascribed to the people, and goes very deep into the
essence of Christian service. There are to be no
pressed men or mercenaries in that host. As Deborah
sang of her warriors, these " offer themselves willingly."
Glad consecration of self, issuing in spontaneous enlist-

ing for the wars of the King, is to characterise all His subjects. The army is the nation. These soldiers are to be priests. They are clad in holy attire, " fine linen, clean and white." That representation goes as deep into the nature of the warfare they have to wage and the weapons they have to wield, as the former did into the impulse which sends them to serve under Messiah's flag. The priestly function is to bring God and man near to one another. Their warfare can only be for the carrying out of their office. Their weapons are sympathy, gentleness, purity. Like the Templars, the Christian soldier must bear the cross on his shield and the hilt of his sword. Another reading of this phrase is " on the holy mountains," which is preferred by many, among whom are Hupfeld and Cheyne. But the great preponderance of evidence is against the change, which obliterates a very striking and profound thought.

Ver. 3 *c, d* gives another picture of the host. The usual explanation of the clause takes " youth" as meaning, not the young vigour of the King, but, in a collective sense, the assembled warriors, whom it paints as in the bloom of early manhood. The principal point of comparison of the army with the dew is probably its multitude (2 Sam. xvii. 12). The warriors have the gift of un-aging youth, as all those have who renew their strength by serving Christ. And it is permissible to take other characteristics of the dew than its abundance, and to think of the mystery of its origin, of the tiny mirrors of the sunshine hanging on every cobweb, of its power to refresh, as well as of the myriads of its drops.

But this explanation, beautiful and deep as it is, is challenged by many. The word rendered " dawn" is unusual. "Youth" is not found elsewhere in the sense thus assigned to it. "Dew" is thought to be an infelicitous emblem. "From a linguistic point of view" Cheyne pronounces both "dawn" and "dew" to be intolerable. Singularly enough, in the next sentence, he deprecates a previous opinion of his own as premature "until we know something certain of the Hebrew of the Davidic age" ("Orig. of Psalt.," p. 482). But if such certainty is lacking, why should these two words be "intolerable"? He approves Bickell's conjectural emendation, "From the womb, from the dawn [of life], Thy youthful band is devoted to Thee."

Ver. 4 again enshrines a Divine utterance, which is presented in an even more solemn manner than that of ver. 1. The oath of Jehovah by Himself represents the thing sworn as guaranteed by the Divine character. God, as it were, pledges His own name, with its fulness of unchanging power, to the fulfilment of the word ; and this irrevocable and omnipotent decree is made still more impressive by the added assurance that He "will not repent." Thus inextricably intertwined with the augustness of God's nature, the union of the royal and priestly offices in the person of Messiah shall endure for ever. Some commentators contend that every theocratic king of Israel was a priest, inasmuch as he was king of a priestly nation. But since the national priestliness did not hinder the appointment of a special order of priests, it is most natural to assume that the special order is here referred to. Why should the singer have gone back into the mists of antiquity, in order to find the type of a priest-king, if the union of offices belonged, by virtue of his kinghood, to every Jewish monarch? Clearly the combination was un- exampled ; and such an incident as that of Uzziah's leprosy shows how carefully the two great offices were kept apart. Their opposition has resulted in many tragedies: probably their union would be still more fatal, except in the case of One whose priestly sacrifice of Himself as a willing offering is the basis of His royal sway. The "order of Melchizedek" has received unexpected elucidation from the Tel-el-Amarna tablets, which bring to light, as a correspondent of the Pharaoh, one Ebed-tob, king of Uru-salim (the city of Salim, the god of peace). In one of his letters he says, "Behold, neither my father nor my mother have exalted me in this place; the prophecy [or perhaps, arm] of the mighty King has caused me to enter the house of my father." By the mighty King is meant the god whose sanctuary stood on the summit of Mount Moriah. He was king of Jerusalem, because he was priest of its god (Sayce, "Criticism and the Monuments," p. 175). The psalm lays stress on the eternal duration of the royalty and priesthood of Messiah; and although in other Messianic psalms the promised perpetuity may be taken to refer to the dynasty rather than the individual monarch, that explanation is impossible here, where a person is the theme.

Many attempts have been made to fit the language of the psalm to one or other of the kings of Israel; but, not to mention other difficulties, this ver. 4 remains as an insuperable obstacle. In default of Israelite kings, one or other of the Maccabean family has been thought of. Cheyne strongly pronounces for Simon Maccabæus, and refers, as others have done, to a popular decree in his favour, declaring him "ruler and high priest for ever" ("Orig. of Psalt.," p. 26). On this identification, Baethgen asks if it is probable that the singer should have taken his theme from a popular decree, and have transformed it (*umgestempelt*) into a Divine oath.   It may be added that Simon was not a king, and that he was by birth a priest.

The second part of the psalm carries the King into the battle-field.   He comes forth from the throne, where He sat at Jehovah's right hand, and now Jehovah stands at His right hand.   The word rendered *Lord* in ver. 5 is never used of any but God, and it is best to take it so here, even though to do so involves the necessity of supposing a change in the subject either in ver. 6 or ver. 7, which latter verse can only refer to the Messiah.   The destructive conflict described is said to take place " in the day of His wrath "—*i.e.*, of Jehovah's.   If this is strictly interpreted, the period intended is not that of " the day of Thine army," when by His priestly warriors the Priest-King wages a warfare among His enemies, which wins them to be His lovers, but that dread hour when He comes forth from His ascended glory to pronounce doom among the nations and to crush all opposition.   Such a final apocalypse of the wrath of the Lamb is declared to us in clearer words, which may well be permitted to cast a light back on this psalm (Rev. xix. 11).   " He has crushed kings " is the perfect of prophetic certainty or intuition, the scene being so vividly bodied before the singer that he regards it as accomplished.   " He shall judge " or give doom " among the nations,"— the future of pure prediction.   Ver. 6 *b* is capable of various renderings.   It may be rendered as above, or the verb may be intransitive and the whole clause translated, *It becomes full of corpses* (so Delitzsch) ; or the word may be taken as an adjective, in which case the meaning would be the same as if it were an intransitive verb.   " The head over a wide land " is also ambiguous. If " head " is taken as a collective noun, it means rulers. But it may be also regarded as referring to a person, the principal antagonist of the Messiah. This is the explanation of many of the older interpreters, who think of Death or " the prince of this world," but is too fanciful to be adopted.

Ver. 7 is usually taken as depicting the King as pausing in His victorious pursuit of the flying foe, to drink, like Gideon's men, from the brook, and then with renewed vigour pressing on. But is not the idea of the Messiah needing refreshment in that final conflict somewhat harsh?—and may there not be here a certain desertion of the order of sequence, so that we are carried back to the time prior to the enthronement of the King? One is tempted to suggest the possibility of this closing verse being a full parallel with Phil. ii. 7–9. Christ on the way to His throne drank of " waters of affliction," and precisely therefore is He " highly exalted."

The choice for every man is, being crushed beneath His foot, or being exalted to sit with Him on His throne. " He that overcometh, to him will I give to sit down with Me on My throne, even as I also overcame, and am set down with My Father on His throne." It is better to sit on His throne than to be His footstool.

PSALM CXI.

Hallelujah.

1 א I will thank Jehovah with my whole heart,
  ב In the council of the upright and in the congregation.
2 ג Great are the works of Jehovah,
  ד Inquired into by all who delight in them.
3 ה Honour and majesty is His working,
  ו And His righteousness stands fast for aye.
4 ז He has made a memorial for His wonders,
  ח Gracious and compassionate is Jehovah.
5 ט Food has He given to those who fear Him,
  י He remembers His covenant for ever.
6 כ The power of His works has He showed to His people,
  ל In giving them the inheritance of the nations.
7 מ The works of His hands are truth and judgment
  נ Trustworthy are all His commandments;
8 ס Established for aye and for ever,
  ע Done in truth and uprightness.
9 פ Redemption has He sent to His people,
  צ He has ordained His covenant for ever,
  ק Holy and dread is His name.
10 ר The fear of Jehovah is the beginning of wisdom,
  ש Good understanding [belongs] to all who do them
  ת His praise stands fast for aye.

ANOTHER series of psalms headed with Hallelujah begins here, and includes the two following psalms. The prefix apparently indicates liturgical use. The present psalm is closely allied to the next. Both are acrostic, and correspond verse to verse, as will appear in the exposition. Together they represent God and the godly, this psalm magnifying the Divine character and acts, the other painting the ideal godly man as, in some real fashion, an "imitator of God as a beloved child." Both are gnomic, and built up by accumulation of slightly connected particulars, rather than flowing continuously in a sequence which springs from one pregnant thought. Both have allusions to other psalms and to the Book of Proverbs, and share with many of the psalms of Book V. the character of being mainly working over of old materials.

The Psalmist begins by a vow to thank Jehovah with his whole heart, and immediately proceeds to carry it out. "The upright" is by some understood as a national designation, and "council" taken as equivalent to "congregation." But it is more in accordance with usage to regard the psalmist as referring first to a narrower circle of like-minded lovers of good, to whose congenial ears he rejoices to sing. There was an Israel within Israel, who would sympathise with his song. The "congregation" is then either the wider audience of the gathered people, or, as Delitzsch takes it, equivalent to "*their* congregation"— *i.e.*, of the upright.

The theme of thanksgiving is, as ever, God's works for Israel ; and the first characteristic of these which the psalmist sings is their greatness. He will come closer presently, and discern more delicate features, but now, the magnitude of these colossal manifestations chiefly animates his song. Far-stretching in their mass and in their consequences, deep-rooted in God's own character, His great deeds draw the eager search of "those who delight in them." These are the same sympathetic auditors to whom the song is primarily addressed. There were indolent beholders in Israel, before whom the works of God were passed without exciting the faintest desire to know more of their depth. Such careless onlookers, who see and see not, are rife in all ages. God shines out in His deeds, and they will not give one glance of sharpened interest. But the test of caring for His doings is the effort to comprehend their greatness, and plunge oneself into their depths. The more one gazes, the more one sees. What was at first but dimly apprehended as great resolves itself, as we look ; and, first, " Honour and majesty," the splendour of His reflected character, shine out from His deeds, and then, when still more deeply they are pondered, the central fact of their righteousness, their conformity to the highest standard of rectitude, becomes patent. Greatness and majesty, divorced from righteousness, would be no theme for praise. Such greatness is littleness, such splendour is phosphorescent corruption.

These general contemplations are followed in vv. 4–6 by references to Israel's history as the greatest example of God's working. " He has made a memorial for His wonders." Some find here a reference to the Passover and other feasts commemorative of the deliverance from Egypt. But it is better to think of Israel itself as the " memorial," or of the deeds themselves, in their remembrance by men, as being, as it were, a monument of His power. The men whom God has blessed are standing evidences of His wonders. " Ye are My witnesses, saith the Lord." And the great attribute, which is commemorated by that " memorial," is Jehovah's gracious compassion. The psalmist presses steadily towards the centre of the Divine nature. God's works become eloquent of more and more precious truth as he listens to their voice. They spoke of greatness, honour, majesty, righteousness, but tenderer qualities are revealed to the loving and patient gazer. The two standing proofs of Divine kindness are the miraculous provision of food in the desert and the possession of the promised land. But to the psalmist these are not past deeds to be remembered only, but continually repeated operations. "He remembers His covenant for ever," and so the experiences of the fathers are lived over again by the children, and to-day is as full of God as yesterday was. Still He feeds *us*, still He gives us *our* heritage.

From ver. 7 onwards a new thought comes in. God has spoken as well as wrought. His very works carry messages of "truth and judgment," and they are interpreted further by articulate precepts, which are at once a revelation of what He is and a law for what we should be. His law stands as fast as His righteousness (vv. 3, 8). A man may utterly trust His commandments. They abide eternally, for Duty is ever Duty, and His Law, while it has a surface of temporary ceremonial, has a core of immutable requirement. His commandments are *done—i.e.*, appointed by Him—"in truth and uprightness." They are tokens of His grace and revelations of His character.

The two closing verses have three clauses each, partly from the exigencies of the acrostic structure, and partly to secure a more impressive ending. Ver. 9 sums up all God's works in the two chief manifestations of His goodness which should ever live in Israel's thanks, His sending redemption and His establishing His everlasting covenant—the two facts which are as fresh to-day, under new and better forms, as when long ago this unknown psalmist sang. And he gathers up the total impression which God's dealings should leave, in the great saying, "Holy and dread is His name." In ver. 10 he some-

what passes the limits of his theme, and trenches on
the territory of the next psalm, which is already
beginning to shape itself in his mind.   The designation
of the fear of the Jehovah as " the beginning of
wisdom " is from Prov. i. 7, ix. 10.   " Beginning"
may rather mean " principal part" (Prov. iv. 7, " principal thing ").   The " them " of ver. 10 *b* is best
referred, though the expression is awkward, to " commandments " in ver. 7.   Less probably it is taken to
allude to the " fear " and " wisdom " of the previous
clause.   The two clauses of this verse descriptive of
the godly correspond in structure to *a* and *b* of ver. 9,
and the last clause corresponds to the last of that verse,
expressing the continual praise which should rise to
that holy and dread Name.   Note that the perpetual
duration, which has been predicated of God's attributes,
precepts, and covenant (vv. 3, 5, 8, 9), is here ascribed to
His praise.   Man's songs cannot fall dumb, so long as
God pours out Himself in such deeds.   As long as that
Sun streams across the desert, stony lips will part in
music to hail its beams.

PSALM CXII.

Hallelujah.

1 א Happy the man who fears Jehovah,
  ב [Who] delights exceedingly in His **commandments.**
2 ג Mighty on the earth shall his seed be,
  ד The generation of the upright shall **be blessed.**
3 ה Wealth and riches are in his house,
  ו And his righteousness stands fast for aye.
4 ז There riseth in the darkness light to the upright,—
  ח Gracious and pitiful and righteous is he.
5 ט Well is the man who pities and lends,
  י He shall maintain his causes in [the] judgment.
6 כ For he shall not be moved for ever,
  ל In everlasting remembrance shall the righteous be held.
7 מ Of evil tidings he shall not be afraid,
  נ Steadfast is his heart, trusting in Jehovah.
8 ס Established is his heart, he shall not fear,
  ע Until he looks on his adversaries.
9 פ He has scattered abroad, he has given to the poor,
  צ His righteousness stands fast for aye,
  ק His horn shall be exalted with glory.
10 ר The wicked man shall see it and be grieved,
  ש He shall gnash his teeth and melt away,
  ת The desire of wicked men shall perish.

"BE ye perfect, as your Father in heaven is perfect," might be inscribed on this picture of a godly man, which, in structure and substance, reflects the contemplation of God's character and works contained in the preceding psalm. The idea that the godly man is, in some real sense, an image of God runs through the whole, and comes out strongly, at several points, in the repetition of the same expressions in reference to both. The portrait of the ideal good man, outlined in this psalm, may be compared with those in Psalms xv. and xxiv. Its most characteristic feature is the prominence given to beneficence, which is regarded as eminently a reflection of God's. The foundation of righteousness is laid in ver. 1, in devout awe and inward delight in the commandments. But the bulk of the psalm describes the blessed consequences, rather than the essential characteristics, of godliness.

The basis of righteousness and beneficence to men must be laid in reverence and conformity of will towards God. Therefore the psalm begins with proclaiming that, apart from all external consequences, these dispositions carry blessedness in themselves. The close of the preceding psalm had somewhat overpassed its limits, when it declared that "the fear of Jehovah" was the beginning of wisdom and that to do His commandments was sound discretion.

This psalm echoes these sayings, and so links itself to the former one. It deepens them by pointing out that the fear of Jehovah is a fountain of joy as well as of wisdom, and that inward delight in the Law must precede outward doing of it. The familiar blessing attached in the Old Testament to godliness, namely, prosperous posterity, is the first of the consequences of righteousness which the psalm holds out. That promise belongs to another order of things from that of the New Testament; but the essence of it is true still, namely, that the only secure foundation for permanent prosperity is in the fear of Jehovah. "The generation of the upright" (ver. 2) does not merely mean the natural descendants of a good man—"It is a moral rather than a genealogical term" (Hupfeld)—as is usually the case with the word "generation." Another result of righteousness is declared to be "wealth and riches" (ver. 3), which, again, must be taken as applying more fully to the Old Testament system of Providence than to that of the New.

A parallelism of the most striking character between God and the godly emerges in ver. 3 *b*, where the same words are applied to the latter as were used of the former, in the corresponding verse of Psalm cxi. It would be giving too great evangelical definiteness to the psalmist's words, to read into them the Christian teaching that man's righteousness is God's gift through Christ, but it unwarrantably eviscerates them of their meaning, if we go to the other extreme, and, with Hupfeld, suppose that the psalmist put in the clause under stress of the exigencies of the acrostic structure, and regard it as a "makeshift" and "stop-gap." The psalmist has a very definite and noble thought. Man's righteousness is the reflection of God's ; and has in it some kindred with its original, which guarantees stability not all unlike the eternity of that source. Since ver. 3 *b* thus brings into prominence the ruling thought of the two psalms, possibly we may venture to see a fainter utterance of that thought, in the first clause of the verse, in which the "wealth and riches" in the righteous man's house may correspond to the "honour and majesty" attendant on God's works (cxi. 3 *a*).

Ver. 4 blends consequences of righteousness and characterisation of it, in a remarkable way. The construction is doubtful. In *a*, "upright" is in the plural, and the adjectives in *b* are in the singular number. They are appended abruptly to the preceding clause ; and the loose structure has occasioned difficulty

to expositors, which has been increased by the scruples
of some, who have not given due weight to the leading
thought of correspondence between the human and
Divine, and have hesitated to regard ver. 4 *b* as
referring to the righteous man, seeing that in Psalm
cxi. 4 *b* it refers to God.   Hence efforts have been
made to find other renderings.   Delitzsch would refer
the clause to God, whom he takes to be meant by
" light " in the previous clause, while Hitzig, followed
by Baethgen, would translate, " As a light, he (the
righteous) rises in darkness for the upright," and
would then consider " gracious," etc., as in apposition
with " light," and descriptive of the righteous man's
character as such.   But the very fact that the words
are applied to God in the corresponding verse of
the previous psalm suggests their application here to
the godly man, and the sudden change of number is
not so harsh as to require the ordinary translation to
be abandoned.   However dark may be a good man's
road, the very midnight blackness is a prophecy of
sunrise ; or, to use another figure,

"If winter comes, can spring be far behind?"

(Compare Psalm xcvii. 11.)   The fountain of pity in
human hearts must be fed from the great source of
compassion in God's, if it is to gush out unremittingly
and bless the deserts of sorrow and misery.   He who
has received " grace " will surely exercise grace.   " Be
ye merciful, even as your Father is merciful " (Luke
vi. 36).

Ver. 5 blends characteristics and consequences of
goodness in reverse order from that in ver. 4.   The
compassionate man of ver. 4 *b* does not let pity evapo-
rate, but is moved by it to act and to lend (primarily

money, but secondarily) any needful help or solace. Benevolence which is not translated into beneficence is a poor affair. There is no blessing in it or for it; but it is well with the man who turns emotions into deeds. Lazy compassion hurts him who indulges in it, but that which "lends" gets joy in the act of bestowing aid. The result of such active compassion is stated in ver. 5 *b* as being that such a one will "maintain his causes in judgment," by which seems to be meant the judgment of earthly tribunals. If compassion and charity guide a life, it will have few disputes, and will contain nothing for which a judge can condemn. He who obeys the higher law will not break the lower.

Vv. 6–8 dwell mainly on one consequence of righteousness, namely, the stability which it imparts. While such a man lives, he shall be unmoved by shocks, and after he dies, his memory will live, like a summer evening's glow which lingers in the west till a new morning dawns. In ver. 7 the resemblance of the godly to God comes very beautifully to the surface. Psalm cxi. 7 deals with God's commandments as "trustworthy." The human parallel is an *established* heart. He who has learned to lean upon Jehovah (for such is the literal force of "trusting" here), and has proved the commandments utterly reliable as basis for his life, will have his heart steadfast. The same idea is repeated in ver. 8 with direct quotation of the corresponding verse of Psalm cxi. In both the word for "established" is the same. The heart that delights in God's established commandments is established by them, and, sooner or later, will look in calm security on the fading away of all evil things and men, while it rests indeed, because it rests in God. He who builds his transient life on and into the Rock of Ages wins rocklike steadfastness, and some share in the perpetuity of his Refuge. Lives rooted in God are never uprooted.

The two final verses are elongated, like the corresponding ones in Psalm cxi. Again, beneficence is put in the forefront, as a kind of shorthand summing up of all virtues. And, again, in ver. 9 the analogy is drawn out between God and the godly. "He has sent redemption to His people"; and they, in their degree, are to be communicative of the gifts of which they have been made recipient. Little can they give, compared with what they have received; but what they have they hold in trust for those who need it, and the sure test of having obtained "redemption" is a "heart open as day to melting charity." In the former psalm, ver. 9 *b* declared that God has "ordained His covenant for ever"; and here the corresponding clause re-affirms that the good man's righteousness endures for ever. The final clauses of both verses also correspond, in so far as, in the former psalm, God's Name is represented as "holy and dread"—*i.e.*, the total impression made by His deeds exalts Him —and in the latter, the righteous man's "horn" is represented as "exalted in glory" or honour—*i.e.*, the total impression made by his deeds exalts *him*. Paul quotes the two former clauses of ver. 9 in 2 Cor. ix. 9 as involving the truth that Christian giving does not impoverish. The exercise of a disposition strengthens it; and God takes care that the means of beneficence shall not be wanting to him who has the spirit of it. The later Jewish use of "righteousness" as a synonym for *almsgiving* has probably been influenced by this psalm, in which beneficence is the principal trait in the righteous man's character, but there is no reason for supposing that the psalmist uses the word in that restricted sense.

Ver. 10 is not parallel with the last verse of Psalm cxi., which stands, as we have seen, somewhat beyond the scope of the rest of that psalm. It gives one brief glimpse of the fate of the evil-doer, in opposition to the loving picture of the blessedness of the righteous. Thus it too is rather beyond the immediate object of the psalm of which it forms part. The wicked *sees*, in contrast with the righteous man's *seeing* in ver. 8. The one looks with peace on the short duration of antagonistic power, and rejoices that there is a God of recompenses ; the other grinds his teeth in envious rage, as he beholds the perpetuity of the righteous. He "shall melt away," *i.e.*, in jealousy or despair. Opposition to goodness, since it is enmity towards God, is self-condemned to impotence and final failure. Desires turned for satisfaction elsewhere than to God are sure to perish. The sharp contrast between the righteousness of the good man, which endures for ever, in his steadfast because trustful heart, and the crumbling schemes and disappointed hopes which gnaw the life of the man whose aims go athwart God's will, solemnly proclaims an eternal truth. This psalm, like Psalm i., touches the two poles of possible human experience, in its first and last words, beginning with " happy the man " and ending with " shall perish."

PSALM CXIII.

Hallelujah.

1 Praise, ye servants of Jehovah,
  Praise the name of Jehovah.
2 Be the name of Jehovah blessed
  From henceforth and for evermore!
3 From the rising of the sun to its going down,
  Praised be the name of Jehovah.

4 High above all nations is Jehovah,
  Above the heavens His glory.
5 Who is like Jehovah our God?
  Who sits enthroned on high,
6 Who looks far below
  On the heavens and on the earth;

7 Who raises the helpless from the dust,
  From the rubbish-heap He lifts the needy,
8 To seat him with nobles,
  With the nobles of His people;
9 Who seats the barren [woman] in a house,
  —A glad mother of her children.

THIS pure burst of praise is the first of the psalms composing the Hallel, which was sung at the three great feasts (Passover, Pentecost, and the Feast of Tabernacles), as well as at the festival of Dedication and at the new moons. "In the domestic celebration of the Passover night 'the Hallel' is divided into two parts; the one half, Psalms cxiii., cxiv., being sung before the repast, before the emptying of the second festal cup, and the other half, Psalms cxv.-cxviii., after

the repast, after the filling of the fourth cup, to which
the 'having sung an hymn' in Matt. xxvi. 30, Mark
xiv. 26, . . . may refer" (Delitzsch, *in loc.*).

Three strophes of three verses each may be recognised, of which the first summons Israel to praise
Jehovah, and reaches out through all time and over all
space, in longing that God's name may be known and
praised. The second strophe (vv. 4–6) magnifies God's
exalted greatness; while the third (vv. 7–9) adores
His condescension, manifested in His stooping to lift
the lowly. The second and third of these strophes,
however, overlap in the song, as the facts which they
celebrate do. God's loftiness can never be adequately
measured, unless His condescension is taken into
account; and His condescension never sufficiently
wondered at, unless His loftiness is felt.

The call to praise is addressed to Israel, whose
designation "servants of Jehovah" recalls Isaiah II.'s
characteristic use of that name in the singular number
for the nation. With strong emphasis, the *name* of
Jehovah is declared as the theme of praise. God's
revelation of His character by deed and word must
precede man's thanksgiving. They, to whom that
Name has been entrusted, by their reception of His
mercies are bound to ring it out to all the world. And
in the Name itself, there lies enshrined the certainty
that through all ages it shall be blessed, and in every
spot lit by the sun shall shine as a brighter light, and
be hailed with praises. The psalmist has learned the
world-wide significance of Israel's position as the
depository of the Name, and the fair vision of a
universal adoration of it fills his heart. Ver. 3 *b* may
be rendered "worthy to be praised is the name," but
the context seems to suggest the rendering above.

The infinite exaltation of Jehovah above all dwellers
on this low earth and above the very heavens does not
lift Him too high for man's praise, for it is wedded to
condescension as infinite.   Incomparable is He ; but
still adoration can reach Him, and men do not clasp
mist, but solid substance, when they grasp His Name.
That incomparable uniqueness of Jehovah is celebrated
in ver. 5 *a* in strains borrowed from Exod. xv. 11, while
the striking description of loftiness combined with condescension in vv. 5 *b* and 6 resembles Isa. lvii. 15.
The literal rendering of vv. 5 *b* and 6 *a* is, " Who
makes high to sit, Who makes low to behold," which is
best understood as above.   It may be questioned whether
" On the heavens and on the earth " designates the
objects on which His gaze is said to be turned ; or
whether, as some understand the construction, it is to
be taken with " Who is like Jehovah our God ? " the
intervening clauses being parenthetical ; or whether, as
others prefer, " in heaven " points back to "enthroned
on high," and " on earth " to " looks far below."   But
the construction which regards the totality of created
things, represented by the familiar phrase " the heavens
and the earth," as being the objects on which Jehovah
looks down from His inconceivable loftiness, accords
best with the context and yields an altogether worthy
meaning.   Transcendent elevation, condescension, and
omniscience are blended in the poet's thought.   So
high is Jehovah that the highest heavens are far
beneath Him, and, unless His gaze were all-discerning,
would be but a dim speck.   That He should enter into
relations with creatures, and that there should be
creatures for Him to enter into relations with, are due
to His stooping graciousness.   These far-darting looks
are looks of tenderness, and signify care as well as

knowledge. Since all things lie in His sight, all receive from His hand.

The third strophe pursues the thought of the Divine condescension as especially shown in stooping to the dejected and helpless and lifting them. The effect of the descent of One so high must be to raise the lowliness to which He bends. The words in vv. 7, 8, are quoted from Hannah's song (1 Sam. ii. 8). Probably the singer has in his mind Israel's restoration from exile, that great act in which Jehovah had shown His condescending loftiness, and had lifted His helpless people as from the ash-heap, where they lay as outcasts. The same event seems to be referred to in ver. 9, under a metaphor suggested by the story of Hannah, whose words have just been quoted. The "barren" is Israel (comp. Isa. liv. 1). The expression in the original is somewhat obscure. It stands literally "the barren of the house," and is susceptible of different explanations; but probably the simplest is to regard it as a contracted expression for the unfruitful wife in a house, "a housewife, but yet not a mother. Such an one has in her husband's house no sure position. . . . If God bestows children upon her, He by that very fact makes her for the first time thoroughly at home and rooted in her husband's house" (Delitzsch, *in loc.*). The joy of motherhood is tenderly touched in the closing line, in which the definite article is irregularly prefixed to "sons," as if the poet "points with his finger to the children with whom God blesses her" (Delitzsch, *u.s.*). Thus Israel, with her restored children about her, is secure in her home. That restoration was the signal instance of Jehovah's condescension and delight in raising the lowly. It was therefore the great occasion for world-wide and age-long praise.

The singer did not know how far it would be tran-scended by a more wonderful, more heart-touching manifestation of stooping love, when " The Word became flesh." How much more exultant and world-filling should be the praises from the lips of those who do know how low that Word has stooped, how high He has risen, and how surely all who hold His hand will be lifted from any ash-heap and set on His throne, sharers in the royalty of Him who has been partaker of their weakness!

PSALM CXIV.

1 When Israel went forth from Egypt,
The house of Jacob from a stammering people
2 Judah became His sanctuary,
Israel His dominion.

3 The sea beheld and fled,
Jordan turned back.
4 The mountains leaped like rams,
The hills like the sons of a flock.

5 What ails thee, Sea, that thou fleest?
Jordan, that thou art turned back?
6 Mountains, that ye leap like rams?
Hills, like the sons of a flock?

7 At the presence of the Lord, writhe in pangs, O earth,
At the presence of the God of Jacob,
8 Who turns the rock into a pool of water,
The flint into a fountain of waters.

IT is possible that in this psalm Israel, restored from Babylon, is looking back to the earlier Exodus, and thrilling with the great thought that that old past lives again in the present. Such a historical parallel would minister courage and hope. But the eyes of psalmists were ever turning to the great days when a nation was born, and there are no data in this psalm which connect it with a special period, except certain peculiarities in the form of the words "turns" and "fountain" in ver. 8, both of which have a vowel appended (*i* in the former, *o* in the latter word), which is probably an archaism, used by a late poet for ornament's sake. The same peculiarity is found in Psalm cxiii. 5–9, where it occurs five times.

A familiar theme is treated here with singular force and lyric fervour. The singer does not heap details together, but grasps one great thought. To him there are but two outstanding characteristics of the Exodus one, its place and purpose as the beginning of Israel's prerogative, and another, its apocalypse of the Majesty of Jehovah, the Ruler of Nature in its mightiest forms. These he hymns, and then leaves them to make their own impression. He has no word of "moral," no application, counsel, warning, or encouragement to give. Whoso will can draw these. Enough for him to lift his soaring song, and to check it into silence in the midst of its full music. He would be a consummate artist, if he were not something much better. The limpid clearness, the eloquent brevity of the psalm are not more obvious than its masterly structure. Its four pairs of verses, each laden with one thought, the dramatic vividness of the sudden questions in the third pair, the skilful suppression of the Divine name till the close, where it is pealed out in full tones of triumph, make this little psalm a gem.

In vv. 1, 2, the slighting glance at the land left by the ransomed people is striking. The Egyptians are to this singer "a stammering people," talking a language which sounded to him barely articulate. The word carries a similar contempt to that in the Greek "barbarian," which imitates the unmeaning babble of a foreign tongue. To such insignificance in the psalmist's mind had the once dreaded oppressors sunk ! The great fact about the Exodus was that it was the birthday of the Nation, the beginning of its entrance on its high prerogatives. If the consecration of Judah as

" His sanctuary " took place when Israel went forth from Egypt, there can be no reference to the later erection of the material sanctuary in Jerusalem, and the names of Judah and Israel must both apply to the people, not to the land, which it would be an anachronism to introduce here. That deliverance from Egypt was in order to God's dwelling in Israel, and thereby sanctifying or setting it apart to Himself, "a kingdom of priests and an holy nation." Dwelling in the midst of them, He wrought wonders for them, as the psalm goes on to hymn ; but this is the grand foundation fact, that Israel was brought out of bondage to be God's temple and kingdom. The higher deliverance of which that Exodus is a foreshadowing is, in like manner, intended to effect a still more wonderful and intimate indwelling of God in His Church. Redeemed humanity is meant to be God's temple and realm.

The historical substratum for vv. 3, 4, is the twin miracles of drying up the Red Sea and the Jordan, which began and closed the Exodus, and the "quaking" of Sinai at the Theophany accompanying the giving of the Law. These physical facts are imaginatively conceived as the effects of panic produced by some dread vision ; and the psalmist heightens nis representation by leaving unnamed the sight which dried the sea, and shook the steadfast granite cliffs. In the third pair of verses he changes his point of view from that of narrator to that of a wondering spectator, and asks what terrible thing, unseen by him, strikes such awe ? All is silent now, and the wonders long since past. The sea rolls its waters again over the place where Pharaoh's host lie. Jordan rushes down its steep valley as of old, the savage peaks of Sinai know no tremors ;—but these momentary wonders proclaimed an eternal truth.

So the psalmist answers his own question, and goes beyond it in summoning the whole earth to tremble, as sea, river, and mountain had done, for the same Vision before which they had shrunk is present to all Nature. Now the psalmist can peal forth the Name of Him, the sight of whom wrought these wonders. It is "the Lord," the Sovereign Ruler, whose omnipotence and plastic power over all creatures were shown when His touch made rock and flint forget their solidity and become fluid, even as His will made the waves solid as a wall. and His presence shook Sinai. He is still Lord of Nature. And, more blessed still, the Lord of Nature is the God of Jacob. Both these names were magnified in the two miracles (which, like those named in ver. 3, are a pair) of giving drink to the thirsty pilgrims. With that thought of omnipotence blended with gracious care, the singer ceases. He has said enough to breed faith and hearten courage, and he drops his harp without a formal close. The effect is all the greater, though some critics prosaically insist that the text is defective and put a row or two of asterisks at the end of ver. 8, " since it is not discernible what purpose the representation [*i.e.*, the whole psalm] is to serve " (Graetz)!

PSALM CXV.

1 Not to us, not to us, Jehovah,
  But to Thy name give glory,
  For the sake of Thy lovingkindness, for the sake of Thy troth.
2 Why should the nations say,
  "Where, then, is their God?"

3 But our God is in the heavens,
  Whatsoever He willed, He has done.
4 Their idols are silver and gold,
  The work of the hands of men.
5 A mouth is theirs—and they cannot speak,
  Eyes are theirs—and they cannot see,
6 Ears are theirs—and they cannot hear,
  A nose is theirs—and they cannot smell.
7 Their hands—[with them] they cannot handle
  Their feet—[with them] they cannot walk,
  Not a sound can they utter with their throat.
8 Like them shall those who make them be,
  [Even] every one that trusts in them.

9 Israel, trust thou in Jehovah,
    Their help and shield is He.
10 House of Aaron, trust in Jehovah,
    Their help and shield is He.
11 Ye who fear Jehovah, trust in Jehovah,
    Their help and shield is He.

12 Jehovah has remembered us—He will bless,
    He will bless the house of Israel,
    He will bless the house of Aaron,
13 He will bless those who fear Jehovah,
    The small as well as the great.

14 Jehovah will add to you,
   To you and to your children.
15 Blessed be ye of Jehovah,
   Who made heaven and earth!

16 The heavens are Jehovah's heavens,
   But the earth He has given to the children of men.
17 It is not the dead who praise Jehovah,
   Neither all they who descend into silence.
18 But we—we will bless Jehovah,
   From henceforth and for evermore.

Hallelujah.

ISRAEL is in straits from heathen enemies, and cries to Jehovah to vindicate His own Name by delivering it. Strengthened by faith, which has been stung into action by taunts aimed at both the nation and its Protector, the psalmist triumphantly contrasts Jehovah in the heavens, moving all things according to His will, with idols which had the semblance of powers the reality of which was not theirs. Sarcastic contempt, indignation, and profound insight into the effect of idolatry in assimilating the worshipper to his god, unite in the picture (vv. 3–8). The tone swiftly changes into a summons to withdraw trust from such vanities, and set it on Jehovah, who can and will bless His servants (vv. 9–15); and the psalm closes with recognition of Jehovah's exaltation and beneficence, and with the vow to return blessing to Him for the blessings, already apprehended by faith, which He bestows on Israel.

Obviously the psalm is intended for temple worship, and was meant to be sung by various voices. The distribution of its parts may be doubtful. Ewald would regard vv. 1–11 as the voice of the congregation while the sacrifice was being offered; vv. 12–15 as that of the priest announcing its acceptance; and vv. 16–18 as again the song of the congregation. But there is plainly a change of singer at ver. 9 ; and the threefold summons to trust in Jehovah in the first clauses of vv. 9, 10, 11, may with some probability be allotted to a ministering official, while the refrain, in the second clause of each of these verses, may be regarded as pealed out with choral force. The solo voice next pronounces the benediction on the same three classes to whom it had addressed the call to trust. And the congregation, thus receiving Jehovah's blessing, sends back its praise, as sunshine from a mirror, in vv. 16–18.

The circumstances presupposed in the psalm suit many periods of Israel's history. But probably this, like the neighbouring psalms, is a product of the early days after the return from Babylon, when the feeble settlers were ringed round by scoffing foes, and had brought back from exile a more intimate knowledge and contemptuous aversion for idols and idolatry than had before been felt in Israel. Cheyne takes the psalm to be Maccabean, but acknowledges that there is nothing in it to fix that date, which he seeks to establish for the whole group mainly because he is sure of it for one member of the group, namely, Psalm cxviii. (*Orig. of Psalt.*, 18 *sq.*).

The prayer in vv. 1, 2, beautifully blends profound consciousness of demerit and confidence that, unworthy as Israel is, its welfare is inextricably interwoven with Jehovah's honour. It goes very deep into the logic of supplication, even though the thing desired is but deliverance from human foes. Men win their pleas with God, when they sue *in formâ pauperis*. There must be thorough abnegation of all claims based on self, before there can be faithful urging of the one prevalent motive, God's care for His own fair fame.

The under side of faith is self-distrust, the upper side
is affiance on Jehovah.   God has given pledges for His
future by His past acts of self-revelation, and cannot
but be true to His Name.   His lovingkindness is no
transient mood, but rests on the solid basis of His
faithfulness, like flowers rooted in the clefts of a rock.
The taunts that had tortured another psalmist long
before (Psalm xlii. 3) have been flung now from heathen
lips, with still more bitterness, and call for Jehovah's
thunderous answer.   If Israel goes down before its
foes, the heathen will have warrant to scoff.

But, from their bitter tongues and his own fears,
the singer turns, in the name of the sorely harassed
congregation, to ring out the proclamation which answers
the heathen taunt, before God answers it by deeds.
" Our God is in heaven "—that is where He is ; and
He is not too far away to make His hand felt on earth.
He is no impotent image ; He does what He wills,
executing to the last tittle His purposes ; and conversely,
He wills what He does, being constrained by no
outward force, but drawing the determinations of His
actions from the depths of His being.   Therefore, whatever evil has befallen Israel is not a sign that it has
lost Him, but a proof that He is near.   The brief,
pregnant assertion of God's omnipotence and sovereign
freedom, which should tame the heathens' arrogance
and teach the meaning of Israel's disasters, is set in
eloquent opposition to the fiery indignation which
dashes off the sarcastic picture of an idol.   The tone
of the description is like that of the manufacture of an
image in Isa. xliv. 9–20.   Psalm cxxxv. 15–18 repeats
it verbatim.   The vehemence of scorn in these verses
suggests a previous, compelled familiarity with idolatry
such as the exiles had.   It corresponds with the

revolution which that familiarity produced, by extirpating for ever the former hankering after the gods of the nations. No doubt, there are higher weapons than sarcasm ; and, no doubt, a Babylonian wise man could have drawn distinctions between the deity and its image, but such cobwebs are too fine-spun for rough fingers to handle, and the idolatry both of pagans and of Christians identifies the two.

But a deeper note is struck in ver. **8**, in the assertion that, as is the god, so becomes the worshipper. The psalmist probably means chiefly, if not exclusively, in respect to the impotence just spoken of. So the worshipper and his idol are called by the same name (Isa. xliv. 9, *vanity*), and, in the tragic summary of Israel's sins and punishment in 2 Kings xvii. 15, it is said, that "they followed after vanity and became vain." But the statement is true in a wider sense. Worship is sure to breed likeness. A lustful, cruel god will make his devotees so. Men make gods after their own image, and, when made, the gods make men after theirs. The same principle which degrades the idolater lifts the Christian to the likeness of Christ. The aim and effect of adoration is assimilation.

Probably the congregation is now silent, and a single voice takes up the song, with the call, which the hollowness of idolatry makes so urgent and reasonable, to trust in Jehovah, not in vanities. It is thrice repeated, being first addressed to the congregation, then to the house of Aaron, and finally to a wider circle, those who "fear Jehovah." These are most naturally understood as proselytes, and, in the prominence given to them, we see the increasing consciousness in Israel of its Divine destination to be God's witness to the world. Exile had widened the horizon, and fair hopes that men who were not of Israel's blood would share Israel's faith and shelter under the wings of Israel's God stirred in many hearts. The crash of the triple choral answer to the summons comes with magnificent effect, in the second clauses of vv. 9, 10, 11, triumphantly telling how safe are they who take refuge behind that strong buckler. The same threefold division into *Israel, house of Aaron*, and *they who fear Jehovah* occurs in Psalm cxviii. 2–4, and, with the addition of "house of Levi," in Psalm cxxxv.

Promises of blessing occupy vv. 12–15, which may probably have been sung by priests, or rather by Levites, the musicians of the Temple service. In any case, these benedictions are authoritative assurances from commissioned lips, not utterances of hopeful faith. They are Jehovah's response to Israel's obedience to the preceding summons; swiftly sent, as His answers ever are. Calm certainty that He will bless comes at once into the heart that deeply feels that He is its shield, however His manifestation of outward help may be lovingly delayed. The blessing is parted among those who had severally been called to trust, and had obeyed the call. Universal blessings have special destinations. The fiery mass breaks up into cloven tongues, and sits on each. Distinctions of position make no difference in its reception. Small vessels are filled, and great ones can be no more than full. Cedars and hyssop rejoice in impartial sunshine. Israel, when blessed, increases in number, and there is an inheritance of good from generation to generation. The seal of such hopes is the Name of Him who blesses, "the Maker of heaven and earth," to whose omnipotent, universal sway these impotent gods in human form are as a foil.

Finally, we may hear the united voices of the congregation thus blessed breaking into full-throated praise in vv. 16–18. As in ver. 3 God's dwelling in heaven symbolised His loftiness and power, so here the thought that "the heavens are Jehovah's heavens" implies both the worshippers' trust in His mighty help and their lowliness even in trust. The earth is man's, but by Jehovah's gift. Therefore its inhabitants should remember the terms of their tenure, and thankfully recognise His giving love. But heaven and earth do not include all the universe. There is another region, the land of silence, whither the dead descend. No voice of praise wakes its dumb sleep. (Comp. Isa. xxxviii. 18, 19.) That pensive contemplation, on which the light of the New Testament assurance of Immortality has not shone, gives keener edge to the bliss of present ability to praise Jehovah. We who know that to die is to have a new song put into immortal lips may still be stimulated to fill our brief lives here with the music of thanksgiving, by the thought that, so far as our witness for God to men is concerned, most of us will "descend into silence" when we pass into the grave. Therefore we should shun silence, and bless Him while we live here.

PSALM CXVI.

1 I love—for Jehovah hears
   My voice, my supplications.
2 For He has bent His ear to me,
   And throughout my days will I call.
3 The cords of death ringed me round,
   And the narrows of Sheol found me,
   Distress and trouble did I find.
4 And on the name of Jehovah I called,
   "I beseech Thee, Jehovah, deliver my soul."

5 Gracious is Jehovah and righteous,
   And our God is compassionate.
6 The keeper of the simple is Jehovah,
   I was brought low and He saved me.
7 Return, my soul, to thy rest,
   For Jehovah has lavished good on thee.
8 For Thou hast delivered my soul from death,
   My eye from tears,
   My foot from stumbling.
9 I shall walk before Jehovah in the lands of the living.

10 I believed when I [thus] spake,
   "I am greatly afflicted."
11 I said in my agitation,
   "All men deceive."
12 What shall I return to Jehovah,
   [For] all His goodness lavished on me?
13 The cup of salvations will I lift,
   And on the name of Jehovah will I call.
14 My vows will I repay to Jehovah,
   Oh! may I [do it] before all His people!

15 Precious in the eyes of Jehovah
   Is the death of His favoured ones.

16 I beseech Thee, Jehovah—for I am Thy servant,
  I am Thy servant, the son of Thy handmaid,
  Thou hast loosed my bonds.
17 To Thee will I offer a sacrifice of thanksgiving,
  And on the name of Jehovah will I call.
18 My vows will I repay to Jehovah,
  Oh! may I [do it] before all His people!
19 In the courts of the house of Jehovah,
  In the midst of thee, Jerusalem.

Hallelujah.

THIS psalm is intensely individual. "I," "me," or "my" occurs in every verse but two (vv. 5, 19). The singer is but recently delivered from some peril, and his song heaves with a ground-swell of emotion after the storm. Hupfeld takes offence at its "continual alternation of petition and recognition of the Divine beneficence and deliverance, or vows of thanksgiving," but surely that very blending is natural to one just rescued and still panting from his danger. Certain grammatical forms indicate a late date, and the frequent allusions to earlier psalms point in the same direction. The words of former psalmists were part of this singer's mental furniture, and came to his lips, when he brought his own thanksgivings. Hupfeld thinks it "strange" that "such a patched-up (*zusammengestoppelter*) psalm" has "imposed" upon commentators, who speak of its depth and tenderness; it is perhaps stranger that its use of older songs has imposed upon so good a critic and hid these characteristics from him. Four parts may be discerned, of which the first (vv. 1–4) mainly describes the psalmist's peril; the second (vv. 5–9), his deliverance; the third glances back to his alarm and thence draws reasons for his vow of praise (vv. 10–14); and the fourth bases the same vow on the remembrance of Jehovah's having loosed his bonds.

The early verses of Psalm xviii. obviously colour the psalmist's description of his distress. That psalm begins with an expression of love to Jehovah, which is echoed here, though a different word is employed. "I love" stands in ver. 1 without an object, just as "I will call" does in ver. 2, and "I believed" and "I spoke" in ver. 10. Probably "Thee" has fallen out, which would be the more easy, as the next word begins with the letter which stands for it in Hebrew. Cheyne follows Graetz in the conjectural adoption of the same beginning as in ver. 10, "I am confident." This change necessitates translating the following "for" as "that," whereas it is plainly to be taken, like the "for" at the beginning of ver. 2, as causal. Ver. 3 is moulded on Psalm xviii. 5, with a modification of the metaphors by the unusual expression "the narrows of Sheol." The word rendered *narrows* may be employed simply as = distress or straits, but it is allowable to take it as picturing that gloomy realm as a confined gorge, like the throat of a pass, from which the psalmist could find no escape. He is like a creature caught in the toils of the hunter Death. The stern rocks of a dark defile have all but closed upon him, but, like a man from the bottom of a pit, he can send out one cry before the earth falls in and buries him. He cried to Jehovah, and the rocks flung his voice heavenwards. Sorrow is meant to drive to God. When cries become prayers, they are not in vain. The revealed character of Jehovah is the ground of a desperate man's hope. His own Name is a plea which Jehovah will certainly honour. Many words are needless when peril is sore and the suppliant is sure of God. To name Him and to cry for deliverance are enough. "I beseech Thee" represents a particle which is used frequently in this psalm, and by some peculiarities in its use here indicates a late date.

The psalmist does not pause to say definitely that he was delivered, but breaks into the celebration of the Name on which he had called, and from which the certainty of an answer followed. Since Jehovah is gracious, righteous (as strictly adhering to the conditions He has laid down), and merciful (as condescending in love to lowly and imperfect men), there can be no doubt how He will deal with trustful suppliants. The psalmist turns for a moment from his own experience to sun himself in the great thought of the Name, and thereby to come into touch with all who share his faith. The cry for help is wrung out by personal need, but the answer received brings into fellowship with a great multitude. Jehovah's character leads up in ver. 6 to a broad truth as to His acts, for it ensures that He cannot but care for the "simple," whose simplicity lays them open to assailants, and whose single-hearted adhesion to God appeals unfailingly to His heart. Happy the man who, like the psalmist, can give confirmation from his own experience to the broad truths of God's protection to ingenuous and guileless souls! Each individual may, if he will, thus narrow to his own use the widest promises, and put " I " and " me " wherever God has put " whosoever." If he does he will be able to turn his own experience into universal maxims, and encourage others to put " whosoever " where his grateful heart has put " I " and " me."

The deliverance, which is thus the direct result of the Divine character, and which extends to all the simple, and therefore included the psalmist, leads to calm repose. The singer does not say so in cold words, but beautifully wooes his "soul," his sensitive nature, which had trembled with fear in death's net, to come back to its rest. The word is in the plural, which may be only another indication of late date, but is more worthily understood as expressing the completeness of the repose, which in its fulness is only found in God, and is made the more deep by contrast with previous "agitation."

Vv. 8, 9, are quoted from Psalm lvi. 13 with slight variations, the most significant of which is the change of "light" into "lands." It is noticeable that the Divine deliverance is thus described as surpassing the psalmist's petition. He asked, "Deliver my soul." Bare escape was all that he craved, but he received, not only the deliverance of his soul from death, but, over and above, his tears were wiped away by a loving hand, his feet stayed by a strong arm. God over-answers trustful cries, and does not give the minimum consistent with safety, but the maximum of which we are capable. What shall a grateful heart do with such benefits? "I will walk before Jehovah in the lands of the living," joyously and unconstrainedly (for so the form of the word "walk" implies), as ever conscious of that presence which brings blessedness and requires holiness. The paths appointed may carry the traveller far, but into whatever lands he goes, he will have the same glad heart within to urge his feet and the same loving eye above to beam guidance on him.

The third part (vv. 10–14) recurs to the psalmist's mood in his trouble, and bases on the retrospect of that and of God's mercy the vow of praise. Ver. 10 may be variously understood. The "speaking" may be taken as referring to the preceding expressions of trust or thanksgivings for deliverance. The sentiment would then be that the psalmist was confident that he should

one day thus speak. So Cheyne ; or the rendering may
be " I believed in that I spake thus "—*i.e.*, that he spake
those trustful words of ver. 9 was the result of sheer
faith (so Kay). The thing spoken may also be the
expressions which follow, and this seems to yield the
most satisfactory meaning. " Even when I said, I am
afflicted and men fail me, I had not lost my faith." He
is re-calling the agitation which shook him, but feels
that, through it all, there was an unshaken centre of
rest in God. The presence of doubt and fear does not
prove the absence of trust. There may live a spark of
it, though almost buried below masses of cold unbelief.
What he said was the complaint that he was greatly
afflicted, and the bitter wail that all men deceive or
disappoint. He said so in his agitation (Psalm xxxi. 22).
But even in recognising the folly of trusting in men,
he was in some measure trusting God, and the trust,
though tremulous, was rewarded.

Again he hurries on to sing the issues of deliverance,
without waiting to describe it. That little dialogue of the
devout soul with itself (vv. 12, 13) goes very deep. It
is an illuminative word as to God's character, an eman-
cipating word as to the true notion of service to Him,
a guiding word as to common life. For it declares that
men honour God most by taking His gifts with recognition of the Giver, and that the return which He in
His love seeks is only our thankful reception of His
mercy. A giver who desires but these results is
surely Love. A religion which consists first in accepting God's gift and then in praising by lip and life Him
who gives banishes the religion of fear, of barter, of
unwelcome restrictions and commands. It is the exact
opposite of the slavery which says, " Thou art an
austere man, reaping where thou didst not sow." It

is the religion of which the initial act is faith, and the continual activity, the appropriation of God's spiritual gifts.   In daily life there would be less despondency and weakening regrets over vanished blessings, if men were more careful to take and enjoy thankfully all that God gives.   But many of us have no eyes for other blessings, because some one blessing is withdrawn or denied.   If we treasured all that is given, we should be richer than most of us are.

In ver. 14 the particle of beseeching is added to "before," a singular form of expression which seems to imply desire that the psalmist may come into the temple with his vows.   He may have been thinking of the "sacrificial meal in connection with the peace-offerings."   In any case, blessings received in solitude should impel to public gratitude.   God delivers His suppliants that they may magnify Him before men.

The last part (vv. 15-19) repeats the refrain of ver. 14, but with a different setting.   Here the singer generalises his own experience, and finds increase of joy in the thought of the multitude who dwell safe under the same protection.   The more usual form of expression for the idea in ver. 15 is "their *blood* is precious" (Psalm lxxii. 14).   The meaning is that the death of God's saints is no trivial thing in God's eyes, to be lightly permitted. (Compare the contrasted thought, xliv. 12.)   Then, on the basis of that general truth, is built ver. 16, which begins singularly with the same beseeching word which has already occurred in vv. 4 and 14.   Here it is not followed by an expressed petition, but is a yearning of desire for continued or fuller manifestation of God's favour.   The largest gifts, most fully accepted and most thankfully recognised, still leave room for longing which is not pain, because it is conscious of tender relations with

God that guarantee its fulfilment. " I am Thy servant."
Therefore the longing which has no words needs none.
" Thou hast loosed my bonds." His thoughts go back
to " the cords of death " (ver. 3), which had held him
so tightly. God's hand has slackened them, and, by
freeing him from that bondage, has bound him more
closely than before to Himself. " Being made free
from sin, ye became the slaves of righteousness." So,
in the full blessedness of received deliverance, the
grateful heart offers itself to God, as moved by His
mercies to become a living sacrifice, and calls on the
Name of Jehovah, in its hour of thankful surrender, as
it had called on that Name in its time of deep distress.
Once more the lonely suppliant, who had waded such
deep waters without companion but Jehovah, seeks to
feel himself one of the glad multitude in the courts of
the house of Jehovah, and to blend his single voice in
the shout of a nation's praise. We suffer and struggle
for the most part alone. Grief is a hermit, but Joy is
sociable; and thankfulness desires listeners to its
praise. The perfect song is the chorus of a great
" multitude which no man can number."

PSALM CXVII.

1 Praise Jehovah, all nations,
  Laud Him, all peoples.
2 For great is His lovingkindness over us,
  And the troth of Jehovah endures for ever.

Hallelujah.

THIS shortest of the psalms is not a fragment, though some MSS. attach it to the preceding and some to the following psalm. It contains large "riches in a narrow room," and its very brevity gives force to it. Paul laid his finger on its special significance, when he quoted it in proof that God meant His salvation to be for the whole race. Jewish narrowness was an after-growth and a corruption. The historical limitations of God's manifestation to a special nation were means to its universal diffusion. The fire was gathered in a grate, that it might warm the whole house. All men have a share in what God does for Israel. His grace was intended to fructify through it to all The consciousness of being the special recipients of Jehovah's mercy was saved from abuse, by being united with the consciousness of being endowed with blessing that they might diffuse blessing.

Nor is the psalmist's thought of what Israel's experience proclaimed concerning God's character less noteworthy. As often, lovingkindness is united with troth or faithfulness as twin stars which shine out in all God's dealings with His people. That loving-kindness is "mighty over us"—the word used for *being mighty* has the sense of *prevailing*, and so "where sin abounded, grace did much more abound." The permanence of the Divine Lovingkindness is guaranteed by God's Troth, by which the fulfilment of every promise and the prolongation of every mercy are sealed to men. These two fair messengers have appeared in yet fairer form than the psalmist knew, and the world has to praise Jehovah for a world-wide gift, first bestowed on and rejected by a degenerate Israel, which thought that it owned the inheritance, and so lost it.

PSALM CXVIII.

1 Give thanks to Jehovah, for He is good,
  For His lovingkindness endures for ever.
2 O let Israel say,
  That His lovingkindness endures for ever.
3 O let the house of Aaron say,
  That His lovingkindness endures for ever.
4 O let those who fear Jah say,
  That His lovingkindness endures for ever.

5 Out of the strait place I called on Jah,
  Jah answered me [by bringing me out] into an open place.
6 Jehovah is for me, I will not fear,
  What can man do to me ?
7 Jehovah is for me, as my helper,
  And I shall gaze on my haters.

8 Better is it to take refuge in Jehovah
  Than to trust in man.
9 Better is it to take refuge in Jehovah
  Than to trust in princes.

10 All nations beset me round about ;
  In the name of Jehovah will I cut them down.
11 They have beset me round about, yea, round about beset me ;
  In the name of Jehovah will I cut them down.
12 They beset me round about like bees,
  They were extinguished like a thorn fire;
  In the name of Jehovah will I cut them down.
13 Thou didst thrust sore at me that I might fall,
  But Jehovah helped me.
14 Jah is my strength and song,
  And He is become my salvation.

15 The sound of shrill shouts of joy and salvation is [heard] in
    the tents of the righteous;
  The right hand of Jehovah does prowess.
16 The right hand of Jehovah is exalted,
  The right hand of Jehovah does prowess.

17 I shall not die, but live,
  And I tell forth the works of Jah.
18 Jah has chastened me sore,
  But to death He has not given me up.
19 Open ye to me the gates of righteousness,
  I will go in by them, I will thank Jah.

20 This is the gate of Jehovah:
  The righteous may go in by it.

21 I will thank Thee, for Thou hast answered me
  And art become my salvation.

22 The stone [which] the builders rejected
  Is become the head [stone] of the corner.
23 From Jehovah did this come to pass,
  It is wonderful in our eyes.
24 This is the day [which] Jehovah has made,
  Let us leap for joy and be glad in it.

25 O, I beseech Thee, Jehovah, save, I beseech;
  O, I beseech Thee, Jehovah, give prosperity.

26 Blessed be he that comes in the name of Jehovah,
  We bless you from the house of Jehovah.
27 Jehovah is God, and He has given us light;
  Order the bough-bearing procession,—
  To the horns of the altar!

28 My God art Thou, and I will thank Thee,
  My God, I will exalt Thee.

29 Give thanks to Jehovah, for He is good,
  For His lovingkindness endures for ever.

THIS is unmistakably a psalm for use in the Temple worship, and probably meant to be sung antiphonally, on some day of national rejoicing (ver. 24). A general concurrence of opinion points to the period of the Restoration from Babylon as its date, as in the case of many psalms in this Book V., but different events connected with that restoration have been selected. The psalm implies the completion of the Temple, and therefore shuts out any point prior to that. Delitzsch fixes on the dedication of the Temple as the occasion ; but the view is still more probable which supposes that it was sung on the great celebration of the Feast of Tabernacles, recorded in Neh. viii. 14–18. In later times ver. 25 was the festal cry raised while the altar of burnt-offering was solemnly compassed, once on each of the first six days of the Feast of Tabernacles, and seven times on the seventh. This seventh day was called the " Great Hosanna ; and not only the prayers at the Feast of Tabernacles, but even the branches of osiers (including the myrtles), which are bound to the palm branch (*Lulab*), were called Hosannas " (Delitzsch). The allusions in the psalm fit the circumstances of the time in question. Stier, Perowne, and Baethgen concur in preferring this date : the last-named critic, who is very slow to recognise indications of specific dates, speaks with unwonted decisiveness, when he writes, " I believe that I can say with certainty, Psalm cxviii. was sung for the first time at the Feast of Tabernacles in the year 444 B.C." Cheyne follows his usual guides in pointing to the purification and reconstruction of the Temple by Judas Maccabæus as " fully adequate to explain alike the tone and the expressions." He is " the terrible hero," to whose character the refrain, " In the name, of Jehovah I will cut them down," corresponds. But the allusions in the psalm are quite as appropriate to any other times of national jubilation and yet of danger, such as that of the Restoration, and

Judas the Maccabee had no monopoly of the warrior trust which flames in that refrain.

Apparently the psalm falls into two halves, of which the former (vv. 1–16) seems to have been sung as a processional hymn while approaching the sanctuary, and the latter (vv. 17–29), partly at the Temple gates, partly by a chorus of priests within, and partly by the procession when it had entered. Every reader recognises traces of antiphonal singing ; but it is difficult to separate the parts with certainty. A clue may possibly be found by noting that verses marked by the occurrence of " I," " me," and " my " are mingled with others more impersonal. The personified nation is clearly the speaker of the former class of verses, which tells a connected story of distress, deliverance, and grateful triumph ; while the other less personal verses generalise the experience of the first speaker, and sustain substantially the part of the chorus in a Greek play. In the first part of the psalm we may suppose that a part of the procession sang the one and another portion the other series ; while in the second part (vv. 17–29) the more personal verses were sung by the whole *cortège* arrived at the Temple, and the more generalised other part was taken by a chorus of priests or Levites within the sanctuary. This distribution of verses is occasionally uncertain, but on the whole is clear, and aids the understanding of the psalm.

First rings out from the full choir the summons to praise, which peculiarly belonged to the period of the Restoration (Ezra iii. 11 ; Psalms cvi. 1, cvii. 1). As in Psalm cxv., three classes are called on : the whole house of Israel, the priests, and "those who fear Jehovah"—*i.e.*, aliens who have taken refuge beneath the wings of Israel's God. The threefold designation expresses the thrill of joy in the recovery of national life ; the high estimate of the priesthood as the only remaining God-appointed order, now that the monarchy was swept away ; and the growing desire to draw the nations into the community of God's people.

Then, with ver. 5, the single voice begins. His experience, now to be told, is the reason for the praise called for in the previous verses. It is the familiar sequence reiterated in many a psalm and many a life,— distress, or "a strait place" (Psalm cxvi. 3), a cry to Jehovah, His answer by enlargement, and a consequent triumphant confidence, which has warrant in the past for believing that no hand can hurt him whom Jehovah's hand helps. Many a man passes through the psalmist's experience without thereby achieving the psalmist's settled faith and power to despise threatening calamities. We fail both in recounting clearly to ourselves our deliverances and in drawing assurance from them for the future. Ver. 5 *b* is a pregnant construction. He "answered me in [or, into] an open place"—*i.e.*, by bringing me into it. The contrast of a narrow gorge and a wide plain picturesquely expresses past restraints and present freedom of movement. Ver. 6 is taken from Psalm lvi. 9, 11 ; and ver. 7 is influenced by Psalm liv. 4, and reproduces the peculiar expression occurring there, "Jehovah is among my helpers,"—on which compare remarks on that passage.

Vv. 8, 9, are impersonal, and generalise the experience of the preceding verses. They ring out loud, like a trumpet, and are the more intense for reiteration. Israel was but a feeble handful. Its very existence seemed to depend on the caprice of the protecting kings who had permitted its return. It had had bitter experience of the unreliableness of a monarch's whim

Now, with superb reliance, which was felt by the psalmist to be the true lesson of the immediate past, it peals out its choral confidence in Jehovah with a " heroism of faith which may well put us to the blush." These verses surpass the preceding in that they avow that faith in Jehovah makes men independent of human helpers, while the former verses declared that it makes superior to mortal foes. Fear of and confidence in man are both removed by trust in God. But it is perhaps harder to be weaned from the confidence than to rise above the fear.

The individual experience is resumed in vv. 10—14. The energetic reduplications strengthen the impression of multiplied attacks, corresponding with the facts of the Restoration period. The same impression is accentuated by the use in ver. 11 *a* of two forms of the same verb, and in ver. 12 *a* by the metaphor of a swarm of angry bees (Deut. i. 44). Numerous, venomous, swift, and hard to strike at as the enemies were, buzzing and stinging around, they were but insects after all, and a strong hand could crush them. The psalmist does not merely look to God to interpose for him, as in vv. 6, 7, but expects that God will give him power to conquer by the use of his own strengthened arm. We are not only objects of Divine protection, but organs of Divine power. Trusting in the revealed character of Jehovah, we shall find conquering energy flowing into us from Him, and the most fierce assaults will die out as quickly as a fire of dry thorn twigs, which sinks into ashes the sooner the more it crackles and blazes. Then the psalmist individualises the multitude of foes, just as the collective Israel is individualised, and brings assailants and assailed down to two antagonists, engaged in desperate duel. But a third Person intervenes. "Jehovah helped me" (ver. 13); as in old legends, the gods on their immortal steeds charged at the head of the hosts of their worshippers. Thus delivered, the singer breaks into the ancient strain, which had gone up on the shores of the sullen sea that rolled over Pharaoh's army, and is still true after centuries have intervened : " Jah is my strength and song, and He is become my salvation." Miriam sang it, the restored exiles sang it, tried and trustful men in every age have sung and will sing it, till there are no more foes ; and then, by the shores of the sea of glass mingled with fire, the calm victors will lift again the undying "song of Moses and of the Lamb."

Vv. 15, 16, are probably best taken as sung by the chorus, generalising and giving voice to the emotions excited by the preceding verses. The same reiteration which characterised vv. 8, 9, reappears here. Two broad truths are built on the individual voice's auto-biography : namely, that trust in Jehovah and consequent conformity to His law are never in vain, but always issue in joy ; and that God's power, when put forth, always conquers. " The tents of the righteous " may possibly allude to the " tabernacles " constructed for the feast, at which the song was probably sung.

Vv. 17–19 belong to the individual voice. The procession has reached the Temple. Deeper thoughts than before now mark the retrospect of past trial and deliverance. Both are recognised to be from Jehovah. It is He who has corrected, severely indeed, but still "in measure, not to bring to nothing, but to make capable and recipient of fuller life." The enemy thrust sore, with intent to make Israel fall ; but God's strokes are meant to make us stand the firmer. It is beautiful that all thought of human foes has faded away, and God only is seen in all the sorrow. But His chastisement has wider purposes than individual blessedness. It is intended to make its objects the heralds of His name to the world. Israel is beginning to lay to heart more earnestly its world-wide vocation to "tell forth the works of Jehovah." The imperative obligation of all who have received delivering help from Him is to become missionaries of His name. The reed is cut and pared thin and bored with hot irons, and the very pith of it extracted, that it may be fit to be put to the owner's lips, and give out music from his breath. Thus conscious of its vocation and eager to render its due of sacrifice and praise, Israel asks that "the gates of righteousness" may be opened for the entrance of the long procession. The Temple doors are so called, because Righteousness is the condition of entrance (Isa. **xxvi.** 2 : compare Psalm **xxiv.**).

Ver. 20 may belong to the individual voice, but is perhaps better taken as the answer from within the Temple, of the priests or Levites who guarded the closed doors, and who now proclaim what must be the character of those who would tread the sacred courts. The gate (not as in ver. 19, *gates*) belongs to Jehovah, and therefore access by it is permitted to none but the righteous. That is an everlasting truth. It is possible to translate, "This is the gate *to* Jehovah" —*i.e.,* by which one comes to His presence ; and that rendering would bring out still more emphatically the necessity of the condition laid down : "Without holiness no man shall see the Lord."

The condition is supposed to be met ; for in ver. **21** the individual voice again breaks into thanksgiving, for being allowed once more to stand in the house of

Jehovah. " Thou hast answered me " : the psalmist
had already sung that Jah had answered him (ver. 5).
" And art become my salvation " : he had already hailed
Jehovah as having become such (ver. 14).   God's deliverance is not complete till full communion with Him is
enjoyed.   Dwelling in His house is the crown of all
His blessings.   We are set free from enemies, from
sins and fears and struggles, that we may abide for
ever with Him, and only then do we realise the full
sweetness of His redeeming hand, when we stand in
His presence and commune evermore with Him.

Vv. 22, 23, 24, probably belong to the priestly chorus.
They set forth the great truth made manifest by
restored Israel's presence in the rebuilt Temple.   The
metaphor is suggested by the incidents connected with
the rebuilding.   The " stone " is obviously Israel,
weak, contemptible, but now once more laid as the very
foundation stone of God's house in the world.   The
broad truth taught by its history is that God lays as
the basis of His building—*i.e.*, uses for the execution
of His purposes—that which the wisdom of man
despises and tosses aside.   There had been abundant
faint-heartedness among even the restored exiles.   The
nations around had scoffed at these " feeble Jews," and
the scoffs had not been without echoes in Israel itself.
Chiefly, the men of position and influence, who ought
to have strengthened drooping courage, had been infected with the tendency to rate low the nation's power,
and to think that their enterprise was destined to
disaster.   But now the Temple is built, and the
worshippers stand in it.   What does that teach but
that all has been God's doing ?   So wonderful is it, so
far beyond expectation, that the very objects of such
marvellous intervention are amazed to find themselves

where they stand. So rooted is our tendency to unbelief that, when God does what He has sworn to do, we are apt to be astonished with a wonder which reveals the greatness of our past incredulity. No man who trusts God ought to be surprised at God's answers to trust.

The general truth contained here is that of Paul's great saying, "God hath chosen the weak things of the world that He might put to shame the things that are strong." It is the constant law, not because God chooses unfit instruments, but because the world's estimates of fitness are false, and the qualities which it admires are irrelevant with regard to His designs, while the requisite qualities are of another sort altogether. Therefore, it is a law which finds its highest exemplification in *the* foundation for God's true temple, other than which can no man lay. "Israel is not only a figure of Christ—there is an organic unity between Him and them. Whatever, therefore, is true of Israel in a lower sense is true in its highest sense of Christ. If Israel is the rejected stone made the head of the corner, this is far truer of Him who was indeed rejected of men, but chosen of God and precious, the corner stone of the one great living temple of the redeemed " (Perowne).

Ver. 24 is best regarded as the continuation of the choral praise in vv. 22, 23. "The day" is that of the festival now in process, the joyful culmination of God's manifold deliverances. It is a day in which joy is duty, and no heart has a right to be too heavy to leap for gladness. Private sorrows enough many of the jubilant worshippers no doubt had, but the sight of the Stone laid as the head of the corner should bring joy even to such. If sadness was ingratitude and almost treason then, what sorrow should now be so dense that it cannot be pierced by the Light which lighteth every man ?   The joy of the Lord should float, like oil on stormy waves, above our troublous sorrows, and smooth their tossing.

Again the single voice rises, but not now in thanksgiving, as might have been expected, but in plaintive tones of earnest imploring (ver. 25).   Standing in the sanctuary, Israel is conscious of its perils, its need, its weakness, and so with pathetic reiteration of the particle of entreaty, which occurs twice in each clause of the verse, cries for continued deliverance from continuing evils, and for prosperity in the course opening before it.   The "day" in which unmingled gladness inspires our songs has not yet dawned, fair as are the many days which Jehovah has made.   In the earthly house of the Lord thanksgiving must ever pass into petition.   An unending day comes, when there will be nothing to dread, and no need for the sadder notes occasioned by felt weakness and feared foes.

Vv. 26, 27, come from the chorus of priests, who welcome the entering procession, and solemnly pronounce on them the benediction of Jehovah.   They answer, in His name, the prayer of ver. 25, and bless the single leader of the procession and the multitudes following.   The use of ver. 26 *a* and of the "Hosanna" (an attempted transliteration of the Hebrew "Save I beseech") from ver. 25 at Christ's entrance into Jerusalem probably shows that the psalm was regarded as Messianic.   It is so, in virtue of the relation already referred to between Israel and Christ.   He "cometh in the name of Jehovah" in a deeper sense than did Israel, the servant of the Lord.

Ver. 27 *a* recalls the priestly benediction (Numb. vi.

25), and thankfully recognises its ample fulfilment in Israel's history, and especially in the dawning of new prosperity now. Ver. 27 *b*, *c*, is difficult. Obviously it should be a summons to worship, as thanksgiving for the benefits acknowledged in *a*. But what is the act of worship intended is hard to say. The rendering " Bind the sacrifice with cords, even unto the horns of the altar," has against it the usual meaning of the word rendered *sacrifice*, which is rather *festival*, and the fact that the last words of the verse cannot possibly be translated " *to* the horns," etc., but must mean " as far as " or " even up to the horns," etc. There must therefore be a good deal supplied in the sentence ; and commentators differ as to how to fill the gap. Delitzsch supposes that " the number of the sacrificial animals is to be so great that the whole space of the courts of the priests becomes full of them, and the binding of them has therefore to take place even up to the horns of the altar." Perowne takes the expression to be a pregnant one for " till [the victim] is sacrificed and its blood sprinkled on the horns of the altar." So Hupfeld, following Chaldee and some Jewish interpreters. Others regard the supposed ellipsis as too great to be natural, and take an entirely different view. The word rendered *sacrifice* in the former explanation is taken to mean a *procession* round the altar, which is etymologically justifiable, and is supported by the known custom of making such a circuit during the Feast of Tabernacles. For " cords " this explanation would read *branches* or *boughs*, which is also warranted. But what does " binding a procession with boughs " mean ? Various answers are given. Cheyne supposes that the branches borne in the hands of the members of the procession were in some unknown way used to bind or link them together before they left the Temple. Baethgen takes "with boughs" as = "bearing boughs," with which he supposes that the bearers touched the altar horns, for the purpose of transferring to themselves the holiness concentrated there. Either explanation has difficulties, —the former in requiring an unusual sense for the word rendered *sacrifice*; the latter in finding a suitable meaning for that translated *bind*. In either *c* is but loosely connected with *b*, and is best understood as an exclamation. The verb rendered *bind* is used in 1 Kings xx. 14, 2 Chron. xiii. 3, in a sense which fits well with "procession" here—*i.e.*, that of marshalling an army for battle. If this meaning is adopted, *b* will be the summons to order the bough-bearing procession, and *c* a call to march onwards, so as to encircle the altar. This meaning of the obscure verse may be provisionally accepted, while owning that our ignorance of the ceremonial referred to prevents complete understanding of the words.

Once more Miriam's song supplies ancient language of praise for recent mercies, and the personified Israel compasses the altar with thanksgiving (ver. 28). Then the whole multitude, both of those who had come up to the Temple and of those who had welcomed them there, join in the chorus of praise with which the psalm begins and ends, and which was so often pealed forth in those days of early joy for the new manifestations of that Lovingkindness which endures through all days, both those of past evil and those of future hoped-for good.

PSALM CXIX.

IT is lost labour to seek for close continuity or
progress in this psalm. One thought pervades it —
the surpassing excellence of the Law ; and the beauty
and power of the psalm lie in the unwearied reiteration
of that single idea. There is music in its monotony,
which is subtilely varied. Its verses are like the ripples
on a sunny sea, alike and impressive in their continual
march, and yet each catching the light with a difference,
and breaking on the shore in a tone of its own. A
few elements are combined into these hundred and
seventy-six gnomic sentences. One or other of the usual
synonyms for the Law—viz., word, saying, statutes,
commandments, testimonies, judgments—occurs in
every verse, except vv. 122 and 132. The prayers
" Teach me, revive me, preserve me—according to Thy
word," and the vows " I will keep, observe, meditate on,
delight in—Thy law," are frequently repeated. There
are but few pieces in the psalmist's kaleidoscope, but
they fall into many shapes of beauty ; and though all
his sentences are moulded after the same general plan,
the variety within such narrow limits is equally a
witness of poetic power which turns the fetters of the
acrostic structure into helps, and of devout heartfelt
love for the Law of Jehovah.

The psalm is probably of late date ; but its allusions

to the singer's circumstances, whether they are taken as autobiographical or as having reference to the nation, are too vague to be used as clues to the period of its composition. An early poet is not likely to have adopted such an elaborate acrostic plan, and the praises of the Law naturally suggest a time when it was familiar in an approximately complete form. It may be that the rulers referred to in vv. 23, 46, were foreigners, but the expression is too general to draw a conclusion from. It may be that the double-minded (ver. 113), who err from God's statutes (ver. 118) and forsake His law (ver. 53), are Israelites who have yielded to the temptations to apostatise, which came with the early Greek period, to which Baethgen, Cheyne, and others would assign the psalm. But these expressions, too, are of so general a nature that they do not give clear testimony of date.

§ א

1 Blessed the perfect in [their] way,
   Who walk in the law of Jehovah !
2 Blessed they who keep His testimonies,
   That seek Him with the whole heart,
3 [Who] also have done no iniquity,
   [But] have walked in His ways !
4 Thou hast commanded Thy precepts,
   That we should observe them diligently.
5 O that my ways were established
   To observe Thy statutes!
6 Then shall I not be ashamed,
   When I give heed to all Thy commandments.
7 I will thank Thee with uprightness of heart,
   When I learn Thy righteous judgments.
8 Thy statutes will I observe;
   Forsake me not utterly.

The first three verses are closely connected. They set forth in general terms the elements of the blessed-

ness of the doers of the Law. To walk in it—*i.e.,* **to**
order the active life in conformity with its requirements
—ensures perfectness. To keep God's testimonies is at
once the consequence and the proof of seeking Him
with whole-hearted devotion and determination. To
walk in His ways is the preservative from evil-doing.
And such men cannot but be blessed with a deep
sacred blessedness, which puts to shame coarse and
turbulent delights, and feeds its pure fires from God
Himself. Whether these verses are taken as exclamation or declaration, they lead up naturally to ver. 4,
which reverently gazes upon the loving act of God in
the revelation of His will in the Law, and bethinks
itself of the obligations bound on us by that act. It
is of God's mercy that He has commanded, and His
words are meant to sway our wills, since He has
broken the awful silence, not merely to instruct us, but
to command ; and nothing short of practical obedience
will discharge our duties to His revelation. So the
psalmist betakes himself to prayer, that he may be
helped to realise the purpose of God in giving the Law.
His contemplation of the blessedness of obedience and
of the Divine act of declaring His will moves him
to longing, and his consciousness of weakness and
wavering makes the longing into prayer that his wavering may be consolidated into fixity of purpose and
continuity of obedience. When a man's ways are
established to observe, they will be established by
observing, God's statutes. For nothing can put to the
blush one whose eye is directed to these.

> " Whatever record leap to light,
>   He never shall be shamed."

Nor will he cherish hopes that fail, nor desires that

when accomplished, are bitter of taste. To give heed
to the commandments is the condition of learning them
and recognising how righteous they are; and such
learning makes the learner's heart righteous like them,
and causes it to run over in thankfulness for the boon
of knowledge of God's will. By all these thoughts the
psalmist is brought to his fixed resolve in ver. 8, to do
what God meant him to do when He gave the Law;
and what the singer had just longed that he might be
able to do—namely, to observe the statutes. But in
his resolve he remembers his weakness, and therefore
he glides into prayer for that Presence without which
resolves are transient and abortive.

§ ב

9 Wherewith shall a young man cleanse his path ?
   By taking heed, according to Thy word.
10 With my whole heart have I sought Thee,
   Let me not wander from Thy commandments.
11 In my heart have I hid Thy saying,
   That I may not sin against Thee.
12 Blessed art Thou, Jehovah,
   Teach me Thy statutes.
13 With my lips have I rehearsed
   All the judgments of Thy mouth.
14 In the way of Thy testimonies have I rejoiced,
   As over all [kinds of] wealth.
15 In Thy precepts will I meditate,
   And will have respect to all Thy paths.
16 In Thy statutes will I delight myself,
   I will not forget Thy word.

The inference drawn from ver. 9, that the psalmist
was a young man, is precarious. The language would
be quite as appropriate to an aged teacher desirous of
guiding impetuous youth to sober self-control. While
some verses favour the hypothesis of the author's youth
(ver. 141, and perhaps vv. 99, 100), the tone of the whole,

its rich experience and comprehensive grasp of the manifold relations of the Law to life, imply maturity of years and length of meditation. The psalm is the ripe fruit of a life which is surely past its spring. But it is extremely questionable whether these apparently personal traits are really so. Much rather is the poet " thinking . . . of the individuals of different ages and spiritual attainments who may use his works " (Cheyne, *in loc.*).

The word rendered " By taking heed " has already occurred in vv. 4, 5 (" observe "). The careful study of the Word must be accompanied with as careful study of self. The object observed there was the Law ; here, it is the man himself. Study God's law, says the psalmist, and study Thyself in its light ; so shall youthful impulses be bridled, and the life's path be kept pure. That does not sound so like a young man's thought as an old man's maxim, in which are crystallised many experiences.

The rest of the section intermingles petitions, professions, and vows, and is purely personal. The psalmist claims that he is one of those whom he has pronounced blessed, inasmuch as he *has* " sought " God with his " whole heart." Such longing is no mere idle aspiration, but must be manifested in obedience, as ver. 2 has declared. If a man longs for God, he will best find Him by doing His will. But no heart-desire is so rooted as to guarantee that it shall not die, nor is past obedience a certain pledge of a like future. Wherefore the psalmist prays, not in reliance on his past, but in dread that he may falsify it, " Let me not wander." He had not only sought God in his heart, but had there hid God's law, as its best treasure, and as an inward power controlling and stimulating. Evil cannot flow from a heart in which God's law is lodged. That is the tree which sweetens the waters of the fountain. But the cry " Teach me Thy statutes " would be but faltering, if the singer could not rise above himself, and take heart by gazing upon God, whose own great character is the guarantee that He will not leave a seeking soul in ignorance.

Professions and vows now take the place of petitions. " From the abundance of the heart the mouth speaketh," and the word hid in it will certainly not be concealed. It is buried deep, that it may grow high. It is hidden, that it may come abroad. Therefore ver. 13 tells of bold utterance, which is as incumbent on men as obedient deeds.

A sane estimate of earthly good will put it decisively below the knowledge of God and of His will. Lives which despise what the world calls riches, because they are smitten with the desire of any sort of wisdom, are ever nobler than those which keep the low levels. And highest of all is the life which gives effect to its conviction that man's true treasure is to know God's mind and will. To rejoice in His testimonies is to have wealth that cannot be lost and pleasures that cannot wither. That glad estimate will surely lead to happy meditation on them, by which their worth shall be disclosed and their sweep made plain. The miser loves to tell his gold ; the saint, to ponder his wealth in God. The same double direction of the mind, already noted, reappears in ver. 15, where quiet meditation on God's statutes is associated with attention to the ways which are called His, as being pointed out by, and pleasing to, Him, but are ours, as being walked in by us. Inward delight in, and practical remembrance of, the Law are vowed in ver. 16, which covers the whole field of contemplative and active life.

§ 3

17 Deal bountifully with Thy servant, that I may live,
   So will I observe Thy word.
18 Open my eyes, that I may behold
   Wonders out of Thy law.
19 A stranger am I on the earth,
   Hide not from me Thy commandments.
20 Crushed is my soul with longing
   Towards Thy judgments at all times.
21 Thou hast rebuked the proud [so that they are] cursed,
   Those who wander from Thy commandments.
22 Remove from me reproach and shame,
   For Thy testimonies do I keep.
23 Princes also sit and speak with one another against me,
   Thy servant meditates on Thy statutes.
24 Also Thy testimonies are my delight,
   The men of my counsel.

In ver. 17 the psalmist desires continued life, mainly
because it affords the opportunity of continued obedience.   He will "observe Thy word," not only in token
of gratitude, but because to him life is precious chiefly
because in its activities he can serve God.   Such a
reason for wishing to live may easily change to a
willingness to die, as it did with Paul, who had learned
that a better obedience was possible when he had
passed through the dark gates, and therefore could
say, "To die is gain."   Vv. 18, 19, are connected, in
so far as the former desires subjective illumination and
the latter objective revelation.   Opened eyes are useless, if commandments are hidden ; and the disclosure
of the latter is in vain unless there are eyes to see
them.   Two great truths lie in the former petition—
namely, that scales cover our spiritual vision which
only God can take away, and that His revelation has
in its depths truths and treasures which can only be
discerned by His help.   The cognate petition in ver. 19

is based upon the pathetic thought that man is a
stranger on earth, and therefore needs what will take
away his sense of homelessness and unrest. All other
creatures are adapted to their environments, but he
has a consciousness that he is an exile here, a haunting,
stinging sense, which vaguely feels after repose in his
native land. "Thy commandments" can still it. To
know God's will, with knowledge which is acceptance
and love, gives rest, and makes every place a mansion
in the Father's house.

There may possibly be a connection between vv. 20
and 21—the terrible fate of those who wander from
the commandments, as described in the latter verse,
being the motive for the psalmist's longing expressed
in the former. The "judgments" for which he longed,
with a yearning which seemed to bruise his soul are
not, as might be supposed, God's judicial acts, but the
word is a synonym for "commandments," as throughout
the psalm.

The last three verses of the section appear to be
linked together. They relate to the persecutions of the
psalmist for his faithfulness to God's law. In ver. 22
he prays that reproach and shame, which wrapped
him like a covering, may be lifted from him; and his
plea in ver. 22 b declares that he lay under these
because he was true to God's statutes. In ver. 23 we
see the source of the reproach and shame, in the con-
clave of men in authority, whether foreign princes or
Jewish rulers, who were busy slandering him and
plotting his ruin; while, with wonderful beauty, the
contrasted picture in b shows the object of that busy talk,
sitting silently absorbed in meditation on the higher
things of God's statutes. As long as a man can do that,
he has a magic circle drawn round him, across which

fears and cares cannot step. Ver. 24 heightens the
impression of the psalmist's rest. "Also Thy testimonies are my delight"—not only the subjects of his
meditation, but bringing inward sweetness, though
earth is in arms against him ; and not only are they his
delights, but "the men of his counsel," in whom he,
solitary as he is, finds companionship that arms him
with resources against that knot of whispering enemies.

§ ד

25 My soul cleaves to the dust,
    Revive me according to Thy word.
26 My ways I told and Thou answeredst me,
    Teach me Thy statutes.
27 The way of Thy precepts make me understand,
    And I will meditate on Thy wonders.
28 My soul weeps itself away for grief,
    Raise me up according to Thy word.
29 The way of lying remove from me,
    And [with] Thy law be gracious to me.
30 The way of faithfulness I have chosen,
    Thy judgments have I set [before me].
31 I have cleaved to Thy testimonies ;
    Jehovah, put me not to shame.
32 The way of Thy commandments will I run,
    For Thou dost enlarge my heart.

The exigencies of the acrostic plan are very obvious
in this section, five of the verses of which begin with
"way" or "ways," and two of the remaining three
with "cleaves." The variety secured under such
conditions is remarkable. The psalmist's soul cleaves
to the dust—*i.e.*, is bowed in mourning (cf. xliv. 25); but
still, though thus darkened by sorrow and weeping
itself away for grief (ver. 28), it cleaves to "Thy
testimonies" (ver. 31). Happy in their sorrow are
they who, by reason of the force which bows their
sensitive nature to the dust, cling the more closely in

their true selves to the declared will of God! Their
sorrow appeals to God's heart, and is blessed if it
dictates the prayer for His quickening (ver. 25). Their
cleaving to His law warrants their hope that He will
not put them to shame.

The first pair of verses in which "way" is the
acrostic word (vv. 26, 27) sets "my ways" over against
"the way of Thy precepts." The psalmist has made
God his confidant, telling Him all his life's story,
and has found continual answers, in gifts of mercy
and inward whispers. He asks, therefore, for further
illumination, which will be in accordance with these
past mutual communications. Tell God thy ways and
He will teach thee His statutes. The franker our
confession, the more fervent our longing for fuller
knowledge of His will. "The way of Thy precepts"
is the practical life according to these, the ideal which
shall rebuke and transform "my ways." The singer's
crooked course is spread before God, and he longs to
see clearly the straight path of duty, on which he vows
that he will meditate, and find wonders in the revelation of God's will. Many a sunbeam is wasted for
want of intent eyes. The prayer for understanding is
vain without the vow of pondering. The next pair of
"way-" verses (vv. 29, 30) contrasts ways of "lying"
and of "faithfulness"—*i.e.*, sinful life which is false
towards God and erroneous in its foundation maxims,
and life which is true in practice to Him and to man's
obligations. The psalmist prays that the former may
be put far from him; for he feels that it is only too
near, and his unhelped feet too ready to enter on it.
He recognises the inmost meaning of the Law as an
outcome of God's favour. It is not harsh, but glowing
with love, God's best gift. The prayer in ver. 29 has

the psalmist's deliberate choice in ver. 30 as its plea.
That choice does not lift him above the need of God's
help, and it gives him a claim thereon.   Our wills may
seem fixed, but the gap between choice and practice is
wide, and our feebleness will not bridge it, unless He
strengthens us.   So the last verse of this section
humbly vows to transform meditation and choice into
action, and to "run the way of God's commandments,"
in thanksgiving for the joy with which, while the
psalmist prays, he feels that his heart swells.

§ ה

33 Teach me, Jehovah, the way of Thy statutes,
    And I will keep it to the end.
34 Make me understand so that I may keep Thy law,
    And I will observe it with [my] whole heart.
35 Make me walk in the path of Thy commandments,
    For in it I delight.
36 Incline my heart to Thy testimonies,
    And not to plunder.
37 Make my eyes go aside from beholding vanity,
    In Thy ways revive me.
38 Confirm to Thy servant Thy promise,
    Which tends to Thy fear.
39 Make my reproach pass away which I dread,
    For Thy judgments are good.
40 Behold, I have longed for Thy precepts,
    In Thy righteousness revive me.

Vv. 33 and 34 are substantially identical in their
prayer for enlightenment and their vow of obedience.
Both are based on the conviction that outward revelation is incomplete without inward illumination.   Both
recognise the necessary priority of enlightened reason
as condition of obedient action, and such action as the
test and issue of enlightenment.   Both vow that
knowledge shall not remain barren.   They differ in
that the former verse pledges the psalmist to obedience

unlimited in time and the latter to obedience without
reservation.   But even in uttering his vow the singer
remembers his need of God's help to keep it, and turns
it, in ver. 35, into petition, which he very significantly
grounds on his heart's delight in the Law.   Warm as
that delight may be, circumstances and flesh will cool
it, and it is ever a struggle to translate desires into
deeds.   Therefore we need the sweet constraint of our
Divine Helper to make us walk in the right way.
Again, in ver. 36 the preceding profession is caught
up and modulated into petition.   " Incline my heart "
stands to " In it I delight," just as " Make me walk "
does to " I will observe it."   Our purest joys in God
and in His Will depend on Him for their permanence
and increase.   Our hearts are apt to spill their affection
on the earth, even while we would bear the cup filled
to God.   And one chief rival of " Thy testimonies " is
worldly gain, from which there must be forcible detach-
ment in order to, and as accompaniment of, attachment
to God.   All possessions which come between us and
Him are " plunder," unjust gain.

The heart is often led astray by the eyes.   The
senses bring fuel to its unholy flames.   Therefore, the
next petition (ver. 37) asks that they may be made, as
it were, to pass on one side of tempting things, which
are branded as being " vanity," without real substance
or worth, however they may glitter and solicit the gaze.
To look longingly on earth's good makes us torpid in
God's ways ; and to be earnest in the latter makes us
dead to the former.   There is but one real life for men,
the life of union with God and of obedience to His
commandments.   Therefore, the singer prays to be
revived in God's ways.   Experience of God's faithfulness to His plighted word will do much to deliver from

earth's glamour, as ver. 38 implies.   The second clause
is elliptical in Hebrew, and is now usually taken as
above, meaning that God's promise fulfilled leads men
to reverence Him.   But the rendering " who is [devoted]
to Thy fear" is tenable and perhaps better.   The
" reproach " in ver. 39 is probably that which would
fall on the psalmist if he were unfaithful to God's law.
This interpretation gives the best meaning to ver. 39 *b*,
which would then contain the reason for his desire to
keep the "judgments "—*i.e.*, the commandments, not
the judicial acts—which he feels to be good.   The
section ends with a constantly recurring strain.   God's
righteousness, His strict discharge of all obligations,
guarantees that no longing, turned to Him, can be left
unsatisfied.   The languishing desire will be changed
into fuller joy of more vigorous life.   The necessary
precursor of deeper draughts from the Fountain of
Life is thirst for it, which faithfully turns aside from
earth's sparkling but drugged potions.

§ ૧

41 And let Thy lovingkindnesses come to me, Jehovah,
   Thy salvation according to Thy promise.
42 And I shall have a word to answer him that reproaches me,
   For I trust in Thy word.
43 And pluck not the word of truth out of my mouth utterly,
   For I have waited for Thy judgments.
44 And I would observe Thy law continually,
   For ever and aye.
45 And I would walk at liberty,
   For I have sought Thy precepts.
46 And I would speak of Thy testimonies before kings,
   And not be ashamed.
47 And I will delight myself in Thy judgments,
   Which I love.
48 And I will lift up my palms to Thy commandments [which I
   love],
   And meditate on Thy statutes.

There are practically no Hebrew words beginning with the letter required as the initial in this section, except the copula "and.' Each verse begins with it, and it is best to retain it in translation, so as to reproduce in some measure the original impression of uniformity. The verses are aggregated rather than linked. "And" sometimes introduces a consequence, as probably in ver. 42, and sometimes is superfluous in regard to the sense. A predominant reference to the duty of bearing witness to the Truth runs through the section. The prayer in ver. 41 for the visits of God's lovingkindnesses which, in their sum, make salvation, and are guaranteed by His word of promise, is urged on the ground that, by experience of these, the psalmist will have his answer ready for all carpers who scoff at him and his patient faith. Such a prayer is entirely accordant with the hypothesis that the speaker is the collective Israel, but not less so with the supposition that he is an individual. "Whereas I was blind, now I see" is an argument that silences sarcasm. Ver. 43 carries on the thought of witnessing and asks that "the word of truth"—*i.e.*, the Law considered as disclosure of truth rather than of duty—may not be snatched from the witness's mouth, as it would be if God's promised lovingkindnesses failed him. The condition of free utterance is rich experience. If prayers had gone up in vain from the psalmist's lips, no glad proclamation could come from them.

The verbs at the beginnings of vv. 44-46 are best taken as optatives, expressing what the psalmist would fain do, and, to some extent, has done. There is no true religion without that longing for unbroken conformity with the manifest will of God. Whoever makes that his deepest desire, and seeks after God's precepts,

will "walk at liberty," or *at large*, for restraints that
are loved are not bonds, and freedom consists not in
doing as I would, but in willing to do as I ought.
Strong in such emancipation from the hindrances of one's
own passions, and triumphant over external circumstances which may mould, but not dominate, a God-
obeying life, the psalmist would fain open his mouth
unabashed before rulers. The "kings" spoken of in
ver. 46 may be foreign rulers, possibly the representa-
tives of the Persian monarch, or later alien sovereigns,
or the expression may be quite general, and the
speaker be a private person, who feels his courage
rising as he enters into the liberty of perfect submission.

Vv. 47, 48, are general expressions of delight in the
Law. Lifting the hands towards the commandments
seems to be a figure for reverent regard, or longing,
as one wistfully stretches them out towards some dear
person or thing that one would fain draw closer. The
phrase "which I love" in ver. 48 overweights the
clause, and is probably a scribe's erroneous repetition
of 47 *b*.

§ ?

49 Remember the word to Thy servant,
   On which Thou hast caused me to hope.
50 This is my comfort in my affliction,
   That Thy promise has given me life.
51 The proud have derided me exceedingly,
   From Thy law I have not declined.
52 I have remembered Thy judgments [which are] from of old,
      Jehovah,
   And I have comforted myself.
53 Fiery anger has seized me because of the wicked,
   Who forsake Thy law.
54 Thy statutes have been songs for me,
   In my house of sojourning.

55 I remembered Thy name in the night, Jehovah,
     And observed Thy law.
56 This good has been mine,
     That I have kept Thy precepts.

This section has only one verse of petition, the others being mainly avowals of adherence to the Law in the face of various trials. The single petition (ver. 49) pleads the relation of servant, as giving a claim on the great Lord of the household, and adduces God's having encouraged hope as imposing on Him an obligation to fulfil it. Expectations fairly deduced from His word are prophets of their own realisation. In ver. 50, " This " points to the fact stated in *b*—namely, that the Word had already proved its power in the past by quickening the psalmist to new courage and hope—and declares that that remembered experience solaces his present sorrow. A heart that has been revived by life-giving contact with the Word has a hidden warmth beneath the deepest snows, and cleaves the more to that Word.

Vv. 51–53 describe the attitude of the lover of the Law in presence of the ungodly. He is as unmoved by shafts of ridicule as by the heavier artillery of slander and plots (ver. 23). To be laughed out of one's faith is even worse than to be terrified out of it. The lesson is not needless in a day when adherence and obedience to the Word are smiled at in so many quarters as indicating inferior intelligence. The psalmist held fast by it, and while laughter, with more than a trace of bitterness, rung about him, threw himself back on God's ancient and enduring words, which made the scoffs sound very hollow and transient (ver. 52). Righteous indignation, too, rises in a devout soul at sight of men's departure from God's law (ver. 53). The word rendered "fiery anger" is found in xi. 6 ("a wind of *burning*"), and is best taken as above, though some would render *horror*. The wrath was not unmingled with compassion (ver. 136), and, whilst it is clearly an emotion belonging to the Old Testament rather than to the Christian type of devotion, it should be present, in softened form, in our feelings towards evil.

In ver. 54 the psalmist turns from gainsayers. He strikes again the note of ver. 19, calling earth his place of transitory abode, or, as we might say, his inn. The brevity of life would be crushing, if God had not spoken to us. Since He has, the pilgrims can march "with songs and everlasting joy upon their heads," and all about their moving camp the sound of song may echo. To its lovers, God's law is not "harsh and crabbed . . . but musical as is Apollo's lute." This psalm is one of the poet's songs. Even those of us who are not singers can and should meditate on God's law, till its melodious beauty is disclosed and its commandments, that sometimes sound stern, set themselves to rhythm and harmony. As God's words took bitterness out of the thought of mortality, so His name remembered in the night brought light into darkness, whether physical or other. We often lose our memory of God and our hold of His hand when in sorrow, and grief sometimes thinks that it has a dispensation from obedience. So we shall be the better for remembering the psalmist's experience, and should, like him, cling to the Name in the dark, and then we shall have light enough to "observe Thy law." Ver. 56 looks back on the mingled life of good and evil, of which some of the sorrows have just been touched, and speaks deep contentment with its portion. Whatever else is withheld or withdrawn, that lot is blessed which has been helped by God to keep His precepts, and they are happy and wise who deliberately prefer that good to all beside.

§ ‌ח

57 My portion is Jehovah,
   I have said that I would observe Thy words.
58 I have sought Thy favour with my whole heart,
   Be merciful to me according to Thy promise.
59 I have thought on my ways,
   And turned my feet to Thy testimonies.
60 I hasted and delayed not
   To observe Thy commandments.
61 The cords of the wicked have enwrapped me,
   Thy law have I not forgotten.
62 At midnight will I rise to thank Thee,
   Because of Thy righteous judgments.
63 A companion am I of all who fear Thee,
   And of those who observe Thy precepts.
64 Of Thy lovingkindness, Jehovah, the earth is full,
   Thy statutes do Thou teach me.

Ver. 57 goes to the root of the matter in setting forth the resolve of obedience as the result of the consciousness of possessing God. He who feels, in his own happy heart, that Jehovah is his portion will be moved thereby to vow to keep His words. This psalmist had learned the evangelical lesson that he did not win God by keeping the Law, but that he was moved to keep the Law because he had won God; and he had also learned the companion truth, that the way to retain that possession is obedience.

Ver. 58 corresponds in some measure to ver. 57, but the order of clauses is inverted, *a* stating the psalmist's prayer, as ver. 57 *b* did his resolve, and *b* building on his cry the hope that God would be truly his portion and bestow His favour on him. But the true ground of our hope is not our most whole-hearted prayers, but God's promise. The following five verses change from the key of petition into that of profession of obedience to, and delight in, the Law. The fruit of wise consideration of one's conduct is willing acceptance of God's law as His witness of what is right for us. The only "ways" which sober consideration will approve are those marked out in mercy by Him, and meditation on conduct is worthless if it does not issue in turning our feet into these. Without such meditation we shall wander on bye-ways and lose ourselves. Want of thought ruins men (ver. 59). But such turning of our feet to the right road has many foes, and chief among them is lingering delay. Therefore resolve must never be let cool, but be swiftly carried into action (ver. 60). The world is full of snares, and they lie thick round our feet whenever these are turned towards God's ways. The only means of keeping clear of them is to fix heart and mind on God's law. Then we shall be able to pick our steps among traps and pits (ver. 61). Physical weariness limits obedience, and needful sleep relaxes nervous tension, so that many a strenuous worker and noble aspirant falls beneath his daylight self in wakeful night seasons. Blessed they who in the night see visions of God and meditate on His law, not on earthly vanities or aims (ver. 62). Society has its temptations as solitude has. The man whose heart has fed in secret on God and His law will naturally gravitate towards like-minded people. Our relation to God and His uttered will should determine our affinities with men, and it is a bad sign when natural impulses do not draw us to those who fear God. Two men who have that fear in common are liker each other in their deepest selves, however different they may be in other respects, than either of them is to those to whom he is likest in surface characteristics and unlike in this

supreme trait (ver. 63).   One pathetic petition closes
the section.   In ver. 19 the psalmist had based his
prayer for illumination on his being a stranger on earth;
here he grounds it on the plenitude of God's loving-
kindness, which floods the world.   It is the same plea
in another form.   All creatures bask in the light of
God's love, which falls on each in a manner appropriate
to its needs.   Man's supreme need is the knowledge
of God's statutes; therefore, the same all-embracing
Mercy, which cares for these happy, careless creatures,
will not be implored in vain, to satisfy his nobler and
more pressing want.   All beings get their respective
boons unasked; but the pre-eminence of ours is partly
seen in this, that it cannot be given without the co-
operation of our desire.   It will be given wherever that
condition is fulfilled (ver. 64).

§ ט

65 Good hast Thou done with Thy servant,
   Jehovah, according to Thy word.
66 Good judgment and knowledge teach me,
   For I have believed Thy commandments.
67 Before I was afflicted, I went astray,
   But now have I observed Thy saying.
68 Good art Thou and doing good,
   Teach me Thy statutes.
69 The proud have trumped up a lie against me,
   I, I with all [my] heart will keep Thy precepts.
70 Gross as fat is their heart,
   I, I delight in Thy law.
71 Good for me was it that I was afflicted,
   That I might learn Thy statutes.
72 Good for me is the law of Thy mouth,
   Above thousands of gold and silver.

The restrictions of the acrostic structure are very
obvious in this section, five of the eight verses of which
begin with "Good."   The epithet is first applied in

ver. 65 to the whole of God's dealings with the
psalmist.   To the devout soul all life is of one piece,
and its submission and faith exercise transmuting
power on pains and sorrows, so that the psalmist can
say—

> "Let one more attest,
> I have lived, seen God's hand through a lifetime,
> And all was for best."

The epithet is next applied (ver. 66) to the perception
(lit. taste) or faculty of discernment of good and evil,
for which the psalmist prays, basing his petition on his
belief of God's word.   Swift, sure, and delicate apprehension of right and wrong comes from such belief.   The
heart in which it reigns is sensitive as a goldsmith's
scales or a thermometer which visibly sinks when a
cloud passes before the sun.   The instincts of faith
work surely and rapidly.   The settled judgment that
life had been good includes apparent evil (ver. 67),
which is real evil in so far as it pains, but is, in a
deeper view, good, inasmuch as it scourges a wandering
heart back to true obedience and therefore to well-being.
The words of ver. 67 are specially appropriate as the
utterance of the Israel purified from idolatrous tenden-
cies by captivity, but may also be the expression of
individual experience.   The epithet is next applied to
God Himself (ver. 68).   How steadfast a gaze into the
depths of the Divine nature and over the broad field of
the Divine activity is in that short, all-including clause,
containing but three words in the Hebrew, "Good art
Thou and doing good"!   The prayer built on it is the
one which continually recurs in this psalm, and is
reached by many paths.   Every view of man's condition, whether it is bright or dark, and every thought
of God, bring the psalmist to the same desire.   Here

God's character and beneficence, widespread and continual, prompt to the prayer, both because the knowledge of His will is our highest good, and because a
good God cannot but wish His servants to be like
Himself, in loving righteousness and hating iniquity.

Vv. 69 and 70 are a pair, setting forth the antithesis,
frequent in the psalm, between evil men's conduct to
the psalmist and his tranquil contemplation of, and
delight in, God's precepts. False slanders buzz about
him, but he cleaves to God's Law, and is conscious
of innocence. Men are dull and insensible, as if their
hearts were waterproofed with a layer of grease,
through which no gentle rain from heaven could steal;
but the psalmist is all the more led to open his heart
to the gracious influences of that law, because others
close theirs. If a bad man is not made worse by
surrounding evil, he is made better by it.

Just as in vv. 65 and 68 the same thought of God's
goodness is expressed, ver. 71 repeats the thought of
ver. 67, with a slight deepening. There the beneficent
influence of sorrow was simply declared as a fact;
here it is thankfully accepted, with full submission and
consent of the will. "Good for me" means not only
good in fact, but *in my estimate*. The repetition of
the phrase at the beginning of the next verse throws
light on its meaning in ver. 71. The singer thinks
that he has two real goods, pre-eminent among the
uniform sequence of such, and these are, first, his
sorrows, which he reckons to be blessings, because
they have helped him to a firmer grasp of the other,
the real good for every man, the Law which is sacred
and venerable, because it has come from the very lips
of Deity. That is our true wealth. Happy they whose
estimate of it corresponds to its real worth, and who

have learned, by affliction or anyhow, that material
riches are dross, compared with its solid preciousness !

§ ›

73 Thy hands have made me and fashioned me,
   Give me understanding that I may learn Thy commandments.
74 Let those who fear Thee see me and rejoice,
   For I have waited for Thy word.
75 I know, Jehovah, that Thy judgments are in righteousness,
   And that [in] faithfulness Thou hast afflicted me.
76 Oh let Thy lovingkindness be [sent] to comfort me,
   According to Thy promise to Thy servant.
77 Let Thy compassions come to me that I may live,
   For Thy law is my delight.
78 Let the proud be shamed, for they have lyingly dealt perversely
    with me ;
   I, I meditate on Thy precepts.
79 Let those who fear Thee turn to me,
   And they shall know Thy testimonies.
80 Let my heart be sound in Thy statutes,
   That I be not shamed.

Prayer for illumination is confined to the first and
last verses of this section, the rest of which is mainly
occupied with petitions for gracious providences, based
upon the grounds of the psalmist's love of the Law,
and of the encouragement to others to trust, derivable
from his experience.   Ver. 73 puts forcibly the thought
that man is evidently an incomplete fragment, unless
the gift of understanding is infused into his material
frame. God has begun by shaping it, and therefore
is pledged to go on to bestow spiritual discernment,
when His creature asks it.   But that prayer will only
be answered if the suppliant intends to use the gift
for its right purpose of learning God's statutes. Ver. 74
prays that the psalmist may be a witness that hope
in His word is never vain, and so that his deliverances
may be occasions of widespread gladness.   God's
honour is involved in answering His servant's trust.

Vv. 75-77 are linked together. " Judgments " (ver. 75) seem to mean here providential acts, not, as generally in this psalm, the Law. The acknowledgment of the justice and faithfulness which send sorrows precedes the two verses of petition for " lovingkindness " and "compassions." Sorrows still sting and burn, though recognised as sent in love, and the tried heart yearns for these other messengers to come from God to sustain and soothe. God's promise and the psalmist's delight in God's law are the double ground of the twin petitions. Then follow three verses which are discernibly connected, as expressing desires in regard to " the proud," the devout, and the psalmist himself. He prays that the first may be shamed—*i.e.*, that their deceitful or causeless hostility may be balked—and, as in several other verses, contrasts his own peaceful absorption in the Law with their machinations. He repeats the prayer of ver. 74 with a slight difference, asking that his deliverance may draw attention to him, and that others may, from contemplating his security, come to know the worth of God's testimonies. In ver. 79 *b* the text reads " they shall know " (as the result of observing the psalmist), which the Hebrew margin needlessly alters into " those who know." For himself he prays that his heart may be sound, or thoroughly devoted to keep the law, and then he is sure that nothing shall ever put him to shame. " Who is he who will harm you, if ye be zealous for that which is good ? "

§ ⊃

81 My soul has pined for Thy salvation,
   For Thy word have I waited.
82 My eyes have pined for Thy promise,
   Saying, When wilt Thou comfort me ?

83 For I am become like a wine-skin in the smoke;
    Thy statutes have I not forgotten.
84 How many are the days of Thy servant?
    When wilt Thou execute judgment on my persecutors?
85 The proud have digged pits for me,
    —They who are not according to Thy law.
86 All Thy commandments are faithfulness,
    Lyingly they persecute me, help Thou me.
87 They had all but made an end of me on earth,
    But I, I have not forgotten Thy precepts.
88 According to Thy lovingkindness revive me,
    And I will observe the testimonies of Thy mouth.

This section has more than usual continuity. The psalmist is persecuted, and in these eight verses pours out his heart to God. Taken as a whole, they make a lovely picture of patient endurance and submissive longing. Intense and protracted yearning for deliverance has wasted his very soul, but has not merged in impatience or unbelief, for he has "waited for Thy word." His eyes have ached with straining for the signs of approaching comfort, the coming of which he has not doubted, but the delay of which has tried his faith. This longing has been quickened by troubles, which have wrapped him round like pungent smoke-wreaths eddying among the rafters, where disused wine-skins hang and get blackened and wrinkled. So has it been with him, but, through all, he has kept hold of God's statutes. So he plaintively reminds God of the brevity of his life, which has so short a tale of days that judgment on his persecutors must be swift, if it is to be of use. Vv. 85-87 describe the busy hostility of his foes. It is truculently contrary to God's law, and therefore, as is implied, worthy of God's counter-working. Ver. 85 *b* is best taken as a further description of the "proud," which is spread before God as a reason for His judicial action. The antithesis in

ver. 86, between the "faithfulness" of the Law and
the "lying" persecutors, is the ground of the prayer,
"Help Thou me." Even in extremest peril, when he
was all but made away with, the psalmist still clung to
God's precepts (ver. 87), and therefore he is heartened
to pray for reviving, and to vow that then, bound by
new chains of gratitude, he will, more than ever,
observe God's testimonies. The measure of the new
wine poured into the shrivelled wine-skin is nothing
less than the measureless lovingkindness of God ; and
nothing but experience of His benefits melts to
obedience.

ל

89 For ever, Jehovah,
      Thy word is set fast in the heavens.
90 To generation after generation lasts Thy faithfulness,
      Thou hast established the earth, and it stands firm.
91 According to Thy ordinances they stand firm to-day,
      For all [things] are Thy servants.
92 Unless Thy law had been my delight,
      Then had I perished in my affliction.
93 Never will I forget Thy precepts,
      For with them Thou hast revived me.
94 To Thee do I belong, save me,
      For Thy precepts have I sought.
95 For me have the wicked waited to destroy me,
      Thy testimonies will I consider.
96 To all perfection have I seen a limit,
      Thy commandment is exceeding broad.

The stability of nature witnesses to the steadfastness
of the Word which sustains it. The Universe began
and continues, because God puts forth His will. The
heavens with their pure depths would collapse, and all
their stars would flicker into darkness, if that uttered
Will did not echo through their overwhelming spaces.
The solid earth would not be solid, but for God's

power immanent in it. Heaven and earth are thus His servants. Ver. 91 *a* may possibly picture them as standing waiting "*for* Thine ordinances," but the indefinite preposition is probably better regarded as equivalent to *In accordance with*. The psalmist has reached the grand conceptions of the universal reign of God's law, and of the continuous forth-putting of God's will as the sustaining energy of all things. He seeks to link himself to that great band of God's servants, to be in harmony with stars and storms, with earth and ocean, as their fellow-servant; but yet he feels that his relation to God's law is closer than theirs, for he can delight in that which they unconsciously obey. Such delight in God's uttered will changes affliction from a foe, threatening life, to a friend, ministering strength (ver. 92). Nor does that Law when loved only avert destruction; it also increases vital power (ver. 93) and re-invigorates the better self. There is a sense in which the law *can* give life (Gal. iii. 21), but it must be welcomed and enshrined in the heart, in order to do so. The frequently recurring prayer for "salvation" has a double plea in ver. 94. The soul that has yielded itself to God in joyful obedience thereby establishes a claim on Him. He cannot but protect His own possession. Ownership has its obligations, which He recognises. The second plea is drawn from the psalmist's seeking after God's precepts, without which seeking there would be no reality in his profession of being God's. To seek them is the sure way to find both them and salvation (ver. 94). Whom God saves, enemies will vainly try to destroy, and, while they lurk in waiting to spring on the psalmist, his eyes are directed, not towards them, but to God's testimonies. To give heed to these is the sure way to escape snares (ver. 95).   Lifelong experience has taught the psalmist that there is a flaw in every human excellence, a limit soon reached and never passed to all that is noblest in man ; but high above all achievements, and stretching beyond present vision, is the fair ideal bodied forth in the Law.   Since it is God's commandment, it will not always be an unreached ideal, but may be indefinitely approximated to ; and to contemplate it will be joy, when we learn that it is prophecy because it is commandment.

§ ן

97 How I love Thy law !
    All the day is it my meditation.
98 Wiser than my enemies do Thy commandments make me,
    For they are mine for ever.
99 More than all my teachers am I prudent,
    For Thy testimonies are my meditation.
100 More than the aged do I understand,
    For Thy precepts have I kept.
101 From every evil path have I held back my feet,
    That I might observe Thy word.
102 From Thy judgments have I not departed,
    For Thou, Thou hast instructed me.
103 How sweet are Thy promises to my palate,
    More than honey to my mouth !
104 By Thy precepts I have understanding,
    Therefore I hate every path of falsehood.

One thought pervades this section, that the Law is the fountain of sweetest wisdom.   The rapture of love with which it opens is sustained throughout.   The psalmist knows that he has not merely more wisdom of the same sort as his enemies, his teachers, and the aged have, but wisdom of a better kind.   His foes were wise in craft, and his teachers drew their instructions from earthly springs, and the elders had learned that bitter, worldly wisdom, which has been disillusioned of youth's unsuspectingness and dreams, without being thereby led to grasp that which is no illusion. But a heart which simply keeps to the Law reaches, in its simplicity, a higher truth than these know, and has instinctive discernment of good and evil. Worldly wisdom is transient. "Whether there be knowledge, it shall be done away," but the wisdom that comes with the commandment is enduring as it (ver. 98). Meditation must be accompanied with practice, in order to make the true wisdom one's own. The depths of the testimonies must be sounded by patient brooding on them, and then the knowledge thus won must be carried into act. To do what we know is the sure way to know it better, and to know more (vv. 99, 100). And that positive obedience has to be accompanied by abstinence from evil ways; for in such a world as this "Thou shalt not" is the necessary preliminary to "Thou shalt." The psalmist has a better teacher than those whom he has outgrown, even God Himself, and His instruction has a graciously constraining power, which keeps its conscious scholars in the right path (ver. 102). These thoughts draw another exclamation from the poet, who feels, as he reflects on his blessings, that the law beloved ceases to be harsh and is delightsome s well as healthgiving. It is promise as well as law, for God will help us to be what He commands us to be. They who love the Lawgiver find sweetness in the law (ver. 103). And this is the blessed effect of the wisdom which it gives, that it makes us quick to detect sophistries which tempt into forbidden paths, and fills us with wholesome detestation of these (ver. 104).

§ 5

105 A lamp to my foot is Thy word,
   And a light to my path.
106 I have sworn, and have fulfilled it,
   To observe Thy righteous judgments.
107 I am afflicted exceedingly,
   Jehovah, revive me according to Thy word.
108 The free-will offerings of my mouth accept, I pray Thee,
      Jehovah,
   And teach me Thy judgments.
109 My soul is continually in my hand,
   But Thy law I do not forget.
110 The wicked have laid a snare for me,
   Yet from Thy precepts I do not stray.
111 Thy testimonies have I taken as my heritage for ever,
   For the joy of my heart are they.
112 I have inclined my heart to perform Thy statutes,
   For ever, [to the] end.

A lamp is for night; light shines in the day. The
Word is both, to the psalmist. His antithesis may be
equivalent to a comprehensive declaration that the Law
is light of every sort, or it may intend to lay stress on
the varying phases of experience, and turn our thoughts
to that Word which will gleam guidance in darkness,
and shine, a better sun, on bright hours. The psalmist's
choice, not merely the inherent power of the Law, is
expressed in ver. 105. He has taken it for his guide,
or, as ver. 106 says, has sworn and kept his oath, that
he would observe the righteous decisions, which would
point to his foot the true path. The affliction bemoaned
in ver. 107 is probably the direct result of the conduct
professed in ver. 106. The prayer for reviving, which
means deliverance from outward evils rather than
spiritual quickening, is, therefore, presented with confidence, and based upon the many promises in the Word
of help to sufferers for righteousness. Whatever our
afflictions, there is ease in telling God of them, and if

our desires for His help are " according to Thy word,"
they will be as willing to accept help to bear as help
which removes the sorrow, and thus will not be offered
unanswered.   That cry for reviving is best understood
as being " the free-will offerings " which the psalmist
prays may be accepted.   Happy in their afflictions are
they whose chief desire even then is to learn more of
God's statutes !   They will find that their sorrows are
their best teachers.   If we wish most to make advances
in His school, we shall not complain of the guides to
whom He commits us.   Continual alarms and dangers
tend to foster disregard of Duty, as truly as does the
opposite state of unbroken security.   A man absorbed in
keeping himself alive is apt to think he has no attention
to spare for God's law (ver. 109), and one ringed about
by traps is apt to take a circuit to avoid them, even at
the cost of divergence from the path marked out by
God (ver. 110).   But, even in such circumstances, the
psalmist did what all good men have to do, deliberately
chose his portion, and found God's law better than any
outward good, as being able to diffuse deep, sacred, and
perpetual joy through all his inner nature.   The heart
thus filled with serene gladness is thereby drawn to
perform God's statutes with lifelong persistency, and
the heart thus inclined to obedience has tapped the
sources of equally enduring joy.

§ ס

113 **The double-minded I hate,**
   But Thy law I love.
114 **My shelter and my shield art Thou,**
   For Thy word have I waited.
115 Depart from me, ye evil-doers,
   That I may keep the commandments of my God.
116 Uphold me according to Thy promise that I may live,
   And let me not be ashamed of my hope.

117 Hold me up and I shall be saved,
    And have regard to Thy statutes continually.
118 Thou makest light of all those who stray from Thy statutes,
    For their deceit is a lie.
119 [Like] dross Thou hast cast aside all the wicked of the earth,
    Therefore I love Thy testimonies.
120 My flesh creeps for fear of Thee,
    And of Thy judgments I am afraid.

This section is mainly the expression of firm resolve
to cleave to the Law.   Continuity may be traced in it,
since vv. 113–115 breathe love and determination, which
pass in vv. 116, 117, into prayer, in view of the psalmist's
weakness and the strength of temptation, while in
vv. 118–120 the fate of the despisers of the Law inten-
sifies the psalmist's clinging grasp of awe-struck love.
Hatred of "double-minded" who waver between God
and idols, and are weak accordingly, rests upon, and in
its turn increases, whole-hearted adherence to the Law.

It is a tepid devotion to it which does not strongly
recoil from lives that water down its precepts and try
to walk on both sides of the way at once.   Whoever
has taken God for his defence can afford to bide God's
time for fulfilment of His promises (ver. 114).   And the
natural results of such love to, and waiting for, His word
are resolved separation from the society of those whose
lives are moulded on opposite principles, and the order-
ing of external relations in accordance with the supreme
purpose of keeping the commandments of Him whom
love and waiting claim as "my God" (ver. 115).   But
resolves melt in the fire of temptation, and the psalmist
knows life and himself too well to trust himself.   So
he betakes himself to prayer for God's upholding, without which he cannot live.   A hope built on God's promise has a claim on Him, and its being put to shame in
disappointment would be dishonour to God (ver. 116).

The psalmist knows that his wavering will can only be fixed by God, and that experience of His sustaining hand will make a stronger bond between God and him than anything besides. The consciousness of salvation must precede steadfast regard to the precepts of the God who saves (ver. 117). To stray from the Law is ruin, as is described in vv. 118, 119. They who wander are despised or made light of, " for their deceit is a lie " —*i.e.*, the hopes and plans with which they deceive themselves are false. It is a gnarled way of saying that all godless life is a blunder as well as a sin, and is fed with unrealisable promises. Dross is flung away when the metal is extracted. Slag from a furnace is hopelessly useless, and this psalmist thinks that the wicked of the earth are "thrown as rubbish to the void." He is not contemplating a future life, but God's judgments as manifested here in providence, and his faith is assured that, even here, that process is visible. Therefore, gazing upon the fate of evil-doers, his flesh creeps and every particular hair stands on end (as the word means). His dread is full of love, and love is full of dread. Profoundly are the two emotions yoked together in vv. 119 *b* and 120 *b*, " I *love* Thy testimonies . . . of Thy judgments I am *afraid*."

§ v

121 I have done judgment and righteousness,
    Thou wilt not leave me to my oppressors.
122 Be surety for Thy servant for good,
    Let not the proud oppress me.
123 My eyes pine for Thy salvation
    And for Thy righteous promise.
124 Deal with Thy servant according to Thy lovingkindness,
    And teach me Thy statutes.
125 Thy servant am I; give me understanding,
    That I may know Thy testimonies.

126 It is time for Jehovah to work,
     They have made void Thy law.
127 Therefore I love Thy commandments
     More than gold and more than fine gold.
128 Therefore I esteem all Thy precepts to be right,
     Every false way do I hate.

The thought of evil-doers tinges most of this section.
It opens with a triplet of verses, occasioned by their
oppressions of the psalmist, and closes with a triplet
occasioned by their breaches of the Law. In the former,
he is conscious that he has followed the "judgment"
or law of God, and hence hopes that he will not be
abandoned to his foes. The consciousness and the
hope equally need limitation, to correspond with true
estimates of ourselves and with facts; for there is no
absolute fulfilment of the Law, and good men are often
left to be footballs for bad ones. But in its depths the
confidence is true. Precisely because he has it, the
psalmist prays that it may be vindicated by facts.
"Be surety for Thy servant"—a profound image,
drawn from legal procedure, in which one man becomes
security for another and makes good his deficiencies.
Thus God will stand between the hunted man and his
foes, undertaking for him. "Thou shalt answer, Lord,
for me." How much the fulfilment in Christ has ex-
ceeded the desire of the psalmist! "The oppressors
wrong" had lasted long, and the singer's weary eyes
had been strained in looking for the help which seemed
to tarry (compare ver. 82), and that fainting gaze
humbly appeals to God. Will He not end the wistful
watching speedily? Vv. 124, 125, are a pair, the
psalmist's relation of servant being adduced in both as
the ground of his prayer for teaching. But they differ,
in that the former verse lays stress on the consonance
of such instruction with God's lovingkindness, and the

latter, on its congruity with the psalmist's position and character as His servant. God's best gift is the knowledge of His will, which He surely will not withhold from spirits willing to serve, if they only knew how. Vv. 126-128 are closely linked. The psalmist's personal wrongs melt into the wider thought of wickedness which does its little best to make void that sovereign, steadfast law. Delitzsch would render " It is time to work for Jehovah "; and the meaning thus obtained is a worthy one. But that given above is more in accordance with the context. It is bold—and would be audacious if a prayer did not underlie the statement— to undertake to determine when evil has reached such height as to demand God's punitive action. But, however slow we should be to prescribe to Him the when or the how of His intervention, we may learn from the psalmist's emphatic " Therefores," which stand co-ordinately at the beginnings of vv. 127, 128, that the more men make void the Law, the more should God's servants prize it, and the more should they bind its precepts on their moral judgment, and heartily loathe all paths which, specious as they may be, are "paths of falsehood," though all the world may avow that they are true.

§ ᴅ

129 Wonderful are Thy testimonies,
   Therefore my soul keeps them.
130 The opening of Thy words gives light,
   It gives understanding to the simple.
131 My mouth did I open wide, and panted,
   For I longed for Thy commandments.
132 Turn to me and be gracious to me,
   According to the right of those who love Thy name.
133 Establish my steps by Thy promise,
   And let not iniquity lord it over me.
134 Redeem me from the oppression of men,
   That I may observe Thy precepts.

135 Cause Thy face to shine upon Thy servant,
    And teach me Thy statutes.
136 My eyes run down [in] streamlets of water,
    Because men observe not Thy law.

Devout souls do not take offence at the depths and
difficulties of God's word, but are thereby drawn to
intenser contemplation of them. We weary of the
Trivial and Obvious. That which tasks and outstrips
our powers attracts. But the obscurity must not be
arbitrary, but inherent, a clear obscure, like the depths
of a pure sea. These wonderful testimonies give light,
notwithstanding, or rather because of, their wonderful-
ness, and it is the simple heart, not the sharpened
intellect, that penetrates furthest into them and finds
light most surely (ver. 130). Therefore the psalmist
longs for God's commandments, like a wild creature
panting open-mouthed for water. He puts to shame
our indifference. If his longing was not excessive,
how defective is ours! Ver. 132, like ver. 122, has no
distinct allusion to the Law, though the word rendered
in it "right" is that used in the psalm for the Law
considered as "judgments." The prayer is a bold one,
pleading what is justly due to the lovers of God's
name. Kay appropriately quotes " God is not *unrighteous* to forget your work and labour of *love*, which ye
have showed towards His *name*" (Heb. vi. 10). One
would have expected "Law" instead of "name" in the
last word of the verse, and possibly the conception of
Law may be, as it were, latent in "name," for the latter
does carry in it imperative commandments and plain
revelations of duty. God's Name holds the Law in
germ. The Law is but the expansion of the meaning
of the Name. "Promise" in ver. 133 (lit. saying) must
be taken in a widened sense, as including all God's

revealed will. The only escape from the tyranny of sin is to have our steps established by God's word, and His help is needed for such establishment. Rebellion against sin's dominion is already victory over it, if the rebel summons God's heavenly reinforcements to his help. It is a high attainment to desire deliverance from men, chiefly in order to observe, unhindered, God's commandments (ver. 134). And it is as high a desire to seek the light of God's face mainly as the means of seeing His will more clearly. The psalmist did not merely wish for outward prosperity or inward cheer and comfort, but that these might contribute to fulfilling his deepest wish of learning better what God would have him to do (ver. 135). The moods of indignation (ver. 53) and of hatred (vv. 104, 113, 128) have given place to softer emotions, as they ever should (ver. 136). Tears and dewy pity should mingle with righteous anger, as when Jesus " looked round about on them with anger, being with the anger grieved at the hardening of their heart " (Mark iii. 5).

§ צ

137 Righteous art Thou, Jehovah,
   And upright are Thy judgments.
138 In righteousness Thou hast commanded Thy testimonies
   And in exceeding faithfulness.
139 My zeal has consumed me,
   For my adversaries have forgotten Thy words.
140 Well tried by fire is Thy promise,
   And Thy servant loves it.
141 Small and despised am I,
   Thy precepts have I not forgotten.
142 Thy righteousness is righteousness for ever,
   And Thy law is truth.
143 Distress and anguish have found me,
   Thy commandments are my delight.
144 Righteousness for ever are Thy testimonies,
   Give me understanding that I may live.

The first word suggested to the psalmist under this letter is Righteousness. That august conception was grasped by devout Israelites with a tenacity, and assumed a prominence in their thoughts, unparalleled elsewhere. It is no mere yielding to the requirements of the acrostic scheme which sets that great word in four of the eight verses of this section (137, 138, 142, 144). Two thoughts are common to them all, that Righteousness has its seat in the bosom of God, and that the Law is a true transcript of that Divine right-eousness. These things being so, it follows that the Law is given to men in accordance with the Divine "faithfulness"—*i.e.*, in remembrance and discharge of the obligations which God has undertaken towards them. Nor less certainly does it follow that that Law, which is the "eradiation" of God's righteousness, is eternal as its fontal source (vv. 142, 144). The beam must last as long as the sun. No doubt, there are transient elements in the Law which the psalmist loved, but its essence is everlasting, because its origin is God's everlasting Righteousness. So absorbed is he in adoring contemplation of it, that he even forgets to pray for help to keep it, and not till ver. 144 does he ask for understanding that he may live. True life is in the knowledge of the Law by which God is known, as Jesus has taught us that to know the only true God is life eternal. A faint gleam of immortal hope perhaps shines in that prayer, for if the "testimonies" are for ever, and the knowledge of them is life, it cannot be that they shall outlast the soul that knows and lives by them. One more characteristic of God's righteous testimonies is celebrated in ver. 140—namely, that they have stood sharp tests, and, like metal in the furnace, have not been dissolved but brightened by the heat.

They have been tested, when the psalmist was afflicted and found them to hold true. The same fire tried him and them, and he does not glorify his own endurance, but the promise which enabled him to stand firm. The remaining verses of the section describe the psalmist's afflictions and clinging to the Law. Ver. 139 recurs to his emotions on seeing men's neglect of it. "Zeal" here takes the place of grief (ver. 136) and of indignation and hatred. Friction against widespread godlessness generates a flame of zeal, as it should always do. "Small and despised" was Israel among the great powers of the ancient world, but he who meditates on the Law is armed against contempt and contented in insignificance (ver. 141). "Distress and anguish" may surround him, but hidden springs of "delight" well up in the heart that cleaves to the Law, like outbursts of fresh water rising to the surface of a salt sea (ver. 144).

§ פ

145 I have called with my whole heart; answer me, Jehovah;
    Thy statutes will I keep.

146 I have called unto Thee, save me,
    And I will observe Thy testimonies.

147 I anticipated the morning twilight and cried aloud,
    For Thy word I waited.

148 My eyes anticipated the night watches,
    That I might meditate on Thy promise.

149 Hear my voice according to Thy lovingkindness,
    Jehovah, according to Thy judgments revive me.

150 They draw near who follow after mischief,
    From Thy law they are far off.

151 Near art Thou, Jehovah,
    And all Thy commandments are truth.

152 Long ago have I known from Thy testimonies,
    That Thou hast founded them for ever.

The first two verses are a pair, in which former prayers

for deliverance and vows of obedience are recalled and repeated. The tone of supplication prevails through the section. The cries now presented are no new things. The psalmist's habit has been prayer, whole-hearted, continued, and accompanied with the resolve to keep by obedience and to observe with sharpened watchfulness the utterances of God's will. Another pair of verses follows (vv. 147, 148), which recall the singer's wakeful devotion. His voice rose to God ere the dim morning broke, and his heart kept itself in submissive expectance. His eyes saw God's promises shining in the nightly darkness, and making meditation better than sleep. The petitions in ver. 149 may be taken as based upon the preceding pairs. The psalmist's patient continuance gives him ground to expect an answer. But the true ground is God's character, as witnessed by His deeds of loving-kindness and His revelation of His "judgments" in the Law.

Another pair of verses follows (vv. 150, 151), in which the hostile nearness of the psalmist's foes, gathering round him with malignant purpose, is significantly contrasted, both with their remoteness in temper from the character enjoined in the Law, and with the yet closer proximity of the assailed man's defender. He who has God near him, and who realises that His "commandments are truth," can look untrembling on mustering masses of enemies. This singer had learned that before danger threatened. The last verse of the section breathes the same tone of long-continued and habitual acquaintance with God and His Law as the earlier pairs of verses do. The convictions of a life-time were too deeply rooted to be disturbed by such a passing storm. There is, as it were, a calm smile of triumphant certitude in that "Long ago." Experience teaches that the foundation, laid for trust as well as for conduct in the Law, is too stable to be moved, and that we need not fear to build our all on it. Let us build rock on that rock, and answer God's everlasting testimonies with our unwavering reliance and submission.

ק

153 See my affliction, and deliver me,
   For Thy law do I not forget.
154 Plead my plea and redeem me,
   Revive me according to Thy promise.
155 Far from the wicked is salvation,
   For they seek not Thy statutes.
156 Thy compassions are many, Jehovah,
   According to Thy judgments revive me.
157 Many are my pursuers and my adversaries,
   From Thy testimonies I have not declined.
158 I beheld the faithless and loathed [them]
   Because they observed not Thy promise.
159 See how I love Thy precepts,
   Jehovah, according to Thy lovingkindness revive me.
160 The sum of Thy word is truth,
   And every one of Thy righteous judgments endures for ever.

The prayer "revive me" occurs thrice in this section. It is not a petition for spiritual quickening so much as for removal of calamities, which restrained free, joyous life. Its repetition accords with other characteristics of this section, which is markedly a cry from a burdened heart. The psalmist is in affliction; he is, as it were, the defendant in a suit, a captive needing a strong avenger (ver. 154), compassed about by a swarm of enemies (ver. 157), forced to endure the sight of the faithless and to recoil from them (ver. 158). His thoughts vibrate between his needs and God's compassions, between his own cleaving to the Law and its grand comprehensiveness and perpetuity. His prayer now is not for fuller knowledge of the Law, but for rescue from his troubles. It is worth while to follow his swift turns of thought, which, in their windings, are shaped by the double sense of need and of Divine fulness. First come two plaintive cries for rescue, based in one case on his adherence to the Law, and in the other on God's promise. Then his eye turns on those who do not, like him, seek God's statutes, and these he pronounces, with solemn depth of insight, to be far from the salvation which he feels is his, because they have no desire to know God's will. That is a pregnant word. Swiftly he turns from these unhappy ones to gaze on the multitude of God's compassions, which hearten him to repeat his prayer for revival, according to God's "judgments"—*i.e.*, His decisions contained in the Law. But, again, his critical position among enemies forces itself into remembrance, and he can only plead that, in spite of them, he has held fast by the Law, and, when compelled to see apostates, has felt no temptation to join them, but a wholesome loathing of all departure from God's word. That loathing was the other side of his love. The more closely we cleave to God's precepts, the more shall we recoil from modes of thought and life which flout them. And then the psalmist looks wistfully up once more, and asks that his love may receive what God's lovingkindness emboldens it to look for as its result—namely, the reviving, which he thus once more craves. That love for the Law has led him into the depths of understanding God's Word, and so his lowly petitions swell into the declaration, which he has verified in life, that its sum-total is truth, and a perpetual possession for loving hearts, however ringed round by enemies and "weighed upon by sore distress."

§ ע

161 Princes have persecuted me without a cause,
But at Thy words my heart stands in awe.

162 I rejoice over Thy promise,
As one that finds great booty.

163 Lying I hate and abhor,
Thy law do I love.

164 Seven times a day I praise Thee,
Because of Thy righteous judgments.

165 Great peace have they that love Thy law,
And they have no stumbling-block.

166 I have hoped for Thy salvation, Jehovah,
And Thy commandments have I done.

167 My soul has observed Thy testimonies,
And I love them exceedingly.

168 I have observed Thy precepts and Thy testimonies,
For all my ways are before Thee.

The tone of this section is in striking contrast with that of the preceding. Here, with the exception of the first clause of the first verse, all is sunny, and the thunder-clouds are hull down on the horizon. Joy, peace, and hope breathe through the song. Beautifully are reverential awe and exuberant gladness blended as contemporaneous results of listening to God's word. There is rapture in that awe; there is awe in that bounding gladness. To possess that Law is better than to win rich booty. The spoils of the conflict, which we wage with our own negligence or disobedience, are our best wealth. The familiar connection between love of the Law and hatred of lives which depart from it, and are therefore lies and built on lies, re-appears, yet not as the ground of prayer for help, but as part of the blessed treasures which the psalmist is recounting. His life is accompanied by music of perpetual praise. Seven times a day—*i.e.*, unceasingly—his glad heart breaks into song, and "the o'ercome of his song" is ever God's righteous

judgments. His own experience gives assurance of
the universal truth that the love of God's law secures
peace, inasmuch as such love brings the heart into
contact with absolute good, inasmuch as submission to
God's will is always peace, inasmuch as the fountain of
unrest is dried up, inasmuch as all outward things are
allies of such a heart and serve the soul that serves
God. Such love saves from falling over stumbling-
blocks, and enables a man " to walk firmly and safely
on the clear path of duty." Like the dying Jacob,
such a man waits for God's salvation, patiently expecting that each day will bring its own form of help and
deliverance, and his waiting is no idle anticipation, but
full of strenuous obedience (ver. 166), and of watchful
observance, such as the eyes of a servant direct to his
master (ver. 167 a). Love makes such a man keen to
note the slightest indications of God's will, and eager
to obey them all (vv. 167 b., 168 a). All this joyous
profession of the psalmist's happy experience he spreads
humbly before God, appealing to Him whether it is
true. He is not flaunting his self-righteousness in
God's face, but gladly recounting to God's honour all
the " spoil " that he has found, as he penetrated into
the Law and it penetrated into his inmost being.

§ ת

169 Let my cry come near before Thy face, Jehovah,
   According to Thy word give me understanding.
170 Let my supplication come before Thy face,
   According to Thy promise deliver me.
171 My lips shall well forth praise,
   For Thou teachest me Thy statutes.
172 My tongue shall sing of Thy promise,
   For all Thy commandments are righteousness.
173 Let Thy hand be [stretched out] to help me,
   For Thy precepts have I chosen.

174 I long for Thy salvation, Jehovah,
    And Thy law is my delight.
175 Let my soul live and it shall praise Thee,
    And let Thy judgments help me.
176 I have strayed like a lost sheep, seek Thy servant,
    For Thy commandments do I not forget.

The threads that have run through the psalm are knotted firmly together in this closing section, which falls into four pairs of verses. In the first, the manifold preceding petitions are concentrated into two for understanding and deliverance, the twin needs of man, of which the one covers the whole ground of inward illumination, and the other comprises all good for outward life, while both are in accordance with the large confidence warranted by God's faithful words. Petition passes into praise. The psalmist instinctively obeys the command, "By prayer and supplication with thanksgiving let your requests be made known." His lips give forth not only shrill cries of need, but well up songs of thanks; and, while a thousand mercies impel the sparkling flood of praise, the chief of these is God's teaching him His righteous statutes (vv. 171, 172). In the next pair of verses, the emphasis lies, not on the prayer for help, so much as on its grounds in the psalmist's deliberate choice of God's precepts, his patient yearning for God's salvation, and his delight in the Law, all of which characteristics have been over and over again professed in the psalm. Here, once more, they are massed together, not in self-righteousness, but as making it incredible that, God being the faithful and merciful God which He is, His hand should hang idle when His servant cries for help (vv. 173, 174). The final pair of verses sets forth the relations of the devout soul with God in their widest and most permanent forms. The true life of the soul must come from Him, the Fountain of Life. A soul thus made to live by communion with, and derivation of life from, God lives to praise, and all its motions are worship. To it the Law is no menace nor unwelcome restriction but a helper. Life drawn from God, turned to God in continual praise, and invigorated by unfailing helps ministered through His uttered will, is the only life worth living. It is granted to all who ask for it. But a lower, sadder note must ever mingle in our prayers. Aspiration and trust must be intertwined with consciousness of weakness and distrust of one's self. Only those who are ignorant of the steps of the soul's pilgrimage to God can wonder that the psalmist's last thoughts about himself blend confession of wandering like a straying sheep, and profession of not forgetting God's commandments. Both phases of consciousness co-exist in the true servant of God, as, alas! both have grounds in his experience. But our sense of having wandered should ever be accompanied with the tender thought that the lost sheep *is* a sheep, beloved and sought for by the great Shepherd, in whose search, not in our own docile following of His footsteps, lies our firmest hope. The psalmist prayed "Seek Thy servant," for he knew how continually he would be tempted to stray. But we know better than he did how wonderfully the answer has surpassed his petition. "The Son of Man is come to seek and to save that which was lost."

PSALMS CXX.—CXXXIV.

THESE fifteen psalms form a short psalter within the Psalter, each having the same title (with a slight grammatical variation in Psalm cxxi.). Its meaning is very doubtful. Many of the older authorities understand it to signify "a song of steps," and explain it by a very uncertain tradition that these psalms were sung on fifteen steps leading from the court of the women to that of the men, each on one step. The R.V.'s rendering, "degrees," uses that word in this sense (like the Latin *gradus*). But though undoubtedly the word means steps, there is no sufficient support for the tradition in question; and, as Delitzsch well observes, if this were the meaning of the title, "it would be much more external than any of the other inscriptions to the Psalms."

Another explanation fixes on the literal meaning of the word—*i.e.*, "goings up"—and points to its use in the singular for the Return from Babylon (Ezra vii. 9), as supporting the view that these were psalms sung by the returning exiles. There is much in the group of songs to favour this view; but against it is the fact that Psalms cxxii. and cxxxiv. imply the existence of the Temple, and the fully organised ceremonial worship.

A third solution is that the name refers to the structure of these psalms, which have a "step-like, progressive rhythm." This is Gesenius' explanation, adopted by Delitzsch. But the peculiar structure in question, though very obvious in several of these psalms, is scarcely perceptible in others, and is entirely absent from Psalm cxxxii.

The remaining explanation of the title is the most probable—that the " goings up " were those of the worshippers travelling to Jerusalem for the feasts. This little collection is, then, " The Song Book of the Pilgrims," a designation to which its contents well correspond.

PSALM CXX.

1 To Jehovah in my straits I cried,
  And He answered me.

2 Jehovah, deliver my soul from the lying lip,
  From the deceitful tongue.
3 What shall He give to thee, and what more
      shall He give thee,
  Deceitful tongue ?
4 Arrows of the Mighty, sharpened ones,
  With coals of broom.

5 Woe is me that I sojourn in Meshech,
  [That] I dwell beside the tents of Kedar!
6 Long has my soul had her dwelling
  With him who hates peace.
7 I am—peace; but when I speak,
  They are for war.

THE collection of pilgrim songs is appropriately
    introduced by one expressive of the unrest arising
from compulsory association with uncongenial and
hostile neighbours. The psalmist laments that his
sensitive "soul" has been so long obliged to be a
"sojourner" where he has heard nothing but lying and
strife. Weary of these, his soul stretches her wings
towards a land of rest. His feeling ill at ease amidst
present surroundings stings him to take the pilgrim's
staff. "In" this singer's "heart are the ways."

The simplicity of this little song scarcely admits of
separation into parts; but one may note that an intro-

ductory verse is followed by two groups of three verses each,—the former of which is prayer for deliverance from the "deceitful tongue," and prediction that retribution will fall on it (vv. 2–4); while the latter bemoans the psalmist's uncongenial abode among enemies (vv. 5–7).

The verbs in ver. 1 are most naturally referred to former experiences of the power of prayer, which encourage renewed petition. Devout hearts argue that what Jehovah has done once He will do again. Since His mercy endureth for ever, He will not weary of bestowing, nor will former gifts exhaust His stores. Men say, "I have given so often that I can give no more"; God says, "I have given, therefore I will give." The psalmist was not in need of defence against armed foes, but against false tongues. But it is not plain whether these were slanderous, flattering, or untrustworthy in their promises of friendship. The allusions are too general to admit of certainty. At all events, he was surrounded by a choking atmosphere of falsehood, from which he longed to escape into purer air. Some commentators would refer the allusions to the circumstances of the exiles in Babylon; others to the slanders of the Samaritans and others who tried to hinder the rebuilding of the Temple; others think that his own hostile fellow-countrymen are the psalmist's foes. May we not rather hear in his plaint the voice of the devout heart, which ever painfully feels the dissonance between its deep yearnings and the Babel of vain words which fills every place with jangling and deceit? To one who holds converse with God, there is nothing more appalling or more abhorrent than the flood of empty talk which drowns the world. If there was any specific foe in the psalmist's mind, he has not described him so as to enable us to identify him.

Ver. 3 may be taken in several ways, according as "deceitful tongue" is taken as a vocative or as the nominative of the verb "give," and as that verb is taken in a good or a bad sense, and as "thee" is taken to refer to the tongue or to some unnamed person. It is unnecessary to enter here on a discussion of the widely divergent explanations given. They fall principally into two classes. One takes the words "deceitful tongue" as vocative, and regards the question as meaning, "What retribution shall God give to thee, O deceitful tongue?" while the other takes it as asking what the tongue shall give unto an unnamed person designated by "thee." That person is by some considered to be the owner of the tongue, who is asked what profit his falsehood will be to him; while others suppose the "thee" to mean Jehovah, and the question to be like that of Job (x. 3). Baethgen takes this view, and paraphrases, "What increase of Thy riches canst Thou expect therefrom, that Thou dost permit the godless to oppress the righteous?" Grammatically either class of explanation is warranted; and the reader's feeling of which is most appropriate must decide. The present writer inclines to the common interpretation, which takes ver. 3 as addressed to the deceitful tongue, in the sense, "What punishment shall God inflict upon thee?" Ver. 4 is the answer, describing the penal consequences of falsehood, as resembling the crimes which they avenge. Such a tongue is likened to sharp arrows and swords in Psalms lvii. 4, lxiv. 3, etc. The punishment shall be like the crime. For the sentiment compare Psalm cxl. 9, 10. It is not necessary to suppose that the "Mighty" is God, though such a reference gives force to the words. " The tongue which shot piercing arrows is pierced by the sharpened arrows of an irresistibly strong One ; it, which set its neighbour in a fever of arguish, must endure a lasting heat of broom-coals, which consumes it surely " (Delitzsch).

In the group of vv. 5–7, the psalmist bemoans his compulsory association with hostile companions, and longs to " flee away and be at rest." Meshech was the name of barbarous tribes who, in the times of Sargon and Sennacherib, inhabited the highlands to the east of Cilicia, and in later days retreated northwards to the neighbourhood of the Black Sea (Sayce, " Higher Criticism and Monuments," p. 130). Kedar was one of the Bedawin tribes of the Arabian desert. The long distance between the localities occupied by these two tribes requires an allegorical explanation of their names. They stand as types of barbarous and truculent foes— as we might say, Samoyeds and Patagonians. The psalmist's plaint struck on Cromwell's heart, and is echoed, with another explanation of its meaning which he had, no doubt, learned from some Puritan minister : " I live, you know where, in Meshech, which they say signifies prolonging ; in Kedar, which signifies blackness ; yet the Lord forsaketh me not " (Carlyle, " Letters and Speeches," i. 127 : London, 1846). The peace-loving psalmist describes himself as stunned by the noise and quarrelsomeness of those around him. " I am—peace " (compare Psalm cix. 4). But his gentlest word is like a spark on tinder. If he but speaks, they fly to their weapons, and are ready without provocation to answer with blows.

So the psalm ends as with a long-drawn sigh. It inverts the usual order of similar psalms, in which the description of need is wont to precede the prayer for deliverance. It thus sets forth most pathetically the sense of discordance between a man and his environment, which urges the soul that feels it to seek a better home. So this is a true pilgrim psalm.

PSALM CXXI.

1 I will lift mine eyes to the hills;
   Whence cometh my help?
2 My help [comes] from Jehovah,
   The Maker of heaven and earth.

3 May He not suffer thy feet to totter,
   May thy Keeper not slumber!
4 Behold, thy Keeper slumbers not;
   Behold, He slumbers not nor sleeps
   [Who is] the Keeper of Israel.

5 Jehovah is thy Keeper,
   Jehovah is thy shade on thy right hand.
6 By day the sun shall not smite thee,
   Nor the moon by night.

7 Jehovah shall keep thee from all evil,
   He shall keep thy soul.
8 Jehovah shall keep thy going out and thy
     coming in,
   From now, even for evermore.

HOW many timid, anxious hearts has this sweet outpouring of quiet trust braced and lifted to its own serene height of conscious safety! This psalmist is so absorbed in the thought of his Keeper that he barely names his dangers. With happy assurance of protection, he says over and over again the one word which is his amulet against foes and fears. Six times in these few verses does the thought recur that Jehovah is the Keeper of Israel or of the single soul. The quietness that comes of confidence is the singer's strength.   Whether he is an exile, looking across the plains of Mesopotamia towards the blue hills, which the eye cannot discern, or a pilgrim catching the first sight of the mountain on which Jehovah sits enshrined, is a question which cannot be decisively answered ; but the power and beauty of this little breathing of peaceful trust are but slightly affected by any hypothesis as to the singer's circumstances.   Vv. 1 and 2 stand apart from the remainder, in so far as in them the psalmist speaks in the first person, while in the rest of the psalm he is spoken to in the second.   But this does not necessarily involve the supposition of an antiphonal song.   The two first verses may have been sung by a single voice, and the assurances of the following ones by a chorus or second singer.   But it is quite as likely that, as in other psalms, the singer is in vv. 3–8 himself the speaker of the assurances which confirm his own faith.

His first words describe the earnest look of longing. He will lift his eyes from all the coil of troubles and perils to the heights.   *Sursum corda* expresses the true ascent which these psalms enjoin and exemplify.   If the supposition that the psalmist is an exile on the monotonous levels of Babylon is correct, one feels the pathetic beauty of his wistful gaze across the dreary flats towards the point where he knows that the hills of his father-land rise.   To look beyond the low levels where we dwell, to the unseen heights where we have our home, is the condition of all noble living amid these lower ranges of engagement with the Visible and Transient.   " Whence comes my help ? " is a question which may be only put in order to make the assured answer more emphatic, but may also be an expression of momentary despondency, as the thought of the distance between the gazer and the mountains chills his aspirations. 'It is easy to look, but hard to journey thither. How shall I reach that goal? I am weak; the way is long and beset with foes." The loftier the ideal, the more needful, if it is ever to be reached, that our consciousness of its height and of our own feebleness should drive us to recognise our need of help in order to attain it.

Whoever has thus high longings sobered by lowly estimates of self is ready to receive the assurance of Divine aid. That sense of impotence is the precursor of faith. We must distrust ourselves, if we are ever to confide in God. To know that we need His aid is a condition of obtaining it. Bewildered despondency asks, "Whence comes my help?" and scans the low levels in vain. The eye that is lifted to the hills is sure to see Him coming to succour; for that question on the lips of one whose looks are directed thither is a prayer, rather than a question; and the assistance he needs sets out towards him from the throne, like a sunbeam from the sun, as soon as he looks up to the light.

The particle of negation in ver. 3 is not that used in ver. 4, but that which is employed in commands or wishes. The progress from subjective desire in ver. 3, to objective certainty of Divine help as expressed in ver. 4 and the remainder of the psalm, is best exhibited if the verbs in the former verse are translated as expressions of wish—"May He not," etc. Whether the speaker is taken to be the psalmist or another makes little difference to the force of ver. 3, which lays hold in supplication of the truth just uttered in ver. 2, and thereby gains a more assured certainty that it is true, as the following verses go on to declare. It is no drop to a lower mood to pass from assertion of God's help

to prayer for it. Rather it is the natural progress of
faith. Both clauses of ver. 2 become specially significant if this is a song for pilgrims. Their daily march
and their nightly encampment will then be placed under
the care of Jehovah, who will hold up their feet unwearied on the road and watch unslumbering over their
repose. But such a reference is not necessary. The
language is quite general. It covers the whole ground
of toil and rest, and prays for strength for the one and
quiet security in the other.

The remainder of the psalm expands the one thought
of Jehovah the Keeper, with sweet reiteration, and yet
comprehensive variation. First, the thought of the
last clause of the preceding verse is caught up again.
Jehovah is the keeper of the community, over which
He watches with unslumbering care. He keeps Israel,
so long as Israel keeps His law; for the word so
frequently used here is the same as is continually
employed for observance of the commandments. He
had seemed to slumber while Israel was in exile, and
had been prayed to awake, in many a cry from the
captives. Now they have learned that He never
slumbers: His power is unwearied, and needs no recu-
peration; His watchfulness is never at fault. But
universal as is His care, it does not overlook the single
defenceless suppliant. He is "*thy* Keeper," and will
stand at thy right hand, where helpers stand, to shield
thee from all dangers. Men lose sight of the individual
in the multitude, and the wider their benevolence or
beneficence, the less it takes account of units; but God
loves all because He loves each, and the aggregate is
kept because each member of it is. The light which
floods the universe gently illumines every eye. The
two conceptions of defence and impartation of power

are smelted together in the pregnant phrase of ver. 5 *b*, " thy shade at thy right hand."

The notion of shelter from evils predominates in the remainder of the psalm. It is applied in ver. 6 to possible perils from physical causes : the fierce sunlight beat down on the pilgrim band, and the moon was believed, and apparently with correctness, to shed malignant influences on sleepers. The same antithesis of day and night, work and rest, which is found in ver. 3 appears again here. The promise is widened out in ver. 7 so as to be all-inclusive. " All evil " will be averted from him who has Jehovah for his keeper ; therefore, if any so-called Evil comes, he may be sure that it is God with a veil on. We should apply the assurances of the psalm to the interpretation of life, as well as take them for the antidote of fearful anticipations.

Equally comprehensive is the designation of that which is to be kept. It is " thy soul," the life or personal being. Whatever may be shorn away by the sharp shears of Loss, that will be safe ; and if it is, nothing else matters very much. The individual soul is of large account in God's sight : He keeps it as a deposit entrusted to Him by faith. Much may go ; but His hand closes round us when we commit ourselves into it, and none is able to pluck us thence.

In the final verse, the psalmist recurs to his favourite antithesis of external toil and repose in the home, the two halves of the pilgrim life for every man ; and while thus, in the first clause of the verse, he includes all varieties of circumstance, in the second he looks on into a future of which he does not see the bounds, and triumphs over all possible foes that may lurk in its dim recesses, in the assurance that, however far it may extend, and whatever strange conditions it may hide, the Keeper will be there, and all will be well. Whether or not he looked to the last " going out," our exodus from earth (Luke ix. 31 ; 2 Peter i. 15), or to that abundant entrance (2 Peter i. 11) into the true home which crowns the pilgrimage here, we cannot but read into his indefinite words their largest meaning, and rejoice that we have One who " is able to keep that which we have committed to Him against that day."

PSALM CXXII.

1 I rejoiced when they said to me,
  To the house of Jehovah let us go.
2 Standing are our feet
  In thy gates, Jerusalem.

3 Jerusalem that art built [again]
  As a city that is compact together.
4 Whither went up the tribes, the tribes of Jah,
  —[According to] the precept for Israel—
  To give thanks to the name of Jehovah.
5 For there were set thrones of judgment,
  Thrones for the house of David.

6 Pray for the peace of Jerusalem;
  Prosperous be they who love thee!
7 Be peace within thy bulwark,
  Prosperity within thy palaces.
8 Because of my brethren and my companions' sake
  Let me now wish thee peace.
9 Because of the house of Jehovah our God
  Let me now seek thy good.

THIS is very distinctly a pilgrim psalm. But there is difficulty in determining the singer's precise point of view, arising from the possibility of understanding the phrase in ver. 2, "are standing," as meaning either "are" or "were standing" or "have stood." If it is taken as a present tense, the psalm begins by recalling the joy with which the pilgrims began their march, and in ver. 2 rejoices in reaching the goal. Then, in vv. 3, 4, 5 the psalmist paints the sight of the city which gladdened the gazers' eyes, remembers ancient glories when Jerusalem was the rallying-point for united worship and the seat of the Davidic monarchy, and finally pours out patriotic exhortations to love Jerusalem and prayers for her peace and prosperity. This seems the most natural construing of the psalm. If, on the other hand, ver. 2 refers to a past time, " the poet, now again returning home or actually returned, remembers the whole pilgrimage from its beginning onwards." This is possible ; but the warmth of emotion in the exclamation in ver. 3 is more appropriate to the moment of rapturous realisation of a long-sought joy than to the paler remembrance of it.

Taking, then, the former view of the verse, we have the beginning and end of the pilgrimage brought into juxtaposition in vv. 1 and 2. It was begun in joy ; it ends in full attainment and a satisfied rapture, as the pilgrim finds the feet which have traversed many a weary mile planted at last within the city. How fading the annoyances of the road ! Happy they whose life's path ends where the psalmist's did ! The joy of fruition will surpass that of anticipation, and difficulties and dangers will be forgotten.

Vv. 3–5 give voice to the crowding thoughts and memories waked by that moment of supreme joy, when dreams and hopes have become realities, and the pilgrim's happy eyes do actually see the city. It stands " built," by which is best understood *built anew*, rising from the ruins of many years. It is " compact together," the former breaches in the walls and the melancholy gaps in the buildings being filled up. Others take the reference to be to the crowding of its houses, which its site, a narrow peninsula of rock with deep ravines on three sides, made necessary. But fair to his eyes as the Jerusalem of to-day looked, the poet-patriot sees auguster forms rising behind it, and recalls vanished glories, when all the twelve tribes came up to worship, according to the commandment, and there was yet a king in Israel. The religious and civil life of the nation had their centres in the city; and Jerusalem had become the seat of worship because it was the seat of the monarchy. These days were past; but though few in number, the tribes still were going up; and the psalmist does not feel the sadness but the sanctity of the vanished past.

Thus moved to the depths of his soul, he breaks forth into exhortation to his companion pilgrims to pray for the peace of the city. There is a play on the meaning of the name in ver. 6 a; for, as the Tel-el-Amarna tablets have told us, the name of the city of the priest-king was Uru Salim—the city of [the god of] peace. The prayer is that the *nomen* may become *omen*, and that the hope that moved in the hearts that had so long ago and in the midst of wars given so fair a designation to their abode, may be fulfilled now at last. A similar play of words lies in the interchange of "peace" and "prosperity," which are closely similar in sound in the Hebrew. So sure is the psalmist that God will favour Zion, that he assures his companions that individual well-being will be secured by loyal love to her. The motive appealed to may be so put as to be mere selfishness, though, if any man loved Zion not for Zion's sake but for his own, he could scarcely be deemed to love her at all. But rightly understood, the psalmist proclaims an everlasting truth, that the highest good is realised by sinking self in a passion of earnest love for and service to the City of God. Such love is in itself well-being; and while it may have no rewards appreciable by sense, it cannot fail of sharing in the good of Zion and the prosperity of God's chosen.

The singer puts forth the prayers which he enjoins on others, and rises high above all considerations of self. His desires are winged by two great motives,—on the one hand, his self-oblivious wish for the good of those who are knit to him by common faith and worship; on the other, his loving reverence for the sacred house of Jehovah. That house hallowed every stone in the city. To wish for the prosperity of Jerusalem, forgetting that the Temple was in it, would have been mere earthly patriotism, a very questionable virtue. To wish and struggle for the growth of an external organisation called a Church, disregarding the Presence which gives it all its sanctity, is no uncommon fault in some who think that they are actuated by " zeal for the Lord," when it is a much more earthly flame that burns in them.

PSALM CXXIII.

1 To Thee lift I mine eyes,
  O Thou that art enthroned in the heavens.
2 Behold, as the eyes of slaves are towards the hand of their masters,
  As the eyes of a maid are towards the hand of her mistress,
  So [are] our eyes towards Jehovah our God,
  Till He be gracious to us.

3 Be gracious to us, Jehovah, be gracious to us,
  For we are abundantly filled with contempt.
4 Abundantly is our soul filled
  With the scorn of them that are at ease,
  The contempt of the proud.

A SIGH and an upward gaze and a sigh! No period is more appropriate, as that of this psalm, than the early days after the return from exile, when the little community, which had come back with high hopes, found themselves a laughing-stock to their comfortable and malicious neighbours. The contrast of tone with the joy of the preceding psalm is very striking. After the heights of devout gladness have been reached, it is still needful to come down to stern realities of struggle, and these can only be faced when the eye of patient dependence and hope is fixed on God.

That attitude is the great lesson of this brief and perfect expression of wistful yet unfaltering trust joined with absolute submission. The upward look here is like, but also unlike, that in Psalm cxxi., in that this is less triumphant, though not less assured, and has an expression of lowly submission in the appealing gaze. Commentators quote illustrations of the silent observance of the master's look by his rows of slaves ; but these are not needed to elucidate the vivid image. It tells its own story. Absolute submission to God's hand, whether it wields a rod or lavishes gifts or points to service, befits those whose highest honour is to be His slaves. They should stand where they can see Him ; they should have their gaze fixed upon Him ; they should look with patient trust, as well as with eager willingness to start into activity when He indicates His commands.

The sigh for deliverance, in the second half of the psalm, is no breach of that patient submission. Trust and resignation do not kill natural shrinking from contempt and scorn. It is enough that they turn shrinking into supplication and lamentations into appeals to God. He lets His servants make their moan to Him, and tell how full their souls have long been of men's scorn. As a plea with Him the psalmist urges the mockers' "ease." In their security and full-fed complacency, they laughed at the struggling band, as men gorged with material good ever do at enthusiasts ; but it is better to be contemned for the difficulties which cleaving to the ruins of God's city brings, than to be the contemners in their selfish abundance. They are further designated as "haughty," by a word which the Hebrew margin reads as two words, meaning "proud ones of the oppressors" ; but this is unnecessary, and the text yields a good meaning as it stands, though the word employed is unusual.

This sweet psalm, with all its pained sense of the mockers' gibes and their long duration, has no accent of impatience. Perfect submission, fixed observance, assured confidence that, "till He is gracious," it is best to bear what He sends, befit His servants, and need not hinder their patient cry to Him, nor their telling Him how long and hard their trial has been.

PSALM CXXIV.

1 Had not Jehovah been for us,
  —Thus let Israel say—
2 Had not Jehovah been for us,
  When men rose against us :
3 Then had they swallowed us alive,
  When their wrath blazed out upon us;
4 Then had the waters overwhelmed us,
  The torrent had gone over our soul ;
5 Then had gone over our soul
  The proud waters.

6 Blessed be Jehovah,
  Who has not given us [as] a prey to their teeth.
7 Our soul is like a bird escaped from the fowlers' snare ;
  The snare is broken, and we—we are escaped.
8 Our help is in the name of Jehovah,
  Maker of heaven and earth.

A SEQUENCE may be traced connecting this with the two adjacent psalms. In Psalm cxxiii., patient resignation sighed for deliverance, which here has been received and has changed the singer's note into jubilant and wondering praise ; while, in the next little lyric, we have the escaped Israel established in Jerusalem, and drawing omens of Divine guardianship from its impregnable position, on a mountain girt by mountains. This psalm is an outgush of the first rapture of astonishment and joy for deliverance so sudden and complete. It is most naturally taken as the expression of the feelings of the exiles on their restoration from Babylon. One thought runs through it all, that the

sole actor in their deliverance has been Jehovah. No
human arm has been bared for them ; no created might
could have rescued them from the rush of the swelling
deluge. Like a bird in a net panting with fear and
helplessness, they waited the fowler's grasp ; but, lo, by
an unseen Power the net was broken, and they are free
to wing their flight to their nest. So, triumphantly they
ring out at last the Name which has been their help,
abjuring any share in their own rescue, and content to
owe it all to Him.

The step-like structure is very obvious in this psalm.
As Delitzsch puts it, " In order to take a step forward,
it always goes back half a step." But the repetitions
are not mere artistic embellishments ; they beautifully
correspond to the feelings expressed. A heart running
over with thankful surprise at its own new security
and freedom cannot but reiterate the occasion of its
joy. It is quite as much devotion as art which says
twice over that Jehovah was on the singers' side, which
twice recalls how nearly they had been submerged in
the raging torrent, and twice remembers their escape
from the closely wrapping but miraculously broken
snare. A suppliant is not guilty of vain repetitions
though he asks often for the same blessing, and
thanksgiving for answered petitions should be as persistent as the petitions were. That must be a shallow
gratitude which can be all poured out at one gush.

The psalmist's metaphors for Israel's danger are
familiar ones. " They had swallowed us alive " may
refer to the open jaws of Sheol, as in other psalms, but
more probably is simply a figure drawn from beasts of
prey, as in ver. 6. The other image of a furious swollen
torrent sweeping over the heads (or, as here, over the
soul) recalls the grand contrast drawn by Isaiah

between the gently flowing "waters of Siloam" and the devastating rush of the "river," symbolising the King of Assyria, which, like some winter torrent swollen by the rains, suddenly rises and bears on its tawny bosom to the sea the ruins of men's works and the corpses of the workers.

The word rendered "proud" is a rare word, coming from a root meaning *to boil over*, and may be used here in its literal sense, but is more probably to be taken in its metaphorical meaning of haughty, and applied rather to the persons signified by the waters than to the flood itself. Vv. 6 and 7 are an advance on the preceding, inasmuch as those described rather the imminence of danger, and these magnify the completeness of Jehovah's delivering mercy. The comparison of the soul to a bird is beautiful (Psalm xi. 1). It hints at tremors and feebleness, at alternations of feeling like the flutter of some weak-winged songster, at the utter helplessness of the panting creature in the toils. One hand only could break the snare, and then the bruised wings were swiftly spread for flight once more, and up into the blue went the ransomed joy, with a song instead o harsh notes of alarm. "We—we are escaped." That is enough : we are out of the net. Whither the flight may be directed does not concern the singer in the first bliss of recovered freedom. All blessedness is contained in the one word "escaped," which therefore he reiterates, and with which the song closes, but for that final ascription of the glory of the escape to the mighty Name of Him whc made heaven and earth.

PSALM CXXV.

1 They who trust in Jehovah
  Are like Mount Zion, [which] cannot be moved,
  For ever it shall sit steadfast.
2 Jerusalem—mountains are round her,
  And Jehovah is round His people
  From now and for ever.
3 For the sceptre of the wicked shall not rest on the lot
      of the righteous ones,
  Lest the righteous put forth their hands to iniquity.

4 Do good, Jehovah, to the good,
  And to the upright in their hearts.
5 And those who warp their crooked paths,
  Jehovah shall make them go with the workers of iniquity.
  Peace be upon Israel !

THE references to the topography of Jerusalem in
vv. 1, 2, do not absolutely require, though they
recommend, the supposition, already mentioned, that this
psalm completes a triad which covers the experience
of the restored Israel from the time just prior to its
deliverance up till the period of its return to Jerusalem.
The strength of the city perched on its rocky peninsula,
and surrounded by guardian heights, would be the
more impressive to eyes accustomed to the plains of
Babylon, where the only defence of cities was artificial.
If this hypothesis as to the date of the psalm is
accepted, its allusions to a foreign domination and to
half-hearted members of the community, as distinguished
from manifest workers of evil, fall in with the facts

of the period. The little band of faithful men was surrounded by foes, and there were faint hearts among themselves, ready to temporise and "run with the hare," as well as "hunt with the hounds." In view of deliverance accomplished and of perils still to be faced, the psalmist sings this strong brief song of commendation of the excellence of Trust, anticipates as already fulfilled the complete emancipation of the land from alien rule, and proclaims, partly in prayer and partly in prediction, the great law of retribution—certain blessedness for those who are good, and destruction for the faithless.

The first of the two grand images in vv. 1, 2, sets forth the stability of those who trust in Jehovah. The psalmist pictures Mount Zion somewhat singularly as "sitting steadfast," whereas the usual expression would be "stands firm." But the former conveys still more forcibly the image and impression of calm, effortless immobility. Like some great animal couched at ease, the mountain lies there, in restful strength. Nothing can shake it, except One Presence, before which the hills "skip like young rams." Thus quietly steadfast and lapped in repose, not to be disturbed by any external force, should they be who trust in Jehovah, and shall be in the measure of their trust.

But trust could not bring such steadfastness, unless the other figure in ver. 2 represented a fact. The steadfastness of the trustful soul is the consequence of the encircling defence of Jehovah's power. The mountain fortress is girdled by mountains; not, indeed, as if it was ringed about by an unbroken circle of manifestly higher peaks; but still Olivet rises above Zion on the east, and a spur of higher ground runs out thence and overlooks it on the north, while the

levels rise to the west, and the so-called Hill of Evil
Counsel is on the south. They are not conspicuous
summits, but they hide the city from those approaching,
till their tops are reached. Perhaps the very incon-
spicuousness of these yet real defences suggested to the
poet the invisible protection which to purblind eyes
looked so poor, but was so valid. The hills of Bashan
might look scornfully across Jordan to the humble
heights round Jerusalem ; but they were enough to
guard the city. The psalmist uses no words of comparison, but lays his two facts side by side : the
mountains round Jerusalem—Jehovah round His people.
That circumvallation is their defence. They who have
the everlasting hills for their bulwark need not trouble
themselves to build a wall such as Babylon needed.
Man's artifices for protection are impertinent when God
flings His hand round His people. Zechariah, the
prophet of the Restoration, drew that conclusion from
the same thought, when he declared that Jerusalem
should be " inhabited as villages without walls," because
Jehovah would be " unto her a wall of fire round
about " (Zech. ii. 4, 5).

Ver. 3 seems at first sight to be appended to the
preceding in defiance of logical connection, for its
" for " would more naturally have been " therefore,"
since the deliverance of the land from foreign invaders
is a consequence of Jehovah's protection. But the
psalmist's faith is so strong that he regards that
still further deliverance as already accomplished, and
adduces it as a confirmation of the fact that Jehovah
ever guards His people. In the immediate historical
reference this verse points to a period when the lot of
the righteous—*i.e.*, the land of Israel—was, as it were,
weighed down by the crushing sceptre of some alien

power that had long lain on it. But the psalmist is sure that that is not going to last, because his eyes are lifted to the hills whence his aid comes. With like tenacity and longsightedness, Faith ever looks onward to the abolition of present evils, however stringent may be their grip, and however heavy may be the sceptre which Evil in possession of the heritage of God wields. The rod of the oppressor shall be broken, and one more proof given that they dwell safely who dwell encircled by God.

The domination of evil, if protracted too long, may tempt good men, who are righteous because they trust, to lose their faith and so to lose their righteousness, and make common cause with apparently triumphant iniquity. It needs Divine wisdom to determine how long a trial must last in order that it may test faith, thereby strengthening it, and may not confound faith, thereby precipitating feeble souls into sin. He knows when to say, It is enough.

So the psalm ends with prayer and prediction, which both spring from the insight into Jehovah's purposes which trust gives. The singer asks that the good may receive good, in accordance with the law of retribution. The expressions describing these are very noticeable, especially when connected with the designation of the same persons in ver. 1 as those who trust in Jehovah. Trust makes righteous and good and upright in heart. If these characteristics are to be distinguished, *righteous* may refer to action in conformity with the law of God, *good* to the more gentle and beneficent virtues, and *upright in heart* to inward sincerity. Such persons will get "good" from Jehovah, the God of recompenses, and that good will be as various as their necessities and as wide as their capacities. But the righteous

Protector of those who trust in Him is so, partly
because He smites as well as blesses, and therefore
the other half of the law of retribution comes into
view, not as a petition, but as prediction.   The psalmist
uses a vivid image to describe half-hearted adherents
to the people of Jehovah: "they bend their ways," so
as to make them crooked.   Sometimes the tortuous
path points towards one direction, and then it swerves
to almost the opposite.   "These crooked, wandering
ways," in which irresolute men, who do not clearly
know whether they are for Jehovah or for the other
side, live lives miserable from vacillation, can never
lead to steadfastness or to any good.   The psalmist
has taken his side.   He knows whom he is for; and
he knows, too, that there is at bottom little to choose
between the coward who would fain be in both camps
and the open antagonist.   Therefore they shall share
the same fate.

Finally the poet, stretching out his hands over all
Israel, as if blessing them like a priest, embraces all his
hopes, petitions, and wishes in the one prayer "Peace
be upon Israel!"   He means the true Israel of God
(Gal. vi. 16), upon whom the Apostle, with a reminiscence
possibly of this psalm, invokes the like blessing, and
whom he defines in the same spirit as the psalmist
does, as those who walk according to this rule, and not
according to the crooked paths of their own devising.

PSALM CXXVI.

1 When Jehovah brought back the captives of Zion,
  We were like as if dreaming.
2 Then was our mouth filled with laughter,
  And our tongues with joyful cries ;
  Then said they among the nations,
  Jehovah has done great things with these [people].
3 Jehovah has done great things with us ;
  We were glad.

4 Bring back, Jehovah, our captives,
  Like watercourses in the Southland.
5 They who sow with tears
  With joyful cries shall reap.
6 [The husbandman] goes, going and weeping,
  [While] bearing the handful of seed ;
  He shall surely come with joyful cries,
  [When] bearing his sheaves.

AS in Psalm lxxxv., the poet's point of view here is in the midst of a partial restoration of Israel. In vv. 1–3 he rejoices over its happy beginning, while in vv. 4–6 he prays for and confidently expects its triumphant completion. Manifestly the circumstances fit the period to which most of these pilgrim psalms are to be referred—namely, the dawn of the restoration from Babylon. Here the pressure of the difficulties and hostility which the returning exiles met is but slightly expressed. The throb of wondering gratitude is still felt ; and though tears mingle with laughter, and hard work which bears no immediate result has to be done, the singer's confidence is unfaltering.

His words set a noble example of the spirit in which
inchoate deliverances should be welcomed, and toil for
their completion encountered with the lightheartedness
which is folly if it springs from self-trust, but wisdom
and strength if its ground is the great things which
Jehovah has begun to do.

The word in ver. 1 rendered captives is capable of
other meanings. It is an unusual form, and is probably an error for the more common word which occurs
in ver. 4. It is most probable that the expressions
should be identical in both instances, though small
changes in a refrain are not infrequent. But if this
correction is adopted, there is room for difference of
opinion as to the meaning of the phrase. Cheyne, with
the support of several other commentators, takes the
phrase to mean "turn the fortunes" (lit., a turning),
but allows that the "debate is not absolutely closed"
(Critical Note on Psalm xiv. 7). The ordinary rendering is, however, more natural, "captivity" being
the mass of captives. Others would regard the two
words in vv. 1 and 4 as different, and render the
former "those who return" (Delitzsch) or "the
returned" (Perowne).

Sudden and great revolutions for the better have for
their first effect bewilderment and a sense of unreality.
Most men have some supreme moment of blessedness
in their memories with which they were stunned; but,
alas! it is oftener the rush of unexpected miseries
that makes them wonder whether they are awake
or dreaming. It is not lack of faith, but slowness in
accommodating oneself to surprising new conditions,
which makes these seem unreal at first. "The sober
certainty of waking bliss" is sweeter than the first
raptures. It is good to have had such experience of

walking, as it were, on air; but it is better to plant
firm feet on firm ground.

The mood of the first part of this little psalm is
momentary; but the steadfast toil amid discourage-
ments, not uncheered by happy confidence, which
is pictured in the second part, should be the permanent
temper of those who have once tasted the brief emotion.
The jubilant laughter and ringing cries with which
the exiles streamed forth from bondage, and made
the desert echo as they marched, witnessed to the
nations that Jehovah had magnified His dealings with
them.   Their extorted acknowledgment is caught up
triumphantly by the singer.   He, as it were, thanks
the Gentiles for teaching him that word.   There is a
world of restrained feeling, all the more impressive for
the simplicity of the expression, in that quiet "We
became glad."   When the heathen attested the reality
of the deliverance, Israel became calmly conscious of it.
These exclamations of envious onlookers sufficed to
convince the returning exiles that it was no dream
befooling them.   Tumultuous feeling steadied itself into
conscious joy.   There is no need to say more.   The
night of weeping was past, and Joy was their companion in the fresh morning light.

But the work was but partly done.   Difficulties and
hardships were not abolished from the world, as Israel
had half expected in the first flush of joy.   We all are
apt to think so, when some long wished and faintly
hoped-for good is ours at last.   But not such is the
Divine purpose for any life here.   He gives moments
of untroubled joy, when no cloud stains the blue and
all the winds are still, in order to prepare us for toil
amid tempests and gloomy skies.   So the second half
of the psalm breathes petitions for the completion of

the Restoration, and animates the returned exiles with
assurances that, whatever may be their toils, and however rough the weather in which they have to sow the
seed, and however heavy the hearts with which they
do it, "the slow result of winter showers" is sure.
Lessons of persevering toil, or contented doing of preparatory work, of confidence that no such labour can
fail to be profitable to the doer and to the world, have
been drawn for centuries from the sweet words of this
psalm. Who can tell how many hearts they have
braced, how much patient toil they have inspired? The
psalmist was sowing seed, the fruit of which he little
dreamed of, when he wrote them, and his sheaves will
be an exceeding weight indeed.

The metaphor in ver. 4 brings before the imagination
the dried torrent-beds in the arid Negeb, or Southland,
which runs out into the Arabian desert. Dreary and
desolate as these dried wadies lie bleaching in the
sunshine, so disconsolate and lonely had the land been
without inhabitants. The psalmist would fain see, not
the thin trickle of a streamlet, to which the returned
captives might be compared, but a full, great rush of
rejoicing fellow-countrymen coming back, like the torrents that fill the silent watercourses with flashing life.

He prays, and he also prophesies. "They who sow
with tears" are the pioneers of the return, to whom
he belonged. Vv. 6, 7, merely expand the figure of
ver. 5 with the substitution of the image of a single
husbandman for the less vivid, clear-cut plural. The
expression rendered "handful of seed" means literally
a "draught of seed"—*i.e.*, the quantity taken out of the
basket or cloth at one grasp, in order to be sown. It
is difficult to convey the force of the infinitives in combination with participles and the finite verb in ver. 6.

But the first half of the verse seems to express repeated actions on the part of the husbandman, who often goes forth to sow, and weeps as he goes; while the second half expresses the certainty of his glad coming in with his arms full of sheaves. The meaning of the figure needs no illustration. It gives assurances fitted to animate to toil in the face of dangers without, and in spite of a heavy heart—namely, that no seed sown and watered with tears is lost; and further, that, though it often seems to be the law for earth that one soweth and another reapeth, in deepest truth "every man shall receive his own reward, according to his own labour," inasmuch as, hereafter, if not now, whatsoever of faith and toil and holy endeavour a man soweth, trusting to God to bless the springing thereof, that shall he also reap. In the highest sense and in the last result the prophet's great words are ever true: "They shall not plant, and another eat . . . for My chosen shall long enjoy the work of their hands" (Isa. lxv. 22).

PSALM CXXVII.

1 **If Jehovah** build not a house,
　Vainly do its builders toil upon **it;**
　If Jehovah keeps not a city,
　Vainly wakes the keeper.
2 Vain is it for you, ye that make early [your] rising
　　and your sitting down late,
　That eat the bread of painful toil;
　Even so He gives [it] to His beloved while in sleep.

3 Behold, sons are an heritage from Jehovah,
　The fruit of the womb is [His] reward.
4 Like arrows in the hand of a mighty man,
　So are sons of [a father's] youth.
5 Happy the man who has filled his quiver with them,
　They shall not be ashamed
　When they speak with enemies in the gate.

THIS pure expression of conscious dependence on
　God's blessing for all well-being may possibly
have special reference to the Israel of the Restoration.
The instances of vain human effort and care would
then have special force, when the ruins of many generations had to be rebuilt and the city to be guarded.
But there is no need to seek for specific occasion, so
general is this psalm.　It sings in a spirit of happy trust
the commonplace of all true religion, that God's blessing
prospers all things, and that effort is vain without it.
There is no sweeter utterance of that truth anywhere,
till we come to our Lord's parallel teaching, lovelier

still than that of our psalm, when He points us to the flowers of the field and the fowls of the air, as our teachers of the joyous, fair lives that can be lived, when no carking care mars their beauty.

In ver. 1 the examples chosen by the singer are naturally connected. The house when built is one in the many that make the city. The owner's troubles are not over when it is built, since it has to be watched. It is as hard to keep as to acquire earthly goods. The psalmist uses the past tenses in describing the vanity of building and watching unblessed by God. "They" have built in vain, and watched in vain. He, as it were, places us at the point of time when the failure is developed.—the half-built house a ruin, the city sacked and in flames.

Ver. 2 deals with domestic life within the built house and guarded city. It is vain to eke out the laborious day by early beginning and late ending. Long hours do not mean prosperous work. The evening meal may be put off till a late hour ; and when the toil-worn man sits down to it, he may eat bread made bitter by labour. But all is in vain without God's blessing. The last clause of the verse must be taken as presenting a contrast to the futile labour reprehended in the former clauses ; and therefore the beautiful rendering of the A.V. must be abandoned, though it has given many sweet thoughts to trustful souls, and none sweeter than in Mrs. Browning's pathetic lines. But clearly the contrast is between labour which effects nothing, but is like spinning ropes out of sea-sand, and God's gift of the good which the vain toil had aimed at, and which He gives to His beloved in their sleep. "So" seems here to be equivalent to "Even so," and the thought intended is probably that God's gift to His

beloved secures to them the same result as is in-
effectually sought by godless struggles.

This is no preaching of laziness masquerading as
religious trust. The psalmist insists on one side of
the truth. Not work, but self-torturing care and work,
without seeking God's blessing, are pronounced vanity.

The remainder of the psalm dwells on one special
instance of God's gifts, that of a numerous family, which,
in accordance with the Hebrew sentiment, is regarded
as a special blessing. But the psalmist is carried
beyond his immediate purpose of pointing out that that
chief earthly blessing, as he and his contemporaries
accounted it, is God's gift, and he lingers on the picture
of a father surrounded in his old age by a band of
stalwart sons born unto him in his vigorous youth, and
so now able to surround him with a ring of strong protectors of his declining days. "They shall speak with
their enemies in the gate." Probably "they" refers to
the whole band, the father in the midst and his sons
about him. The gate was the place where justice was
administered, and where was the chief place of concourse.
It is therefore improbable that actual warfare is meant :
rather, in the disputes which might arise with neighbours, and in the intercourse of city life, which would
breed enmities enough, the man with his sons about
him could hold his own. And such blessing is God's
gift.

The lesson of the psalm is one that needs to be
ever repeated. It is so obvious that it is unseen by
many, and apt to be unnoticed by all. There are two
ways of going to work in reference to earthly good.
One is that of struggling and toiling, pushing and
snatching, fighting and envying, and that way comes
to no successful issue ; for if it gets what it has wriggled

and wrestled for, it generally gets in some way or other
an incapacity to enjoy the good won, which makes it
far less than the good pursued.   The other way is the
way of looking to God and doing the appointed tasks
with quiet dependence on Him, and that way always
succeeds; for, with its modest or large outward results,
there is given likewise a quiet heart set on God, and
therefore capable of finding water in the desert and
extracting honey from the rock.   The one way is that
of "young lions," who, for all their claws and strength,
"do lack and suffer hunger"; the other is that of
"them that seek the Lord," who "shall not want any
good."

PSALM CXXVIII.

1 Happy is every one that fears Jehovah,
   That walks in His ways.
2 The labour of thy hands shalt thou surely eat,—
   Happy art thou, and it is well with thee.
3 Thy wife [shall be] like a fruitful vine in the inmost
         chambers of thy house,
   Thy children like young olive plants round thy table.
4 Behold, that thus shall the man be blessed
   Who fears Jehovah.

5 Jehovah bless thee out of Zion!
   And mayest thou look on the prosperity of Jerusalem
   All the days of thy life,
6 And see children to thy children!
   Peace be upon Israel!

THE preceding psalm traced all prosperity and
domestic felicity to God's giving hand. It painted
in its close the picture of a father surrounded by his
sons able to defend him. This psalm presents the
same blessings as the result of a devout life, in which
the fear of Jehovah leads to obedience and diligence
in labour. It presents the inner side of domestic
happiness. It thus doubly supplements the former,
lest any should think that God's gift superseded man's
work, or that the only blessedness of fatherhood was
that it supplied a corps of sturdy defenders. The first
four verses describe the peaceful, happy life of the
God-fearing man, and the last two invoke on him
the blessing which alone makes such a life his. Blended

with the sweet domesticity of the psalm is glowing love
for Zion. However blessed the home, it is not to
weaken the sense of belonging to the nation.

No purer, fairer idyll was ever penned than this
miniature picture of a happy home life. But its calm,
simple beauty has deep foundations. The poet sets
forth the basis of all noble, as of all tranquil, life when
he begins with the fear of Jehovah, and thence advances
to practical conformity with His will, manifested by
walking in the paths which He traces for men. Thence
the transition is easy to the mention of diligent labour,
and the singer is sure that such toil done on such
principles and from such a motive cannot go unblessed.
Outward prosperity does not follow good men's work
so surely as the letter of the psalm teaches, but the
best fruits of such work are not those which can be
stored in barns or enjoyed by sense ; and the labourer
who does his work " heartily, as to the Lord," will
certainly reap a harvest in character and power and
communion with God, whatever transitory gain may be
attained or missed.

The sweet little sketch of a joyous home in ver. 3
is touched with true grace and feeling. The wife is
happy in her motherhood, and ready, in the inner
chambers (literally *sides*) of the house, where she does
her share of work, to welcome her husband returning
from the field. The family gathers for the meal won
and sweetened by his toil ; the children are in vigorous
health, and growing up like young " layered " olive
plants. It may be noted that this verse exhibits a
home in the earlier stages of married life, and reflects
the happy hopes associated with youthful children, all
still gathered under the father's roof; while, in the
latter part of the psalm, a later stage is in view, when

the father sits as a spectator rather than a worker, and sees children born to his children. Ver. 4 emphatically dwells once more on the foundation of all as laid in the fear of Jehovah. Happy a nation whose poets have such ideals and sing of such themes! How wide the gulf separating this "undisturbed song" of pure home joys from the foul ideals which baser songs try to adorn! Happy the man whose ambition is bounded by its limits, and whose life is

"True to the kindred points of heaven and home"!

Israel first taught the world how sacred the family is; and Christianity recognises "a church in the house" of every wedded pair whose love is hallowed by the fear of Jehovah.

In vv. 5, 6, petitions take the place of assurances, for the singer knows that none of the good which he has been promising will come without that blessing of which the preceding psalm had spoken. All the beautiful and calm joys just described must flow from God, and be communicated from that place which is the seat of His self-revelation. The word rendered above "mayest thou look" is in the imperative form, which seems here to be intended to blend promise, wish, and command. It is the duty of the happiest husband and father not to let himself be so absorbed in the sweets of home as to have his heart beat languidly for the public weal. The subtle selfishness which is but too commonly the accompaniment of such blessings is to be resisted. From his cheerful hearth the eyes of a lover of Zion are to look out, and be gladdened when they see prosperity smiling on Zion. Many a Christian is so happy in his household that his duties to the Church, the nation, and the world are neglected. This ancient singer had a truer conception of the obligations flowing from personal and domestic blessings. He teaches us that it is not enough to " see children's children," unless we have eyes to look for the prosperity of Jerusalem, and tongues which pray not only for those in our homes, but for " peace upon Israel."

PSALM CXXIX.

1 Sorely have they oppressed me from my youth,
   Let Israel now say,
2 Sorely have they oppressed me from my youth,
   But they have not also prevailed against me.
3 On my back the ploughers ploughed,
   They made their furrows long.
4 Jehovah the righteous
   Has cut the cord of the wicked.

5 Let them be shamed and turned back,
   All they who hate Zion.
6 Let them be as the grass of the housetops,
   Which, before it shoots forth, withers:
7 With which the mower fills not his hand,
   Nor the sheaf-binder his bosom ;
8 And the passers-by say not,
   " The blessing of Jehovah be to you ! "
   " We bless you in the name of Jehovah ! "

THE point of view here is the same as in Psalm
cxxiv., with which the present psalm has much
similarity both in subject and in expression. It is a
retrospect of Israel's past, in which the poet sees a uniform exemplification of two standing facts—sore affliction and wonderful deliverance. The bush burned, *nec
tamen consumebatur.* " Cast down, but not destroyed,"
is the summary of the Church's history. No doubt
the recent deliverance from captivity underlies this, as
most of the pilgrim psalms. The second part (vv. 5–8)
blends confidence and wish, founded on the experience
recorded in the first part, and prophesies and desires

331

the overthrow of Israel's foes. The right use of retrospect is to make it the ground of hope. They who
have passed unscathed through such afflictions may
well be sure that any to-morrow shall be as the
yesterdays were, and that all future assaults will fail
as all past ones have failed.

The words which Israel is called upon to say twice
with triumphant remembrance are the motto of the
Ecclesia pressa in all ages. Ever there is antagonism ;
never is there overthrow. Israel's " youth " was far
back in the days of Egyptian bondage ; and many an
affliction has he since met, but he lives still, and his
existence proves that " they have not prevailed against "
him. Therefore the backward look is gladsome, though
it sees so many trials. Survived sorrows yield joy and
hope, as gashes in trees exude precious gums.

Ver. 3 expresses Israel's oppressions by a strong
metaphor, in which two figures are blended—a slave
under the lash, and a field furrowed by ploughing.
Cruel lords had laid on the whip, till the victim's back
was scored with long wounds, straight and parallel, like
the work of a ploughman. The Divine deliverance
follows in ver. 4. The first words of the verse do not
stand in the usual order, if rendered " Jehovah is
righteous," and are probably to be taken as above ;
" righteous " standing in apposition to " Jehovah," and
expressing the Divine characteristic which guaranteed
and, in due time, accomplished Israel's deliverance.
God could not but be true to His covenant obligations.
Therefore He cut the " cord of the wicked." The
figure is here changed to one occasioned by the former.
Israel is now the draught ox harnessed to the plough ;
and thus both sides of his bondage are expressed—cruel
treatment by the former, and hard toil by the latter,

figure. The same act which, in the parallel 124th Psalm, is described as breaking the fowler's snare, is in view here; and the restoration from Babylon suits the circumstances completely.

The story of past futile attempts against Israel animates the confidence and vindicates the wish breathed in the latter half of the psalm. To hate Zion, which Jehovah so manifestly loves and guards, must be suicidal. It is something far nobler than selfish vengeance which desires and foresees the certain failure of attempts against it. The psalmist is still under the influence of his earlier metaphor of the ploughed field, but now has come to think of the harvest. The graphic image of the grass on flat housetops of clay, which springs quickly because it has no depth of earth, and withers as it springs, vividly describes the short-lived success and rapid extinction of plots against Zion and of the plotters. The word rendered above "shoots forth" is by some translated "is plucked up," and that meaning is defensible, but grass on the housetops would scarcely be worth plucking, and the word is used elsewhere for unsheathing a sword. It may, therefore, be taken here to refer to the shooting out of the spikelets from their covering. The psalmist dilates upon his metaphor in ver. 7, which expresses the fruitlessness of assaults on God's chosen. No harvest is to be reaped from such sowing. The enemies may plot and toil, and before their plans have had time to bud they are smitten into brown dust; and when the contrivers come expecting success, there is nothing to mow or gather. "They look for much, and behold little." So it has been; so it shall be; so it should be; so may it be, wishes the psalmist; and true hearts will say Amen to his aspiration.

Such reapers have no joy in harvest, and no man can invoke Jehovah's blessing on their bad work. Ver. 8 brings up a lovely little picture of a harvest field, where passers-by shout their good wishes to the glad toilers, and are answered by these with like salutations. It is doubtful whether ver. 8 *c* is spoken by by the passers-by or is the reapers' responsive greeting. The latter explanation gives animation to the scene. But in any case the verse suggests by contrast the gloomy silence of Israel's would-be destroyers, who find, as all who set themselves against Jehovah's purposes do find, that He blasts their plans with His breath, and makes their "harvest an heap in the day of grief and desperate sorrow."

PSALM CXXX.

1 Out of the depths have I cried to Thee, Jehovah.
2 Lord, hearken to my voice,
 Be Thine ears attent
 To the voice of my supplications.

3 If Thou, Jah, shouldest mark iniquities,
 Lord, who could stand?—
4 For with Thee is forgiveness,
 That Thou mayest be feared.

5 I have waited for Jehovah,
 And in His word have I hoped.
6 My soul [hopes] for the Lord
 More than watchers for the morning,
 —Watchers for the morning.

7 Let Israel hope in Jehovah,
 For with Jehovah is loving-kindness,
 And in abundance with Him is redemption.
8 And He—He will redeem Israel
 From all his iniquities.

IN a very emphatic sense this is a song of ascents, for it climbs steadily from the abyss of penitence to the summits of hope. It falls into two divisions of four verses each, of which the former breathes the prayer of a soul penetrated by the consciousness of sin, and the latter the peaceful expectance of one that has tasted God's forgiving mercy. These two parts are again divided into two groups of two verses, so that there are four stages in the psalmist's progress from the depths to the sunny heights.

In the first group we have the psalmist's cry.   He
has called, and still calls.   He reiterates in ver. 2 the
prayer that he had long offered and still presents.   It
is not only quotation, but is the cry of present need.
What are these "depths" from which his voice sounds,
as that of a man fallen into a pit and sending up a faint
call ?   The expression does not merely refer to his
creatural lowliness, nor even to his troubles, nor even
to his depression of spirit.   There are deeper pits than
these—those into which the spirit feels itself going
down, sick and giddy, when it realises its sinfulness.
Unless a man has been down in that black abyss, he
has scarcely cried to God as he should do.   The beginning of true personal religion is the sense of personal
sin.   A slight conception of the gravity of that fact
underlies inadequate conceptions of Christ's nature and
work, and is the mother of heresies in creed and super-
ficialities and deadnesses in practice.   A religion that
sits lightly upon its professor, impelling to no acts of
devotion, flashing out in no heroisms, rising to no
heights of communion—that is to say, the average
Christianity of great masses of so-called Christians—
bears proof, in its languor, that the man knows nothing
about the depths, and has never cried to God from
them.   Further, if out of the depths we cry, we shall
cry ourselves out of the depths.   What can a man do
who finds himself at the foot of a beetling cliff, the sea
in front, the wall of rock at his back, without foothold
for a mouse, between the tide at the bottom and the
grass at the top ?   He can do but one thing : he can
shout, and perhaps may be heard, and a rope may
come dangling down that he can spring at and clutch.
For sinful men in the miry pit the rope is already let
down, and their grasping it is the same act as the

psalmist's cry. God has let down His forgiving love in Christ, and we need but the faith which accepts while it asks, and then we are swung up into the light, and our feet set on a rock.

Vv. 3, 4, are the second stage. A dark fear shadows the singer's soul, and is swept away by a joyful assurance. The word rendered above " mark " is literally *keep* or *watch*, as in ver. 6, and here seems to mean to *take account of*, or *retain* in remembrance, in order to punish. If God should take man's sin into account in His dispositions and dealings, " O Lord, who shall stand ? " No man could sustain that righteous judgment. He must go down before it like a flimsy hut before a whirlwind, or a weak enemy before a fierce charge. That thought comes to the psalmist like a blast of icy air from the north, and threatens to chill his hope to death and to blow his cry back into his throat. But its very hypothetical form holds a negation concealed in it. Such an implied negative is needed in order to explain the " for " of ver. 4. The singer springs, as it were, to that confidence by a rebound from the other darker thought. We must have tremblingly entertained the contrary dread possibility, before we can experience the relief and gladness of its counter-truth. The word rendered " forgiveness " is a late form, being found only in two other late passages (Neh. ix. 17 ; Dan. ix. 9). It literally means *cutting off*, and so suggests the merciful surgery by which the cancerous tumour is taken out of the soul. Such forgiveness is " with God," inherent in His nature. And that forgiveness lies at the root of true godliness. No man reverences, loves, and draws near to God so rapturously and so humbly as he who has made experience of His pardoning mercy, lifting a soul from its abysses of sin and misery.   Therefore the psalmist, taught by what pardon has done for him in drawing him lovingly near to God, declares that its great purpose is "that Thou mayest be feared," and that not only by the recipient, but by beholders.   Strangely enough, many commentators have found a difficulty in this idea, which seems sun-clear to those whose own history explains it to them.   Grätz, for instance, calls it "completely unintelligible."   It has been very intelligible to many a penitent who has been by pardon transformed into a reverent lover of God.

The next stage in the ascent from the depths is in vv. 5, 6, which breathe peaceful, patient hope.   It may be doubtful whether the psalmist means to represent that attitude of expectance as prior to and securing forgiveness or as consequent upon it.   The latter seems the more probable.   A soul which has received God's forgiveness is thereby led into tranquil, continuous, ever-rewarded waiting on Him, and hope of new gifts springs ever fresh in it.   Such a soul sits quietly at His feet, trusting to His love, and looking for light and all else needed, to flow from Him.   The singleness of the object of devout hope, the yearning which is not impatience, characterising that hope at its noblest, are beautifully painted in the simile of the watchers for morning.   As they who have outwatched the long night look eagerly to the flush that creeps up in the east, telling that their vigil is past, and heralding the stir and life of a new day with its wakening birds and fresh morning airs, so this singer's eyes had turned to God, and to Him only.   Ver. 6 does not absolutely require the supplement "hopes."   It may read simply "My soul is towards Jehovah"; and that translation gives still more emphatically the notion of complete

turning of the whole being to God.   Consciousness
of sin was as a dark night; forgiveness flushed the
Eastern heaven with prophetic twilight.   So the psalmist
waits for the light, and his soul is one aspiration
towards God.

In vv. 7, 8, the psalmist becomes an evangelist,
inviting Israel to unite in his hope, that they may share
in his pardon.   In the depths he was alone, and felt
as if the only beings in the universe were God and
himself.   The consciousness of sin isolates, and the
sense of forgiveness unites.   Whoever has known that
" with Jehovah is pardon " is impelled thereby to invite
others to learn the same lesson in the same sweet way.
The psalmist has a broad gospel to preach, the general-
isation of his own history.   He had said in ver. 4 that
" with Jehovah is forgiveness " (lit. *the* forgiveness,
possibly meaning *the needed forgiveness*), and he thereby
had animated his own hope.   Now he repeats the form
of expression, only that he substitutes for " forgiveness "
the loving-kindness which is its spring, and the redemption which is its result; and these he presses upon his
fellows as reasons and encouragements for their hope.
It is " abundant redemption," or " multiplied," as the
word might be rendered.   " Seventy times seven "—
the perfect numbers seven and ten being multiplied
together and their sum increased sevenfold—make a
numerical symbol for the unfailing pardons which we
are to bestow; and the sum of the Divine pardon is
surely greater than that of the human.   God's forgiving
grace is mightier than all sins, and able to conquer
them all.

" He will redeem Israel from all his iniquities "; not
only from their consequences in punishment, but from
their power, as well as from their guilt and their

penalty.　The psalmist means something a great deal deeper than deliverance from calamities which conscience declared to be the chastisement of sin.　He speaks New Testament language.　He was sure that God would redeem from all iniquity ; but he lived in the twilight dawn, and had to watch for the morning.　The sun is risen for us ; but the light is the same in quality, though more in degree : " Thou shalt call His name Jesus, for He shall save His people from their sins."

PSALM CXXXI.

1 Jehovah, not haughty is my heart,
   And not lofty are mine eyes;
   And I go not into great things,
   Nor things too wonderful for me.
2 I have calmed and quieted my soul,
   Like a weaned child with its mother,
   Like the weaned child is my soul with me.

3 Let Israel hope in Jehovah,
   From now, even for evermore.

A QUIET, because self-quieted, heart speaks here
in quiet accents, not unlike the "crooning" of
the peaceful child on its mother's bosom, to which the
sweet singer likens his soul. The psalm is the most
perfect expression of the child-like spirit, which, as
Christ has taught, is characteristic of the subjects of the
kingdom of heaven. It follows a psalm of penitence,
in which a contrite soul waited on Jehovah for pardon,
and, finding it, exhorted Israel to hope in His redemption from all iniquity. Consciousness of sin and
conscious reception of redemption therefrom precede
true lowliness, and such lowliness should follow such
consciousness.

The psalmist does not pray; still less does he con-
tradict his lowliness in the very act of declaring it, by
pluming himself on it. He speaks in that serene and
happy mood, sometimes granted to lowly souls, when
fruition is more present than desire, and the child,

341

folded to the Divine heart, feels its blessedness so
satisfyingly that fears and hopes, wishes and dreams,
are still. Simple words best speak tranquil joys. One
note only is sounded in this psalm, which might almost
be called a lullaby. How many hearts it has helped
to hush!

The haughtiness which the psalmist disclaims has
its seat in the heart and its manifestation in supercilious
glances. The lowly heart looks higher than the proud
one does, for it lifts its eyes to the hills, and fixes them
on Jehovah, as a slave on his lord. Lofty thoughts of
self naturally breed ambitions which seek great spheres
and would intermeddle with things above reach. The
singer does not refer to questions beyond solution by
human faculty, but to worldly ambitions aiming at
prominence and position. He aims low, as far as earth
is concerned; but he aims high, for his mark is in the
heavens.

Shaking off such ambitions and loftiness of spirit,
he has found repose, as all do who clear their hearts
of that perilous stuff. But it is to be noted that the
calm which he enjoys is the fruit of his own self-
control, by which his dominant self has smoothed and
stilled the sensitive nature with its desires and passions. It is not the tranquillity of a calm nature which
speaks here, but that into which the speaker has
entered, by vigorous mastery of disturbing elements.
How hard the struggle had been, how much bitter
crying and petulant resistance there had been before the
calm was won, is told by the lovely image of the weaned
child. While being weaned it sobs and struggles, and
all its little life is perturbed. So no man comes to
have a quiet heart without much resolute self-suppres-
sion. But the figure tells of ultimate repose, even more

plainly than of preceding struggle. For, once the process is accomplished, the child nestles satisfied on the mother's warm bosom, and wishes nothing more than to lie there. So the man who has manfully taken in hand his own weaker and more yearning nature, and directed its desires away from earth by fixing them on God, is freed from the misery of hot desire, and passes into calm. He that ceases from his own works enters into rest. If a man thus compels his "soul" to cease its cravings for what earth can give, he will have to disregard its struggles and cries, but these will give place to quietness; and the fruition of the blessedness of setting all desires on God will be the best defence against the recurrence of longings once silenced.

The psalmist would fain have all Israel share in his quietness of heart, and closes his tender snatch of song with a call to them to hope in Jehovah, whereby they, too, may enter into peace. The preceding psalm ended with the same call; but there God's mercy in dealing with sin was principally in question, while here His sufficiency for all a soul's wants is implied. The one secret of forgiveness and deliverance from iniquity is also the secret of rest from tyrannous longings and disturbing desires. Hope in Jehovah brings pardon, purity, and peace.

PSALM CXXXII.

1 Remember, Jehovah, to David
   All the pains he took
2 Who swore to Jehovah,
   [And] vowed to the Mighty One of Jacob,
3 "I will not go into the tent of my house,
   I will not go up to the bed of my couch,
4 I will not give sleep to mine eyes,
   To mine eyelids slumber,
5 Till I find a place for Jehovah,
   A habitation for the Mighty One of Jacob."

6 Behold, we heard [of] it at Ephrathah,
   We found it in the Fields of the Wood.
7 Let us come to His habitation,
   Let us bow ourselves at His footstool.

8 Arise, Jehovah, to Thy rest,
   Thou and the Ark of Thy strength.
9 Let Thy priests be clothed with righteousness,
   And Thy favoured ones utter shrill cries of joy.
10 For the sake of David Thy servant,
   Turn not away the face of Thine anointed.

11 Jehovah has sworn to David,
   It is truth—He will not go back from it—
   "Of the fruit of thy body will I set on thy throne.
12 If thy sons keep My covenant
   And My testimonies which I will teach them,
   Their sons also for ever and aye
   Shall sit on thy throne."

13 For Jehovah has chosen Zion,
   He has desired it for His dwelling.
14 "This is My rest for ever and aye,
   Here will I abide, for I have desired it.

344

15 Her provision blessing I will bless,
   Her poor will I satisfy with bread.
16 Her priests also will I clothe with salvation,
   And her favoured ones uttering will utter shrill cries of joy.
17 There will I cause a horn to sprout for David,
   I have trimmed a lamp for Mine anointed.
18 His enemies will I clothe with shame,
   But upon himself shall his crown glitter."

THE continuance of "the sure mercies of David" to his descendants for his sake is first besought from God, and is then promised, for his sake, by God Himself, speaking in the singer's spirit. The special blessing sought for is Jehovah's dwelling in His house, which is here contemplated as reared after long toil. Expositors differ, as usual, in regard to the date and occasion of this psalm. Its place among the pilgrim psalms raises a presumption in favour of a post-exilic date, and one class of commentators refers it confidently to the period of the rebuilding of the Temple. But the mention of the Ark (which disappeared after the destruction of Solomon's Temple) can be reconciled with that supposed date only by a somewhat violent expedient. Nor is it easy to suppose that the repeated references to David's descendants as reigning in accordance with God's promise could have been written at a time when there was no king in Israel. Zerubbabel has, indeed, been suggested as "the anointed" of this psalm; but he was not king, and neither in fact nor in idea was he anointed. And could a singer in Israel, in the post-exilic period, have recalled the ancient promises without some passing sigh for their apparent falsification in the present? Psalm lxxxix. is often referred to as the "twin" of this psalm. Its wailings over the vanished glories of the Davidic monarchy have nothing corresponding to them here. These considerations are against a post-exilic date, for which the chief argument is the inclusion of the psalm in the collection of pilgrim songs.

If, on the other hand, we disregard its place in the Psalter and look at its contents, it must be admitted that they perfectly harmonise with the supposition that its occasion was the completion of Solomon's Temple. The remembrance of David's long-cherished purpose to build the House, of the many wanderings of the Ark, the glad summons to enter the courts to worship, the Divine promises to David, which were connected with his design of building a Temple, all fit in with this view of the occasion of the psalm. Singularly enough, some advocates of later dates than even the building of the second Temple catch in the psalm tones of depression, and see indications of its having been written when the glowing promises which it quotes appeared to have failed. It is not in reference to "Nature" only that "we receive but what we give.' To other ears, with perhaps equal though opposite bias, glad confidence in a promise, of which the incipient fulfilment was being experienced, sounds in the psalm. To some it is plain that it was written when Ark and king had been swept away ; to others it is equally clear that it presupposes the existence of both. The latter view is to the present writer the more probable.

The psalm is not divided into regular strophes. There is, however, a broad division into two parts, of which vv. 1–10 form the first, the pleading of Israel with Jehovah ; and vv. 11–18 the second, the answer of Jehovah to Israel. The first part is further divided into two : vv. 1–5 setting forth David's vow ; vv. 6–10 the congregation's glad summons to enter the completed sanctuary, and its prayer for blessings on the worshipping nation with its priests and king. The second part is Jehovah's renewed promises, which take up and surpass the people's prayer. It is broken by a single verse (13), which is an interjected utterance of Israel's.

"One remembers anything to another, when one requites him for what he has done, or when one performs for him what one has promised him " (Delitzsch). David's earnest longing to find a fixed place for the Ark, his long-continued and generous amassing of treasure for the purpose of building the Temple, are regarded as a plea with God. The solidarity of the family, which was so vividly realised in old times, reaches its highest expression in the thought that blessings to David's descendants are as if given to him, sleeping in the royal tomb. Beautifully and humbly the singer, as representing the nation, has nothing to say of the toil of the actual builders. Not the hand which executes, but the heart and mind which conceived and cherished the plan, are its true author. The psalmist gives a poetic version of David's words in 2 Sam. vii. 2. "See now, I dwell in an house of cedar, but the Ark of God dwelleth in curtains," contains in germ all which the psalmist here draws out of it. He, the aged king, was almost ashamed of his own ease. "God gave him rest from his enemies," but he will not "give sleep to his eyes" till he finds out a place for Jehovah. Wearied with a stormy life, he might well have left it to others to care for the work which the prophet had told him that he was not to be permitted to begin. But not so does a true man reason. Rather, he will consecrate to God his leisure and his old age, and will rejoice to originate work which he cannot hope to see completed, and even to gather materials which happier natures and times may turn to account.   He will put his own comfort second, God's service first.

Such devotedness does make a plea with God.   The psalmist's prayer goes on that supposition, and God's answer endorses it as valid.   He does not require perfect faithfulness in His servants ere He prospers their work with His smile.   Stained offerings, in which much of the leaven of earthly motives may be fermenting, are not therefore rejected.

Vv. 6–10 are the petitions grounded on the preceding plea, and asking that Jehovah would dwell in the sanctuary and bless the worshippers.   Ver. 6 offers great difficulties.   It seems clear, however, that it and the next verse are to be taken as very closely connected (note the " we " and " us " occurring in them for the only time in the psalm).   They seem to describe continuous actions, of which the climax is entrance into the sanctuary.   The first question as to ver. 6 is what the " it " is, which is spoken of in both clauses ; and the most natural answer is—the Ark, alluded to here by anticipation, though not mentioned till ver. 8.   The irregularity is slight and not unexampled.   The interpretation of the verse mainly depends on the meaning of the two designations of locality, " Ephrathah " and " the fields of the Wood."   Usually the former is part of the name of Bethlehem, but the Ark in all its wanderings is never said to have been there.   Most probably Shiloh, in which the Ark did remain for a time, is intended.   But why should Shiloh be called Ephrathah ?   The answer usually given, but not altogether satisfactory, is that Shiloh lay in the territory of Ephraim, and that we have instances in which an Ephraimite is called an " Ephrathite " (Judg. xii. 5 ; I Sam. i. 1 ; I Kings xi. 26), and therefore it may be presumed that the territory of Ephraim was called Ephrathah. "The fields of the Wood," on the other hand, is taken to be a free poetic variation of the name of Kirjath-jearim (the city of the woods), where the Ark long lay, and whence it was brought up to Jerusalem by David. In this understanding of the verse, the two places where it remained longest are brought together, and the meaning of the whole verse is, "We heard that it lay long at Shiloh, but we found it in Kirjath-jearim." Delitzsch, followed by Cheyne, takes a different view, regarding "Ephrathah" as a name for the district in which Kirjath-jearim lay. He founds this explanation on the genealogies in 1 Chron. ii. 19, 50, according to which Caleb's wife, Ephrath, was the mother of Hur, the ancestor of the Bethlehemites, and whose son Shobal was the ancestor of the people of Kirjath-jearim; Ephrathah was thus a fitting name for the whole district, which included both Bethlehem and Kirjath-jearim. In this understanding of the names, the verse means, "We heard that the Ark was at Kirjath-jearim, and there we found it."

Ver. 7 must be taken as immediately connected with the preceding. If the same persons who found the Ark still speak, the "tabernacle" into which they encourage each other to enter must be the tent within which, as David said, it dwelt "in curtains"; and the joyful utterance of an earlier age will then be quoted by the still happier generation who, at the moment while they sing, see the sacred symbol of the Divine Presence enshrined within the Holy Place of the Temple. At all events, the petitions which follow are most naturally regarded as chanted forth at that supreme moment, though it is possible that the same feeling of the solidity of the nation in all generations, which, as

applied to the reigning family, is seen in ver. I, may
account for the worshippers in the new Temple identify-
ing themselves with the earlier ones who brought up
the Ark to Zion.   The Church remains the same, while
its individual members change.

The first of the petitions is partly taken from the
invocation in Numb. x. 35, when " the Ark set forward";
but there it was a prayer for guidance on the march;
here, for Jehovah's continuance in His fixed abode.   It
had wandered far and long.   It had been planted in
Shiloh, but had deserted that sanctuary which He had
once loved.   It had tarried for a while at Mizpeh and
at Bethel.   It had been lost on the field of Aphek, been
borne in triumph through Philistine cities, and sent
back thence in terror.   It had lain for three months in
the house of Obed-edom, and for twenty years been
hidden at Kirjath-jearim.   It had been set with glad
acclaim in the tabernacle provided by David, and now
it stands in the Temple.   There may it abide and go
no more out!   Solomon and Hiram and all their work-
men may have done their best, and the result of their
toils may stand gleaming in the sunlight in its fresh
beauty; but something more is needed.   Not till the
Ark is in the Shrine does the Glory fill the house.
The lesson is for all ages.   Our organisations and
works are incomplete without that quickening Presence.
It will surely be given if we desire it.   When His
Church prays, "Arise, O Lord, into Thy rest, Thou
and the Ark of Thy strength," His answer is swift and
sure, "Lo, I am with you always."

From this petition all the others flow.   If "the Ark
of Thy strength" dwells with us, we too shall be
strong, and have that Might for our inspiration as well
as our shield.   "Let Thy priests be clothed with

righteousness." The pure vestments of the priests were symbols of stainless character, befitting the ministers of a holy God. The psalmist prays that the symbol may truly represent the inner reality. He distinguishes between priests and the mass of the people; but in the Church to-day, as indeed in the original constitution of Israel, all are priests, and must be clothed in a righteousness which they receive from above. They do not weave that robe, but they must "put on" the garment which Christ gives them. Righteousness is no hazy, theological virtue, having little to do with every-day life and small resemblance to secular morality. To be good, gentle, and just, self-forgetting and self-ruling, to practise the virtues which all men call "lovely and of good report," and to consecrate them all by reference to Him in whom they dwell united and complete, is to be righteous; and that righteousness is the garb required of, and given by God to, all those who seek it and minister in His Temple.

"Let Thy favoured ones utter shrill cries of joy." Surely, if they dwell in the Temple, gladness will not fail them. True religion is joyful. If a man has only to lift his eyes to see the Ark, what but averted eyes should make him sad? True, there are enemies, but we are close to the fountain of strength. True, there are sins, but we can receive the garment of righteousness. True, there are wants, but the sacrifice whereof "the meek shall eat and be satisfied" is at hand. There is much unreached as yet, but there is a present God. So we may "walk all the day in the light of His countenance," and realise the truth of the paradox of always rejoicing, though sometimes we sorrow.

The final petition is for the anointed king, that his

prayers may be heard. To "turn away the face" is a graphic expression, drawn from the attitude of one who refuses to listen to a suppliant. It is harsh in the extreme to suppose that the king referred to is David himself, though Hupfeld and others take that view. The reference to Solomon is natural.

Such are the psalmist's petitions. The answers follow in the remainder of the psalm, which, as already noticed, is parted in two by an interjected verse (ver. 13), breaking the continuity of the Divine Voice. The shape of the responses is determined by the form of the desires, and in every case the answer is larger than the prayer. The Divine utterance begins with a parallel between the oath of David and that of God. David "sware to Jehovah." Yes, but "Jehovah has sworn to David." That is grander and deeper. With this may be connected the similar parallel in vv. 13 and 14 with ver. 5. David had sought to "find a habitation" for Jehovah. But He Himself had chosen His habitation long ago. He is throned there now, not because of David's choice or Solomon's work, but because His will had settled the place of His feet. These correspondences of expression point to the great truth that God is His own all-sufficient reason. He is not won to dwell with men by their importunity, but in the depths of His unchangeable love lies the reason why He abides with us unthankful. The promise given in ver. 12, which has respect to the closing petition of the preceding part, is substantially that contained in 2 Sam. vii. Similar references to that fundamental promise to David are found in Psalm lxxxix., with which this psalm is sometimes taken to be parallel; but that psalm comes from a time when the faithful promise seemed to have failed for evermore, and breathes a sadness which is alien to the spirit of this song.

Ver. 13 appears to be spoken by the people. It breaks the stream of promises. God has been speaking, but now, for a moment, He is spoken of. His choice of Zion for His dwelling is the glad fact, which the congregation feels so borne in on its consciousness that it breaks forth into speech. The " For " at the beginning of the verse gives a striking sequence, assigning, as it does, the Divine selection of Zion for His abode, as the reason for the establishment of the Davidic monarchy. If the throne was set up in Jerusalem, because there God would dwell, how solemn the obligation thereby laid on its occupant to rule as God's viceroy, and how secure each in turn might feel, if he discharged the obligations of his office, that God would grant to the kingdom an equal date with the duration of His own abode ! Throne and Temple are indissolubly connected.

With ver. 14 the Divine Voice resumes, and echoes the petitions of the earlier part. The psalmist asked God to arise into His rest, and He answers by granting the request with the added promise of perpetuity : " Here will I dwell *for ever*." He adds a promise which had not been asked—abundance for all, and bread to fill even the poor. The psalmist asked that the priests might be clothed in righteousness, and the answer promises robes of *salvation*, which is the perfecting and most glorious issue of righteousness. The psalmist asked that God's favoured ones might utter shrill cries of joy, and God replies with an emphatic reduplication of the word, which implies the exuberance and continuance of the gladness. The psalmist asked for favour to the anointed, and God replies by expanded and magnificent promises. The " horn " is an emblem of power. It shall continually " sprout "—*i.e.*, the might of the royal house shall continually increase. The " lamp for Mine anointed " may be simply a metaphor for enduring prosperity and happiness, but many expositors take it to be a symbol of the continuance of the Davidic house, as in 1 Kings xv. 4, where, however, the word employed is not the same as that used here, though closely connected with it. The promise of perpetuity to the house of David does not fit into the context as well as that of splendour and joy, and it has already been given in ver. 12. Victory will attend the living representative of David, his foes being clothed by Jehovah with shame—*i.e.*, being foiled in their hostile attempts—while their confusion is as a dark background, against which the radiance of his diadem sparkles the more brightly. These large promises are fulfilled in Jesus Christ, of the seed of David ; and the psalm is Messianic, as presenting the ideal which it is sure shall be realised, and which is so in Him alone.

The Divine promises teach the great truth that God over-answers our desires, and puts to shame the poverty of our petitions by the wealth of His gifts. He is " able to do exceeding abundantly above all that we ask or think," for the measure of His doing is none other than " according to the Power that worketh in us," and the measure of that Power is none other than " the working of the strength of His might, which He wrought in Christ, when He raised Him from the dead, and set Him at His own right hand in the heavenly places."

PSALM CXXXIII.

1 Behold, how good and how pleasant [it is]
   That brethren dwell in unity !
2 Like the precious oil on the head,
   Flowing down on the beard,
   [Even] Aaron's beard,
   That flows down on the opening of his garments.
3 Like the dew of Hermon, that flows down on the mountains of
     Zion.
   For there Jehovah has commanded the blessing,
   Life for evermore.

IT is natural to suppose that this psalm was occasioned by, or at least refers to, the gathering of
the pilgrims or restored exiles in Jerusalem. The
patriot-poet's heart glows at the sight of the assembled
multitudes, and he points with exultation to the good
and fair sight. Like the other short psalms in this
group, this one is the expression of a single thought—
the blessing of unity, and that not merely as shown
in the family, but in the church-state of the restored
Israel. The remembrance of years of scattering among
the nations, and of the schism of the Northern tribes,
makes the sight of an united Israel the more blessed,
even though its numbers are small.

The psalm begins with a " Behold," as if the poet
would summon others to look on the goodly spectacle
which, in reality or in imagination, is spread before
him. Israel is gathered together, and the sight is good,

as securing substantial benefits, and " pleasant," **as** being lovely. The original in ver. 1 *b* runs, " That brethren dwell *also* together." The " also " suggests that, in addition to local union, there should be heart harmony, as befits brothers. To speak in modern dialect, the psalmist cares little for external unity, if the spirit of oneness does not animate the corporate whole.

His two lovely metaphors or parables set forth the same thought—namely, the all-diffusive, all-blessing nature of such inward concord. The repetition in both figures of the same word, " flows down," is not merely due to the " step-like " structure common to this with other of the pilgrim psalms, but is the key to its meaning.

In the first emblem, the consecrating oil, poured on Aaron's head, represents the gracious spirit of concord between brethren. The emblem is felicitous by reason of the preciousness, the fragrance, and the manifold uses of oil ; but these are only to be taken into account in a subordinate degree, if at all. The one point of comparison is the flow of the oil from the priestly head on to the beard and thence to the garments. It is doubtful whether ver. 2 *d* refers to the oil or to the beard of the high priest. The latter reference is pre-ferred by many, but the former is more accordant with the parallelism, and with the use of the word " flows down," which can scarcely be twice used in regard to oil and dew, the main subjects in the figures, and be taken in an entirely different reference in the inter-vening clause. The " opening " (lit. *mouth*) of the robe is the upper edge or collar, the aperture through which the wearer's head was passed.

The second figure illustrates the same thought of

the diffusive blessing of concord, but it presents some difficulty. How can the dew of Hermon in the far north fall on the mountains of Zion ? Some commentators, as Delitzsch, try to make out that "an abundant dew in Jerusalem might rightly be accounted for by the influence of the cold current of air sweeping down from the north over Hermon." But that is a violent supposition ; and there is no need to demand meteorological accuracy from a poet. It is the one dew which falls on both mountains ; and since Hermon towers high above the lower height of Zion, and is visited with singular abundance of the nightly blessing, it is no inadmissible poetic licence to say that the loftier hill transmits it to the lesser. Such community of blessing is the result of fraternal concord, whereby the high serve the lowly, and no man grudgingly keeps anything to himself, but all share in the good of each. Dew, like oil, is fitted for this symbolic use, by reason of qualities which, though they do not come prominently into view, need not be wholly excluded. It refreshes the thirsty ground and quickens vegetation ; so fraternal concord, falling gently on men's spirits, and linking distant ones together by a mysterious chain of transmitted good, will help to revive failing strength and refresh parched places.

That brotherly unity is blessed, not only because it diffuses itself, and so blesses all in whose hearts it dwells, but also because it is the condition on which still higher gifts are spread among brethren by their brethren's mediation. God Himself pours on men the sacred anointing of His Divine Spirit and the dew of His quickening influences. When His servants are knit together, as they should be, they impart to one another the spiritual gifts received from above. When

Christians are truly one as brethren, God's grace will fructify through each to all.

Ver. 3 *b, c,* seem to assign the reason why the dew of Hermon will descend on Zion—*i.e.,* why the blessings of brotherly concord should there especially be realised.   There God has appointed to be stored His blessing of life ; therefore it becomes those who, dwelling there, receive that blessing, to be knit together in closest bonds, and to impart to their brethren what they receive from the Fountain of all good.   That Zion should not be the home of concord, or that Jerusalem should not be the city of peace, contradicts both the name of the city and the priceless gift which Jehovah has placed there for all its citizens.

PSALM CXXXIV.

1 Behold, bless Jehovah, all ye servants of Jehovah,
   Who stand in the house of Jehovah in the night seasons.
2 Lift up your hands to the sanctuary,
   And bless Jehovah.

3 Jehovah bless thee out of Zion,
   The Maker of heaven and earth!

THIS fragment of song closes the pilgrim psalms
after the manner of a blessing. It is evidently
antiphonal, vv. 1, 2, being a greeting, the givers of
which are answered in ver. 4 by a corresponding
salutation from the receivers. Who are the parties to
the little dialogue is doubtful. Some have thought of
two companies of priestly watchers meeting as they
went their rounds in the Temple; others, more probably, take vv. 1, 2, to be addressed by the congregation
to the priests, who had charge of the nightly service
in the Temple, while ver. 3 is the response of the
latter, addressed to the speakers of vv. 1, 2. I Chron.
ix. 33 informs us that there was such a nightly
service, of the nature of which, however, nothing is
known. The designation " servants of Jehovah " here
denotes not the people, but the priests, for whose
official ministrations " stand " is a common term.
They are exhorted to fill the night with prayer as
well as watchfulness, and to let their hearts go up in
blessing to Jehovah. The voice of praise should echo

through the silent night and float over the sleeping city. The congregation is about to leave the crowded courts at the close of a day of worship, and now gives this parting salutation and charge to those who remain.

The answer in ver. 3 is addressed to each individual of the congregation—" Jehovah bless *thee !* " and it invokes on each a share in the blessing which, according to the preceding psalm, " Jehovah has commanded " in Zion. The watchers who remain in the sanctuary do not monopolise its blessings. These stream out by night, as by day, to all true hearts ; and they are guaranteed by the creative omnipotence of Jehovah, the thought of which recurs so often in these pilgrim psalms, and may be due to the revulsion from idolatry consequent on the Captivity and Restoration.

With this sweet interchange of greeting and exhortation to continual worship, this group of psalms joyously ends.

PSALM CXXXV.

Hallelujah !
Praise the name of Jehovah,
Praise, ye servants of Jehovah,
2 Who stand in the house of Jehovah,
In the courts of the house of our God.
3 Praise Jah, for Jehovah is good ;
Harp to His name, for it is pleasant.
4 For Jah has chosen Jacob for Himself,
Israel for His own possession.

5 For I—I know that Jehovah is great,
And [that] our Lord is above all gods.
6 Whatsoever Jehovah wills He has done,
In the heaven and in the earth,
In the seas and all depths ;
7 Who makes the vapours go up from the end of the earth,
He makes lightnings for the rain,
Who brings forth wind from His storehouses.

8 Who smote the first-born of Egypt,
Both of man and of cattle ;
9 He sent signs and wonders into thy midst, O Egypt,
On Pharaoh and all his servants.

10 Who smote many nations,
And slew mighty kings ;
11 Sihon, king of the Amorites,
And Og, king of Bashan ;
12 And gave their land [as] an inheritance,
An inheritance to Israel His people.

13 Jehovah, Thy name [endures] for ever,
Jehovah, Thy memorial [endures] to generation after
generation.
14 For Jehovah will right His people,
And will relent concerning His servants.

15 The idols of the nations are silver and gold,
   The work of the hands of men.
16 A mouth is theirs—and they cannot speak;
   Eyes are theirs—and they cannot see ;
17 Ears are theirs—and they cannot give ear;
   Yea, there is no breath at all in their mouths.
18 Like them shall those who make them be,
   [Even] every one that trusts in them.

19 House of Israel, bless ye Jehovah,
   House of Aaron, bless ye Jehovah;
20 House of Levi, bless ye Jehovah;
   Ye who fear Jehovah, bless ye Jehovah.
21 Blessed be Jehovah from Zion,
   Who dwells in Jerusalem !
                    Hallelujah!

LIKE Psalms xcvii. and xcviii., this is a cento, or piece of mosaic work, apparently intended as a call to worship Jehovah in the Temple. His greatness, as manifested in Nature, and especially in His planting Israel in its inheritance, is set forth as the reason for praise : and the contemptuous contrast of the nothingness of idols is repeated from Psalm cxv., and followed, as there, by an exhortation to Israel to cleave to Him. We have not here to do with a song which gushed fresh from the singer's heart, but with echoes of many strains which a devout and meditative soul had made its own. The flowers are arranged in a new bouquet, because the poet had long delighted in their fragrance. The ease with which he blends into a harmonious whole fragments from such diverse sources tells how familiar he was with these, and how well he loved them.

Vv. 1–4 are an invocation to praise Jehovah, and largely consist of quotations or allusions. Thus Psalm cxxxiv. 1 underlies vv. 1, 2. But here the reference to nightly praises is omitted, and the summons is

addressed not only to those who stand in the house of
Jehovah, but to those who stand in its *courts*. That
expansion may mean that the call to worship is here
directed to the people as well as to the priests (so in
ver. 19).   Ver. 3 closely resembles Psalm cxlvii. 1,
but the question of priority may be left undecided.
Since the act of praise is said to be "pleasant" in
Psalm cxlvii. 1, it is best to refer the same word here
to the same thing, and not, as some would do, to the
Name, or to take it as an epithet of Jehovah.   To a
loving soul praise is a delight.   The songs which are
not winged by the singer's joy in singing will not rise
high.   True worship pours out its notes as birds do
theirs—in order to express gladness which, unuttered,
loads the heart.   Ver. 4 somewhat passes beyond the
bounds of the invocation proper, and anticipates the
subsequent part of the psalm.   Israel's prerogative is
so great to this singer that it forces utterance at once,
though "out of season," as correct critics would say.
But the throbs of a grateful heart are not always
regular.   It is impossible to keep the reasons for praise
out of the summons to praise.   Ver. 4 joyfully and
humbly accepts the wonderful title given in Deut.
vii. 6.

In vv. 5–7 God's majesty as set forth in Nature is
hymned.   The psalmist says emphatically in ver. 5
"I—I know," and implies the privilege which he shared,
in common with his fellow-Israelites (who appear in the
"our" of the next clause), of knowing what the heathen
did not know—how highly Jehovah was exalted above
all their gods.   Ver. 6 is from Psalm cxv. 3, with the
expansion of defining the all-inclusive sphere of God's
sovereignty.   Heaven, earth, seas, and depths cover
all space.   The enumeration of the provinces of His

dominion prepares for that of the phases of His power in Nature, which is quoted with slight change from Jer. x. 13, li. 16. The mysterious might which gathers from some unknown region the filmy clouds which grow, no man knows how, in the clear blue ; the power which weds in strange companionship the fire of the lightning flash and the torrents of rain ; the controlling hand which urges forth the invisible wind,— these call for praise.

But while the psalmist looks on physical phenomena with a devout poet's eye, he turns from these to expatiate rather on what Jehovah has done for Israel. Psalmists are never weary of drawing confidence and courage for to-day from the deeds of the Exodus and the Conquest. Ver. 8 is copied from Exod. xiii. 15, and the whole section is saturated with phraseology drawn from Deuteronomy. Ver. 13 is from Exod. iii. 15, the narrative of the theophany at the Bush. That Name, proclaimed then as the basis of Moses' mission and Israel's hope, is now, after so many centuries and sorrows, the same, and it will endure for ever. Ver. 14 is from Deut. xxxii. 36. Jehovah will right His people—*i.e.*, deliver them from oppressors—which is the same thing as " relent concerning His servants," since His wrath was the reason of their subjection to their foes. That judicial deliverance of Israel is at once the sign that His Name, His revealed character, continues the same, unexhausted and unchanged for ever, and the reason why the Name shall continue as the object of perpetual adoration and trust.

Vv. 15–20 are taken bodily from Psalm cxv., to which the reader is referred. Slight abbreviations and one notable difference occur. In ver. 17 *b*, " Yea, there is no breath at all in their mouths," takes the place of " A nose is theirs—and they cannot smell." The variation has arisen from the fact that the particle of strong affirmation (yea) is spelt like the noun " nose," and that the word for "breath" resembles the verb "smell." The psalmist plays upon his original, and by his variation makes the expression of the idols' lifelessness stronger.

The final summons to praise, with which the end of the psalm returns to its beginning, is also moulded on Psalm cxv. 9—11, with the addition of "the house of Levi" to the three groups mentioned there, and the substitution of a call to "bless" for the original invitation to "trust." Ver. 21 looks back to the last verse of the preceding psalm, and significantly modifies it. There, as in Psalm cxviii., Jehovah's blessing comes out of Zion to His people. Here the people's blessing in return goes from Zion and rises to Jehovah. They gathered there for worship, and dwelt with Him in His city and Temple. Swift interchange of the God-given blessing, which consists in mercies and gifts of gracious deliverance, and of the human blessing, which consists in thanksgiving and praise, fills the hours of those who dwell with Jehovah, as guests in His house, and walk the streets of the city which He guards and Himself inhabits.

PSALM CXXXVI.

1 Give thanks to Jehovah, for He is good,
   For His loving-kindness endures for ever,
2 Give thanks to the God of gods,
   For His loving-kindness endures for ever,
3 Give thanks to the Lord of lords,
   For His loving-kindness endures for ever.

4 To Him who alone does great wonders,
   For His loving-kindness endures for ever.
5 To Him who made the heavens by understanding,
   For His loving-kindness endures for ever.
6 To Him who spread the earth above the waters,
   For His loving-kindness endures for ever.
7 To Him who made great lights,
   For His loving-kindness endures for ever;
8 The sun to rule by day,
   For His loving-kindness endures for ever;
9 The moon and stars to rule by night,
   For His loving-kindness endures for ever.

10 To Him who smote the Egyptians in their first-born,
   For His loving-kindness endures for ever;
11 And brought forth Israel from their midst,
   For His loving-kindness endures for ever;
12 With mighty strong hand and outstretched arm,
   For His loving-kindness endures for ever.
13 To Him that cut the Red Sea into parts,
   For His loving-kindness endures for ever;
14 And made Israel pass through the midst of it,
   For His loving-kindness endures for ever;
15 And shook out Pharaoh and his host into the Red Sea,
   For His loving-kindness endures for ever.

16 To Him who led His people in the wilderness,
   For His loving-kindness endures for ever.

17 To Him who smote great kings,
   For His loving-kindness endures for ever ;
18 And slew mighty kings,
   For His loving-kindness endures for ever ;
19 Sihon, king of the Amorites,
   For His loving-kindness endures for ever ;
20 And Og, king of Bashan,
   For His loving-kindness endures for ever ;
21 And gave their land for an inheritance,
   For His loving-kindness endures for ever ;
22 An inheritance to Israel His servant,
   For His loving-kindness endures for ever.

23 Who in our low estate remembered us,
   For His loving-kindness endures for ever ;
24 And tore us from the grasp of our adversaries,
   For His loving-kindness endures for ever.
25 Who gives bread to all flesh,
   For His loving-kindness endures for ever.
26 Give thanks to the God of heaven,
   For His loving-kindness endures for ever.

THIS psalm is evidently intended for liturgic use. It contains reminiscences of many parts of Scripture, and is especially based on the previous psalm, which it follows closely in vv. 10–18, and quotes directly in vv. 19–22. Delitzsch points out that if these quoted verses are omitted, the psalm falls into triplets. It would then also contain twenty-two verses, corresponding to the number of letters in the Hebrew alphabet. The general trend of thought is like that of Psalm cxxxv. ; but the addition in each verse of the refrain gives a noble swing and force to this exulting song.

The first triplet is a general invocation to praise, coloured by the phraseology of Deuteronomy. Vv. 2 *a* and 3 *a* quote Deut. x. 17. The second and third triplets (vv. 4–9) celebrate Jehovah's creative power. " Doeth great wonders " (ver. 4) is from Psalm lxxii. 18.

The thought of the Divine Wisdom as the creative
agent occurs in Psalm civ. 24, and attains noble expression in Prov. iii.   In ver. 6 the word rendered *spread* is
from the same root as that rendered " firmament " in
Genesis.   The office of the heavenly bodies to rule day
and night is taken from Gen. i.   But the psalm looks
at the story of Creation from an original point of view,
when it rolls out in chorus, after each stage of that
work, that its motive lay in the eternal loving-kindness
of Jehovah.   Creation is an act of Divine love.   That
is the deepest truth concerning all things visible.
They are the witnesses, as they are the result, of
loving-kindness which endures for ever.

Vv. 10–22 pass from world-wide manifestations of
that creative loving-kindness to those specially affecting Israel.   If vv. 19–22 are left out of notice, there are
three triplets in which the Exodus, desert life, and conquest of Caanan are the themes,—the first (vv. 10–12)
recounting the departure ; the second (vv. 13–15) the
passage of the Red Sea ; the third (vv. 16–18) the
guidance during the forty years and the victories
over enemies.   The whole is largely taken from the
preceding psalm, and has also numerous allusions to
other parts of Scripture.   Ver. 12 *a* is found in
Deut. iv. 34, etc.   The word for dividing the Red Sea
is peculiar.   It means to hew in pieces or in two, and
is used for cutting in halves the child in Solomon's
judgment (1 Kings iii. 25) ; while the word " parts " is
a noun from the same root, and is found in Gen. xv. 17,
to describe the two portions into which Abraham clave
the carcasses.   Thus, as with a sword, Jehovah hewed
the sea in two, and His people passed between the
parts, as between the halves of the covenant sacrifice.
In ver. 15 the word describing Pharaoh's destruction

is taken from Exod. xiv. 27, and vividly describes it as a "shaking out," as one would vermin or filth from a robe.

In the last triplet (vv. 23–25) the singer comes to the Israel of the present. It, too, had experienced Jehovah's remembrance in its time of need, and felt the merciful grasp of His hand plucking it, with loving violence, from the claws of the lion. The word for "low estate" and that for "tore us from the grasp" are only found besides in late writings—the former in Eccles. x. 6, and the latter in Lam. v. 8.

But the song will not close with reference only to Israel's blessings. "He gives bread to all flesh." The loving-kindness which flashes forth even in destructive acts, and is manifested especially in bringing Israel back from exile, stretches as wide in its beneficence as it did in its first creative acts, and sustains all flesh which it has made. Therefore the final call to praise, which rounds off the psalm by echoing its beginning, does not name Him by the Name which implied Israel's special relation, but by that by which other peoples could and did address Him, "the God of heaven," from whom all good comes down on all the earth.

PSALM CXXXVII.

1 By the streams of Babylon, there we sat, yea, wept,
  When we remembered Zion.
2 On the willows in the midst thereof
  We hung our harps.
3 For there our captors required of us words of song,
  And our plunderers [required of us] mirth;
  "Sing us one of the songs of Zion."
4 How can we sing Jehovah's songs
  In a strange land?

5 If I forget thee, Jerusalem,
  May my right hand forget!
6 May my tongue cleave to my palate,
  If I remember thee not,
  If I set not Jerusalem
  Above the summit of my joy!

7 Remember, Jehovah, to the children of Edom
  The day of Jerusalem,
  Who said, "Lay bare, lay bare,
  To the foundation therein."
8 Daughter of Babylon, thou that art laid waste,
  Happy he that requites thee
  Thy doing which thou hast done to us!
9 Happy he that seizes and dashes thy little ones
  Against the rock!

THE Captivity is past, as the tenses in vv. 1–3 show, and as is manifest from the very fact that its miseries have become themes for a psalm. Grief must be somewhat removed before it can be sung. But the strains of triumph heard in other psalms are wanting in this, which breathes passionate love for Jerusalem, tinged with sadness still. The date of the psalm is apparently the early days of the Return, when true-hearted patriots still felt the smart of recent bondage and sadly gazed on the dear ruins of the city. The singer passes in brief compass from tender music breathing plaintive remembrance of the captives' lot, to passionate devotion, and at last to an outburst of vehement imprecation, magnificent in its fiery rush, amply explicable by Israel's wrongs and Babylon's crimes, and yet to be frankly acknowledged as moving on a lower plane of sentiment than is permissible to those who have learned to repay scorn with gentleness, hate with love, and injuries with desires for the injurer's highest good. The coals of fire which this psalmist scatters among Israel's foes are not those which Christ's servants are bidden to heap on their enemies' heads.

Nothing sweeter or sadder was ever written than that delicate, deeply felt picture of the exiles in the early verses of the psalm. We see them sitting, as too heavy-hearted for activity, and half noting, as adding to their grief, the unfamiliar landscape round them, with its innumerable canals, and the monotonous " willows " (rather, a species of poplar) stretching along their banks. How unlike this flat, tame fertility to the dear home-land, with its hills and glens and rushing streams ! The psalmist was probably a Temple singer, but he did not find solace even in " the harp, his sole remaining joy." No doubt many of the exiles made themselves at home in captivity, but there were some more keenly sensitive or more devout, who found that it was better to remember Zion and weep than to enjoy Babylon. " Alas, alas ! how much less it is to hold converse with others than to remember thee !" So they sat, like Michael Angelo's brooding figure of

Jeremiah in the Sistine Chapel, silent, motionless, **lost**
in bitter-sweet memories.

But there was another reason than their own sadness
for hanging their idle harps upon the willows. **Their**
coarse oppressors bade them sing to make mirth. **They**
wished entertainment from the odd sounds of foreign
music, or they were petulantly angry that such dumb
hang-dog people should keep sullen faces, like un-
illuminated windows, when their masters were pleased
to be merry. So, like tipsy revellers, they called out
" Sing ! " The request drove the iron deeper into sad
hearts, for it came from those who had made the misery.
They had led away the captives, and now they bid
them make sport.

The word rendered *plunderers* is difficult. The translation adopted here is that of the LXX. and others.
It requires a slight alteration of reading, which is
approved by Hupfeld (as an alternative), Perowne,
Baethgen, Graetz, etc. Cheyne follows Halevy in
preferring another conjectural alteration which gives
" dancers " (" and of our dancers, festive glee "), but
admits that the other view is " somewhat more natural."
The roystering Babylonians did not care what kind of
songs their slaves sang—Temple music would do as well
as any other ; but the devout psalmist and his fellows
shrank from profaning the sacred songs that praised
Jehovah by making them parts of a heathen banquet.
Such sacrilege would have been like Belshazzar's using
the Temple vessels for his orgy. " Give not that which
is holy to dogs." And the singers were not influenced
by superstition, but by reverence and by sadness, when
they could not sing these songs in that strange land.
No doubt it was a fact that the Temple music fell
into desuetude during the Captivity. There are moods

and there are scenes in which it is profanation to utter the deep music which may be sounding on perpetually in the heart. "Songs unheard" are sometimes not only "sweetest," but the truest worship.

The psalmist's remembrances of Babylon are suddenly broken off. His heart burns as he broods on that past, and then lifts his eyes to see how forlorn and forgotten-like Jerusalem stands, as if appealing to her sons for help. A rush of emotion sweeps over him, and he breaks into a passion of vowed loyalty to the mother city. He has Jerusalem written on his heart. It is noteworthy that her remembrance *was* the exiles' crown of sorrow; it now becomes the apex of the singer's joy. No private occasion for gladness so moves the depths of a soul, smitten with the noble and ennobling love of the city of God, as does its prosperity. Alas that the so-called citizens of the true city of God should have so tepid interest in its welfare, and be so much more keenly touched by individual than by public prosperity or adversity! Alas that so often they should neither weep when they remember its bondage nor exult in its advancement!

Ver. 5 *b* is emphatic by its incompleteness. "May my right hand forget!" What? Some word like "power," "cunning," or "movement" may be supplied. It would be as impossibly unnatural for the poet to forget Jerusalem as for his hand to forget to move or cease to be conscious of its connection with his body.

Ver. 6 *d* reads literally "Above the head of my joy": an expression which may either mean the summit of my joy—*i.e.*, my greatest joy; or the sum of my joy—*i.e.*, my whole joy. In either case the well-being of Jerusalem is the psalmist's climax of gladness; and so utterly does he lose himself in the community founded

by God, that all his springs of felicity are in her.   He
had chosen the better part.   Unselfish gladness is the
only lasting bliss ; and only they drink of an unfailing
river of pleasures whose chiefest delight lies in beholding and sharing in the rebuilding of God's city on earth.

The lightning flashes of the last part of the psalm
need little commenting.   The desire for the destruction
of Zion's enemies, which they express, is not the highest
mood of the loyal citizen of God's city, and is to be
fully recognised as not in accordance with Christian
morality.   But it has been most unfairly judged, as if
it were nothing nobler than ferocious thirsting for
vengeance.   It is a great deal more.   It is desire for
retribution, heavy as the count of crimes which demands it is heavy.   It is a solemn appeal to God to
sweep away the enemies of Zion, who, in hating her,
rebelled against Him.   First, the psalmist turns to the
treacherous kinsmen of Israel, the Edomites, who had,
as Obadiah says, " rejoiced over the children of Judah
in the days of their destruction " (Obad. 12), and stimulated the work of rasing the city.   Then the singer
turns to Babylon, and salutes her as already laid waste ;
for he is a seer as well as a singer, and is so sure of
the judgment to be accomplished that it is as good as
done.   The most repellent part of the imprecation, that
which contemplates the dreadful destruction of tender
infants, has its harshness somewhat softened by the
fact that it is the echo of Isaiah's prophecy concerning
Babylon (Isa. xiii. 16–18), and still further by the consideration that the purpose of the apparently barbarous
cruelty was to make an end of a " seed of evil-doers,"
whose continuance meant misery for wide lands.

Undoubtedly, the words are stern, and the temper
they embody is harsh discord, when compared with the

Christian spirit.   But they are not the utterances of
mere ferocious revenge.   Rather they proclaim God's
judgments, not with the impassiveness, indeed, which
best befits the executors of such terrible sentences, but
still less with the malignant gratification of sanguinary
vengeance which has been often attributed to them.
Perhaps, if some of their modern critics had been under
the yoke from which this psalmist has been delivered,
they would have understood a little better how a good
man of that age could rejoice that Babylon was fallen
and all its race extirpated.   Perhaps, it would do
modern tender-heartedness no harm to have a little
more iron infused into its gentleness, and to lay to
heart that the King of Peace must first be King of
Righteousness, and that Destruction of evil is the
complement of Preservation of Good.

PSALM CXXXVIII.

1 I will thank Thee, Jehovah, with my whole heart,
  In presence of the gods will I harp to Thee.
2 I will worship toward Thy holy Temple,
  And will thank Thy name for Thy loving-kindness and for Thy
    truth,
  For Thou hast magnified Thy promise above all Thy name.
3 In the day [when] I called Thou answeredst me,
  Thou didst make me bold—in my soul [welled up] strength.

4 Jehovah, all the kings of the earth shall thank Thee,
  When they have heard the words of Thy mouth.
5 And they shall sing of the ways of Jehovah,
  For great is the glory of Jehovah.
6 For Jehovah is high, and the lowly He regards,
  And the lofty from afar off He knows.

7 If I walk in the midst of trouble Thou wilt revive me,
  Against the wrath of mine enemies Thou wilt stretch forth Thy
    hand,
  And Thy right hand shall save me.
8 Jehovah will complete [all] that concerns me ;
  Jehovah, Thy loving-kindness [endures] for ever ;
  The works of Thy hands abandon not.

THIS is the first of a group of eight psalms
attributed to David in the superscriptions. It
precedes the closing hallelujah psalms, and thus stands
where a " find " of Davidic psalms at a late date would
naturally be put. In some cases, there is no impro-
bability in the assigned authorship ; and this psalm is
certainly singularly unlike those which precede it, and

376

has many affinities with the earlier psalms ascribed to David.

In reading it, one feels the return to familiar thoughts and tones. The fragrance it exhales wakes memories of former songs. But the resemblance may be due to the imitative habit so marked in the last book of the Psalter. If it is a late psalm, the speaker is probably the personified Israel, and the deliverance which seems to the singer to have transcended all previous manifestations of the Divine name is the Restoration, which has inspired so many of the preceding psalms. The supporters of the Davidic authorship, on the other hand, point to the promise to David by Nathan of the perpetuity of the kinghood in his line, as the occasion of the psalmist's triumph.

The structure of the psalm is simple. It falls into three parts, of which the two former consist of three verses each, and the last of two. In the first, the singer vows praise and recounts God's wondrous dealings with him (vv. 1–3) ; in the second, he looks out over all the earth in the confidence that these blessings, when known, will bring the world to worship (vv. 4–6) ; and in the third, he pleads for the completion to himself of mercies begun (vv. 7, 8).

The first part is the outpouring of a thankful heart for recent great blessing, which has been the fulfilment of a Divine promise. So absorbed in his blessedness is the singer, that he neither names Jehovah as the object of his thanks, nor specifies what has set his heart vibrating. The great Giver and the great gift are magnified by being unspoken. To whom but Jehovah could the current of the psalmist's praise set ? He feels that Jehovah's mercy to him requires him to become the herald of His name ; and therefore he vows, in lofty consciousness of his mission, that he will ring out God's praises in presence of false gods, whose worshippers have no such experience to loose their tongues. Dead gods have dumb devotees; the servants of the living Jehovah receive His acts of power, that they may proclaim His name.

The special occasion for this singer's praise has been some act, in which Jehovah's faithfulness was very conspicuously shown. "Thou hast magnified Thy promise above all Thy name." If the history of David underlies the psalm, it is most natural to interpret the " promise " as that of the establishment of the monarchy. But the fulfilment, not the giving, of a promise is its magnifying, and hence one would incline to take the reference to be to the great manifestation of God's troth in restoring Israel to its land. In any case the expression is peculiar, and has induced many attempts at emendation. Baethgen would strike out " Thy name " as a dittograph from the previous clause, and thus gets the reading "done great things beyond Thy word "— *i.e.*, transcended the promise in fulfilment—which yields a good sense. Others make a slight alteration in the word " Thy name," and read it " Thy heavens," supposing that the psalmist is making the usual comparison between the manifestation of Divine power in Nature and in Revelation, or in the specific promise in question. But the text as it stands, though peculiar, is intelligible, and yields a meaning very appropriate to the singer's astonished thankfulness. A heart amazed by the greatness of recent blessings is ever apt to think that they, glittering in fresh beauty, are greater, as they are nearer and newer, than the mercies which it has only heard of as of old. To-day brings growing revelations of Jehovah to the waiting heart. The psalmist is singing, not dissertating. It is quite true that if his words are measured by the metaphysical theologian's foot-rule, they are inaccurate, for "the name of God cannot be surpassed by any single act of His, since every single act is but a manifestation of that name"; but thankfulness does not speak by rule, and the psalmist means to say that, so great has been the mercy given to him and so signal its confirmation of the Divine promise, that to him, at all events, that whole name blazes with new lustre, and breathes a deeper music. So should each man's experience be the best teacher of what God is to all men.

In ver. 3 *b* the psalmist uses a remarkable expression, in saying that Jehovah had made him bold, or, as the word is literally, *proud*. The following words are a circumstantial or subsidiary clause, and indicate how the consciousness of inbreathed strength welling up in his soul gave him lofty confidence to confront foes.

The second part (vv. 4–6) resembles many earlier psalms in connecting the singer's deliverance with a world-wide manifestation of God's name. Such a consciousness of a vocation to be the world's evangelist is appropriate either to David or the collective Israel. Especially is it natural, and, as a fact, occurs in post-exilic psalms. Here "the words of Thy mouth" are equivalent to the promise already spoken of, the fulfilment of which has shown that Jehovah the High has regard to the lowly—*i.e.*, to the psalmist; and "knows the lofty"—*i.e.*, his oppressors—"afar off." He reads their characters thoroughly, without, as it were, needing to approach for minute study. The implication is that He will thwart their plans and judge the plotters. This great lesson of Jehovah's providence, care for the lowly, faithfulness to His word, has exemplification

in the psalmist's history ; and when it is known, the
lofty ones of the earth shall learn the principles of
Jehovah's ways, and become lowly recipients of His
favours and adoring singers of His great glory.

The glowing vision is not yet fulfilled ; but the singer
was cherishing no illusions when he sang. It *is* true
that the story of God's great manifestation of Himself
in Christ, in which He has magnified His Word above
all His name, is one day to win the world. It *is* true
that the revelation of a God who regards the lowly
is the conquering Gospel which shall bow all hearts.

In the third part (vv. 7, 8), the psalmist comes back
to his own needs, and takes to his heart the calming
assurance born of his experience, that he bears a
charmed life. He but speaks the confidence which
should strengthen every heart that rests on God. Such
an one may be girdled about by troubles, but he will
have an inner circle traced round him, within which
no evil can venture. He may walk in the valley of
the shadow of death unfearing, for God will hold his
soul in life. Foes may pour out floods of enmity and
wrath, but one strong hand will be stretched out
against (or *over*) the wild deluge, and will draw the
trustful soul out of its rush on to the safe shore. So
was the psalmist assured ; so may and should those
be who have yet greater wonders for which to thank
Jehovah.

That last prayer of the psalm blends very beautifully
confidence and petition. Its central clause is the basis
of both the confidence in its first, and the petition in
its last, clause. Because Jehovah's loving-kindness
endures for ever, every man on whom His shaping
Spirit has begun to work, or His grace in any form
to bestow its gifts, may be sure that no exhaustion or

change of these is possible. God is not as the foolish tower-builder, who began and was not able to finish. He never stops till He has completed His work ; and nothing short of the entire conformity of a soul to His likeness and the filling of it with Himself can be the termination of His loving purpose, or of His achieving grace. Therefore the psalmist "found it in his heart to pray" that God would not abandon the works of His own hands. That prayer appeals to His faithfulness and to His honour. It sets forth the obligations under which God comes by what He has done. It is a prayer which goes straight to His heart ; and they who offer it receive the old answer, "I will not leave thee till I have done unto thee that which I have spoken to thee of."

PSALM CXXXIX.

1 Jehovah, Thou hast searched me and known [me].
2 Thou, Thou knowest my down-sitting and my up-rising,
  Thou understandest my thought afar off.
3 My walking and my lying down Thou siftest,
  And with all my ways Thou art familiar.
4 For there is not a word on my tongue,
  —Behold, Thou, Jehovah, knowest it all.
5 Behind and before Thou hast shut me in,
  And hast laid upon me Thy hand.
6 [Such] knowledge is too wonderful for me,
  Too high, I am not able for it.

7 Whither shall I go from Thy spirit ?
  And whither from Thy face shall I flee ?
8 If I climb heaven, there art Thou,
  Or make Sheol my bed, lo, Thou [art there].
9 [If] I lift up the wings of the dawn,
  [If] I dwell at the farthest end of the sea,
10 Even there Thy hand shall lead me,
  And Thy right hand shall hold me.
11 And [if] I say, "Only let darkness cover me,
  And the light about me be [as] night,"
12 Even darkness darkens not to Thee,
  And night lightens like day ;
  As is the darkness, so is the light.

13 For Thou, Thou hast formed my reins,
  Thou hast woven me together in my mother's womb.
14 I will thank Thee for that in dread fashion I am wondrously made
  Wondrous are Thy works,
  And my soul knows [it] well.
15 My bones were not hid from Thee,
  When I was made in secret,
  [And] wrought like embroidery [as] in the depths of the earth.

382

16 Thine eyes saw my shapeless mass,
And in Thy book were they all written,
The days [that] were fashioned,
And yet there was not one among them.

17 And to me how precious are Thy thoughts, O God,
How great is their sum!

18 Would I reckon them, they outnumber the sand;
I awake—and am still with Thee.

19 Oh, if Thou wouldest smite the wicked, O God!
—And [ye] men of blood, depart from me,

20 Who rebel against Thee with wicked deeds,
They lift up [themselves] against Thee vainly (?)

21 Do not I hate them which hate Thee, Jehovah?
And am not I grieved with those who rise against Thee?

22 With perfect hatred I hate them,
They are counted for enemies to me.

23 Search me, O God, and know my heart,
Try me and know my thoughts,

24 And see if there be any way of grief in me,
And lead me in a way everlasting.

THIS is the noblest utterance in the Psalter of pure contemplative theism, animated and not crushed by the thought of God's omniscience and omnipresence. No less striking than the unequalled force and sublimity with which the psalm hymns the majestic attributes of an all-filling, all-knowing, all-creating God, is the firmness with which the singer's personal relation to that God is grasped. Only in the last verses is there reference to other men. In the earlier parts of the psalm, there are but two beings in the universe—God and the psalmist. With impressive reiteration, God's attributes are gazed on in their bearing on him. Not mere omniscience, but a knowledge which knows *him* altogether, not mere omnipresence, but a presence which *he* can nowhere escape, not mere creative power, but a power which shaped *him*, fill and thrill the psalmist's soul. This is no cold theism, but vivid religion. Conscience and the consciousness of individual relation to God penetrate and vitalise the whole. Hence the sudden turn to prayer against evil men and for the singer's direction in the right way, which closes the hymn, is natural, however abrupt.

The course of thought is plain. There are four strophes of six verses each,—of which the first (vv. 1–6) magnifies God's omniscience; the second (vv. 7–12) His omnipresence; the third (vv. 13–18), His creative act, as the ground of the preceding attributes; and the fourth (vv. 19–24) recoils from men who rebel against such a God, and joyfully submits to the searching of His omniscient eye, and the guidance of His ever-present hand.

The psalmist is so thoroughly possessed by the thought of his personal relation to God that his meditation spontaneously takes the form of address to Him. That form adds much to the impressiveness, but is no rhetorical or poetic artifice. Rather, it is the shape in which such intense consciousness of God cannot but utter itself. How cold and abstract the awestruck sentences become, if we substitute " He " for " Thou," and " men " for " I " and " me " ! The first overwhelming thought of God's relation to the individual soul is that He completely knows the whole man. " Omniscience " is a pompous word, which leaves us unaffected by either awe or conscience. But the psalmist's God was a God who came into close touch with him, and the psalmist's religion translated the powerless generality of an attribute referring to the Divine relation to the universe into a continually exercised power having reference to himself. He utters his reverent consciousness of it in ver. 1 in a single clause, and expands that verse in the succeeding ones. " Thou hast searched me " describes a process of minute investigation ; " and known [me]," its result in complete knowledge.

That knowledge is then followed out in various directions, and recognised as embracing the whole man in all his modes of action and repose, in all his inner and outward life.   Vv. 2 and 3 are substantially parallel.   " Down-sitting " and " up-rising " correspond to " walking " and " lying down," and both antitheses express the contrast between action and rest.   " My thought " in ver. 2 corresponds to " my ways " in ver. 3,—the former referring to the inner life of thought, purpose, and will ; the latter to the outward activities which carry these into effect.   Ver. 3 is a climax to ver. 2, in so far as it ascribes a yet closer and more accurate knowledge to God.   " Thou siftest " or *win-nowest* gives a picturesque metaphor for careful and judicial scrutiny which discerns wheat from chaff. " Thou art familiar " implies intimate and habitual knowledge.   But thought and action are not the whole man.   The power of speech, which the Psalter always treats as solemn and a special object of Divine approval or condemnation, must also be taken into account. Ver. 4 brings it, too, under God's cognisance.   The meaning may either be that " There is no word on my tongue [which] Thou dost not know altogether " ; or, " The word is not yet on my tongue, [but] lo ! Thou knowest," etc. " Before it has shaped itself on the tongue, [much less been launched from it], thou knowest all its secret history " (Kay).

The thought that God knows him through and through blends in the singer's mind with the other, that God surrounds him on every side.   Ver. 5 thus anticipates the thought of the next strophe, but presents it rather as the basis of God's knowledge, and as limiting man's freedom.　But the psalmist does not feel that he is imprisoned, or that the hand laid on him is heavy. Rather, he rejoices in the defence of an encompassing God, who shuts off evil from him, as well as shuts him in from self-willed and self-determined action ; and he is glad to be held by a hand so gentle as well as strong. " Thou God seest me " may either be a dread or a blessed thought. It may paralyse or stimulate. It should be the ally of conscience, and, while it stirs to all noble deeds, should also emancipate from all slavish fear.　An exclamation of reverent wonder and confession of the limitation of human comprehension closes the strophe.

Why should the thought that God is ever with the psalmist be put in the shape of vivid pictures of the impossibility of escape from Him ? It is the sense of sin which leads men to hide from God, like Adam among the trees of the garden.　The psalmist does not desire thus to flee, but he supposes the case, which would be only too common if men realised God's knowledge of all their ways. He imagines himself reaching the extremities of the universe in vain flight, and stunned by finding God there. The utmost possible height is coupled with the utmost possible depth. Heaven and Sheol equally fail to give refuge from that moveless Face, which confronts the fugitive in both, and fills them as it fills all the intervening dim distances. The dawn flushes the east, and swiftly passes on roseate wings to the farthest bounds of the Mediterranean, which, to the psalmist, represented the extreme west, a land of mystery. In both places and in all the broad lands between, the fugitive would find himself in the grasp of the same hand (compare ver. 5).

Darkness is the friend of fugitives from men ; but is transparent to God. In ver. 11 the language is some what obscure. The word rendered above " cover " is doubtful, as the Hebrew text reads " bruise," which is quite unsuitable here. Probably there has been textual error, and the slight correction which yields the above sense is to be adopted, as by many moderns. The second clause of the verse carries on the supposition of the first, and is not to be regarded, as in the A.V., as stating the result of the supposition, or, in grammatical language, the apodosis. That begins with ver. 12, and is marked there, as in ver. 10, by " even."

The third strophe (vv. 13–18) grounds the psalmist's relation to God on God's creative act. The mysteries of conception and birth naturally struck the imagination of non-scientific man, and are to the psalmist the direct result of Divine power. He touches them with poetic delicacy and devout awe, casting a veil of metaphor over the mystery, and losing sight of human parents in the clear vision of the Divine Creator. There is room for his thought of the origin of the indivi- dual life, behind modern knowledge of embryology. In ver. 13 the word rendered in the A.V. " possessed " is better understood in this context as meaning " formed," and that rendered there " covered " (as in Psalm cxl. 7) here means to *plait* or *weave together*, and pic- turesquely describes the interlacing bones and sinews, as in Job x. 11. But description passes into adoration in ver. 14. Its language is somewhat obscure. The verb rendered " wondrously made " probably means here " selected " or " distinguished," and represents man as the *chef d'œuvre* of the Divine Artificer. The psalmist cannot contemplate his own frame, God's workmanship, without breaking into thanks, nor without being touched with awe. Every man carries in his own body reasons enough for reverent gratitude.

The word for "bones" in ver. 15 is a collective noun, and might be rendered "bony framework." The mysterious receptacle in which the unborn body takes shape and grows is delicately described as "secret," and likened to the hidden region of the underworld, where are the dead. The point of comparison is the mystery enwrapping both. The same comparison occurs in Job's pathetic words, "Naked came I out of my mother's womb, and naked shall I return thither." It is doubtful whether the word rendered above "wrought like embroidery" refers to a pattern wrought by weaving or by needlework. In any case, it describes "the variegated colour of the individual members, especially of the viscera" (Delitzsch). The mysteries of ante-natal being are still pursued in ver. 16, which is extremely obscure. It is, however, plain that *a* sets forth the Divine knowledge of man in his first rudiments of corporeity. "My shapeless mass" is one word, meaning anything rolled up in a bundle or ball. But in *b* it is doubtful what is referred to in "they all." Strictly, the word should point back to something previously mentioned; and hence the A.V. and R.V. suppose that the "shapeless mass" is thought of as resolved into its component parts, and insert "my members"; but it is better to recognise a slight irregularity here, and to refer the word to the "days" immediately spoken of, which existed in the Divine foreknowledge long before they had real objective existence in the actual world. The last clause of the verse is capable of two different meanings, according as the Hebrew text or margin is followed. This is one of a number of cases in which there is a doubt whether we should

read "not" or "to him" (or "it"). The Hebrew
words having these meanings are each of two letters,
the initial one being the same in both, and both words
having the same sound. Confusion might easily therefore arise, and as a matter of fact there are numerous
cases in which the text has the one and the margin the
other of these two words. Here, if we adhere to the
text, we read the negative, and then the force of the
clause is to declare emphatically that the "days" were
written in God's book, and in a real sense "fashioned,'
when as yet they had not been recorded in earth's
calendars. If, on the other hand, the marginal reading
is preferred, a striking meaning is obtained : "And for
it [*i.e.*, for the birth of the shapeless mass] there was
one among them [predestined in God's book]."

In vv. 17, 18, the poet gathers together and crowns
all his previous contemplations by the consideration
that this God, knowing him altogether, ever near him,
and Former of his being, has great "thoughts" or
purposes affecting him individually. That assurance
makes omniscience and omnipresence joys, and not
terrors. The root meaning of the word rendered
"precious" is *weighty*. The singer would weigh God's
thoughts towards him, and finds that they weigh down
his scales. He would number them, and finds that they
pass his enumeration. It is the same truth of the
transcendent greatness and graciousness of God's purposes as is conveyed in Isaiah's "As the heavens are
higher than the earth, so are . . . My thoughts than
your thoughts." "I awake, and am still with Thee,"—
this is an artless expression of the psalmist's blessedness in realising God's continual nearness. He awakes
from sleep, and is conscious of glad wonder to find that,
like a tender mother by her slumbering child, God has

been watching over him, and that all the blessed communion of past days abides as before.

The fiery hatred of evil and evil men which burns in the last strophe offends many and startles more. But while the vehement prayer that " Thou wouldest slay the wicked " is not in a Christian tone, the recoil from those who could raise themselves against such a God is the necessary result of the psalmist's delight in Him. Attraction and repulsion are equal and contrary. The measure of our cleaving to that which is good, and to Him who is good, settles the measure of our abhorrence of that which is evil. The abrupt passing from petition in ver. 19 *a* to command in *b* has been smoothed away by a slight alteration which reads, " And that men of blood would depart from me " ; but the variation in tense is more forcible, and corresponds with the speaker's strong emotion. He cannot bear companionship with rebels against God. His indignation has no taint of personal feeling, but is pure zeal for God's honour.

Ver. 20 presents difficulties. The word rendered in the A.V. and R.V. (text) " speak against Thee " is peculiarly spelt if this is its meaning, and its construction is anomalous. Probably, therefore, the rendering should be as above. That meaning does not require a change of consonants, but only of vowel points. The difficulty of the last clause lies mainly in the word translated in the A.V. *adversaries* and in the R.V. " *enemies.*" That meaning is questionable ; and if the word is the nominative to the verb in the clause, the construction is awkward, since the preceding " who " would naturally extend its influence to this clause. Textual emendation has been resorted to ; the simplest form of which is to read " against Thee " for " Thine adversaries," a change of one letter. Another form of emendation, which is adopted by Cheyne and Graetz, substitutes " Thy name," and reads the whole, " And pronounce Thy name for falsehoods." Delitzsch adheres to the reading " adversaries," and by a harsh ellipsis makes the whole to run, " Who pronounce [Thy name] deceitfully—Thine adversaries."

The vindication of the psalmist's indignation lies in vv. 21, 22. That soul must glow with fervent love to God which feels wrong done to His majesty with as keen a pain as if it were itself struck. What God says to those who love Him, they in their degree say to God : " He that toucheth Thee toucheth the apple of mine eye." True, hate is not the Christian requital of hate, whether that is directed against God or God's servant. But recoil there must be, if there is any vigour of devotion ; only, pity and love must mingle with it, and the evil of hatred be overcome by their good.

Very beautifully does the lowly prayer for searching and guidance follow the psalmist's burst of fire. It is easier to glow with indignation against evil-doers than to keep oneself from doing evil. Many secret sins may hide under a cloak of zeal for the Lord. So the psalmist prays that God would search him, not because he fancies that there is no lurking sin to be burned by the light of God's eye, like vermin that nestle and multiply under stones and shrivel when the sunbeams strike them, but because he dreads that there is, and would fain have it cast out. The psalm began with declaring that Jehovah had searched and known the singer, and it ends with asking for that searching knowledge.

It makes much difference, not indeed in the reality

or completeness of God's knowledge of us, but in the good we derive therefrom, whether we welcome and submit to it, or try to close our trembling hearts, that do not wish to be cleansed of their perilous stuff, from that loving and purging gaze. God will cleanse the evil which He sees, if we are willing that He should see it. Thoughts of the inner life and " ways " of the outer are equally to be submitted to Him. There are two " ways " in which men can walk. The one is a " way of grief or pain," because that is its terminus. All sin is a blunder. And the inclination to such ways is " in me," as every man who has dealt honestly with himself knows. The other is " a way everlasting," a way which leads to permanent good, which continues uninterrupted through the vicissitudes of life, and even (though that was not in the psalmist's mind) through the darkness of death, and with ever closer approximation to its goal in God, through the cycles of eternity. And that way is not " in me," but I must be led into and in it by the God who knows me altogether and is ever with me, to keep my feet in the way of life, if I will hold the guiding hand which He lays upon me.

PSALM CXL.

1 Deliver me, Jehovah, from the evil man,
From the man of violence guard me,

2 Who plot evils in heart,
Every day they stir up wars.

3 They have sharpened their tongue like a serpent,
Adders' poison is under their lips.   Selah.

4 Keep me, Jehovah, from the hands of the wicked man,
From the man of violences guard me,
Who have plotted to overthrow my steps.

5 The proud have hidden a snare for me and cords,
They have spread a net hard by the path,
They have set gins for me.   Selah.

6 I said to Jehovah, My God art Thou,
Give ear, Jehovah, to the voice of my supplications.

7 Jehovah, Lord, my stronghold of salvation !
Thou hast covered my head in the day of battle

8 Grant not, Jehovah, the desires of the wicked,
Further not his plan.   Selah.

9 They who compass me about lift up the head—
The mischief of their own lips cover them !

10 [Jehovah] rain hot coals on them ! (?)
Let Him cause them to fall into fire,
Into floods, that they rise no more !

11 The man with a [slanderous] tongue shall not continue
on earth ;
The man of violence—evil shall hunt him with blow
upon blow.

12 I know that Jehovah will maintain the cause of the
afflicted,
The right of the needy.

13 Surely the righteous shall thank Thy name,
The upright shall dwell with Thy face.

393

IN tone and contents this psalm has many parallels in the earlier books, especially among the psalms ascribed to David. Its originality lies principally in its use of peculiar words, and in the extreme obscurity of a part of it. The familiar situation of a man ringed about by slanderous enemies, the familiar metaphors of snares and traps, the familiar venture of faith flinging itself into God's arms for refuge, the familiar prayers for retribution, are all here. One cannot argue about impressions, but the present writer receives the impression strongly from the psalm that it is cast in the Davidic manner by a later singer, and is rather an echo than an original voice, while, no doubt, the feelings expressed, both of distress and of confidence, are none the less felt by the singer, though he falls back on familiar forms for their expression.

The arrangement is in four strophes of approximately equal length, the first and third of which consist of three verses of two clauses each, while the fourth is abnormally elongated by having three clauses in ver. 10, and the second (vv. 4, 5) has two verses of three clauses each. Selah again appears as dividing the strophes, but is omitted at the end of the fourth, to which a closing strophe of two verses is appended.

The first two strophes (vv. 1–3 and 4, 5) cover the same ground. Both set forth the psalmist's need, and plead for deliverance. The first verse of the second strophe (ver. 4) is almost identical with ver. 1. Both paint the psalmist's enemies as evil and violent, plotting against him privily. The only difference in the two strophes is in the metaphors describing the foes and their devices, and in the prominence given in the first to their slanderous and sharp tongues. The forms of their malice are like those in earlier psalms. A characteristic of the Psalter is the prominence given to hostility which has but bitter speech for its weapon (Psalm x. 7, lviii. 4). The slanderer's tongue is sharp like a serpent's, with which the popular opinion supposed that the venom was injected. The particular kind of serpent meant in ver. 3 *a* is doubtful, as the word is only found here.

The figures for hostility in the second strophe are the other equally familiar ones of setting snares and traps. The contrivers are here called "proud," since their hostility to God's servant implies haughty antagonism to God. But they are not too proud to resort to tricks. Cunning and pride do not go well together, but they are united in these enemies, who spread a net " by the hand of the path."

In the third strophe, Faith rouses itself to lay hold on God. The psalmist turns from contemplating what his foes are doing, to realise what Jehovah is to him, and is wont to do for him. Since He is the singer's God and protects him in all conflict, he " finds it in his heart " to ask confidently that the plots of the foe may be wrecked. Consciousness of danger drove the poet in the former strophes to prayer; Jehovah's character and loving relations to him draw him, in this one.

" The day of battle " is literally " the day of armour " —when weapons clash and helmets are fitting wear. Then Jehovah will be as a head-piece to him, for He always gives the shape to His help which is required at the moment. The words in ver. 8 for " desires " and " plan " are found here only.

The text here is evidently in some disorder, and the word which is now awkwardly attached to the end of ver. 8 is by most commentators carried over to ver. 9. The change of position clears away difficulties in both verses, but a considerable crop remains in this fourth strophe. The language becomes gnarled and obscure under the stress of the poet's emotion, as he prays for the destruction of his persecutors. If the transference of the word from ver. 8 to ver. 9 is accepted, that verse describes in vivid fashion what in prose would have been cast into the form of, " *When* my encompassers lift up the head [*i.e.*, in proud assault], *then*," etc. The psalmist omits the particles which would give a hypothetical form, and prefers to set the two things side by side, and leave sympathetic readers to feel their connection. Ver. 10 is very obscure. According to the Hebrew text, the first clause would have to be rendered, " Let coals be thrown on them "; but such a rendering is " contrary to the usage of the language." The Hebrew margin, therefore, corrects into, " Let them [*i.e.*, men indefinitely] cast down coals "; but this is harsh, and the office is strange as one attributed to men. The emendation which finds favour with most moderns substitutes for the inappropriate verb of the present text that which is used in precisely the same connection in Psalm xi. 6, and gives the reading, " Let Him [*i.e.*, Jehovah] rain coals on them." The following clause then swiftly adds another element of horror. Fire rains down from above ; fire yawns below. They are beaten down by the burning storm, and they fall into a mass of flame. The noun in ver. 10 *c* is found only here, and is by some rendered " pits," by others " floods," and by others is corrected into " nets." If " floods " is taken as the meaning, destruction by water is set by the side of that by fire, as if the antagonistic elements forgot their opposition and joined in strange amity to sweep the wicked from the earth. The terrible strophe ends with the assured declaration of the

Divinely appointed transiency of the evil-doers, especially of the slanderers against whom the psalmist
took refuge in Jehovah. They shall be soon cut off,
and the hunters (ver. 5) shall become the hunted.
"Evil"—*i.e.*, the punishment of their evil deeds—shall
dog their heels, and with stroke after stroke chase them
as dogs would follow vermin.

In vv. 13, 14, the poet comes back to brighter
thoughts, and his words become limpid again with
his change of mood. He "knows," as the result of
meditation and experience, that not only he, but all
the afflicted and needy, who are righteous and upright,
have God on their side. He will stand by their side in
their hour of distress; He will admit them to dwell by
His side, in deep, still communion, made more real and
sweet by the harassments of earth, which drive them
for shelter and peace to His breast. That confidence
is a certitude for the psalmist. He announces it with
an "I know," and seals it with a "surely." Such is
the issue of trouble which was spread before Jehovah
and vented itself in prayer.

PSALM CXLI.

1 Jehovah, I have called on Thee; haste to me,
   Give ear to my voice when I call to Thee.
2 Let my prayer appear before Thee [as] incense,
   The lifting up of my hands [as] an evening sacrifice.

3 Set a watch, Jehovah, before my mouth,
   Keep guard over the door of my lips.
4 Incline not my heart to any evil thing,
   To practise wicked practices with men that work iniquity;
   And let me not eat of their dainties.

5 Let the righteous smite me in kindness and reprove me,
   [Such] oil for the head shall not my head refuse.
   For so is it that my prayer shall continue in their wickednesses (?)
6 Their judges are thrown down by the sides of the cliff, (?)
   And they hear my sayings, that they are sweet. (?)
7 As a man ploughing and cleaving the earth,
   Our bones are strewn at the mouth of Sheol.

8 For toward Thee, Jehovah, Lord, are mine eyes [turned];
   In Thee do I take refuge—pour not out my soul.
9 Keep me from the hands of the snare which they have laid for me,
   And from the gins of the doers of iniquity.
10 May the wicked fall into their own nets,
   Whilst at the same time I pass by!

PART of this psalm is hopelessly obscure, and the connection is difficult throughout. It is a prayer of a harassed soul, tempted to slacken its hold on God, and therefore betaking itself to Him. Nothing more definite as to author or occasion can be said with certainty.

The allusions in vv. 6, 7, are dark to us, and the psalm must, in many parts, remain an enigma. Probably Baethgen and Cheyne are wise in giving up the attempt to extract any intelligible meaning from ver. 5 c and ver. 6 as the words stand, and falling back on asterisks. Delitzsch regards the psalm as being composed as suitable to "a Davidic situation," either by David himself, or by some one who wished to give expression in strains like David's to David's probable mood. It would thus be a "Dramatic Idyll," referring, according to Delitzsch, to Absalom's revolt. Ver. 2 is taken by him to allude to the king's absence from the sanctuary, and the obscure ver. 6, to the fate of the leaders of the revolt and the return of the mass of the people to loyal submission. But this is a very precarious reference.

The psalm begins with the cry to God to hear, which so often forms the introduction to psalms of complaint and supplications for deliverance. But here a special colouring is given by the petition that the psalmist's prayers may be equivalent to incense and sacrifice. It does not follow that he was shut out from outward participation in worship, but only that he had learned what that worship meant. " Appear " might be rendered " established." The word means to be set firm, or, reflexively, to station oneself, and hence is taken by some as equivalent to "appear" or "come" before Thee ; while others give prominence rather to the notion of stability in the word, and take it to mean *continue—i.e.*, be accepted. There may be a reference to the morning sacrifice in the " incense," so that both morning and evening ritual would be included ; but it is more natural to think of the evening incense, accompanying the evening " meal offering," and to suppose that the psalm is an evening prayer. The penetrating insight into the realities of spiritual worship which the singer has gained is more important to note than such questions about the scope of his figures.

The prayer in vv. 3, 4, is for deliverance not from dangers, but from temptation to sin in word or deed. The psalmist is not suffering from the hostility of the workers of iniquity, but dreads becoming infected with their sin. This phase of trial was not David's in Absalom's revolt, and the prominence given to it here makes Delitzsch's view of the psalm very doubtful. An earlier psalmist had vowed to " put a muzzle on his mouth," but a man's own guard over his words will fail, unless God keeps the keeper, and, as it were, sets a sentry to watch the lips. The prayer for strength to resist temptation to wrong acts, which follows that against wrong speech, is curiously loaded with synonymous terms. The psalmist asks that his heart, which is but too apt to feel the risings of inclination to fall in with the manners around him, may be stiffened into wholesome loathing of every evil—" To practise practices in wickedness with men [perhaps, *great men*] who work iniquity." The clause rather drags, and the proposed insertion of " Let me not sit " before " with men that work iniquity " lightens the weight, and supplies a good parallel with " Let me not eat of their dainties." It is, however, purely conjectural, and the existing reading is intelligible, though heavy. The psalmist wishes to keep clear of association with the corrupt society around him, and desires to be preserved from temptations to fall in with its luxurious sensuality, lest thereby he should slide into imitation of its sins. He chose plain living, because he longed for high thinking, and noble doing, and grave, reverend speech. All this points to a period when the world fought against goodness by proffering vulgar delights, rather than by persecution. Martyrs have little need to pray that they may not be tempted by persecutors' feasts.

This man " scorned delights " and chose to dwell with good men.

The connection of ver. 5 with the preceding seems to be that in it the psalmist professes his preference for the companionship of the righteous, even if they reprove him. It is better, in his judgment, to have the wholesome correction of the righteous than to feast with the wicked. But while this is the bearing of the first part of the verse, the last clause is obscure, almost to unintelligibility, and even the earlier ones are doubtful. If the Hebrew accents are adhered to, the rendering above must be adopted. The division of clauses and rendering adopted by Hupfeld and many others, and in the A.V. and R.V., gives vividness, but requires " it shall be " to be twice supplied. The whole sentence seems to run more smoothly, if the above translation is accepted. " Oil for the head " is that with which the head is anointed as for a feast ; and there is probably a tacit suggestion of a better festival, spread in the austere abodes of the righteous poor, than on the tables loaded with the dainties of the wicked rich.

But what is the meaning and bearing of the last clause of ver. 5 ? No wholly satisfactory answer has been given. It is needless here to travel through the various more or less violent and unsuccessful attempts to unravel the obscurities of this clause and of the next verse. One sympathises with Hupfeld's confession that it is an unwelcome (*sauer*) task to him to quote the whirl of varying conjectures. The rendering adopted above, as, on the whole, the least unlikely, is substantially Delitzsch's. It means that the psalmist " will oppose no weapon but prayer to his enemies' wickedness, and is therefore in the spiritual mood susceptible to well-meaning reproof." The logic of

the clause is not very clear, even with this explanation.   The psalmist's continuance in prayer against the
wicked is not very obviously a reason for his accepting
kindly rebuke.   But no better explanation is proposed.

The darkness thickens in ver. 6.   The words indeed
are all easily translatable ; but what the whole sentence
means, or what an allusion to the destruction of some
unnamed people's rulers has to do here, or who they
are who hear the psalmist's words, are questions as
yet unanswered.   To cast men down " by the sides
[lit., *hands*] of a rock " is apparently an expression for
the cruel punishment mentioned as actually inflicted on
ten thousand of the " children of Seir " (2 Chron. **xxv.**
12).   Those who, with Delitzsch, take the revolt under
Absalom to be the occasion of the psalm, find in the
casting down of these judges an imaginative description
of the destruction of the leaders of the revolt, who are
supposed to be hurled down the rocks by the people
whom they had misled ; while the latter, having again
come to their right mind, attend to David's word, and
find it pleasant and beneficent.   But this explanation
requires much supplementing of the language, and
does not touch the difficulty of bringing the verse into
connection with the preceding.

Nor is the connection with what follows more clear.
A various reading substitutes " Their " for " Our " in
ver. 7, and so makes the whole verse a description of
the bones of the ill-fated " judges " lying in a litter at
the base of the precipice.   But apparently the reading
is merely an attempt to explain the difficulty.   Clearly
enough the verse gives an extraordinarily energetic and
graphic picture of a widespread slaughter.   But who
are the slain, and what event or events in the history
of Israel are here imaginatively reproduced, is quite

unknown. All that is certain is the tremendous force of the representation, the Æschylean ruggedness of the metaphor, and the desperate condition to which it witnesses. The point of the figure lies in the resemblance of the bones strewn at the mouth of Sheol to broken clods turned up by a plough. *Sheol* seems here to waver between the meanings of the unseen world of souls and the grave. The unburied bones of slaughtered saints " lie scattered," as unregarded as the lumps of soil behind the ploughman.

In vv. 8–10 the familiar psalm-tone recurs, and the language clears itself. The stream has been foaming among rocks in a gorge, but it has emerged into sunlight, and flows smoothly. Only the " For " at the beginning of ver. 8 is difficult, if taken to refer to the immediately preceding verses. Rather, it overleaps the obscure middle part of the psalm, and links on to the petitions of vv. 1–4. Patient, trustful expectance is the psalmist's temper, which gazes not interrogatively, but with longing which is sure of satisfaction, towards God from amidst the temptations or sorrows of earth. The reason for that fixed look of faith lies in the Divine names, so rich in promise, which are here blended in an unusual combination. The devout heart pleads its own act of faith in conjunction with God's names, and is sure that, since He is Jehovah, Lord, it cannot be vain to hide oneself in Him. Therefore, the singer prays for preservation from destruction. " Pour not out my soul " recalls Isa. liii. 12, where the same vivid metaphor is used. The prayer of the earlier verses was for protection from temptation ; here, circumstances have darkened, and the psalmist's life is in danger. Possibly the " snares " and " gins " of ver. 9 mean both temptations and perils.

The final petition in ver. 10 is like many in earlier psalms. It was a fundamental article of faith for all the psalmists that a great *Lex Talionis* was at work, by which every sin was avenged in kind ; and if one looks deeper than the outside of life, the faith is eternally warranted. For nothing is more certain than that, whomsoever else a man may harm by his sin, he harms himself most. Nets woven and spread for others may or may not ensnare them, but their meshes cling inextricably round the feet of their author, and their tightening folds will wrap him helpless, like a fly in a spider's web. The last clause presents some difficulties. The word rendered above " at the same time " is literally " together," but seems to be used here, as in Psalm iv. 8 (*at once*), with the meaning of *simultaneously*. The two things are co-temporaneous—the enemies' ensnaring and the psalmist's escape. The clause is abnormal in its order of words. It stands thus : " At the same time I, while [until] I pass by." Probably the irregularity arose from a desire to put the emphatic word " at the same time " in the prominent place. It is doubtful whether we should translate " while " or " until." Authorities are divided, and either meaning is allowable. But though the rendering *until* gives picturesqueness to the representation of the snared foe restrained and powerless, until his hoped-for prey walks calmly through the toils, the same idea is conveyed by " while," and that rendering avoids the implication that the snaring lasted only as long as the time taken for the psalmist's escape. What is uppermost in the psalmist's mind is, in any case, not the destruction of his enemies, but their being made powerless to prevent his " passing by " their snares uncaptured.

PSALM CXLII.

1 With my voice to Jehovah will I cry,
  With my voice to Jehovah will I make supplication.
2 I will pour out before Him my complaint,
  My straits before Him will I declare.
3 When my spirit wraps itself in gloom upon me,
  Then Thou—Thou knowest my path;
  In the way wherein I have to go
  They have hidden a snare for me.
4 Look on the right hand and see,
  There is none that knows me,
  Shelter is perished from me,
  There is no one that makes inquiry after my soul.

5 I have cried unto Thee, Jehovah,
  I have said, Thou art my refuge,
  My portion in the land of the living.
6 Attend to my shrill cry,
  For I am become very weak;
  Deliver me from my pursuers,
  For they are too strong for me.
7 Bring out from prison my soul,
  That I may thank Thy name;
  In me shall the righteous glory,
  For Thou dealest bountifully with me.

THE superscription not only calls this a psalm of
David's, but specifies the circumstances of its
composition. It breathes the same spirit of mingled
fear and faith which characterises many earlier psalms;
but one fails to catch the unmistakable note of freshness,
and there are numerous echoes of preceding singers.
This psalmist has as deep sorrows as his predecessors,
and as firm a grasp of Jehovah, his helper. His song

runs naturally in well-worn channels, and is none the less genuine and acceptable to God because it does. Trouble and lack of human sympathy or help have done their best work on him, since they have driven him to God's breast. He has cried in vain to man ; and now he has gathered himself up in a firm resolve to cast himself upon God. Men may take offence that they are only appealed to as a last resort, but God does not. The psalmist is too much in earnest to be content with unspoken prayers. His voice must help his thoughts. Wonderful is the power of articulate utterance in defining, and often in diminishing, sorrows. Put into words, many a burden shrinks. Speaking his grief, many a man is calmed and braced to endure. The complaint poured out before God ceases to flood the spirit ; the straits told to Him begin to grip less tightly.

Ver. 1 resembles Psalm lxxvii. 1, and ver. 3 has the same vivid expression for a spirit swathed in melancholy as Psalm lxxvii. 3. Hupfeld would transfer ver. 3 *a* to ver. 2, as being superfluous in ver. 3, and, in connection with the preceding, stating the situation or disposition from which the psalmist's prayer flows. If so taken, the copula (And) introducing *b* will be equivalent to " But," and contrasts the omniscience of God with the psalmist's faintheartedness. If the usual division of verses is retained, the same contrast is presented still more forcibly, and the copula may be rendered " Then." The outpouring of complaint is not meant to tell Jehovah what He does not know. It is for the complainer's relief, not for God's information. However a soul is wrapped in gloom, the thought that God knows the road which is so dark brings a little creeping beam into the blackness. In the strength of

that conviction the psalmist beseeches Jehovah to
behold what He does behold. That is the paradox
of faithful prayer, which asks for what it knows that
it possesses, and dared not ask for unless it knew.
The form of the word rendered above " Look " is
irregular, a " hybrid " (Delitzsch) ; but when standing
beside the following " see," it is best taken as an
imperative of petition to Jehovah. The old versions
render both words as first person singular, in which they
are followed by Baethgen, Graetz, and Cheyne. It is
perhaps more natural that the psalmist should represent
himself as looking round in vain for help, than that he
should ask God to look ; and, as Baethgen remarks,
the copula before " There is none " in ver. 4 *b* favours
this reading, as it is superfluous with an imperative.
In either case the drift of ver. 4 is to set forth the
suppliant's forlorn condition. The " right hand " is the
place for a champion or helper, but this lonely sufferer's
is unguarded, and there is none who knows him, in
the sense of recognising him as one to be helped (Ruth
ii. 10, 19). Thus abandoned, friendless, and solitary,
confronted by foes, he looks about for some place to
hide in ; but that too has failed him (Job xi. 20 ; Jer.
xxv. 35 ; Amos ii. 14). There is no man interested
enough in him to make inquiry after his life. Whether
he is alive or dead matters not a straw to any..

Thus utterly naked of help, allies, and earthly hiding-
place, what can a man do but fling himself into the
arms of God ? This one does so, as the rest of the
psalm tells. He had looked all round the horizon in
vain for a safe cranny to creep into and escape. He
was out in the open, without a bush or rock to hide
behind, on all the dreary level. So he looks up, and
suddenly there rises by his side an inexpugnable

fortress, as if a mountain sprang at once from the flat earth. "I have said, Thou art my refuge!" Whoso says thus has a shelter, Some One to care for him, and the gloom begins to thin off from his soul. The psalmist is not only safe in consequence of his prayer, but rich; for the soul which, by strong resolve, even in the midst of straits, claims God as its portion will at once realise its portion in God.

The prayer for complete deliverance in vv. 6, 7, passes into calmness, even while it continues fully conscious of peril and of the power of the pursuers. Such is the reward of invoking Jehovah's help. Agitation is soothed, and, even before any outward effect has been manifest, the peace of God begins to shed itself over heart and mind. The suppliant still spreads his needs before God, is still conscious of much weakness, of strong persecutors, and feels that he is, as it were, in prison (an evident metaphor, though Graetz, with singular prosaicness, will have it to be literal); but he has hold of God now, and so is sure of deliverance, and already begins to shape his lips for songs of praise, and to anticipate the triumph which his experience will afford to those who are righteous, and so are his fellows. He was not, then, so utterly solitary as he had wailed that he was. There were some who would joy in his joy, even if they could not help his misery. But the soul that has to wade through deep waters has always to do it alone; for no human sympathy reaches to full knowledge of, or share in, even the best loved one's grief. We have companions in joy; sorrow we have to face by ourselves. Unless we have Jesus with us in the darkness, we have no one.

The word rendered above "shall glory" is taken in different meanings. According to some, it is to be rendered here " surround "—*i.e.*, with congratulations ; others would take the meaning to be " shall crown themselves "—*i.e.*, " triumph on my account " (Delitzsch, etc.). Graetz suggests a plausible emendation, which Cheyne adopts, reading "glory in," the resulting meaning being the same as that of Delitzsch. The notion of participation in the psalmist's triumph is evidently intended to be conveyed ; and any of these renderings preserves that. Possibly *surround* is most in accordance with the usage of the word. Thus the psalmist's plaints end, as plaints which are prayers ever do, in triumph anticipated by faith, and one day to be realised in experience.

PSALM CXLIII.

1 Jehovah, hear my prayer, give ear to my supplications,
  In Thy faithfulness answer me, in Thy righteousness;
2 And enter not into judgment with Thy servant,
  For before Thee shall no man living be righteous.
3 For the enemy has pursued my soul,
  Crushed my life to the ground,
  Made me to dwell in dark places, like the dead of
      long ago.

4 Therefore my spirit wraps itself in gloom in me,
  Within me is my heart benumbed.
5 I remember the days of old,
  I muse on all Thy doings,
  On the work of Thy hands I brood.
6 I spread my hands to Thee,
  My soul is towards Thee like a thirsty land. Selah.

7 Make haste, answer me, Jehovah; my spirit faints;
  Hide not Thy face from me,
  Lest I become like those that descend into the pit.
8 Make me hear Thy loving-kindness in the morning,
  For in Thee do I trust;
  Make me know the way in which I should go,
  For to Thee do I lift my soul.
9 Deliver me from mine enemies, Jehovah,
  For to Thee do I flee for refuge. (?)

10 Teach me to do Thy will, for Thou art my God;
   Let Thy good spirit lead me in a level land.
11 For Thy name's sake, Jehovah, quicken me;
   In Thy righteousness bring my soul out of all straits;
12 And in Thy loving-kindness cut off my foes,
   And destroy all who oppress my soul,
   For I am Thy servant.

THIS psalm's depth of sadness and contrition, blended with yearning trust, recalls the earlier psalms attributed to David. Probably this general resemblance in inwardness and mood is all that is meant by the superscription in calling it "a psalm of David." Its copious use of quotations and allusions indicate a late date. But there is no warrant for taking the speaker to be the personified Israel. It is clearly divided into two equal halves, as indicated by the Selah, which is not found in Books IV. and V., except here, and in Psalm cxl. The former half (vv. 1-6) is complaint; the latter (vv. 7-12), petition. Each part may again may be regarded as falling into two equal portions, so that the complaint branches out into a plaintive description of the psalmist's peril (vv. 1-3), and a melancholy disclosure of his feelings (vv. 4-6); while the prayer is similarly parted into cries for deliverance (vv. 7-9), and for inward enlightenment and help (vv. 10-12). But we are not reading a logical treatise, but listening to the cry of a tried spirit, and so need not wonder if the discernible sequence of thought is here and there broken.

The psalmist knows that his affliction is deserved. His enemy could not have hunted and crushed him (ver. 3) unless God had been thereby punishing him. His peril has forced home the penitent conviction of his sin, and therefore he must first have matters set right between him and God by Divine forgiveness. His cry for help is not based upon any claims of his own, nor even on his extremity of need, but solely on God's character, and especially on the twin attributes of Faithfulness and Righteousness. By the latter is not meant the retributive righteousness which gives according to desert, but that by which He maintains the order of salvation established by His holy love. The prayer anticipates St. John's declaration that God is "faithful and just to forgive us our sins." That answer in righteousness is as eagerly desired as God's dealing on the footing of retributive justice is shrunk from. " Enter not into judgment with Thy servant " is not a prayer referring to a future appearance before the Judge of all, but the judgment deprecated is plainly the enmity of men, which, as the next verse complains, is crushing the psalmist's life out of him. His cry is for deliverance from it, but he feels that a more precious gift must precede outward deliverance, and God's forgiveness must first be sealed on his soul. The conviction that, when the light of God's face is turned on the purest life, it reveals dark stains which retributive justice cannot but condemn, is not, in the psalmist's mouth, a palliation of his guilt. Rather, it drives him to take his place among the multitude of offenders, and from that lowly position to cry for pardon to the very Judge whose judgment he cannot meet. The blessedness of contrite trust is that it nestles the closer to God, the more it feels its unworthiness. The child hides its face on the mother's bosom when it has done wrong. God is our refuge from God. A little beam of light steals into the penitent's darkness, while he calls himself God's servant, and ventures to plead that relation, though he has done what was unworthy of it, as a reason for pardon. The significant " For " beginning ver. 3 shows that the enemy's acts were, to the contrite psalmist, those of God's stern justice. **Vv.** 3 *a, b,* are moulded on Psalm vii. 5, and *c* is verbally identical with Lam. iii. 6. " The dead of long ago " is by some rendered *dead for ever*; but the translation adopted above adds force to the psalmist's sad description of himself, by likening him to those forgotten ones away back in the mists of bygone ages.

In vv. 4–6 the record of the emotions caused by his

peril follows.   They begin with the natural gloom.   As
in Psalm cxlii. 3 (with which this has many points
of resemblance, possibly indicating identity of author),
he describes his "spirit" as swathed in dark robes of
melancholy.   His heart, too, the centre of personality,
was *stunned* or *benumbed*, so that it almost ceased to
beat.   What should a "servant" of Jehovah's, brought
to such a pass, do ?   If he is truly God's, he will do
precisely what this man did.   He will compel his thoughts
to take another direction, and call Memory in to fight
Despair and feed Hope.   His own past and God's past
are arguments enough to cheer the most gloom-wrapped
sufferer.   "A sorrow's crown of sorrow" may be
"remembering happier things," but the remembrance
will be better used to discrown a sorrow which
threatens to lord it over a life.   Psalm lxxvii. 5, 6,
11, 12, has shaped the expressions here.   Both the
contrast of present misery with past mercy, and the
assurances of present help given by that past mercy,
move the psalmist to appeal to God, stretching out his
hands in entreaty.   Psalm lxiii. 1 echoes in ver. 6 *b*,
the pathos and beauty of which need no elucidation.
The very cracks in parched ground are like mouths
opened for the delaying rains ; so the singer's soul was
gaping wide in trouble for God's coming, which would
refresh and fertilise.   Blessed is that weariness which
is directed to Him ; it ever brings the showers of grace
for which it longs.   The construction of ver. 6 *b* is
doubtful, and the supplement "thirsteth" (A.V. and
R.V.) is possibly better than the "is" given above.

The second half of the psalm is purely petition.
Vv. 7–9 ask especially for outward deliverance.   They
abound with reminiscences of earlier psalms.   "Make
haste, answer me" recalls Psalm lxix. 17 ; "my spirit

faints " is like Psalm lxxxiv. 2 ; " Hide not Thy face
from me " is a standing petition, as in Psalms xxvii. 9,
cii. 2, etc. ; " Lest I become like those who descend
into the pit " is exactly reproduced from Psalm xxviii. 1.
The prayer for the manifestation of God's loving-kindness in the morning is paralleled in Psalm xc. 14, and
that for illumination as to the way to walk in is like
Exod. xxxiii. 13 ; Psalm xxv. 4. The plea "To
Thee do I lift my soul" is found in Psalms xxv. 1,
lxxxvi. 4.

The plea appended to the petition in ver. 9 *b* is
difficult. Literally, the words run, " To Thee have I
covered [myself]," which can best be explained as a
pregnant construction, equivalent to " I have fled to
Thee and hid myself in Thee." Much divergence exists
in the renderings of the clause. But a slight emendation, adopted by Hupfeld and Cheyne from an ancient
Jewish commentator, reads the familiar expression, " I
have fled for refuge." Baethgen prefers to read " have
waited," which also requires but a trivial alteration ;
while Graetz reaches substantially the same result by
another way, and would render " I have hope."

A glance at these three verses of petition as a whole
brings out the sequence of the prayers and of their
pleas. The deepest longing of the devout soul is for
the shining of God's face, the consciousness of His
loving regard, and that not only because it scatters
fears and foes, but because it is good to bathe in that
sunshine. The next longing is for the dawning of a
glad morning, which will bring to a waiting heart sweet
whispers of God's loving-kindness, as shown by outward deliverances. The night of fear has been dark
and tearful, but joy comes with the morning. The
next need is for guidance in the way in which a man

should go, which here must be taken in the lower
sense of practical direction, rather than in any higher
meaning.   That higher meaning follows in vv. 10–12 ;
but in ver. 8 the suppliant asks to be shown the path by
which he can secure deliverance from his foes.   That
deliverance is the last of his petitions.   His pleas are
beautiful as examples of the logic of supplication.   He
begins with his great need.   His spirit faints, and he
is on the edge of the black pit into which so much
brightness and strength have gone down.   The margin
is slippery and crumbling ; his feet are feeble.   One
Helper alone can hold him up.   But his own exceeding
need is not all that he pleads.   He urges his trust, his
fixing of his desires, hopes, and whole self, by a dead
lift of faith, on God.   That is a reason for Divine help.
Anything is possible rather than that such hope should
be disappointed.   It cannot be that any man, who has
fled for sanctuary to the asylum of God's heart, should
be dragged thence and slain before the God whose altar
he has vainly clasped.

The last part (vv. 10–12) puts foremost the prayer
for conformity of will with God's, and, though it closes
with recurring prayer for outward deliverance, yet
breathes desires for more inward blessings.   As in
the preceding verses, there are, in these closing ones,
many echoes of other psalms.   The sequence of petitions and pleas is instructive.   To do, not merely to
know, God's will is the condition of all blessedness,
and will be the deepest desire of every man who is
truly God's servant.   But that obedience of heart and
hand must be taught by God, and He regards our
taking Him for our God as establishing a claim on
Him to give all illumination of heart and all bending of
will and all skill of hand which are necessary to make

us doers of His will. His teaching is no mere outward communication of knowledge, but an inbreathing of power to discern, and of disposition and ability to perform, what is His will. Ver. 10 *b* is best taken as a continuous sentence, embodying a prayer for guidance. The plea on which it rests remains the same, though the statement of it as a separate clause is not adopted in our translation. For the fact that God's spirit is "good "—*i.e.*, beneficently self-communicative—heartens us to ask, and binds Him to give, all such direction as is needed. This is not a mere repetition of the prayer in ver. 8, but transcends it. "A level land " (or, according to a possible suggested emendation, *path*) is one in which the psalmist can freely walk, unhindered in doing God's will. His next petition goes deepest of the three, inasmuch as it asks for that new Divine life to be imparted, without which no teaching to do God's will can be assimilated, and no circumstances, however favourable, will conduce to doing it. He may not have known all the depth which his prayer sounded ; but no man who has real desires to conform heart and life to the supreme will of God but must have felt his need of a purer life to be poured into his spirit. As this prayer is deep, so its plea is high. "For Thy name's sake "—nothing can be pleaded of such force as that. God supremely desires the glory of His name ; and, for the sake of men whose blessedness depends on their knowing and loving it, will do nothing that can dim its lustre. His name is the record of His past acts, the disclosure of that in Him which is knowable. That name contains the principles of all His future acts. He will be what He has been. He will magnify His name ; and the humblest, most tormented soul that can say, "Thou art my God," may be sure that Divinely given life will throb in it, and that even its lowliness may contribute to the honour of the name.

The hunted psalmist cannot but come back, in the close of his psalm, to his actual circumstances, for earthly needs do clog the soul's wings. He unites righteousness and loving-kindness as co-operating powers, as in ver. 1 he had united faithfulness and righteousness. And as in the first verses he had blended pleas drawn from God's character with those drawn from his relation to God, so he ends his petitions with pleading that he is God's servant, and, as such, a fit object of God's protection

PSALM CXLIV.

1 Blessed be Jehovah my rock, who trains my hands for battle,
My fingers for war ;
2 My loving-kindness and my fortress, my high tower and my
deliverer,
My shield and He in whom I take refuge,
Who subdues my people under me.

3 Jehovah, what is man, that Thou takest knowledge of him?
The son of frail man, that Thou takest account of him?
4 Man—he is like to a breath,
His days are like a shadow passing away.

5 Jehovah, bow Thy heavens and come down,
Touch the mountains that they smoke.
6 Lighten lightning and scatter them,
Shoot Thy arrows and confound them.
7 Stretch Thy hands from on high,
Pluck me [out] and deliver me from many waters,
From the hands of the sons of the alien,
8 Whose mouth speaks falsehood,
And whose right hand is a right hand of lies.

9 O God, a new song will I sing to Thee,
On a ten-stringed harp will I harp to Thee,
10 Who giveth salvation to kings,
Who snatches David His servant from the evil sword.
11 Pluck me [out] and deliver me from the hand of the sons of
the alien,
Whose mouth speaks falsehood,
And whose right hand is a right hand of lies.

12 So that (? or Because) our sons [may be] as plants,
Grown tall in their youth ;
Our daughters like corner-pillars,
Carved after the fashion of a palace ;
13 Our granaries full, giving forth kind after kind [of supply] ;

418

Our flocks producing thousands,
Producing tens of thousands in our fields ;
14 Our kine heavy with young ;
No breach and no sally,
And no [battle-] cry in our open spaces.
15 Happy the people that is in such a case !
Happy the people whose God is Jehovah !

THE force of compilation could no further go than in this psalm, which is, in the first eleven verses, simply a *réchauffé* of known psalms, and in vv. 12–15 is most probably an extract from an unknown one of later date. The junctions are not effected with much skill, and the last is tacked on very awkwardly (ver. 12). It is completely unlike the former part, inasmuch as there the speaker is a warlike king praying for victory, while in the latter the nation sings of the tranquil blessings of peaceful expansion. The language of the later portion is full of late forms and obscurities. But the compiler's course of thought is traceable. He begins by praising Jehovah, who has taught him war-like skill ; then adoringly thinks of his own weakness, made strong by God's condescending regard ; next prays for complete victory, and vows fresh praises for new mercies ; and closes with a picture of the prosperity which follows conquest, and is secured to Israel because Jehovah is its God.

Vv. 1, 2, are echoes of Psalm xviii. 2, 34, 46, with slight variations. The remarkable epithet " My loving-kindness " offends some critics, who emend so as to read " My stronghold " ; but it has a parallel in Jonah ii. 9, and is forcible as an emotional abbreviation of the fuller " God of my loving-kindness " (Psalm lix. 10). The original passage reads " people," which is the only appropriate word in this connection, and should probably be read in ver. 2 c.

Psalm viii. supplies the original of vv. 3, 4, with a reminiscence of Psalm xxxix. 5, and of Psalm cii. 11, from which comes the pathetic image of the fleeting shadow. The link between this and the former extract seems to be the recognition of God's condescension in strengthening so weak and transient a creature for conflict and conquest.

The following prayer for further Divine help in further struggles is largely borrowed from the magnificent picture of a theophany in Psalm xviii. 9, 14–16. The energetic " Lighten lightning " is peculiar to this psalm, as is the use of the word for " Pluck out." The description of the enemies as "sons of the alien" is like Psalm xviii. 44, 45. As in many other psalms, the treachery of the foe is signalised. They break their oaths. The right hand which they had lifted in swearing is a lying hand. The vow of new praise recalls Psalms xxxiii. 2, 3, and xcvi. 1, xcviii. 1. Ver. 10 is a reproduction of Psalm xviii. 50. The mention of David's deliverance from the " evil sword " has apparently been the reason for the LXX. referring the psalm to the victory over Goliath—an impossible view. The new song is not here sung ; but the psalm drops from the level of praise to renew the petition for deliverance, in the manner of a refrain caught up in ver. 11 from ver. 7. This might make a well-rounded close, and may have originally been the end of the psalm.

The appended fragment (vv. 12–15) is attached to the preceding in a most embarrassing fashion. The first word of ver. 12 is the sign of the relative. The LXX. accordingly translates " Whose sons are," etc., and understands the whole as a description of the prosperity of the enemies, which view necessarily involves the alteration of " our " into " their" in the following clauses. Others supply an antecedent to the relative by inserting *save us* or the like expression at the beginning of the verse. Others, again—*e.g.*, Ewald, followed by Perowne—connect the relative with ver. 15: "We whose sons are," etc. . . . "Happy is the people," etc. Delitzsch takes the relative to signify here "because," and compares Judg. ix. 17; Jer. xvi. 13. The prosperity subsequently described would then be alleged as the occasion of the enemies' envy. Others would slightly emend the text so as to read, "I pronounce happy," or "Happy are we." The latter, which makes all smooth, and corresponds with ver. 15, is Graetz's proposal. The rendering of the A.V., "that" or "in order that," has much in its favour. The word which is the sign of the relative is a component of the full expression usually so rendered, and stands alone as equivalent to it in Deut. iv. 40, Gen. xi. 7. It is true, as Delitzsch objects to this rendering, that the following verbs are usually finite, while here they are participles; but that is not a fatal objection. The whole that follows would then be dependent on the petition of ver. 11, and would describe the purpose of the desired deliverance. "This is, in fact, the poet's meaning. He prays for deliverance from enemies, in order that the happy condition pictured in ver. 12 *sqq.* may come to pass" (Baethgen). On the whole, that rendering presents least difficulty, but in any case the seam is clumsy.

The substance of the description includes three things—a vigorous, growing population, agricultural prosperity, and freedom from invasion. The language is obscure, especially in ver. 14, but the general drift is plain. The characteristic Jewish blessing of numerous offspring is first touched on in two figures, of which the former is forcible and obvious, and the latter obscure. The comparison of the virgin daughters of Israel to " corners " is best understood by taking the word to mean " corner-pillars," not necessarily caryatides, as is usually supposed—an architectural decoration unknown in the East. The points of comparison would then be slender uprightness and firm grace. Delitzsch prefers to take the word as meaning *cornices*, such as, to the present day, are found in the angles of Eastern rooms, and are elaborately carved in mazy patterns and brightly coloured. He would also render " variegated " instead of " carved." But such a comparison puts too much stress on gay dresses, and too little on qualities corresponding to those of the " well-grown " youths in the former clause.

The description of a flourishing rural community is full of difficult words. " Granaries " is found only here, and " kind " is a late word. " Fields " is the same word as is usually rendered " streets " ; it literally means " places outside," and here obviously must refer to the open pastures without the city, in contrast to the "open spaces " within it, mentioned in the next verse. In that verse almost every word is doubtful. That rendered " kine " is masculine in form, but is generally taken as being applicable to both sexes, and here used for the milky mothers of the herd. The word translated above " heavy with young " means *laden*, and if the accompanying noun is masculine, must mean laden with the harvest sheaves ; but the parallel of the increasing flocks suggests the other rendering. The remainder of ver. 14 would in form make a complete verse, and it is possible that something has fallen out between the first clause and the two latter. These paint tranquil city life when enemies are far away.

"No breach"—*i.e.*, in the defences, by which besiegers could enter; "No going forth"—*i.e.*, sally of the besieged, as seems most probable, though *going forth as captured* or *surrendering* has been suggested; "No cry"—*i.e.*, of assailants who have forced an entrance, and of defenders who make their last stand in the open places of the city.

The last verse sums up all the preceding picture of growth, prosperity, and tranquillity, and traces it to the guardian care and blessing of Jehovah. The psalmist may seem to have been setting too much store by outward prosperity. His last word not only points to the one Source of it, but sets high above the material consequences of God's favour, joyous as these are, that favour itself, as the climax of human blessedness.

PSALM CXLV.

1 א I will exalt Thee, my God, O King,
   And I will bless Thy name for ever and aye.
2 ב Every day will I bless Thee,
   And I will praise Thy name for ever and aye.
3 ג Great is Jehovah and much to be praised,
   And of His greatness there is no searching.
4 ד Generation to generation shall loudly praise Thy works
   And Thy mighty acts shall they declare.
5 ה The splendour of the glory of Thy majesty,
   And the records of Thy wonders will I meditate.
6 ו And the might of Thy dread acts shall they speak,
   And Thy greatness will I tell over.

7 ז The memory of Thy abundant goodness shall they well
       forth,
   And Thy righteousness shall they shout aloud.
8 ח Gracious and full of compassion is Jehovah,
   Slow to anger and great in loving-kindness.
9 ט Good is Jehovah to all,
   And His compassions are upon all His works.
10 י All Thy works thank Thee, Jehovah,
   And Thy favoured ones shall bless Thee.

11 כ The glory of Thy kingdom shall they speak,
   And talk of Thy might ;
12 ל To make known to the sons of men His mighty deeds
   And the glory of the splendour of His kingdom.
13 מ Thy kingdom is a kingdom for all ages,
   And Thy dominion [endures] through every generation
       after generation.

14 ם Jehovah upholds all the falling,
   And raises all the bowed down.
15 ע The eyes of all look expectantly to Thee,
   And Thou givest them their food in its season.

16 ‫ס‬ Thou openest Thy hand,
    And satisfiest every living thing [with] its desire.
17 ‫צ‬ Jehovah is righteous in all His ways,
    And loving in all His works.
18 ‫ק‬ Jehovah is near to all who call on Him,
    To all who call on Him in truth.
19 ‫ר‬ The desire of them that fear Him He will fulfil,
    And their cry He will hear and will save them.
20 ‫ש‬ Jehovah keeps all who love Him,
    And all the wicked will He destroy.

21 ‫ת‬ The praise of Jehovah my mouth shall speak,
    And let all flesh bless His holy name for ever and aye.

THIS is an acrostic psalm. Like several others of that kind, it is slightly irregular, one letter (Nun) being omitted. The omission is supplied in the LXX. by an obviously spurious verse inserted in the right place between vv. 13 and 14. Though the psalm has no strophical divisions, it has distinct sequence of thought, and celebrates the glories of Jehovah's character and deeds from a fourfold point of view. It sings of His greatness (vv. 1–6), goodness (vv. 7–10), His kingdom (vv. 11–13), and the universality of His beneficence (vv. 14–21). It is largely coloured by other psalms, and is unmistakably of late origin.

The first group of verses has two salient characteristics—the accumulation of epithets expressive of the more majestic aspects of Jehovah's self-revelation, and the remarkable alternation of the psalmist's solo of song and the mighty chorus, which takes up the theme and sends a shout of praise echoing down the generations.

The psalmist begins with his own tribute of praise, which he vows shall be perpetual. Ver. 1 recalls Psalms xxx. 1 and xxxiv. 1. We "exalt" God, when we recognise that He is King, and worthily adore Him as such. A heart suffused with joy in the thought of

God would fain have no other occupation than the loved one of ringing out His name. The singer sets "for ever and aye" at the end of both ver. 1 and ver. 2, and while it is possible to give the expression a worthy meaning as simply equivalent to *continually*, it is more in harmony with the exalted strain of the psalm and the emphatic position of the words to hear in them an expression of the assurance which such delight in God and in the contemplation of Him naturally brings with it, that over communion so deep and blessed, Death has no power. " Every day will I bless Thee "—that is the happy vow of the devout heart. " And I will praise Thy name for ever and ever "—that is the triumphant confidence that springs from the vow. The experiences of fellowship with God are prophets of their own immortality.

Ver. 3 *a* is from Psalm xlviii. 1, and *b* is tinged by Isaiah xl., but substitutes " greatness," the key-note of the first part of this psalm, for " understanding." That note having been thus struck, is taken up in vv. 4–6, which set forth various aspects of that greatness, as manifested in works which are successively described as " mighty "—*i.e.*, instinct with conquering power such as a valiant hero wields ; as, taken together, constituting the " splendour of the glory of Thy majesty," the flashing brightness with which, when gathered, as it were, in a radiant mass, they shine out, like a great globe of fire ; as " wonders," not merely in the narrower sense of miracles, but as being productive of lowly astonishment in the thoughtful spectator ; and as being " dread acts "—*i.e.*, such as fill the beholder with holy awe. In ver. 5 *b* the phrase rendered above " records of His wonders " is literally " words of His wonders," which some regard as being like the similar phrase in Psalm lxv. 3 (words or matters of iniquities), a pleonasm, and others would take as they do the like expression in Psalm ·v. 27, as equivalent to " *deeds* of the Divine wonders " (Delitzsch). But " words " may very well here retain its ordinary sense, and the poet represent himself as meditating on the records of God's acts in the past as well as gazing on those spread before his eyes in the present.

His passing and repassing from his own praise in vv. 1, 2, to that of successive generations in ver. 4, and once more to his own in ver. 5, and to that of others in ver. 6, is remarkable. Does he conceive of himself as the chorus leader, teaching the ages his song ? Or does he simply rejoice in the less lofty consciousness that his voice is not solitary ? It is difficul to say, but this is clear, that the Messianic hope ƒ the world's being one day filled with the praises which were occasioned by God's manifestation in Israel burned in this singer's heart. He could not bear to sing alone, and his hymn would lack its highest note, if he did not believe that the world was to catch up the song.

But greatness, majesty, splendour, are not the Divinest parts of the Divine nature, as this singer had learned. These are but the fringes of the central glory. Therefore the song rises from greatness to celebrate better things, the moral attributes of Jehovah (vv. 7–10). The psalmist has no more to say of himself, till the end of his psalm. He gladly listens rather to the chorus of many voices which proclaims Jehovah's widespread goodness. In ver. 7 the two attributes which the whole Old Testament regards as inseparable are the themes of the praise of men. Goodness and righteousness are not antithetic, but complementary, as green and red rays blend in white light. The exuberance of praise evoked by these attributes is strikingly represented by the two strong words describing it ; of which the former, " well forth," compares its gush to the clear waters of a spring bursting up into sunlight, dancing and flashing, musical and living, and the other describes it as like the shrill cries of joy raised by a crowd on some festival, or such as the women trilled out when a bride was brought home. Ver. 8 rests upon Exod. xxxiv. 6 (compare Psalm ciii. 8). It is difficult to de-synonymise "gracious" and "full of compassion." Possibly the former is the wider, and expresses love in exercise towards the lowly in its most general aspect, while the latter specialises graciousness as it reveals itself to those afflicted with any evil. As "slow to anger," Jehovah keeps back the wrath which is part of His perfection, and only gives it free course after long waiting and wooing. The contrast in ver. 8 *b* is not so much between anger and loving-kindness, which to the psalmist are not opposed, as between the slowness with which the one is launched against a few offenders and the plenitude of the other. That thought of abundant loving-kindness is still further widened, in ver. 9, to universality. God's goodness embraces all, and His compassions hover over all His works, as the broad wing and warm breast of the mother eagle protect her brood. Therefore the psalmist hears a yet more multitudinous voice of praise from all creatures ; since their very existence, and still more their various blessednesses, give witness to the all-gladdening Mercy which encompasses them. But Creation's anthem is a song without words, and needs to be made articulate by the conscious thanksgivings of those who, being blessed by possession of Jehovah's loving-kindness, render blessing to Him with heart and lip.

The Kingship of God was lightly touched in ver. 1
It now becomes the psalmist's theme in vv. 11–13. It
is for God's favoured ones to *speak*, while Creation can
but *be*. It is for men who can recognise God's sovereign
Will as their law, and know Him as Ruler, not only
by power, but by goodness, to proclaim that kingdom
which psalmists knew to be "righteousness, peace, and
joy." The purpose for which God has lavished His
favour on Israel is that they might be the heralds of
His royalty to "the sons of men." The recipients
of His grace should be the messengers of His grace.
The aspects of that kingdom which fill the psalmist's
thoughts in this part of his hymn, correspond with that
side of the Divine nature celebrated in vv. 1–6—namely,
the more majestic—while the graciousness magnified in
vv. 7–10 is again the theme in the last portion (vv.
14–20). An intentional parallelism between the first
and third parts is suggested by the recurrence in ver. 12
of part of the same heaped-together phrase which
occurs in ver. 5. There we read of "the splendour of
the glory of Thy majesty"; here of "the glory of the
splendour of Thy kingdom,"—expressions substantially
identical in meaning. The very glory of the kingdom
of Jehovah is a pledge that it is eternal. What corruption or decay could touch so radiant and mighty a
throne? Israel's monarchy was a thing of the past;
but as, "in the year that King Uzziah died," Isaiah saw
the true King of Israel throned in the Temple, so the
vanishing of the earthly head of the theocracy seems to
have revealed with new clearness to devout men in
Israel the perpetuity of the reign of Jehovah. Hence
the psalms of the King are mostly post-exilic. It is
blessed when the shattering of earthly goods or the
withdrawal of human helpers and lovers makes more

plain the Unchanging Friend and His abiding power to
succour and suffice.

The last portion of the psalm is marked by a frequent repetition of "all," which occurs eleven times in
these verses. The singer seems to delight in the very
sound of the word, which suggests to him boundless
visions of the wide sweep of God's universal mercy,
and of the numberless crowd of dependents who wait
on and are satisfied by Him. He passes far beyond
national bounds.

Ver. 14 begins the grand catalogue of universal blessings by an aspect of God's goodness which, at first
sight, seems restricted, but is only too wide, since
there is no man who is not often ready to fall and
needing a strong hand to uphold him. The universality of man's weakness is pathetically testified by this
verse. Those who are in the act of falling are upheld
by Him; those who have fallen are helped to regain
their footing. Universal sustaining and restoring grace
are His. The psalmist says nothing of the conditions
on which that grace in its highest forms is exercised;
but these are inherent in the nature of the case, for,
if the falling man will not lay hold of the outstretched
hand, down he must go. There would be no place for
restoring help, if sustaining aid worked as universally
as it is proffered. The word for "raises" in ver. 14 *b*
occurs only here and in Psalm cxlvi. 8. Probably
the author of both Psalms is one. In vv. 15, 16, the
universality of Providence is set forth in language
partly taken from Psalm civ. 27, 28. The petitioners
are all creatures. They mutely appeal to God, with
expectant eyes fixed on Him, like a dog looking for
a crust from its master. He has but to "open His
hand" and they are satisfied. The process is repre-

sented as easy and effortless. Ver. 16 *b* has received different explanations. The word rendered "desire" is often used for "favour"—*i.e.*, God's—and is by some taken in that meaning here. So Cheyne translates "fillest everything that lives with goodwill." But seeing that the same word recurs in ver. 19, in an obvious parallel with this verse, and has there necessarily the meaning of *desire*, it is more natural to give it the same signification here. The clause then means that the opening of God's hand satisfies every creature, by giving it that which it desires in full enjoyment.

These common blessings of Providence avail to interpret deeper mysteries. Since the world is full of happy creatures nourished by Him, it is a reasonable faith that His work is all of a piece, and that in all His dealings the twin attributes of righteousness and loving-kindness rule. There are enough plain tokens of God's character in plain things to make us sure that mysterious and apparently anomalous things have the same character regulating them. In ver. 17 *b* the word rendered *loving* is that usually employed of the objects of loving-kindness, God's "favoured ones." It is used of God only here and in Jer. iii. 12, and must be taken in an active sense, as *One who exercises loving-kindness.* The underlying principle of all His acts is Love, says the psalmist, and there is no antagonism between that deepest motive and Righteousness. The singer has indeed climbed to a sun-lit height, from which he sees far and can look down into the deep of the Divine judgments and discern that they are clear-obscure.

He does not restrict this universal beneficence when he goes on to lay down conditions on which the reception of its highest forms depend. These conditions are not arbitrary ; and within their limits, the same universality is displayed. The lower creation makes its mute appeal to God, but men have the prerogative and obligation of calling upon Him with real desire and trust. Such suppliants will universally be blessed with a nearness of God to them, better than His proximity through power, knowledge, or the lower manifestations of His loving-kindness, to inferior creatures. Just as the fact of life brought with it certain wants, which God is bound to supply, since He gives it, so the fear and love of Him bring deeper needs, which He is still more (if that were possible) under pledge to satisfy. The creatures have their desires met. Those who fear Him will certainly have theirs ; and that, not only in so far as they share physical life with worm and bee, whom their heavenly Father feeds, but in so far as their devotion sets in motion a new series of aspirations, longings, and needs, which will certainly not be left unfulfilled. " Food " is all the boon that the creatures crave, and they get it by an easy process. But man, especially man who fears and loves God, has deeper needs, sadder in one aspect, since they come from perils and ills from which he has to be saved, but more blessed in another, since every need is a door by which God can enter a soul. These sacreder necessities and more wistful longings are not to be satisfied by simply opening God's hand. More has to be done than that. For they can only be satisfied by the gift of Himself, and men need much disciplining before they will to receive Him into their hearts. They who love and fear Him will desire Him chiefly, and that desire can never be balked. There is a region, and only one, in which it is safe to set our hearts on unattained good. They who long

for God will always have as much of God as they long
for and are capable of receiving.

But notwithstanding the universality of the Divine
loving-kindness, mankind still parts into two sections,
one capable of receiving the highest gifts, one incapable,
because not desiring them.   And therefore the One
Light, in its universal shining, works two effects, being
lustre and life to such as welcome it, but darkness
and death to those who turn from it.   It is man's
awful prerogative that he can distil poison out of the
water of life, and can make it impossible for himself
to receive from tender, universal Goodness anything
but destruction.

The singer closes his song with the reiterated vow
that his songs shall never close, and, as in the earlier
part of the psalm, rejoices in the confidence that his
single voice shall, like that of the herald angel at
Bethlehem, be merged in the notes of "a multitude
praising God and saying, Glory to God in the highest."

PSALM CXLVI.

1   Hallelujah!
Praise Jehovah, my soul.
2 I will praise Jehovah while I live,
I will harp to Jehovah as long as I exist.

3 Trust not in nobles,
In a son of Adam, who has no deliverance [to give].
4 His spirit goes forth, he returns to his earth,
In that same day his schemes perish.

5 Blessed he who has the God of Jacob for his help,
Whose hope is on Jehovah his God!
6 Who made heaven and earth,
The sea—and all that is in them;
Who keeps troth for ever;
7 Who executes judgment for the oppressed;
Who gives bread to the hungry.
Jehovah looses captives;
8 Jehovah opens the eyes of the blind;
Jehovah raises the bowed down;
Jehovah loves the righteous;
9 Jehovah preserves the strangers;
Orphans and widows He sets up;
But the way of the wicked He thwarts.
10 Jehovah shall be King for ever,
Thy God, O Zion, to generation after generation.
Hallelujah!

THE long-drawn music of the Psalter closes with five Hallelujah psalms, in which, with constantly swelling diapason, all themes of praise are pealed forth, until the melodious thunder of the final psalm, which calls on everything that has breath to praise Jehovah.

434

Possibly the number of these psalms may have reference to the five books into which the Psalter is divided.

This is the first of the five. It is largely coloured by earlier songs, but still throbs with fresh emotion. Its theme is the blessedness of trust in Jehovah, as shown by His character and works. It deals less with Israel's special prerogatives than its companions do, while yet it claims the universally beneficent Ruler as Israel's God.

The singer's full heart of thanksgiving must first pour itself out in vows of perpetual praise, before he begins to woo others to the trust which blesses him. Exhortations are impotent unless enforced by example. Ver. 2 is borrowed with slight variation from Psalm civ. 33.

The negative side of the psalmist's exhortation follows in vv. 3, 4, which warn against wasting trust on powerless men. The same antithesis between men and God as objects of confidence occurs in many places of Scripture, and here is probably borrowed from Psalm cxviii. 8. The reason assigned for the dehortation is mainly man's mortality. However high his state, he is but a " son of Adam " (the earth-born), and inherits the feebleness and fleetingness which deprive him of ability to help. " He has no salvation " is the literal rendering of the last words of ver. 3 b. Psalm lx. 11 gives the same thought, and almost in the same words. Ver. 4 sets forth more fully man's mortality, as demonstrating the folly of trusting in him. His breath or spirit escapes; he goes back to " his earth," from which he was created ; and what becomes of all his busy schemes ? They " perish " as he does. The psalmist has a profound sense of the phantasmal character of the solid-seeming realities of human glory and power. But it wakes no bitterness in him, nor does it breathe any sadness into his song. It only teaches him to cling the more closely to the permanent and real. His negative teaching, if it stood alone, would be a gospel of despair, the reduction of life to a torturing cheat; but taken as the prelude to the revelation of One whom it is safe to trust, there is nothing sad in it. So the psalm springs up at once from these thoughts of the helplessness of mortal man, to hymn the blessedness of trust set upon the undying God, like a song-bird from its lair in a grave-yard, which pours its glad notes above the grassy mounds, as it rises in spirals towards the blue, and at each gives forth a more exultant burst of music.

The exclamation in ver. 5 is the last of the twenty-five "Blesseds" in the Psalter. Taken together, as any concordance will show, beginning with Psalm i., they present a beautiful and comprehensive ideal of the devout life. The felicity of such a life is here gathered up into two comprehensive considerations, which supplement each other. It is blessed to have the God of Jacob on our side; but it is not enough for the heart to know that He bore a relation to another in the far-off past or to a community in the present. There must be an individualising bond between the soul and God, whereby the "God of Jacob" becomes the God who belongs to the single devout man, and all the facts of whose protection in the past are renewed in the prosaic present. It is blessed to have Jehovah for one's "help," but that is only secured when, by the effort of one's own will, He is clasped as one's "hope." Such hope is blessed, for it will never be put to shame, nor need to shift its anchorage. It brings into any life the all-sufficient help which is the ultimate source of all felicity, and makes the hope that grasps it blessed, as the hand that holds some fragrant gum is perfumed by the touch.

But the psalmist passes swiftly from celebrating trust to magnify its object, and sets forth in an impressive series the manifold perfections and acts which witness that Jehovah is worthy to be the sole Confidence of men.

The nine Divine acts, which invite to trust in Him, are divided into two parts, by a change in construction. There is, first, a series of participles (vv. 6–7 *b*), and then a string of brief sentences enumerating Divine deeds (vv. 7 *c*–9). No very clear difference in thought can be established as corresponding to this difference in form. The psalmist begins with God's omnipotence as manifested in creation. The first requisite for trust is assurance of power in the person trusted. The psalmist calls heaven and earth and sea, with all their inhabitants, as witnesses that Jehovah is not like the son of man, in whom there is no power to help.

But power may be whimsical, changeable, or may shroud its designs in mystery; therefore, if it is to be trusted, its purposes and methods must be so far known that a man may be able to reckon on it. Therefore the psalm adds unchangeable faithfulness to His power. But Power, however faithful, is not yet worthy of trust, unless it works according to righteousness, and has an arm that wars against wrong; therefore to creative might and plighted troth the psalmist adds the exercise of judgment. Nor are these enough, for the conception which they embody may be that of a somewhat stern and repellent Being, who may be reverenced, but not approached with the warm heart of trust; therefore the psalmist adds beneficence, which ministers their appropriate food to all desires, not only of the flesh, but of the spirit. The hungry hearts of men, who are all full of needs and longings, may turn to this mighty, faithful, righteous Jehovah, and be sure that He never sends mouths but He sends meat to fill them. All our various kinds of hunger are doors for God to come into our spirits.

The second series of sentences deals mainly with the Divine beneficence in regard to man's miseries. The psalmist does not feel that the existence of these sad varieties of sorrow clouds his assurance in God's goodness. To him, they are occasions for the most heart-touching display of God's pitying, healing hand. If there is any difference between the two sets of clauses descriptive of God's acts, the latter bring into clearer light His personal agency in each case of suffering. This mighty, faithful, righteous, beneficent Jehovah, in all the majesty which that name suggests, comes down to the multitude of burdened ones and graciously deals with each, having in His heart the knowledge of, and in His hand the remedy for, all their ills. The greatness of His nature expressed by His name is vividly contrasted with the tenderness and lowliness of His working. Captives, blind persons, and those bowed down by sorrows or otherwise appeal to Him by their helplessness, and His strong hand breaks the fetters, and His gentle touch opens without pain the closed eyes and quickens the paralysed nerve to respond to the light, and His firm, loving hold lifts to their feet and establishes the prostrate. All these classes of afflicted persons are meant to be regarded literally, but all may have a wider meaning, and be intended to hint at spiritual bondage, blindness, and abjectness.

The next clause (ver. 8 c) seems to interrupt the representation of forms of affliction, but it comes in with great significance in the centre of that sad catalogue ; for its presence here teaches that not merely affliction, whether physical or other, secures Jehovah's gracious help, but that there must be the yielding of heart to Him, and the effort at conformity of life with His precepts and pattern, if His aid is to be reckoned on in men's sorrows. The prisoners will still languish in chains, the blind will grope in darkness, the bowed down will lie prone in the dust, unless they are righteous.

The series of afflictions which God alleviates is resumed in ver. 9 with a pathetic triad—strangers, widows, and fatherless. These are forlorn indeed, and the depth of their desolation is the measure of the Divine compassion. The enumeration of Jehovah's acts, which make trust in God blessed in itself, and the sure way of securing help which is not vain, needs but one more touch for completion, and that is added in the solemn thought that He, by His providences and in the long run, turns aside (*i.e.* from its aim) the way of the wicked. That aspect of God's government is lightly handled in one clause, as befits the purpose of the psalm. But it could not be left out. A true likeness must have shadows. God were not a God for men to rely on, unless the trend of His reign was to crush evil and thwart the designs of sinners.

The blessedness of trust in Jehovah is gathered up into one great thought in the last verse of the psalm, The sovereignty of God to all generations suggests the swift disappearance of earthly princes, referred to in ver. 4. To trust in fleeting power is madness ; to trust in the Eternal King is wisdom and blessedness, and in some sense makes him who trusts a sharer in the eternity of the God in whom is his hope, and from whom is his help.

PSALM CXLVII.

1   Hallelujah!
    For it is good to harp unto our God,
    For it is pleasant: praise is comely.
2 Jehovah is the builder up of Jerusalem,
    The outcasts of Israel He gathers together;
3 The healer of the broken-hearted,
    And He binds their wounds;
4 Counting a number for the stars,
    He calls them all by names.
5 Great is our Lord and of vast might,
    To His understanding there is no number.
6 Jehovah helps up the afflicted,
    Laying low the wicked to the ground.

7 Sing to Jehovah with thanksgiving,
    Harp to our God on the lyre,
8 Covering heaven with clouds,
    Preparing rain for the earth;
    Making the mountains shoot forth grass,
9 Giving to the beast its food,
    To the brood of the raven which croak.
10 Not in the strength of the horse does He delight,
    Not in the legs of a man does He take pleasure.
11 Jehovah takes pleasure in them that fear Him,
    Them that wait for His loving-kindness.

12 Extol Jehovah, O Jerusalem,
    Praise thy God, O Zion.
13 For He has strengthened the bars of thy gates,
    He has blessed thy children in thy midst.
14 Setting thy borders in peace,
    With the fat of wheat He satisfies thee;
15 Sending forth His commandment on the earth,
    Swiftly runs His word;

16 Giving snow like wool,
  Hoar frost He scatters like ashes;
17 Flinging forth His ice like morsels,
  Before His cold who can stand?
18 He sends forth His word and melts them,
  He causes His wind to blow—the waters flow;
19 Declaring His word to Jacob,
  His statutes and judgments to Israel.
20 He has not dealt thus to any nation;
  And His judgments—they have not known them.

THE threefold calls to praise Jehovah (vv. 1, 7, 12) divide this psalm into three parts, the two former of which are closely connected, inasmuch as the first part is mainly occupied with celebrating God's mercy to the restored Israel, and the second takes a wider outlook, embracing His beneficence to all living things. Both these points of view are repeated in the same order in the third part (vv. 12–20), which the LXX. makes a separate psalm. The allusions to Jerusalem as rebuilt, to the gathering of the scattered Israelites, and to the fortifications of the city naturally point to the epoch of the Restoration, whether or not, with Delitzsch and others, we suppose that the psalm was sung at the feast of the dedication of the new walls. In any case, it is a hymn of the restored people, which starts from the special mercy shown to them, and rejoices in the thought that "Our God" fills the earth with good and reigns to bless, in the realm of Nature as in that of special Revelation. The emphasis placed on God's working in nature, in this and others of these closing psalms, is probably in part a polemic against the idolatry which Israel had learned to abhor, by being brought face to face with it in Babylon, and in part a result of the widening of conceptions as to His relation to the world outside Israel which the

Exile had also effected. The two truths of His special relation to His people and of His universal lovingkindness have often been divorced, both by His people and by their enemies. This psalm teaches a more excellent way.

The main theme of vv. 1–6 is God's manifestation of transcendent power and incalculable wisdom, as well as infinite kindness, in building up the ruined Jerusalem and collecting into a happy band of citizens the lonely wanderers of Israel. For such blessings praise is due, and the psalm summons all who share them to swell the song. Ver. 1 is somewhat differently construed by some, as Hupfeld, who would change one letter in the word rendered above "to harp," and, making it an imperative, would refer "good" and "pleasant" to God, thus making the whole to read, "Praise Jehovah, for He is good; harp to our God, for He is pleasant: praise is comely." This change simplifies some points of construction, but labours under the objection that it is contrary to usage to apply the adjective "pleasant" to God; and the usual rendering is quite intelligible and appropriate. The reason for the fittingness and delightsomeness of praise is the great mercy shown to Israel in the Restoration, which mercy is in the psalmist's thoughts throughout this part. He has the same fondness for using participles as the author of the previous psalm, and begins vv. 2, 3, 4, and 6 with them. Possibly their use is intended to imply that the acts described by them are regarded as continuous, not merely done once for all. Jehovah is ever building up Jerusalem, and, in like manner, uninterruptedly energising in providence and nature. The collocation of Divine acts in ver. 2 bears upon the great theme that fills the singer's heart and lips. It is the outcasts

of Israel of whom he thinks, while he sings of binding
up the broken-hearted. It is they who are the "afflicted,"
helped up by that strong, gentle clasp; while their
oppressors are the wicked, flung prone by the very
wind of God's hand. The beautiful and profound
juxtaposition of gentle healing and omnipotence in vv.
3, 4, is meant to signalise the work of restoring Israel
as no less wondrous than that of marshalling the stars,
and to hearten faith by pledging that incalculable Power
to perfect its restoring work. He who stands beside the
sick-bed of the broken-hearted, like a gentle physician,
with balm and bandage, and lays a tender hand on
their wounds, is He who sets the stars in their places
and tells them as a shepherd his flock or a commander
his army. The psalmist borrows from Isa. xl. 26–29,
where several of his expressions occur. "Counting a
number for the stars" is scarcely equivalent to number-
ing them as they shine. It rather means determining
how many of them there shall be. Calling them all
by names (lit., He calls names to them all) is not giving
them designations, but summoning them as a captain
reading the muster-roll of his band. It may also imply
full knowledge of each individual in their countless
hosts. Ver. 5 is taken from the passage in Isaiah
already referred to, with the change of "no number"
for "no searching," a change which is suggested by
the preceding reference to the number of the stars.
These have a number, though it surpasses human
arithmetic; but His wisdom is measureless. And all
this magnificence of power, this minute particularising
knowledge, this abyss of wisdom, are guarantees for
the healing of the broken-hearted. The thought goes
further than Israel's deliverance from bondage. It has
a strong voice of cheer for all sad hearts, who will let

Him probe their wounds that He may bind them up. The mighty God of Creation is the tender God of Providence and of Redemption. Therefore "praise is comely," and fear and faltering are unbefitting.

The second part of the psalm (ver. 7–11) passes out from the special field of mercy to Israel, and comes down from the glories of the heavens, to magnify God's universal goodness manifested in physical changes, by which lowly creatures are provided for. The point of time selected is that of the November rains. The verbs in vv. 8, 9, 11, are again participles, expressive of continuous action. The yearly miracle which brings from some invisible storehouse the clouds to fill the sky and drop down fatness, the answer of the brown earth which mysteriously shoots forth the tender green spikelets away up on the mountain flanks, where no man has sown and no man will reap, the loving care which thereby provides food for the wild creatures, owned by no one, and answers the hoarse croak of the callow fledgelings in the ravens' nests— these are manifestations of God's power and revelations of His character worthy to be woven into a hymn which celebrates His restoring grace, and to be set beside the apocalypse of His greatness in the nightly heavens. But what has ver. 10 to do here? The connection of it is difficult to trace. Apparently, the psalmist would draw from the previous verses, which exhibit God's universal goodness and the creatures' dependence on Him, the lesson that reliance on one's own resources or might is sure to be smitten with confusion, while humble trust in God, which man alone of earth's creatures can exercise, is for him the condition of his receiving needed gifts. The beast gets its food, and it is enough that the young ravens should croak, but man has to "fear Him" and to wait on His "loving-kindness." Ver. 10 is a reminiscence of Psalm xxxiii. 16, 17, and ver. 11 of the next verse of the same psalm.

The third part (vv. 12–20) travels over substantially the same ground as the two former, beginning with the mercy shown to the restored Israel, and passing on to wider manifestations of God's goodness. But there is a difference in this repeated setting forth of both these themes. The fortifications of Jerusalem are now complete, and their strength gives security to the people gathered into the city. Over all the land once devastated by war peace broods, and the fields that lay desolate now have yielded harvest. The ancient promise (Psalm lxxxi. 16) has been fulfilled, its condition having been complied with, and Israel having hearkened to Jehovah. Protection, blessing, tranquillity, abundance, are the results of obedience, God's gifts to them that fear Him. So it was in the psalmist's experience; so, in higher form, it is still. These Divine acts are continuous, and as long as there are men who trust, there will be a God who builds defences around them, and satisfies them with good.

Again the psalmist turns to the realm of nature; but it is nature at a different season which now yields witness to God's universal power and care. The phenomena of a sharp winter were more striking to the psalmist than to us. But his poet's eye and his devout heart recognise even in the cold, before which his Eastern constitution cowered shivering, the working of God's Will. His "commandment" or Word is personified, and compared to a swift-footed messenger. As ever, power over material things is attributed to the Divine word, and as ever, in the Biblical view of nature, all intermediate links are neglected, and the Almighty cause at one end of the chain and the physical effect at the other are brought together. There is between these two clauses room enough for all that meteorology has to say.

The winter-piece in vv. 16, 17, dashes off the dreary scene with a few bold strokes. The air is full of flakes like floating wool, or the white mantle covers the ground like a cloth; rime lies everywhere, as if ashes were powdered over trees and stones. Hail-stones fall, as if He flung them down from above. They are like "morsels" of bread, a comparison which strikes us as violent, but which may possibly describe the more severe storms, in which flat pieces of ice fall. As by magic, all is changed when He again sends forth His word. It but needs that He should let a warm wind steal gently across the desolation, and every sealed and silent brook begins to tinkle along its course. And will not He who thus changes the face of the earth in like manner breathe upon frost-bound lives and hearts,

> "And every winter merge in spring"?

But the psalm cannot end with contemplation of God's universal beneficence, however gracious that is. There is a higher mode of activity for His word than that exercised on material things. God sends His commandment forth and earth unconsciously obeys, and all creatures, men included, are fed and blessed. But the noblest utterance of His word is in the shape of statutes and judgments, and these are Israel's prerogative. The psalmist is not rejoicing that other nations have not received these, but that Israel has. Its privilege is its responsibility. It has received them that it may obey them, and then that it may make them known. If the God who scatters lower blessings broad-cast, not forgetting beasts and ravens, has restricted His highest gift to His people, the restriction is a clear call to them to spread the knowledge of the treasure entrusted to them. To glory in privilege is sin; to learn that it means responsibility is wisdom. The lesson is needed by those who to-day have been served as heirs to Israel's prerogative, forfeited by it because it clutched it for itself, and forgot its obligation to carry it as widely as God had diffused His lower gifts.

PSALM CXLVIII.

1   Hallelujah !
   Praise Jehovah from the heavens,
   Praise Him in the heights.
2 Praise Him, all His angels,
   Praise Him, all His host.
3 Praise Him, sun and moon,
   Praise Him, all stars of light.
4 Praise Him, heavens of heavens,
   And waters that are above the heavens—
5 Let them praise the name of Jehovah,
   For He, He commanded and they were created.
6 And He established them for ever and aye,
   A law gave He [them] and none transgresses.

7 Praise Jehovah from the earth,
   Sea-monsters, and all ocean-depths;
8 Fire and hail, snow and smoke,
   Storm-wind doing His behest;
9 Mountains and all hills,
   Fruit trees and all cedars;
10 Wild beast and all cattle,
   Creeping thing and winged fowl;
11 Kings of the earth and all peoples,
   Princes and all judges of the earth;
12 Young men and also maidens,
   Old men with children—
13 Let them praise the name of Jehovah,
   For His name alone is exalted,
   His majesty above earth and heaven.
14 And He has lifted up a horn for His people,
   A praise for all His beloved,
   [Even] for the children of Israel, the people near to Him.
       Hallelujah !

THE mercy granted to Israel (ver. 14) is, in the psalmist's estimation, worthy to call forth strains of praise from all creatures. It is the same conception as is found in several of the psalms of the King (xciii.–c.), but is here expressed with unparalleled magnificence and fervour. The same idea attains the climax of its representation in the mighty anthem from "every creature which is in heaven and on the earth, and under the earth, and such as are in the sea, and all that are in them," whom John heard saying, "Blessing and honour and glory and power unto Him that sitteth upon the throne, and unto the Lamb for ever and ever." It may be maintained that this psalm is only a highly emotional and imaginative rendering of the truth that all God's works praise Him, whether consciously or not, but its correspondence with a line of thought which runs through Scripture from its first page to its last— namely, that, as man's sin subjected the creatures to "vanity," so his redemption shall be their glorifying— leads us to see prophetic anticipation, and not mere poetic rapture, in this summons pealed out to heights and depths, and all that lies between, to rejoice in what Jehovah has done for Israel.

The psalm falls into two broad divisions, in the former of which heaven, and in the latter earth, are invoked to praise Jehovah. Ver. 1 addresses generally the subsequently particularised heavenly beings. "From the heavens" and "in the heights" praise is to sound; the former phrase marks the place of origin, and may imply the floating down to a listening earth of that ethereal music; the latter thinks of all the dim distances as filled with it. The angels, as conscious beings, are the chorus-leaders, and even to "principalities and powers in heavenly places" Israel's restoration reveals new phases of the "manifold wisdom of God." The "host" (or *hosts*, according to the amended reading of the Hebrew margin) are here obviously angels, as required by the parallelism with *a*. The sun, moon, and stars, of which the psalmist knows nothing but that they burn with light and roll in silence through the dark expanse, are bid to break the solemn stillness that fills the daily and nightly sky. Finally, the singer passes in thought through the lower heavens, and would fain send his voice whither his eye cannot pierce, up into that mysterious watery abyss, which, according to ancient cosmography, had the firmament for its floor. It is absurd to look for astronomical accuracy in such poetry as this; but a singer who knew no more about sun, moon, and stars, and depths of space, than that they were all God's creatures and in their silence praised Him, knew and felt more of their true nature and charm than does he who knows everything about them except these facts.

Vv. 5, 6, assign the reason for the praise of the heavens —Jehovah's creative act, His sustaining power and His " law," the utterance of His will to which they conform. Ver. 6 *a* emphatically asserts, by expressing the " He," which is in Hebrew usually included in the verb, that it is Jehovah and none other who " preserves the stars from wrong." " Preservation is continuous creation." The meaning of the close of ver. 6 *b* is doubtful, if the existing text is adhered to. It reads literally "and [it ?] shall not pass." The unexpressed nominative is by some taken to be the before-mentioned "law," and "pass" to mean *cease to be in force* or *be transgressed*. Others take the singular verb as being used distributively, and so render " None of them transgresses." But a very slight alteration gives the plural verb, which makes all plain.

In these starry depths obedience reigns; it is only on earth that a being lives who can and will break the merciful barriers of Jehovah's law. Therefore, from that untroubled region of perfect service comes a purer song of praise, though it can never have the pathetic harmonies of that which issues from rebels brought back to allegiance.

The summons to the earth begins with the lowest places, as that to the heavens did with the highest. The psalmist knows little of the uncouth forms that may wallow in ocean depths, but he is sure that they too, in their sunless abodes, can praise Jehovah. From the ocean the psalm rises to the air, before it, as it were, settles down on earth. Ver. 8 may refer to contemporaneous phenomena, and, if so, describes a wild storm hurtling through the lower atmosphere. The verbal arrangement in ver. 8 *a* is that of inverted parallelism, in which "fire" corresponds to "smoke" and "hail" to "snow." Lightning and hail, which often occur together, are similarly connected in Psalm xviii. 12. But it is difficult to explain "snow and smoke," if regarded as accompaniments of the former pair—fire and hail. Rather they seem to describe another set of meteorological phenomena, a winter storm, in which the air is thick with flakes as if charged with smoke, while the preceding words refer to a summer's thunderstorm. The resemblance to the two pictures in the preceding psalm, one of the time of the latter rains and one of bitter winter weather, is noticeable. The storm-wind, which drives all these formidable agents through the air, in its utmost fury is a servant. As in Psalm cvii. 25, it obeys God's command.

The solid earth itself, as represented by its loftiest

summits which pierce the air; vegetable life, as represented by the two classes of fruit-bearing and forest trees; animals in their orders, wild and domestic; the lowest worm that crawls and the light-winged bird that soars,—these all have voices to praise God. The song has been steadily rising in the scale of being from inanimate to animated creatures, and last it summons man, in whom creation's praise becomes vocal and conscious.

All men, without distinction of rank, age, or sex, have the same obligation and privilege of praise. Kings are most kingly when they cast their crowns before Him. Judges are wise when they sit as His vice-gerents. The buoyant vigour of youth is purest when used with remembrance of the Creator; the maiden's voice is never so sweet as in hymns to Jehovah. The memories and feebleness of age are hallowed and strengthened by recognition of the God who can renew failing energy and soothe sad remembrances; and the child's opening powers are preserved from stain and distortion, by drawing near to Him in whose praise the extremes of life find common ground. The young man's strong bass, the maiden's clear alto, the old man's quavering notes, the child's fresh treble, should blend in the song.

Ver. 13 gives the reason for the praise of earth, but especially of man, with very significant difference from that assigned in vv. 5, 6. "His name is exalted." He has manifested Himself to eyes that can see, and has shown forth His transcendent majesty. Man's praise is to be based not only on the Revelation of God in Nature, but on that higher one in His dealings with men, and especially with Israel. This chief reason for praise is assigned in ver. 14, and indeed underlies the whole psalm. "He has lifted up a horn for His people," delivering them from their humiliation and captivity, and setting them again in their land. Thereby He has provided all His favoured ones with occasion for praise. The condensed language of ver. 14 *b* is susceptible of different constructions and meanings. Some would understand the verb from *a* as repeated before "praise," and take the meaning to be "He exalts the praise [*i.e.*, the glory] of His beloved," but it is improbable that praise here should mean anything but that rendered to God. The simplest explanation of the words is that they are in apposition to the preceding clause, and declare that Jehovah, by "exalting a horn to His people," has given them especially occasion to praise Him. Israel is further designated as "a people near to Him." It is a nation of priests, having the privilege of access to His presence ; and, in the consciousness of this dignity, "comes forward in this psalm as the leader of all the creatures in their praise of God, and strikes up a hallelujah that is to be joined in by heaven and earth" (Delitzsch).

PSALM CXLIX.

1 Sing to Jehovah a new song,
His praise in the congregation of His favoured ones.
2 Let Israel rejoice in his Maker,
Let the children of Zion be glad in their King.
3 Let them praise His name in [the] dance,
With timbrel and lyre let them play to Him.
4 For Jehovah takes pleasure in His people,
He adorns the meek with salvation.
5 Let His favoured ones exult in glory,
Let them shout aloud on their beds—
6 The high praises of God in their throat,
And a two-edged sword in their hand;
7 To execute vengeance on the nations,
Chastisements on the peoples;
8 To bind their kings in chains
And their nobles in bonds of iron;
9 To execute on them the sentence written—
An honour is this to all His favoured ones.
Hallelujah !

IN the preceding psalm Israel's restoration was connected with the recognition by all creatures, and especially by the kings of the earth and their people, of Jehovah's glory. This psalm presents the converse thought, that the restored Israel becomes the executor of judgments on those who will not join in the praise which rings from Israel that it may be caught up by all. The two psalms are thus closely connected. The circumstances of the Restoration accord with the tone of both, as of the other members of this closing group.

The happy recipients of new mercy are, as in Psalms xcvi. and xcviii., summoned to break into new songs. Winter silences the birds; but spring, the new " life re-orient out of dust," is welcomed with music from every budding tree.

Chiefly should God's praise sound out from "the congregation of His favoured ones," the long-scattered captives who owe it to His favour that they *are* a congregation once more. The jubilant psalmist delights in that name for Israel, and uses it thrice in his song. He loves to set forth the various names, which each suggest some sweet strong thought of what God is to the nation and the nation to God—His favoured ones, Israel, the children of Zion, His people, the afflicted. He heaps together synonyms expressive of rapturous joy—rejoice, be glad, exult. He calls for expressions of triumphant mirth in which limbs, instruments, and voices unite. He would have the exuberant gladness well over into the hours of repose, and the night be made musical with ringing shouts of joy. " Praise is better than sleep," and the beds which had often been privy to silent tears may well be witnesses of exultation that cannot be dumb.

The psalmist touches very lightly on the reason for this outburst of praise, because he takes it for granted that so great and recent mercy needed little mention. One verse (ver. 4) suffices to recall it. The very absorption of the heart in its bliss may make it silent about the bliss. The bride needs not to tell what makes her glad. Restored Israel requires little reminder of its occasion for joy. But the brief mention of it is very beautiful. It makes prominent, not so much the outward fact, as the Divine pleasure in His people, of which the fact was effect and indication.

Their affliction had been the token that God's complacency did not rest on them ; their deliverance is
the proof that the sunlight of His face shines on them
once more. His chastisements rightly borne are ever
precursors of deliverance, which adorns the meek
afflicted, giving " beauty for ashes." The qualification
for receiving Jehovah's help is meekness, and the
effect of that help on the lowly soul is to deck it with
strange loveliness. Therefore God's favoured ones may
well exult in glory—*i.e.*, on account of the glory with
which they are invested by His salvation.

The stern close of the psalm strikes a note which
many ears feel to be discordant, and which must be
freely acknowledged to stand on the same lower level
as the imprecatory psalms, while, even more distinctly
than these, it is entirely free from any sentiment of
personal vengeance. The picture of God's people going
forth to battle, chanting His praises and swinging two-
edged swords, shocks Christian sentiment. It is not
to be explained away as meaning the spiritual conquest
of the world with spiritual weapons. The psalmist
meant actual warfare and real iron fetters. But, while
the form of his anticipations belongs to the past and
is entirely set aside by the better light of Christianity,
their substance is true for ever. Those who have been
adorned with Jehovah's salvation have the subjugation
of the world to God's rule committed to them. " The
weapons of our warfare are not carnal." There are
stronger fetters than those of iron, even " the cords of
ove " and " the bands of a man."

" The judgment written," which is to be executed
by the militant Israel on the nations, does not seem
to have reference either to the commandment to exterminate the Canaanites or to the punishments threatened

In many places of Scripture. It is better to take it as denoting a judgment " fixed, settled, . . . written thus by God Himself" (Perowne). Ver. 9 *b* may be rendered (as Hupfeld does) " Honour [or, majesty] is He to all His favoured ones," in the sense that God manifests His majesty to them, or that He is the object of their honouring ; but the usual rendering is more in accordance with the context and its high-strung martial ardour. " This "—namely, the whole of the crusade just described—is laid upon all Jehovah's favoured ones, by the fact of their participation in His salvation. They are redeemed from bondage that they may be God'. warriors. The honour and obligation are universal.

PSALM CL.

1   Hallelujah !
  Praise God in His sanctuary,
  Praise Him in the firmament of His strength.
2 Praise Him for His mighty deeds,
  Praise Him according to the abundance of His greatness.
3 Praise Him with blast of horn,
  Praise Him with psaltery and harp,
4 Praise Him with timbrel and dance,
  Praise Him with strings and pipe.
5 Praise Him with clear-sounding cymbals,
  Praise Him with deep-toned cymbals.
6 Let everything that has breath praise Jah.
    Hallelujah !

THIS noble close of the Psalter rings out one clear
  note of praise, as the end of all the many moods
and experiences recorded in its wonderful sighs and
songs. Tears, groans, wailings for sin, meditations on
the dark depths of Providence, fainting faith and foiled
aspirations, all lead up to this. The psalm is more
than an artistic close of the Psalter; it is a prophecy
of the last result of the devout life, and, in its unclouded
sunniness, as well as in its universality, it proclaims
the certain end of the weary years for the individual
and for the world. "Everything that hath breath"

shall yet praise Jehovah. The psalm is evidently meant for liturgic use, and one may imagine that each instrument began to take part in the concert as it was named, till at last all blended in a mighty torrent of praiseful sound, to which the whirling dancers kept time. A strange contrast to modern notions of sobriety in worship!

The tenfold "Praise Him" has been often noticed as symbolic of completeness, but has probably no special significance.

In ver. 1 the psalmist calls on earth and heaven to praise. The "sanctuary" may, indeed, be either the Temple or the heavenly palace of Jehovah, but it is more probable that the invocation, like so many others of a similar kind, is addressed to men and angels, than that the latter only are meant. They who stand in the earthly courts and they who circle the throne that is reared above the visible firmament are parts of a great whole, an antiphonal chorus. It becomes them to praise, for they each dwell in God's sanctuary.

The theme of praise is next touched in ver. 2. "His mighty deeds" might be rendered "His heroic [or, valiant] acts." The reference is to His deliverance of His people as a signal manifestation of prowess or conquering might. The tenderness which moved the power is not here in question, but the power cannot be worthily praised or understood, unless that Divine pity and graciousness of which it is the instrument are apprehended. Mighty acts, unsoftened by loving impulse and gracious purpose, would evoke awe, but not thanks. No praise is adequate to the abundance of His greatness, but yet He accepts such adoration as men can render.

The instruments named in vv. 3–5 were not all used, so far as we know, in the Temple service. There is possibly an intention to go beyond those recognised as sacred, in order to emphasise the universality of praise. The horn was the curved " Shophar," blown by the priests; "harp and psaltery were played by the Levites, timbrels were struck by women; and dancing, playing on stringed instruments and pipes and cymbals, were not reserved for the Levites. Consequently the summons to praise God is addressed to priests, Levites, and people " (Baethgen). In ver. 4 *b* " strings" means stringed instruments, and "pipe" is probably that used by shepherds, neither of which kinds of instrument elsewhere appears as employed in worship.

Too little is known of Jewish music to enable us to determine whether the epithets applied to cymbals refer to two different kinds. Probably they do; the first being small and high-pitched, the second larger, like the similar instrument used in military music, and of a deep tone.

But the singer would fain hear a volume of sound which should drown all that sweet tumult which he has evoked; and therefore he calls on "everything that has breath" to use it in sending forth a thunder-chorus of praise to Jehovah. The invocation bears the prophecy of its own fulfilment. These last strains of the long series of psalmists are as if that band of singers of Israel turned to the listening world, and gave into its keeping the harps which, under their own hands, had yielded such immortal music.

Few voices have obeyed the summons, and the vision of a world melodious with the praise of Jehovah and of Him alone appears to us, in our despondent moments, almost as far off as it was when the last psalmist ceased to sing. But his call is our confidence ; and we know that the end of history shall be that to Him whose work is mightier than all the other mighty acts of Jehovah, " Every knee shall bow, and every tongue confess that Jesus Christ is Lord, to the glory of God the Father."

THE END.

OTHER FINE VOLUMES AVAILABLE

1980-81